The Tozer Topical Reader
Volume Two

The TOZER Topical Reader

Volume Two

COMPILED BY
RON EGGERT

CAMP HILL, PENNSYLVANIA

Christian Publications
3825 Hartzdale Drive, Camp Hill, PA 10711
www.cpi-horizon.com

Faithful, biblical publishing since 1883

The Tozer Topical Reader
In Two Volumes

ISBN: 0-87509-838-X
Copyright 1998, by Ron Eggert
All rights reserved
Printed in the United States of America

99 00 01 02 03   5 4 3 2 1

Selected quotations as submitted from
*The Knowledge of the Holy, The Attributes of God:
Their Meaning in the Christian* by A.W. Tozer
Copyright © 1961 by Alden Wilson Tozer.
Copyright Renewed.
Reprinted by permission of
HarperCollins Publishers, Inc.

Selected quotations are taken from
Keys to the Deeper Life by A.W. Tozer.
Copyright © 1987 by
Zondervan Publishing House.
Used by permission of Zondervan Publishing House.

Scripture taken from the Holy Bible:
King James Version.

Scripture also taken from the HOLY BIBLE:
NEW INTERNATIONAL VERSION ®.
© 1973, 1978, 1984 by the
International Bible Society.
Used by permission of
Zondervan Bible Publishers.

L

709. Laodicea; Backsliding

The church at Laodicea has stood for nineteen hundred years as a serious warning to the whole church of Christ to be most watchful when no enemy is in sight and to remain poor in spirit when earthly wealth increases, yet we appear to have learned nothing from her. We expound the seven letters to the churches of Asia and then return to our own company to live like the Laodicean church. There is in us a bent to backsliding that is all but impossible to cure.

Hosea 12:6-9; Matthew 5:3; Revelation 3:14-22
That Incredible Christian, 86.

710. Layman; Service: motives for

The "layman" need never think of his humbler task as being inferior to that of his minister. Let every man abide in the calling wherein he is called and his work will be as sacred as the work of the ministry. It is not what a man does that determines whether his work is sacred or secular, it is why he does it. The motive is everything. Let a man sanctify the Lord God in his heart and he can thereafter do no common act. All he does is good and acceptable to God through Jesus Christ. For such a man, living itself will be a priestly ministration. As he performs his never-so-simple task, he will hear the voice of the seraphim saying, "Holy, holy, holy, is the LORD of hosts: the whole earth is full of his glory" (Isaiah 6:3).

Isaiah 6:3; 1 Corinthians 7:20; 1 Corinthians 10:31; 1 Peter 3:15
The Pursuit of God, 118.

711. Leaders: attitude toward

I think we make two mistakes in our attitude toward our Christian leaders, one in not being sufficiently grateful to them and the other in following them too slavishly....

In a very real sense we thank God when we thank His people. Gratitude felt and expressed becomes a healing, life-building force in the soul. Something wonderful happens within us when gratitude enters. We cannot be too grateful, for it would be like loving too much or being too kind. And if we are to make a mistake it had better be on the side of humble gratitude for benefits received. Should we in error give credit to someone who does not deserve it we are far better off than if we fail to give credit to one who does. . . .

If it is a sin of omission to be ungrateful toward our God-ordained leaders and benefactors it is as surely a sin to be too dependent upon them. . . .

We make a serious mistake when we become so attached to the preaching or writing of a great Christian leader that we accept his teaching without daring to examine it. No man is that important in the kingdom of God. We should follow men only as they follow the Lord and we should keep an open mind lest we become blind followers of a man whose breath is in his nostrils.

Acts 17:11; 1 Corinthians 11:1; 1 Timothy 5:17-18
The Set of the Sail, 161, 162, 163, 164.

712. Leaders: spiritual need; Church: leadership

Conformity to the Word of God is always right, but obedience to religious leaders is good only if those leaders prove themselves worthy to lead. Leadership in the church of Christ is a spiritual thing and should be so understood by everyone. It takes more than a ballot to make a leader. . . .

If the church is to prosper spiritually she must have spiritual leadership, not leadership by majority vote. It is highly significant that when the apostle Paul found it necessary to ask for obedience among the young churches he never appealed to them on the grounds that he had been duly elected to office. He asserted his authority as an apostle appointed by the Head of the church. He held his position by right of sheer spiritual ascendancy, the only earthly right that should be honored among the children of the new creation.

Acts 9:15-16; 2 Corinthians 11:12-15; 1 Timothy 3:1-7; 1 John 4:1
The Warfare of the Spirit, 162, 163, 164.

713. Leaders: spiritual need; Church: leadership; Prayer: necessity of

Prayer is not a work that can be allocated to one or another group in the church. It is everybody's responsibility; it is everybody's privilege. Prayer is the respiratory function of the church; without it we suffocate and die at last, like a living body deprived of the breath of life. Prayer knows no sex, for the soul has no sex, and it is the soul that must pray. Women can pray, and their prayers will be answered;

but so can man, and so should men if they are to fill the place God has given them in the church.

Let us watch that we do not slide imperceptibly to a state where the women do the praying and the men run the churches. Men who do not pray have no right to direct church affairs. We believe in the leadership of men within the spiritual community of the saints, but that leadership should be won by spiritual worth.

Leadership requires vision, and whence will vision come except from hours spent in the presence of God in humble and fervent prayer? All things else being equal, a praying woman will know the will of God for the church far better than a prayerless man.

We do not here advocate the turning of the churches over to the women, but we do advocate a recognition of proper spiritual qualifications for leadership among the men if they are to continue to decide the direction the churches shall take. The accident of being a man is not enough. Spiritual manhood alone qualifies.

Acts 6:3-7; Ephesians 6:18; 1 Timothy 2:1-8
We Travel an Appointed Way, 16.

714. Leaders: spiritual need; Holy Spirit: need for; Church: Holy Spirit's work; Human wisdom

I have reason to suspect that many people are trying to give leadership in Christian churches today without ever having yielded to the wise and effective leading of the Holy Spirit. He truly is the Spirit of wisdom, understanding and counsel. He alone can bring the gracious presence of the living God into our lives and ministries.

You may think it out of place for me to say so, but in our churches today we are leaning too heavily upon human talents and educated abilities. We forget that the illumination of the Holy Spirit of God is a necessity, not only in our ministerial preparation, but in the administrative and leadership functions of our churches.

We need an enduement of the Spirit of God! We sorely need more of His wisdom, His counsel, His power, His knowledge. We need to reverence and fear the Almighty God. If we knew the full provision and the spiritual anointing that Jesus promised through the Holy Spirit, we would be far less dependent on so many other things.

Psychiatrists, psychologists, anthropologists, sociologists—and most of the other "ologists"—have their place in our society. I do not doubt that. But many of these professionals now have credentials in the church, and I fear that their counsel is put above the ministry of the Holy Spirit. I have said it before, and I say it now: We need the Holy Spirit more and more, and we need human helps less and less!

Isaiah 11:2-4; John 16:13-15; Acts 1:8
Jesus Is Victor!, 48.

715. Leaders: spiritual need; Pastoral ministry: spiritual impact

The history of Israel and Judah points up a truth taught clearly enough by all history, viz., that the masses are or soon will be what their leaders are. The kings set the moral pace for the people....

Whatever sort of man the king turned out to be the people were soon following his leadership. They followed David in the worship of Jehovah, Solomon in the building of the Temple, Jeroboam in the making of a calf and Hezekiah in the restoration of the temple worship.

It is not complimentary to the masses that they are so easily led, but we are not interested in praising or blaming; we are concerned for truth, and the truth is that for better or for worse religious people follow leaders. A good man may change the moral complexion of a whole nation; or a corrupt and worldly clergy may lead a nation into bondage....

Today Christianity in the Western world is what its leaders were in the recent past and is becoming what its present leaders are. The local church soon becomes like its pastor....

1 Kings 12:28-30; 1 Corinthians 4:16; Philippians 3:17; Philippians 4:9
God Tells the Man Who Cares, 59, 60.

716. Leaders: spiritual need; Spiritual discernment; Pastors: prophetic ministry

That so-called Bible religion in our times is suffering rapid decline is so evident as to need no proof, but just what has brought about this decline is not so easy to discover. I can only say that I have observed one significant lack among evangelical Christians which might turn out to be the real cause of most of our spiritual troubles. Of course, if that were true, then the supplying of that lack would be our most critical need.

The great deficiency to which I refer is the lack of spiritual discernment, especially among our leaders. How there can be so much Bible knowledge and so little insight, so little moral penetration, is one of the enigmas of the religious world today. . . .

If not the greatest need, then surely one of the greatest is for the appearance of Christian leaders with prophetic vision. We desperately need seers who can see through the mist. Unless they come soon, it will be too late for this generation. And if they do come, we will no doubt crucify a few of them in the name of our worldly orthodoxy. But the cross is always the harbinger of the resurrection.

1 Kings 3:9; Proverbs 2:3-9; 2 Corinthians 3:14-15; James 1:5-6
We Travel an Appointed Way, 111, 112.

717. Leaders: visionaries; A. B. Simpson

A. B. Simpson had become a world-missionary, whatever men may think of it, and he had come through in the only way a man of his temperament could. For better or for worse that was the way he moved. He would first get an idea, a concept, then must come a heart experience to set it off, to detonate the charge it contained. Until the explosion came, he could wait, sometimes for years, mulling his idea over, half forgetting it, burying it under a mountain of work; then the great day would come and he would be prostrated, almost slain under the impact of that idea, his and yet God's idea, leaping up now, and powerfully compelling as it came out at him like a blast of creative force.

To the earth-walking Christian, ankle-deep in dust, who has never seen heaven opened or beheld a vision of God, this will seem all out of order, too emotional, too extreme. But it is the way of the strong eagles of the kingdom, the prophets, the apostles, the reformers and revivalists. These fly high and see far, and that they are not understood is no great wonder. The sky-loving eagle, screaming in the sun, may be a puzzle to the contented biddy scratching in the yard, but that is no good argument against the eagle.

Wingspread; A. B. Simpson: A Study in Spiritual Altitude, 63, 64.

718. Legalism; Conscience

If the devil cannot succeed in destroying the conscience he will settle for making it sick. I know Christians who live in a state of constant distress, fearing that they may displease God. Their world of permitted acts becomes narrower year by year till at last they fear to engage in the common pursuits of life. They believe this self-torture to be a proof of godliness, but how wrong they are.

John 8:31-32,36; Romans 8:15; 2 Corinthians 3:15-18; Galatians 5:1
That Incredible Christian, 55.

719. Liberty; Freedom; Current issues: misuse of freedom

"Our American way of life" is a phrase constantly heard these days. It is a good phrase, and to many sincere and honest persons it means liberty of conscience, freedom of individual enterprise and the right to worship God after the dictates of our own conscience; it means the rule of law instead of the rule of tyrants; it means a minimum of interference from the state and a maximum of liberty for the individual citizen.

To millions of others, however, it means little more than the right to sin to their heart's content without molestation by the civil authorities. The Constitution may be, as Gladstone said it was, the noblest document ever struck off by the mind of man. But we must remember that there are countless thousands of Americans who use it merely as a place to hide when they are caught in some act of iniquity.

Liberty as used by the American founding fathers meant freedom to do good; many today conceive it to mean freedom to do evil, and they work it for all the traffic will bear.

1 Corinthians 8:9; Galatians 5:13; 1 Peter 2:16
The Next Chapter after the Last, 44, 45.

720. Life purpose

The life ideal was described by the apostle in the Book of Acts: "For David, after he had served his own generation by the will of God, fell on sleep."

We submit that it would be difficult, if not impossible, to improve upon this. It embraces the whole sphere of religion, appearing as it does in its three directions: God, the individual, society. Within that simple triangle all possible human activities are carried on. To each of us there can be but these three dimensions: God, myself, others. Beyond this we cannot go, nor should we even attempt to go. If we serve God according to His own will, and in doing so serve our generation, we shall have accomplished all that is possible for any human being.

Acts 13:36
The Next Chapter after the Last, 67.

721. Life purpose; Priorities

The Associated Press lately carried an interesting if somewhat depressing story out of London about a certain British peer who had died just a few days short of his eighty-ninth birthday.

Having been a man of means and position, it had presumably not been necessary for him to work for a living like the rest of us, so at the time of his death he had had about seventy adult years in which he was free to do whatever he wanted to do, to pursue any calling he wished or to work at anything he felt worthy of his considerable abilities.

And what had he chosen to do? Well, according to the story, he had "devoted his life to trying to breed the perfect spotted mouse."

Now, I grant every man the right to breed spotted mice if he wants to and can get the cooperation of the mice, and I freely admit that it is his business and not mine. Not being a mouse lover (nor a mouse hater for that matter; I am just neutral about mice), I do not know but that a spotted mouse might be more useful and make a more affectionate pet than a common mouse-colored mouse. But still I am troubled....

Made in the image of God, equipped with awesome powers of mind and soul, called to dream immortal dreams and to think the long thoughts of eternity, he chooses the breeding of a spotted mouse as his reason for existing. Invited to walk with God on earth and to dwell at last with the saints and angels in the world above; called to serve his generation by the will of God, to press with holy vigor toward the mark for the prize of the high calling of God in Christ Jesus, he dedicates his life to the spotted mouse—not just evenings or holidays, mind you, but his entire life.

Acts 13:36; Romans 8:28-30; Philippians 3:7-16
Man: The Dwelling Place of God, 91, 92.

722. Life purpose; Priorities; Eternal Perspective

If the spiritual view of the world is the correct one, as Christianity boldly asserts that it is, then for every one of us heaven is more important than earth and eternity more important than time. If Jesus Christ is who He claimed to be; if He is what the glorious company of the apostles and the noble army of martyrs declared that He is; if the faith which the holy church throughout all the world doth acknowledge is the true faith of God, then no man has any right to dedicate his life to anything that can burn or rust or rot or die. No man has any right to give himself completely to anyone but Christ nor to anything but prayer.

Matthew 6:19-21; 1 Corinthians 3:12-14; 1 Timothy 6:17-19
Man: The Dwelling Place of God, 93.

723. Life purpose; Priorities; Philosophy of life

The man who does not know where he is is lost; the man who does not know why he was born is worse lost; the man who cannot find an object worthy of his true devotion is lost utterly; and by this description the human race is lost, and it is a part of our lostness that we do not know how lost we are. So we use up the few precious years allotted to us breeding spotted mice. Not the kind that scurry and squeak, maybe; but viewed in the light of eternity, are not most of our little human activities almost as meaningless? . . .

Back of every wasted life is a bad philosophy, an erroneous conception of life's worth and purpose. The man who believes that he was born to get all he can will spend his life trying to get it; and whatever he gets will be but a cage of spotted mice. The man who believes he was created to enjoy fleshly pleasures will devote himself to pleasure seeking; and if by a combination of favorable circumstances he manages to get a lot of fun out of life, his pleasures will all turn to ashes in his mouth at the last. He will find out too late that God made him too noble to be satisfied with those tawdry pleasures he had devoted his life to here under the sun.

Ecclesiastes 12:1-8; Luke 12:15-21; 1 Timothy 6:17-19
Man: The Dwelling Place of God, 93,94.

724. Listening to God

The Scriptures declare, "Abram fell on his face" as the Lord talked with him (Genesis 17:3). Abraham was reverent and submissive. Probably there is no better picture anywhere in the Bible of the right place for mankind and the right place for God. God was on His throne speaking, and Abraham was on his face listening!

Where God and man are in relationship, this must be the ideal. God must be the communicator, and man must be in the listening, obeying attitude. If men and women are not willing to assume this listening attitude, there will be no meeting with God in living, personal experience.

Genesis 17:1-5; Joshua 5:14; 1 Samuel 3:10
Men Who Met God, 21.

725. Listening to God; Busyness; Meditation; Quakers

The Quakers had many fine ideas about life, and there is a story from them that illustrates the point I am trying to make. It concerns a conversation between Samuel Taylor Coleridge and a Quaker woman he had met. Maybe Coleridge was boasting a bit, but he told the woman how he had arranged the use of time so he would have no wasted hours. He said he memorized Greek while dressing and during breakfast. He went on with his list of other mental activities—making notes, reading, writing, formulating thoughts and ideas—until bedtime.

The Quaker listened unimpressed. When Coleridge was finished with his explanation, she asked him a simple, searching question: "My friend, when dost thee think?"

God is having a difficult time getting through to us because we are a fast-paced generation. We seem to have no time for contemplation. We have no time to answer God when He calls.

Psalm 46:10; Psalm 119:97
Jesus, Author of Our Faith, 46.

726. Listening to God; Meditation

The heart seldom gets hot while the mouth is open. A closed mouth before God and a silent heart are indispensable for the reception of certain kinds of truth. No man is qualified to speak who has not first listened.

Psalm 62:1-8
The Set of the Sail, 15.

727. Listening to God; Pastoral ministry: dependence on God

If while hearing a sermon we can fix on but one real jewel of truth we may consider ourselves well rewarded for the time we have spent.

One such gem was uncovered during a sermon which I heard some time ago. From the sermon I got one worthy sentence and no more, but it was so good that I regret that I cannot remember who the preacher was, that I might give him credit. Here is what he said, "Listen to no man who fails to listen to God."...

No man has any right to offer advice who has not first heard God speak. No man has any right to counsel others who is not ready to hear and follow the counsel of the Lord. True moral wisdom must always be an echo of God's voice. The only safe light for our path is the light which is reflected from Christ, the Light of the World. . . .

God has His chosen men still, and they are without exception good listeners. They can hear when the Lord speaks. We may safely listen to such men. But to no others.

Psalm 119:105; John 8:12; 1 Corinthians 11:1; 1 John 1:1-3
The Root of the Righteous, 17, 18, 19.

728. Listening to God; Prayers

Lord, teach me to listen. The times are noisy and my ears are weary with the thousand raucous sounds which continuously assault them. Give me the spirit of the boy Samuel when he said to Thee, "Speak, for thy servant heareth." Let me hear Thee speaking in my heart. Let me get used to the sound of Thy voice, that its tones may be familiar when the sounds of earth die away and the only sound will be the music of Thy speaking voice. Amen.

1 Samuel 3:18; Psalm 1:1-3; Psalm 6:6; Psalm 46:10; Psalm 119:147-148
The Pursuit of God, 76.

729. Loneliness

Most of the world's great souls have been lonely. Loneliness seems to be one price the saint must pay for his saintliness. . . .

The prophets of pre-Christian times differed widely from each other, but one mark they bore in common was their enforced loneliness. They loved their people and gloried in the religion of the fathers, but their loyalty to the God of Abraham, Isaac and Jacob, and their zeal for the welfare of the nation of Israel drove them away from the crowd and into long periods of heaviness. "I am become a stranger unto my brethren, and an alien unto my mother's children," cried one and unwittingly spoke for all the rest. . . .

Always remember: you cannot carry a cross in company. Though a man were surrounded by a vast crowd, his cross is his alone and his carrying of it marks him as a man apart. Society has turned against him; otherwise he would have no cross. No one is a friend to the man with a cross. "They all forsook him, and fled."

1 Kings 19:9-10; Psalm 69:8; Matthew 26:56
Man: The Dwelling Place of God, 168, 170, 171.

730. Loneliness; Communion with God

The sense of not belonging is a very real part of our Christian heritage. It is easily possible that the loneliest person in the world is a Christian—given the right circumstances....

We know what it means to have made our choice and to know that our Lord is our very best friend. We also know that when we break into tears from time to time, it is not a sign of weakness. It is the sense of the normal loneliness of a committed Christian in the middle of a world that rejected our Lord and now would disown us, His disciples.

Is there an encouraging word? Yes, there is a gracious word for you, fellow believer in the faith.

Being lonely in this world will only drive you to a closer communion with the God who has promised never to leave you or forsake you. He is altogether good and He is faithful. He will never break His covenant or alter that which has gone from His mouth. He has promised to keep you as the apple of His eye. He has promised to watch over you as a mother watches over her child.

Deuteronomy 32:10; John 15:18-21; 1 Thessalonians 5:23-24; Hebrews 13:5
Men Who Met God, 34, 35.

731. Loneliness; Heaven: longing for

This is the reason that it is easily possible for a Christian believer to be the loneliest person in the world under a set of certain circumstances. This sense of not belonging is a part of our Christian heritage. That sense of belonging in another world and not belonging to this one steals into the Christian bosom and marks him off as being different from the people around him....

That is exactly the thing that keeps a Christian separated—knowing that his citizenship is not on earth at all but in heaven above, and that he looks for the Savior to come. Who is there that can look more earnestly for the coming of the Lord Jesus than the one who feels that he is a lonely person in the middle of a lonely world?

Romans 8:19,22-25; 1 Corinthians 1:7; Philippians 3:18-21; Colossians 3:1-4
I Call It Heresy!, 26.

732. Loneliness; Spiritual depth

The loneliness of the Christian results from his walk with God in an ungodly world, a walk that must often take him away from the fellowship of good Christians as well as from that of the unregenerate world. His God-given instincts cry out for companionship with others of his kind, others who can understand his longings, his aspirations, his absorption in the love of Christ; and because within his circle of friends there are so few who share his inner experiences he is forced to walk alone. . . .

The truly spiritual man is indeed something of an oddity. He lives not for himself but to promote the interests of Another. He seeks to persuade people to give all to his Lord and asks no portion or share for himself. He delights not to be honored but to see his Saviour glorified in the eyes of men. His joy is to see his Lord promoted and himself neglected. He finds few who care to talk about that which is the supreme object of his interest, so he is often silent and preoccupied in the midst of noisy religious shoptalk. For this he earns the reputation of being dull and over-serious, so he is avoided and the gulf between him and society widens. He searches for friends upon whose garments he can detect the smell of myrrh and aloes and cassia out of the ivory palaces, and finding few or none he, like Mary of old, keeps these things in his heart.

It is this very loneliness that throws him back upon God.

Luke 2:8-20; John 3:30; Philippians 4:17
Man: The Dwelling Place of God, 172, 173.

733. Loneliness; World: contentment with; Pilgrims

Most of the world's great souls have been lonely. Loneliness seems to be one price the saint must pay for his saintliness. . . .

The weakness of so many modern Christians is that they feel too much at home in the world. In their effort to achieve restful "adjustment" to unregenerate society they have lost their pilgrim character and become an essential part of the very moral order against which they are sent to protest. The world recognizes them and accepts them for what they are. And this is the saddest thing that can be said about them. They are not lonely, but neither are they saints.

Philippians 3:18-21; Colossians 3:1-4; Hebrews 11:13-16; 1 Peter 2:11-12
Man: The Dwelling Place of God, 168, 174.

734. Longing for God

I have been greatly and deeply concerned that you and I do

something more than listen, that we dare to go to God. . . and dare to ask Him to give us a faithful, fatherly wound—maybe three of them, if you please: to wound us with a sense of our own sinful unworthiness that we'll never quite get over; to wound us with the sufferings of the world and the sorrows of the church; and then to wound us with the longing after God, a thirst, a sacred thirst and longing that will carry us on toward perfection. . . .

We don't need to have our doctrine straightened out; we're as orthodox as the Pharisees of old. But this longing for God that brings spiritual torrents and whirlwinds of seeking and self-denial—this is almost gone from our midst. . . .

Remember this: the man that has the most of God is the man who is seeking the most ardently for more of God.

Psalm 42:1-2; Psalm 63:1; 2 Corinthians 11:23-33; 1 Timothy 1:12-15
Man: The Dwelling Place of God, 106, 107.

735. Longing for God

Have any of you ever had a gracious, sudden kindling of desire, when everyone else seemed contented with panel discussions and the usual routine of the church which has to do with externals? How many of us go to church regularly and never feel an extra heartbeat, never any kindling of godly desire? We live like that!

So this kind of desire is not something that can be whipped up—God Himself must put it there. We could never have created ourselves and we could never have redeemed ourselves. We cannot talk ourselves into getting a longing for God. It has to come from God. . . .

If you have accepted a common state of spiritual living and you have no deep desire for Him, no man can give it to you. Unless you are willing for God to move in and have His way, you are never going to have spiritual adventures like those who have been explorers in the kingdom of God.

Psalm 42:1-2; Psalm 63:1-2
I Talk Back to the Devil, 58, 59.

736. Longing for God

These words are addressed to those of God's children who have been pierced with the arrow of infinite desire, who yearn for God with a yearning that has overcome them, who long with a longing that has become pain.

"Blessed are those who hunger and thirst for righteousness, for they will be filled" (Matthew 5:6).

A dead body feels no hunger and the dead soul knows not the pangs of holy desire. "If you want God," said the old saint, "you have already found Him." Our desire for fuller life is proof that some life must be there already. . . .

In nature everything moves in the direction of its hungers. In the spiritual world it is not otherwise. We gravitate toward our inward longing, provided of course that those longings are strong enough to move us. Impotent dreaming will not do. The religious urge that is not followed by a corresponding act of the will in the direction of that urge is a waste of emotion.

Matthew 5:6
The Size of the Soul, 17, 18.

737. Longing for God

It is part of my belief that God wants to get us to a place where we would still be happy if we had only Him! We don't need God and something else. God does give us Himself and lets us have other things, too, but there is that inner loneliness until we reach the place where it is only God that we desire.

Psalm 16:2; Psalm 73:25; John 6:68
The Counselor, 82.

738. Longing for God; Church: spiritual condition; Preaching: watered down

I trust I speak in charity, but the lack in our pulpits is real. Milton's terrible sentence applies to our day as accurately as it did to his: "The hungry sheep look up, and are not fed." It is a solemn thing, and no small scandal in the Kingdom, to see God's children starving while actually seated at the Father's table.

John 21:15-17; Acts 20:28-31; 2 Timothy 4:1-5
The Pursuit of God, 8.

739. Longing for God; Complacency

There are two great evils apparent among us today. The two are related in that both spring from callous, apathetic human attitudes. The first is the prevailing spirit of impenitence. The second is the total willingness to exist day after day without any longing for God.

If we yearned after God even as much as a cow yearns for her calf, we would be the worshiping and effective believers God wants us to be. If we longed for God as a bride looks forward to the return of her husband, we would be a far greater force for God than we are now.

Our hindrance, our difficulty is our lack of desire for God.

Men Who Met God, 67.

740. Longing for God; Godliness

Except in rare and isolated instances current Christianity is not producing godliness. And where an example of true saintliness appears occasionally it will be found to be a throwback to another and more serious type of religion than that to which people have "returned" in such numbers today. My own observation has taught me that the few who are yearning to be Christlike are being forced to dissent from most of what they see around them and go it alone in their holy longing after God. Scarcely any religious activities today conduce to holiness. The hungry seeker after personal godliness must look beyond the current "revival." He'll not find much help there.

Genesis 6:9; Leviticus 19:2; Matthew 5:48; Titus 2:11-14; 1 John 3:2-3
The Price of Neglect, 91, 92.

741. Longing for God; Knowledge of God: continuous pursuit; Prayers

O God, I have tasted Thy goodness, and it has both satisfied me and made me thirsty for more. I am painfully conscious of my need of further grace. I am ashamed of my lack of desire. O God, the Triune God, I want to want Thee; I long to be filled with longing; I thirst to be made more thirsty still. Show me Thy glory, I pray Thee, that so I may know Thee indeed. Begin in mercy a new work of love within me. Say to my soul, "Rise up, my love, my fair one, and come away." Then give me grace to rise and follow Thee up from this misty lowland where I have wandered so long. In Jesus' name. Amen.

Psalm 42:1-2; Psalm 63:6-8; John 17:3; Philippians 3:6-8
The Pursuit of God, 19, 20.

742. Longing for God; Knowledge of God: personal, intimate

Theological knowledge is knowledge about God. While this is indispensable it is not sufficient. It bears the same relation to man's spiritual need as a well does to the need of his physical body. It is not the rock-lined pit for which the dusty traveler longs, but the sweet, cool water that flows up from it. It is not intellectual knowledge about God that quenches man's ancient heart-thirst, but the very Person and Presence of God Himself.

Psalm 42:1-2; Psalm 63:1-2; Psalm 143:5-6; Philippians 3:10
Keys to the Deeper Life, 30, 31.

743. Longing for God; Preaching: watered down

Current evangelicalism has. . . laid the altar and divided the sacrifice into parts, but now seems satisfied to count the stones and rearrange the pieces with never a care that there is not a sign of fire upon the top of lofty Carmel. But God be thanked that there are a few who care. They are those who, while they love the altar and delight in the sacrifice, are yet unable to reconcile themselves to the continued absence of fire. They desire God above all. They are athirst to taste for themselves the "piercing sweetness" of the love of Christ about Whom all the holy prophets did write and the psalmists did sing.

1 Kings 18:37-39; Psalm 5:7; Psalm 92:1-4; Romans 8:35-39
The Pursuit of God, 8.

744. Longing for God; Revival: hopeful signs of

In this hour of all-but-universal darkness one cheering gleam appears: within the fold of conservative Christianity there are to be found increasing numbers of persons whose religious lives are marked by a growing hunger after God Himself. They are eager for spiritual realities and will not be put off with words, nor will they be content with correct "interpretations" of truth. They are athirst for God, and they will not be satisfied till they have drunk deep at the Fountain of Living Water.

This is the only real harbinger of revival which I have been able to detect anywhere on the religious horizon. It may be the cloud the size of a man's hand for which a few saints here and there have been looking. It can result in a resurrection of life for many souls and a recapture of that radiant wonder which should accompany faith in Christ, that wonder which has all but fled the Church of God in our day.

1 Kings 18:44; 2 Chronicles 5:13-14; Psalm 96:1-6; Isaiah 6:1-5
The Pursuit of God, 7.

745. Lordship of Christ; Commitment; Prayers

O God, be Thou exalted over my possessions. Nothing of earth's treasures shall seem dear unto me if only Thou art glorified in my life. Be Thou exalted over my friendships. I am determined that Thou shalt be above all, though I must stand deserted and alone in the midst of the earth. Be Thou exalted above my comforts. Though it mean the loss of bodily comforts and the carrying of heavy crosses, I shall keep my vow made this day before Thee. Be Thou exalted over my reputation. Make me ambitious to please Thee even if as a result I must sink into obscurity and my name be forgotten as a dream. Rise, O Lord, into Thy proper place of honor, above my likes and dislikes, above my family, my health and even my life itself. Let me sink that Thou mayest rise above. Ride forth upon me as Thou didst ride into Jerusalem mounted upon the humble little beast, a colt, the foal of an ass, and let me hear the children cry to Thee, "Hosanna in the highest."

Matthew 6:19-21; Matthew 21:6-9; John 3:30; 2 Corinthians 12:9-10; Philippians 4:11-12; Colossians 1:18
The Pursuit of God, 99, 100.

746. Lordship of Christ; Cross: demands of

We lay out the plans for our own lives and say, "Now, Lord, it is nice to serve You and we love You, Lord, and let's sing a chorus," but we won't change our plans in any way.

But, let me remind you, the cross of Jesus Christ always changes men's plans. The cross of Christ is revolutionary, and if we are not ready to let it be revolutionary in us nor let it cost us anything or control us in any way, we are not going to like a church that takes the things of God seriously.

People want the benefits of the cross but yet they do not want to bow to the control of the cross. They want to take all the cross can offer but they don't want to be under the lordship of Jesus.

Matthew 10:37-39; Luke 9:23-25
The Counselor, 12.

747. Lordship of Christ; Submission; Commitment

Every soul belongs to God and exists by His pleasure. God being who and what He is, and we being who and what we are, the only thinkable relation between us is one of full Lordship on His part and complete submission on ours. We owe Him every honor that is in our power to give Him. Our everlasting grief lies in giving Him anything less.

The pursuit of God will embrace the labor of bringing our total personality into conformity to His. . . . I speak of a voluntary exalting of God to His proper station over us and a willing surrender of our whole being to the place of worshipful submission which the Creator-creature circumstance makes proper.

Romans 9:19-21; 1 Corinthians 6:19-20; Revelation 4:8-11; Revelation 5:8-14
The Pursuit of God, 93, 94.

748. Love for God

The Christian's love for God has by some religious thinkers been divided into two kinds, the love of gratitude and the love of excellence. But we must carry our love to God further than love of gratitude and love of excellence.

There is a place in the religious experience where we love God for Himself alone, with never a thought of His benefits.

1 John 4:19
Renewed Day by Day, Volume 1, Jan. 13.

749. Love for God

The teaching of the Bible is that God is Himself the end for which man was created. "Whom have I in heaven but thee?" cried the psalmist, "and there is none upon earth that I desire beside thee" (Psa. 73:25). The first and greatest commandment is to love God with every power of our entire being. Where love like that exists there can be no place for a second object. If we love God as much as we should surely we cannot dream of a loved object beyond Him which He might help us to obtain.

Bernard of Clairvaux begins his radiant little treatise on the love of God with a question and an answer. The question, Why should we love God? The answer, Because He is God. He develops the idea further, but for the enlightened heart little more need be said. We should love God because He is God. Beyond this the angels cannot think.

Deuteronomy 6:4-9; Psalm 73:25; Matthew 22:37-39
Man: The Dwelling Place of God, 58.

750. Love for God; God: His love

It is a strange and beautiful eccentricity of the free God that He has allowed His heart to be emotionally identified with men. Self-sufficient as He is, He wants our love and will not be satisfied till He gets it. Free as He is, He has let His heart be bound to us forever. "Herein is love, not that we loved God, but that he loved us, and sent his Son to be the propitiation for our sins."

John 3:16; John 15:13; 2 Corinthians 5:12-15; 1 John 4:10
The Knowledge of the Holy, 156.

751. Love for God; Knowledge of God: basis for love

But it is wholly impossible to love the unknown. There must be some degree of experience before there can be any degree of love. Perhaps this accounts for the coldness toward God and Christ evidenced by the average Christian. How can we love a Being whom we have not heard nor felt nor experienced? We may work up some kind of reverence for the noble ideals the thought of God brings to our minds; we may feel a certain awe when we think of the high and holy One that inhabiteth eternity; but what we feel is hardly love. It is rather an appreciation of the sublime, a response of the heart to the mysterious and the grand. It is good and desirable, but it is not love. . . .

The heart that mourns its coldness toward God needs only to repent its sins, and a new, warm and satisfying love will flood into it. For the act of repentance will bring a corresponding act of God in self-revelation and intimate communion. Once the seeking heart finds God in personal experience there will be no further problem about loving Him. To know Him is to love Him and to know Him better is to love Him more.

Joshua 22:5; Isaiah 57:15; Mark 12:30,33
The Root of the Righteous, 142, 143.

752. Love for God; Worship: admiration

In the love which any intelligent creature feels for God there must always be a measure of mystery. It is even possible that it is almost wholly mystery, and that our attempt to find reasons is merely a rationalizing of a love already mysteriously present in the heart as a result of some secret operation of the Spirit within us, working like a miner, toiling unseen in the depths of the earth. But so far as reasons can be given, they would seem to be two: gratitude and excellence. To love God because He has been good to us is one of the most reasonable things possible. The love which arises from the consideration of His kindness to us is valid and altogether acceptable to Him. It is nevertheless a lower degree of love, being less selfless than that love which springs from an appreciation of what God is in Himself apart from His gifts.

Thus the simple love which arises from gratitude, when expressed in any act or conscious utterance, is undoubtedly worship. But the quality of our worship is stepped up as we move away from the thought of what God has done for us and nearer the thought of the excellence of His holy nature. This leads us to admiration.

Deuteronomy 6:4-9; Psalm 92:1-4; Psalm 100; Matthew 22:37-39
That Incredible Christian, 126, 127.

753. Love: importance of; Evangelism: concern for lost; Leaders: spiritual need

Once in private conversation with A.B. Simpson, R.R. Brown, then a young student, ventured to ask about the qualifications of a soul winner. "To be a great soul winner," Simpson replied, "a man must first be a great lover." It was only an impulsive sentence tossed off without too much thought, but it contains a world of spiritual philosophy. Spurgeon had a saying that a minister's congregation would always be the size of his heart. In at least one particular all spiritual leaders have been alike—they have all had large hearts. Nothing can take the place of affection. Those who have it in generous measure possess a magic power over men. Intellect will not do; Bible knowledge is not enough; even an upright life will be found wanting without this greatest of all gifts.

Psalm 126:5-6; Romans 9:1-3; 1 Corinthians 13:1-3
Let My People Go: The Life of Robert A. Jaffray, 32, 33.

754. Love: importance of; Unity

Any religious experience that fails to deepen our love for our fellow Christians may safely be written off as spurious....

As we grow in grace we grow in love toward all God's people. "Every one that loveth him that begat loveth him also that is begotten of him" (I John 5:1). This means simply that if we love God we will love His children. All true Christian experience will deepen our love for other Christians.

Therefore we conclude that whatever tends to separate us in person or in heart from our fellow Christians is not of God, but is of the flesh or of the devil. And conversely, whatever causes us to love the children of God is likely to be of God. "By this shall all men know that ye are my disciples, if you have love one to another" (John 13:35).

John 13:34-35; 1 John 3:17-19; 1 John 4:7-8; 1 John 5:1
Man: The Dwelling Place of God, 130.

755. Love: power of; Grace

There was a woman named Bluebird, who lived in Mulberry Bend in the Bowery in New York City a generation ago. She was a woman whose very life was given to the devil. She used dope; she drank; she used tobacco; she lived every way that Paul says we'll not even talk about. She was that kind of woman—a base, evil woman, and she was in jail. A Salvation Army woman went and stood outside and told her she loved her and kept telling her. And Bluebird cursed her and drove her off, but she came back and told her again. And she cursed her some more and drove her off. And she kept coming back. Always this little woman with the funny hat and the little red band around it kept coming back.

Finally, one day Bluebird said, "You say God loves me. You don't love me."

And she said, "But I do love you."

Bluebird replied, "You don't love me; you're just doing your job. You're paid to do this—you're just slumming. If you love me, you'll kiss me." She was dirty and her hair was matted.

And the little Salvation Army girl reached through the bars and stuck her little face as far as she could through and grabbed Bluebird and pulled her dirty face up to her and kissed her full on the mouth. And Bluebird fell in a sobbing heap on the stone floor of the prison and wept her soul out—wept her soul back to her girlhood days, back to her innocency and her purity when she went to Sunday school and learned "God is love."

And there in a dirty heap, sobbing on the floor, she gave her heart to God.

Matthew 25:34-40; 1 John 3:17-19; 1 John 4:7,8,16
Success and the Christian, 106, 107.

756. Love: power of; Influences

Not only are we all in the process of becoming, *we are becoming what we love.* We are to a large degree the sum of our loves and we will of moral necessity grow into the image of what we love most; for love is among other things a creative affinity; it changes and molds and shapes and transforms. It is without doubt the most powerful agent affecting human nature next to the direct action of the Holy Spirit of God within the soul.

What we love is therefore not a small matter to be lightly shrugged off; rather it is of present, critical and everlasting importance. It is prophetic of our future. It tells us what we shall be, and so predicts accurately our eternal destiny.

Matthew 22:37-39; Philippians 4:8;
Colossians 3:1-4; 1 John 2:15-17
God Tells the Man Who Cares, 196.

757. Love: wrong concept

Millions of young people today are wholly unable to think of love except in terms of the disgraceful promiscuity of Hollywood. Newspapers now report the numerous marriages of the movie crowd by number: "It was the third marriage for her; his fourth." And if it were not so tragic for everyone concerned, it would be hugely comical to read of a movie star being interviewed by the press and solemnly assuring the public that she is not at the moment "in love." Such a use of the word is completely degraded and smacks more of the beasts than of men made in the image of God.

For the millions, love is an emotional attraction, nothing more, as unstable and as unpredictable as sheet lightning. The Bible teaches, on the contrary, that true love is a benevolent principle and *is under the control of the will.*

1 Corinthians 13; Ephesians 5:25-29;
Colossians 3:19
We Travel an Appointed Way, 42.

M

758. Man: alienation from God; Communion with God

From man's standpoint the most tragic loss suffered in the Fall was the vacating of this inner sanctum by the Spirit of God. At the far-in hidden center of man's being is a bush fitted to be the dwelling place of the Triune God. There God planned to rest and glow with moral and spiritual fire. Man by his sin forfeited this indescribably wonderful privilege and must now dwell there alone. For so intimately private is the place that no creature can intrude; no one can enter but Christ, and He will enter only by the invitation of faith.

John 4:23-24; 1 Corinthians 2:11-12; Revelation 3:20
Man: The Dwelling Place of God, 10.

759. Man: alienation from God; Sin: consequences of

Fallen nature is no friend of God. Fallen nature is no friend of God's grace. The winds that blow through the corridors of this world do not blow heavenward; they blow hellward. The man with no place of stability or anchorage goes the way the wind blows.

Job 18:5-15; Psalm 14:1-3; Isaiah 57:20
Echoes from Eden, 91.

760. Man: alienation from God; Sin: consequences of

One of the marks of God's image in man is his ability to exercise moral choice. The teaching of Christianity is that man chose to be independent of God and confirmed his choice by deliberately disobeying a divine command. This act violated the relationship that normally existed between God and His creature; it rejected God as the ground of existence and threw man back upon himself. Thereafter he became not a planet revolving around the central Sun, but a sun in his own right, around which everything else must revolve.

Genesis 1:26-27; Genesis 3:6-7; Romans 1:20-23; Romans 3:10-18
The Knowledge of the Holy, 45.

761. Man: insignificance of

With the understanding that God has given us, we have to agree that the physical body is the least essential part of the man. Some scientist has called the body "a concatenation of atoms," just a group of atoms and molecules that have gotten together for a while.

A man is more than likely to put a hat on the top of his body and walk down the street with a little strut, and say, "What a big boy am I!" But the truth is that he is just a walking concatenation of atoms and that is all.

The truth is that the soul of man is the essential part. Just as soon as the soul decides to wing away there will not be anything there for you to put your hat on. The body will decay and depart.

Genesis 3:14-19; Ecclesiastes 12:1-8; 2 Corinthians 5:1-8
Echoes from Eden, 88, 89.

762. Man: insignificance of; God: His majesty

Compared to Him, everything around us in this world shrinks in stature and significance. It is all a little business compared to Him—little churches with little preachers; little authors and little editors; little singers and little musicians; little deacons and little officials; little educators and little statesmen; little cities and little men and little things!

Brethren, humankind is so smothered under the little grains of dust that make up the world and time and space and matter that we are prone to forget that at one point God lived and dwelt and existed and loved without support, without help, and without creation.

Such is the causeless and self-existent God!

Psalm 8:3-6; Psalm 90:1-2; Isaiah 40:12-15
Christ the Eternal Son, 38, 39.

763. Man: rebellion against God; Redemption; Salvation: sovereign calling

But we have been guilty of that "foul revolt" of which Milton speaks when describing the rebellion of Satan and his hosts. We have broken with God. . . .

The whole work of God in redemption is to undo the tragic effects of that foul revolt, and to bring us back again into right and eternal relationship with Himself. This requires that our sins be disposed of satisfactorily, that a full reconciliation be effected and the way opened for us to return again into conscious communion with God and to live again in the Presence as before. Then by His prevenient working within us He moves us to return. This first comes to our notice when our restless hearts feel a yearning for the presence of God and we say within ourselves, "I will arise and go to my Father." That is the first step, and as the

Chinese sage Lao-tze has said, "The journey of a thousand miles begins with a first step."

Luke 15:18; Romans 5:8; Romans 8:28-30; 2 Corinthians 5:19-21
The Pursuit of God, 32, 33.

764. Man: rebellion against God; Self-assertion

Yet so subtle is self that scarcely anyone is conscious of its presence. Because man is born a rebel, he is unaware that he is one. His constant assertion of self, as far as he thinks of it at all, appears to him a perfectly normal thing. He is willing to share himself, sometimes even to sacrifice himself for a desired end, but never to dethrone himself. No matter how far down the scale of social acceptance he may slide, he is still in his own eyes a king on a throne, and no one, not even God, can take that throne from him.

Proverbs 3:7; Luke 18:9-14; Romans 6:11-14
The Knowledge of the Holy, 46.

765. Man: self-centeredness of; Evangelism: humanistic approach to

Christianity today is man-centered, not God-centered. God is made to wait patiently, even respectfully, on the whims of men. The image of God currently popular is that of a distracted Father, struggling in heartbroken desperation to get people to accept a Saviour of whom they feel no need and in whom they have very little interest. To persuade these self-sufficient souls to respond to His generous offers God will do almost anything, even using salesmanship methods and talking down to them in the chummiest way imaginable. This view of things is, of course, a kind of religious romanticism which, while it often uses flattering and sometimes embarrassing terms in praise of God, manages nevertheless to make man the star of the show.

1 Chronicles 29:11-13; Psalm 2:2-6,10-11; Psalm 24:7-10; Romans 1:20-23
Man: The Dwelling Place of God, 27.

766. Man: sinfulness of; America: sinfulness

Until we have seen ourselves as God sees us, we are not likely to be much disturbed over conditions around us as long as they do not get so far out of hand as to threaten our comfortable way of life. We have learned to live with unholiness and have come to look upon it as the natural and expected thing. We are not disappointed that we do not find all truth in our teachers or faithfulness in our politicians or complete honesty in our merchants or full trustworthiness in our friends. That we may continue to exist we make such laws as are necessary to protect us from our fellow men and let it go at that.

Romans 9:1-3; Romans 10:1-3; 2 Corinthians 5:12-15,19-21
The Knowledge of the Holy, 162.

767. Man: spiritual searching; Man: alienation from God; Purposelessness

The average person in the world today, without faith and without God and without hope, is engaged in a desperate personal search throughout his lifetime. He does not really know where he has been. He does not really know what he is doing here and now. He does not know where he is going.

The sad commentary is that he is doing it all on borrowed time and borrowed money and borrowed strength—and he already knows that in the end he will surely die! It boils down to the bewildered confession of many that "we have lost God somewhere along the way."...

Man, made more like God than any other creature, has become less like God than any other creature. Created to reflect the glory of God, he has retreated sullenly into his cave—reflecting only his own sinfulness.

Certainly it is a tragedy above all tragedies in this world that man, made with a soul to worship and praise and sing to God's glory, now sulks silently in his cave. Love has gone from his heart. Light has gone from his mind. Having lost God, he blindly stumbles on through this dark world to find only a grave at the end.

Psalm 8:3-5; Ephesians 2:12-13; Hebrews 9:27
Whatever Happened to Worship?, 65, 66.

768. Man: value of; Jesus Christ: His incarnation

Occasionally, art collectors will come upon an old masterpiece and will hire men who know how to restore it. And here it is, just an old cracked affair, smoky and terrible looking; nobody can see anything there but these keen, sharp-eyed men. These experts know that it's a da Vinci or a Rubens, and they restore it. They know all the chemicals to use that will remove the dirt without hurting the paints. Pretty soon, shining there before them is an old masterpiece, shining as beautiful as it was the day that it was created. . . .

Godless philosophies are among us today that tell us we're only animals. Out of these philosophies have come the totalitarian states—Nazism, communism, fascism and all the rest. But the Christian honors human life because, as the poor, dirty picture by da Vinci or Rubens, human life has about it the inklings and traces of immortality. When God Almighty, by His Son, Jesus Christ, takes that fallen masterpiece and restores it, you will find shining out of it again the face of Jesus Christ. For Christ became a man and was flesh to walk among us.

John 1:14; Romans 6:4-7; 2 Corinthians 5:13-17
Success and the Christian, 105, 108.

769. Man's approval

The man of faith is so sure of his position before God that he can quietly allow himself to be overlooked, discredited, deflated, without a tremor of anxiety. He is willing to wait out God's own good time and let the wisdom of the future judgment reveal his true size and worth. The man of unbelief dare not do this. He is so unsure of himself that he demands immediate and visible proof of his success. His deep unbelief must have the support of present judgment. He looks eagerly for evidence to assure him that he is indeed somebody. And of course this hunger for present approval throws him open to the temptation to inflate his work for the sake of appearances. . . .

If we have faith, we will be concerned only with what God thinks of us. We can smile off man's opinion, whether it be favorable or unfavorable, and go our God- appointed way in complete confidence.

1 Corinthians 4:2-3; 2 Corinthians 5:12-15; 1 Thessalonians 2:6-7
We Travel an Appointed Way, 108, 109.

770. Marriage

Perhaps you saw the cartoon in which the wife was blocking the doorway of the house while saying to her husband: "The high exalted potentate can't go out tonight because I won't let him!"

Tragedy in the Church: The Missing Gifts, 49.

771. Marriage

What I do want to say about the relationships of husbands and wives will boil down to this: for the Christian of either sex, there is only one rule to follow and that is, "What does the Bible say?"

Christians are first of all children of God, and as children of God we are committed to the Word of God. We are committed to a Man and a Book, the man being the Lord Jesus Christ and the book, of course, the Holy Scriptures.

When we have discovered what the Bible has to say with finality about any subject and have determined what pleases the Man in the glory, there is no room left for arguments.

Psalm 127:1-5; Ephesians 5:22-33; 1 Peter 3:1-7
I Call It Heresy!, 120.

772. Materialism; Advertising

Stimulation is good; overstimulation is a positive evil productive of every kind of physical and mental injury. And overstimulation has in recent years become a recognized part of our civilization. Indeed it is now a *necessary* part of it. The modern edifice we call our way of life would collapse were it not upheld by the pressure of abnormal stimulation.

The beating heart of our economy is the production and sale of consumer goods. The average person is likely to be a sluggish buyer unless he is needled into buying by high-pressure advertising. Hence the vast amounts spent each year and the tricky methods employed to persuade the public to buy. I think we have reached a place in the United States where the country must be overstimulated to prevent a serious depression. Take the pressure off and sales would probably decline sufficiently to throw the national economy into chaos.

Matthew 6:25-33; Luke 16:10-13
The Warfare of the Spirit, 92.

773. Materialism; Humanism

The Bible tells us in a variety of ways of an ancient curse that lingers with us to this very hour—the willingness of human society to be completely absorbed in a godless world! . . .

We have become a "profane" society—absorbed and intent with nothing more than the material and physical aspects of this earthly life. Men and women glory in the fact that they are now able to live in unaccustomed luxury in expensive homes; that they can trade in shiny and costly automobiles every year; and that their tailored suits and silk and satin dresses represent an expenditure never before possible in a society of common working people.

This is the curse that lies upon modern man—he is insensible and blind and deaf in his eagerness to forget that there is a God, in his strange belief that materialism and humanism constitute the "good life."

Matthew 6:19-21; Luke 12:33-34; John 1:10; Colossians 3:1-4; 1 Timothy 6:17-19
Who Put Jesus on the Cross?, 115, 116.

774. Materialism; Possessions; Earthly things

I know that we live in an era when believing disciples of the lowly, humble Nazarene have more of this world's goods and comforts than any other generation in history. These things conspire to make this a dangerous time for God's people. . . .

Moses turned his back on the pleasures and treasures of Egypt. Would we, could we turn our backs on the cash, the comforts, the conveniences we have in order to be the people of God? . . .

I confess that I feel a compulsion to cry out in prayer: "My Lord, I have so many earthly treasures! I must continually give thanks to Thee, my God, for Thy blessings. But I know that I am going to have to leave these things, to give them all up some day. Therefore, I do deliberately choose to earnestly seek spiritual treasures, putting them above all else. They are the only treasures that will not perish."

Matthew 6:19-21; Colossians 3:1-4; Hebrews 11:24-26
Men Who Met God, 84, 85.

775. Mediocrity; Cross: demands of; Convenience

What must our Lord think of us if His work and His witness depend upon the convenience of His people? The truth is that every advance that we make for God and for His cause must be made at our inconvenience. If it does not inconvenience us at all, there is no cross in it! If we have been able to reduce spirituality to a smooth pattern and it costs us nothing—no disturbance, no bother and no element of sacrifice in it—we are not getting anywhere with God. We have stopped and pitched our unworthy tent halfway between the swamp and the peak.

We are mediocre Christians!

Was there ever a cross that was convenient? Was there ever a convenient way to die? I have never heard of any, and judgment is not going to be a matter of convenience, either! Yet we look around for convenience, thinking we can reach the mountain peak conveniently and without trouble or danger to ourselves.

Actually, mountain climbers are always in peril and they are always advancing at their inconvenience.

Luke 9:23-25; 1 Corinthians 9:24-27;
Philippians 3:6-8, 12-14
I Talk Back to the Devil, 48.

776. Mediocrity; Spiritual growth; Complacency

Mediocre—most Christians are mediocre!

Actually, I hate the word—mediocre! I get no pleasure out of using it, but I think I am telling the truth when I say that it describes many Christians.

The word mediocre comes from two Latin words and literally means "halfway to the peak." This makes it an apt description of the progress of many Christians. They are halfway up to the peak. They are not halfway to heaven but halfway up to where they ought to be, halfway between the valley and the peak. They are morally above the hardened sinner but they are spiritually beneath the shining saint.

Many have settled down right there, and the tragedy is that years ago some of you said, "I am not going to fail God. I am going to push my way up the mountain until I am at the top of the peak, at the highest possible point of experience with God in this mortal life!"

But you have done nothing about it. If anything, you have lost spiritual ground since that day. You are now a halfway Christian! You are lukewarm, neither hot nor cold. You are halfway up to the peak, halfway to where you could have been if you had pressed on.

Habakkuk 3:19; Philippians 3:12-14;
Hebrews 6:1; Revelation 3:15-17
I Talk Back to the Devil, 43, 44.

777. Meekness; Peace: inner

The meek man is not a human mouse afflicted with a sense of his own inferiority. Rather, he may be in his moral life as bold as a lion and as strong as Samson; but he has stopped being fooled about himself. He has accepted God's estimate of his own life. He knows he is as weak and helpless as God has declared him to be, but paradoxically, he knows at the same time that he is, in the sight of God, more important than angels. In himself, nothing; in God, everything. That is his motto. He knows well that the world will never see him as God sees him and he has stopped caring. He rests perfectly content to allow God to place His own values. He will be patient to wait for the day when everything will get its own price tag and real worth will come into its own. Then the righteous shall shine forth in the Kingdom of their Father. He is willing to wait for that day.

In the meantime, he will have attained a place of soul rest. As he walks on in meekness he will be happy to let God defend him. The old struggle to defend himself is over. He has found the peace which meekness brings.

Psalm 37:7-11; Daniel 12:3; Matthew 5:5
The Pursuit of God, 104, 105.

778. Mentors

To the one who is advanced enough to hear it I would say, *never let anyone become necessary to you.* Be meek enough to learn from the lowly and wise enough to learn from the enlightened. Be quick to profit by the experiences of others and stay alert to the voice of wisdom from whatever direction it may sound. As the bee soars for nectar where the blossoms are thickest, so you must search for spiritual nectar where it is most likely to be found, which is among those Christians who are the most consecrated, the most prayerful and the most experienced.

Every man has some contributions to make to your life if you know how to receive it; certain men will astonish you with their ability to answer your unexpressed question and tell you what is in your heart. But never attach yourself to any man as a parasite. Adopt no man as a guru. Apart from the inspired writers of Holy Scriptures no man is worthy of such confidence. The sweetest saint can be mistaken. . . .

We may receive help from our fellow Christians as they from us, but our need for them is relative and fleeting. Let anyone become spiritually indispensable to us and we have deserted the Rock to build on shifting sand.

Proverbs 1:5; Acts 17:11; 1 Corinthians 3:21-4:1
The Warfare of the Spirit, 22, 23.

779. Miracles: commercialization of

Some are concerned because there are not more miracles and wonders wrought in our midst through faith. In our day, everything is commercialized. And I must say that I do not believe in commercialized miracles.

"Miracles, Incorporated"— you can have it!

"Healing, Incorporated"—you can have that, too! And the same with "Evangelism, Incorporated" and "Without a Vision the People Perish, Incorporated." I have my doubts about signs and wonders that have to be organized, that demand a letterhead and a president and a big trailer with lights and cameras. God is not in that!

But the person of faith who can go alone into the wilderness and get on his or her knees and command heaven—God is in that. The preacher who will dare to stand and let his preaching cost him something—God is in that. The Christian who is willing to put herself in a place where she must get the answer from God and God alone—the Lord is in that!

1 Kings 19:4-15; John 14:13-14; Acts 4:29-30; Philippians 1:20-26
Faith beyond Reason, 33, 34.

780. Miracles: commercialization of

I am not a miracle preacher. I have been in churches where they announced miracle meetings. If you look in the Saturday newspaper you will see occasionally somebody who will hit town and announce, "Come out and see some miracles." That kind of performing I do not care for.

You cannot get miracles as you would get a chemical reaction. You cannot get a miracle as you get a wonderful act on stage by a magician. God does not sell Himself into the hands of religious magicians. I do not believe in that kind of miracles. I believe in the kind of miracles that God gives to His people who live so close to Him that answers to prayer are common and these miracles are not uncommon.

Rut, Rot or Revival: The Condition of the Church, 118.

781. Missions: cautions about

To be saved, the Lord does not require people to change their common ways—except so far as they may be contrary to simple righteousness—but permits them to live after the accepted customs of their own people.

It would have been well for the church if it had remembered this as it sought to carry truth across ethnic and cultural lines during the last hundreds of years. Too often it has confused pure Christianity with Christianity as modified by a particular culture. Its requirements for a person who desires to become a Christian have frequently followed a narrow and prejudiced conception of what constitutes a good life within one or another social bracket. Often missionaries have attempted unconsciously to make new converts good Canadians or Americans, forgetting entirely that the traits marking people as belonging to a particular nation have nothing whatsoever to do with Christ or salvation. Failure to take this into account has hindered the spread of the gospel in no small degree. The inability of the missionary to accept an alien culture as valid has created barriers to the Christian faith where no such barriers should ever have been erected.

Acts 15:24-29; Romans 14:1-6,17-19; Galatians 5:1
Let My People Go: The Life of Robert A. Jaffray, 37, 38.

782. Missions: cautions about

The task of the church is twofold: to spread Christianity throughout the world and to make sure that the Christianity she spreads is the pure New Testament kind. . . .

The popular notion that the first obligation of the church is to spread the gospel to the uttermost parts of the earth is false. *Her first obligation is to be spiritually worthy to spread it.* Our Lord said "Go ye," but He also said, "Tarry ye," and the tarrying had to come before the going. Had the disciples gone forth as missionaries before the day of Pentecost it would have been an overwhelming spiritual disaster, for they could have done no more than make converts after their likeness, and this would have altered for the worse the whole history of the Western world and had consequences throughout the ages to come.

Matthew 28:18-20; Acts 1:4,8; 1 Thessalonians 1:6-8
Of God and Men, 36, 37.

783. Missions: church planting; Follow-up; Discipleship; Church: necessity of

The law of the wilderness operates universally throughout our fallen world, on the mission field as well as in more sheltered lands. It is therefore an error to believe that our missionary obligation may be discharged by passing through one country after another and proclaiming the Gospel without following it up with thorough teaching and careful church organization. . . .

To make a few converts, only to leave them to their own devices without adequate care, is as foolish as to turn loose a flock of newborn lambs in the middle of a wilderness; it is as absurd as to clear and plant a field in the heart of the deep woods and to leave it to the mercies of undisciplined nature. All this would be a waste of effort and could not possibly result in any real gain.

So it is with any spiritual effort that does not take into account the hunger of the wilderness. The lambs must be shepherded or they will be killed; the field must be cultivated or it will be lost; spiritual gains must be conserved by watchfulness and prayer or they too will fall victim to the enemy.

Acts 14:23; Ephesians 6:18; Titus 1:5; 1 Peter 5:1-4
The Root of the Righteous, 102, 103.

784. Missions: commanded

As God's people were held by Pharaoh in the bondage of Egypt, so God has His people in every known and unknown tribe of the earth, who are held in worse bondage than that of Egypt. God proposes in His plan of redemption to release a people for His name.

All human beings are God's creation and possession. Temporarily Satan has usurped authority and, through sin, holds the race in bondage. As God sent Moses to say over and over again to Pharaoh, "Let my people go!" so He has sent the Lord Jesus to save the world. He has commanded us to be His ministers to the last race of people in the uttermost parts of the earth, saying in the name of the Lord Jesus, the Creator and only Savior, "Let my people go!" This is the gospel message of deliverance.

Exodus 5:1; Luke 4:18-19; Acts 1:8
Let My People Go: The Life of Robert A. Jaffray, 5, 6, quoting Robert A. Jaffray, *The Pioneer.*

785. Missions: commanded

The members of many Christian churches dare to brag about being part of a "missionary-minded congregation," somehow failing to realize that it is the same old story—let the missionaries go out and suffer in the hard places. We say we are vitally interested in missions—and that seems to be true as long as it does not inconvenience us at home and the missionaries are willing to go and endure the hardships in the jungles overseas.

Acts 20:24; Acts 21:13; Philippians 1:12-18
Who Put Jesus on the Cross?, 90, 91.

786. Missions: motives for; Service: motives for; Concept of God

Almighty God, just because He is almighty, needs no support. The picture of a nervous, ingratiating God fawning over men to win their favor is not a pleasant one; yet if we look at the popular conception of God that is precisely what we see. Twentieth-century Christianity has put God on charity. So lofty is our opinion of ourselves that we find it quite easy, not to say enjoyable, to believe that we are necessary to God. . . .

Probably the hardest thought of all for our natural egotism to entertain is that God does not need our help. We commonly represent Him as a busy, eager, somewhat frustrated Father hurrying about seeking help to carry out His benevolent plan to bring peace and salvation to the world. . . .

Too many missionary appeals are based upon this fancied frustration of Almighty God. An effective speaker can easily excite pity in his hearers, not only for the heathen but for the God who has tried so hard and so long to save them and has failed for want of support. I fear that thousands of younger persons enter Christian service from no higher motive than to help deliver God from the embarrassing situation His love has gotten Him into and His limited abilities seem unable to get Him out of.

Psalm 50:10-12; Acts 17:24-25;
Romans 11:33-36
The Knowledge of the Holy, 54, 55.

787. Mistakes; Failure; Criticism

When Simpson succeeded it was in a big way. When he failed he made great failures. It had to be so. Men of his caliber do not make little mistakes. They fly too high and too far to steer their courses by city maps. They ask not, "What street is that?" but "What continent?" And when they get off of the course for a moment they will be sure to pull up a long way from their goal. Their range and speed make this inevitable. Little men who never get outside of their own yards point to these mistakes with great satisfaction. But history has a way of disposing of these critics by filing them away in quiet anonymity. She cannot be bothered to preserve their names. She is too busy chalking up the great successes and huge failures of her favorites.

Wingspread; A.B. Simpson: A Study in Spiritual Altitude, 108, 109.

788. Monday worship; Workplace

On Monday, as we go about our different duties and tasks, are we aware of the Presence of God? The Lord desires still to be in His holy temple, wherever we are. He wants the continuing love and delight and worship of His children, wherever we work.

Is it not a beautiful thing for a businessman to enter his office on Monday morning with an inner call to worship: "The Lord is in my office—let all the world be silent before Him."

If you cannot worship the Lord in the midst of your responsibilities on Monday, it is not very likely that you were worshiping on Sunday! . . .

I guess many people have an idea that they have God in a box. He is just in the church sanctuary, and when we leave and drive toward home, we have a rather faint, homesick feeling that we are leaving God in the big box.

You know that is not true, but what are you doing about it?

Psalm 11:4; Habakkuk 2:20; 1 Corinthians 3:16-23; Colossians 3:23
Whatever Happened to Worship?, 122.

789. Moral bearings

As the sailor locates his position on the sea by "shooting" the sun, so we may get our moral bearings by looking at God. We must begin with God. We are right when, and only when, we stand in a right position relative to God, and we are wrong so far and so long as we stand in any other position.

Much of our difficulty as seeking Christians stems from our unwillingness to take God as He is and adjust our lives accordingly. We insist upon trying to modify Him and to bring Him nearer to our own image.

Proverbs 14:12-13; Isaiah 51:1; Romans 10:1-3
The Pursuit of God, 93.

790. Moral rot; Sin: prevalence of; America: sinfulness

There has never been a time in history when people were good, but there have been times when the masses were ashamed of being bad. We have now degenerated to the point where we make belly-laughing jokes out of our evil ways and our scandalous morals. When the moral philosophy of a whole generation becomes such that people can flaunt their evil and rottenness and wind up being celebrated on the front pages of our newspapers, then God will withhold His hand no longer. We will rot from within.

Psalm 14:1-3; Isaiah 5:18-20; Romans 1:18-32
Faith beyond Reason, 125.

791. Moral rot; Sin: prevalence of; Science; Progress

Years ago our teachers told us that the world was getting better. . . .

But there was a fallacy in their proposition. They supposed that because we had become brilliant toy makers, we had also become morally good toy makers. It is true that we have invented and developed and discovered all kinds of brilliant new toys. We can reach up into the skies, pull down the jagged lightning and put it in a box or run it along wires. We have learned how to transmit the human voice over great distances, at first only along wires, now without wires. We can send the human voice anywhere—even out into space.

A few generations ago toys were plain and simple. A boy would take a wheel and put a spike through it, split a stick and run the spike through the split stick, and he had a toy. A girl would take an old sock that was no longer useful, stuff it with cotton, paint a face on it, and she had a rag doll for her younger sister to play with. Now, such simplicity is left far behind. We live in a day of startling electronic and technological marvels. Artificial daylight instead of candles, supersonic transportation instead of ox-cart. Instant communication worldwide instead of runner or pony express. And so our teachers have concluded that we must be better because we know so much more!

But one little thing has been overlooked in their preoccupation with our wonderful new ability to take the forces of nature and harness them. Our scientific and intellectual advances were not accompanied by similar moral strides. . . . Technology, instead of making us morally better, has been accompanied by a time of moral disintegration.

Jeremiah 10:12-15; John 1:20-23; Romans 1:20-23; 1 Corinthians 1:20-21
Faith beyond Reason, 122, 123, 124.

792. Motives; Priorities

That God should be glorified in us is so critically important that it stands in lonely grandeur, a moral imperative more compelling than any other which the human heart can acknowledge. To bring ourselves into a place where God will be eternally pleased with us should be the first responsible act of every man.

1 Corinthians 10:31; Colossians 3:16-18, 23; 1 Peter 4:11
God Tells the Man Who Cares, 39, 40.

793. Motives; Service: motives for

The big question at last will not be so much, "What did you do?" but "Why did you do it?" In moral acts, motive is everything. Of course it is important to do the right thing, but it is still more important to do the right thing for a right reason.

This World: Playground or Battleground?, 38.

794. Music; Hymnody

It can only be a cause for deep regret that the fear of offending has silenced the voices of so many men of discernment and put Bible Christianity at the mercy of the undiscerning.

Religious music has long ago fallen victim to this weak and twisted philosophy of godliness. Good hymnody has been betrayed and subverted by noisy, uncouth persons who have too long operated under the immunity afforded them by the timidity of the saints. The tragic result is that for one entire generation we have been rearing Christians who are in complete ignorance of the golden treasury of songs and hymns left us by the ages. The tin horn has been substituted for the silver trumpet, and our religious leaders have been afraid to protest.

It is ironic that the modernistic churches which deny the theology of the great hymns nevertheless sing them, and regenerated Christians who believe them are yet not singing them; in their stead are songs without theological content set to music without beauty.

Acts 16:25; 1 Corinthians 14:26;
Ephesians 5:18-19; Colossians 3:16-18
The Size of the Soul, 189.

795. Mysticism

Somehow the mystic has earned himself a doubtful reputation, or rather, he has had a doubtful reputation earned for him. That is why so many people feel that they must shy away from anyone who is said to be a mystic.

But John is the mystic of the New Testament even as Paul is the theologian. . . .

The man Paul possessed an unusual intellect and God was able to pour into his great mind and spirit the great basic doctrines of the New Testament. For God's purposes Paul was able then to think them through and reason them out and set them down logically; thus he holds that reputation as the theologian.

But in the mind of John, God found something different altogether—He found a harp that wanted to sit in the window and catch the wind. He found that John had a birdlike sense about him that wanted to take flight all the time.

Thus, God allowed John, starting from the same premises as the theologian Paul, to mount and soar and sing. . . .

Paul and John do not contradict one another; they do not cancel each other out. They complement each other in such a way that we may describe it by saying that Paul is the instrument and John is the music the instrument brings.

John 21:20; 1 John 1:1-3
Christ the Eternal Son, 5, 6.

796. Mysticism; Communion with God

I refer to the evangelical mystic who has been brought by the gospel into intimate fellowship with the Godhead. His theology is no less and no more than is taught in the Christian Scriptures. . . . He differs from the ordinary orthodox Christian only because he experiences his faith down in the depths of his sentient being while the other does not. He exists in a world of spiritual reality. He is quietly, deeply, and sometimes almost ecstatically aware of the Presence of God in his own nature and in the world around him. His religious experience is something elemental, as old as time and the creation. It is immediate acquaintance with God by union with the Eternal Son. It is to know that which passes knowledge.

The hymns and poems found here [*The Christian Book of Mystical Verse*] are mystical in that they are God-oriented; they begin with God, embrace the worshiping soul and return to God again. And they cover almost the full spectrum of religious feeling: fear, hope, penitence, aspiration, the longing to be holy, yearning after God, gratitude, thanksgiving, pure admiration of the Godhead, love for Christ, worship, praise and adoration. The mood runs from near despair to near ecstasy, and the twin notes of utter sincerity and deepest reverence may be heard throughout.

Psalm 63:1-2; Ephesians 1:4-6; 1 John 1:1-3
The Christian Book of Mystical Verse, vi.

797. Mysticism; Jesus Christ: love for

When I read the writings of the old mystics and the devotional writings and hymn writers of the Middle Ages and later, I get sick in my heart and I tell God, "God, I'm sorry; I apologize and I'm ashamed.

I don't love You the way these loved You." Read the letters of Samuel Rutherford. If you haven't, you should. Read those letters and then see how sick it'll make you. You'll fold that book shut and get down on your knees very likely and say, "Lord Jesus, do I love You at all considering that this was love? Then what have I, what have I got?"

Success and the Christian, 76.

N

798. Nature; Creation

I have long contended that the Creator God is an artist. His design and handiwork may be seen throughout His creation.

Do you have compelling memories from your childhood concerning the beauty of the earth where you grew up? I confess that I continue to think of my native Pennsylvania as a wonderful paradise of nature.

When I go back there, I still delight in the rolling green hills, the peaceful valleys, the flowing streams. I recall with pleasure the mystery in the morning fog hanging ribbon-like and low over the river, only to disappear into the sky as the sun rose. It was not hard to sense the hand of God in the lovely face of nature all around.

Men Who Met God, 28, 29.

799. Nature; Creation

There is an old proverb that says, "If you would be alone, look at the stars."

It was Emerson who commented that if the stars should come out only one night in a thousand years, everyone would drop what he or she was doing and in awe "look at the shining city of God." But because we see them all the time and because we are busy, we pay very little attention to the stars. We have too much noise and too many distractions!

Psalm 8:1; Psalm 19:1-6
Men Who Met God, 70.

800. Nature; God: His glory

Two men stood on the shore watching the sun come up out of the sea. One was a merchant from London, the other was the poet, William Blake. As the bright yellow disk of the sun emerged into view, gilding the water and painting the sky with a thousand colors, the poet turned to the merchant and asked, "What do you see?" "Ah! I see gold," replied the merchant. "The sun looks like a great gold piece. What do you see?" "I see the glory of God," Blake answered, "and I hear a multitude of the heavenly host crying 'Holy, Holy, Holy is the Lord God Almighty. The whole earth is full of His glory.'"

Psalm 19:1-6; Psalm 97:6; Isaiah 6:3
Of God and Men, 147, 148.

801. Nature; God: His majesty

With what joy the Christian turns from even the purest nature poets to the prophets and psalmists of the Scriptures. These saw God first; they rose by the power of faith to the throne of the Majesty on high and observed the created world from above. Their love of natural objects was deep and intense, but they loved them not for their own sakes but for the sake of Him who created them. They walked through the world as through the garden of God. Everything reminded them of Him. They saw His power in the stormy wind and tempest; they heard His voice in the thunder; the mountains told them of His strength and the rocks reminded them that He was their hiding place. The sun by day and the moon and stars by night spoke in the ear of reason and recited the story of their divine birth.

The nature poets are enamored of natural objects; the inspired writers are God-enamored men. That is the difference, and it is a vitally important one.

Job 12:7-10; Psalm 8; Psalm 19:1-6; Romans 1:19-20
Of God and Men, 140.

802. Negatives

It is fitting that we consider the negative before dealing with the positive. How can anyone deny that a portion of our Christian teaching has always taken into account the negative concerns? When we stand up for Jesus, it means that there are some things that we will be against.

This is the way it is in this world. We do not deny it, and we do not apologize for it. To say that we will never discuss anything in the negative would be similar to saying that there is only one side of a coin. If I should try to split all of my Canadian quarters right through the middle because I am impressed with the likeness of the Queen but I want to get rid of the likeness of the elk on the other side, someone might soon appear at 5 Old Orchard Road to deal with me. "A nice old man," they would comment condescendingly, "but he has slipped his trolley."

Joshua 24:14-15; 1 Kings 18:21; Romans 6:1-14
Jesus, Author of Our Faith, 113.

803. New believer

"The happiest man in the world," said a well-known preacher some time ago, "is the new convert before he has met too many Bible teachers and seen too many church members.". . .

The way some Bible teachers injure the new convert is to take away his simplicity; and the way some church members do it is by disillusioning him—before he is ready for it.

Matthew 18:6; 1 Corinthians 8:12
The Size of the Soul, 54, 56.

804. New believer; Christians: in the world

The new Christian is like a man who has learned to drive a car in a country where the traffic moves on the left side of the highway and suddenly finds himself in another country and forced to drive on the right. He must unlearn his old habit and learn a new one and, more serious than all, he must learn in heavy traffic. He must fight his old acquired reflexes and learn new ones, and he has no time or place to practice. He can learn only by driving and the Christian can learn only by living. There is no school of Christianity where the Christian can make his mistakes safely before going out where a mistake will cost him something. The Christian can never afford to be wrong, not even once, though by the good grace of God he can be forgiven if he sins and restored again to fellowship if he does fail his Lord. . . .

Among other things, the Bible is a record of the struggle of twice-born men to live in a world run by the once-born.

Romans 7:15-25; Galatians 5:17; 1 John 1:6-9
Of God and Men, 68, 69.

805. New believer; Discipleship

I think most Christians are simply uninstructed. They may have been talked into the kingdom when they were only half ready. Any convert made within the last thirty years was almost certainly told that he had but to take Jesus as his personal Saviour and all would be well. Possibly some counselor may have added that he now had eternal life and would most surely go to heaven when he died, if indeed the Lord does not return and carry him away in triumph before the unpleasant moment of death arrives.

After that first hurried entrance into the kingdom there is usually not much more said. The new convert finds himself with a hammer and a saw and no blueprint. He has not the remotest notion what he is supposed to build, so he settles down to the dull routine of polishing his tools once each Sunday and putting them back in their box.

Ephesians 4:14-16; Colossians 1:28-29; 1 Peter 2:1-2
Born after Midnight, 102.

806. New believer; Opposition; Christians: in the world

Elijah found out something that we are not teaching very well to new Christians. We ought to tell them that when they follow Jesus all the way, His enemies will be their enemies. We ought to tell them that they will be rejected in this world, just as Elijah—and Jesus—were rejected.

We are getting our new converts off to a bad start. We tell them that following Jesus as Lord is just the smoothest, easiest, slickest thing in the world. "Jesus is not going to lay any burdens on you," we reassure them. "Jesus is going to get you out of all your troubles."

I will come right out and say it: We ought not to tell them such lies!

We ought to tell them that if they will follow on to love and obey the Lord, this world will think the same of them that it thought of Him. What the world thought of Jesus was cruelly demonstrated on a rugged cross atop a hill outside Jerusalem.

1 Kings 19:9-10; John 15:18-21; John 16:33
Men Who Met God, 97, 98.

807. New believer; Salvation: transformation

The newborn Christian is a migrant; he has come into the kingdom of God from his old home in the kingdom of man and he must get set for the violent changes that will inevitably follow.

One of the first changes will be a shift of interest from earth to heaven, from men to God, from time to eternity, from earthly gain to Christ and His eternal kingdom. Suddenly, or slowly but surely, he will develop a new pattern of life. Old things will pass away and behold, all things will become new, first inwardly and then outwardly; for the change within him will soon begin to express itself by corresponding changes in his manner of living. . . .

The change will reveal itself further in what the new Christian reads, in the places he goes and the friends he cultivates, what he does with his time and how he spends his money. Indeed faith leaves no area of the new believer's life unaffected.

The genuinely renewed man will have a new life center.

2 Corinthians 5:17; Philippians 3:18-21; Colossians 3:1-4
Man: The Dwelling Place of God, 62, 63.

808. New believer; Salvation: transformation

The workings of God in the hearts of redeemed men always overflow into observable conduct. Certain moral changes will take place immediately in the life of the new convert. A moral revolution without will accompany the spiritual revolution that has occurred within. As the evangelists tell us, even the cat will know it when the head of the house is converted. And the grocer will know it too, and the old cronies in the haunts where the man used to hang out will suspect that something has happened when they miss the new Christian from his accustomed place. All this is collateral proof of the validity of the man's Christian profession.

Matthew 7:20; Luke 6:44-45; 2 Corinthians 5:17
We Travel an Appointed Way, 89.

809. New believer; Satan; Spiritual warfare

The Christian is a holy rebel loose in the world with access to the throne of God. Satan never knows from what direction the danger will come. Who knows when another Elijah will arise, or another Daniel? or a Luther or a Booth? Who knows when an Edwards or a Finney may go in and liberate a whole town or countryside by the preaching of the Word and prayer? Such a danger is too great to tolerate, so Satan gets to the new convert as early as possible to prevent his becoming too formidable a foe.

The new believer thus becomes at once a principal target for the fiery darts of the devil. Satan knows that the best way to be rid of a soldier is to destroy him before he becomes a man. The young Moses must not be allowed to grow into a liberator to set a nation free. The Baby Jesus dare not be permitted to become a man to die for the sins of the world. The new Christian must be destroyed early, or at least he must have his growth stunted so that he will be no real problem later.

Ephesians 6:10-18; Hebrews 5:12-14;
1 Peter 5:8-9
That Incredible Christian, 71, 72.

810. New man; Salvation: transformation

Man is a born cobbler. When he wants a thing to be better he goes to work to improve it. He improves cattle by careful breeding; cars and planes by streamlining; health by diet, vitamins and surgery; plants by grafting; people by education. But God will have none of this cobbling. He makes a man better by making him a new man, He imparts a higher order of life and sets to work to destroy the old.

2 Corinthians 5:17; Galatians 2:20; Ephesians 2:2-7
That Incredible Christian, 33.

811. New year

I know well enough that at midnight, December 31, nothing unusual will actually happen except in my head and the heads of others like me. I will think a new year that is new only because men have arbitrarily called it so, and feel myself passing over a line that is not really there. The whole thing will be imaginary and yet I cannot quite escape the fascination of it.

The Jews start the New Year on one day, and the Christians on another, and we cannot forget that the calendar has been pushed around quite a bit since men began to count time by years. Still the observation of the New Year is useful if it persuades us to slow down and let our souls catch up. And I think that is the real value of watch night services. We might do the same thing any night, but it is not likely that we will, so we may profit by taking advantage of the New Year service to examine our lives and ask of God strength to do better in the future than we have done in the past.

Psalm 139:23-24; Psalm 143:10; Colossians 1:9-11
The Warfare of the Spirit, 101, 102.

812. New year; Boldness; Evangelism: urgency of

Every new year is an uncharted and unknown sea. No ship has ever sailed this way before. The wisest of earth's sons and daughters cannot tell us what we may encounter on this journey. Familiarity with the past may afford us a general idea of what we may expect, but just where the rocks lie hidden beneath the surface or when that "tempestuous wind called Euroclydon" may sweep down upon us suddenly, no one can say with certainty....

Now more than at any other time in generations, the believer is in a position to go on the offensive. The world is lost on a wide sea, and Christians alone know the way to the desired haven. While things were going well, the world scorned them with their Bible and hymns, but now the world needs them desperately, and it needs that despised Bible, too.

For in the Bible, and there only, is found the chart to tell us where we are going on this rough and unknown ocean. The day when Christians should meekly apologize is over—they can get the world's attention not by trying to please, but by boldly declaring the truth of divine revelation. They can make themselves heard not by compromise, but by taking the affirmative and sturdily declaring, "Thus saith the Lord."

Isaiah 28:16; Isaiah 45:18; Jeremiah 10:23; Acts 27:14
This World: Playground or Battleground?, 9, 10.

813. New year; Failure; Repentance

For some of us last year was one in which we did not acquit ourselves very nobly as Christians, considering the infinite power available to us through the indwelling Spirit. But through the goodness of God we may go to school to our failures. The man of illuminated mind will learn from his mistakes, yes even from his sins. If his heart is trusting and penitent, he can be a better man next year for last year's fault—but let him not return again to folly. Repentance should be radical and thorough, and the best repentance for a wrong act, as Fenelon said, is not to do it again. . . .

Brother Lawrence expressed the highest moral wisdom when he testified that if he stumbled and fell he turned at once to God and said, "O Lord, this is what You may expect of me if You leave me to myself." He then accepted forgiveness, thanked God and gave himself no further concern about the matter.

2 Chronicles 7:14; Romans 7:24-25; Ephesians 4:22-24; 1 John 1:6-9
The Warfare of the Spirit, 102, 103, 104.

814. Noah; Obedience: need for; Doctrine; Faith: daily walk

The Bible gives us a straightforward message concerning Noah. It is simply this: "Demonstrate your faith in God in your everyday life!"

It is evident that God did not say to Noah: "I am depending on you to hold the proper orthodox doctrines. Everything will be just fine if you stand up for the right doctrines!" No, that is not what God demanded of Noah. Yet we have many religiously inclined people in our day who hold to an illusion that the learning of doctrine is enough. They actually think that somehow they are better for having learned the doctrines of religion.

What actually did God ask Noah to do? Just this: to believe, to trust, to obey—to carry out His word. . . .

I have been impressed by a statement on Christian doctrine made by Martin Lloyd-Jones, the English preacher and writer, in a published article. The gist of his message was this: It is perilously close to being sinful for any person to learn doctrine for doctrine's sake. I agree with his conclusion that doctrine is always best when it is incarnated—when it is seen fleshed out in the lives of godly men and women.

Genesis 6:22; Psalm 119:1-2; Hebrews 11:7; James 1:22-25
Jesus, Author of Our Faith, 31.

O

815. Obedience: cost of

But we tend to dicker with God and try to get an easy way. "Lord, I want to be blessed, but I don't want it to cost me this much. Couldn't we talk this thing over?"

"No," says God," we can't talk this thing over. My rules are my rules and my Word is my Word and My will is made known in the Word and there isn't anything to talk over. So you come My way and you will be blessed. Go your way and you'll lose everything."

Matthew 10:10-39; Luke 9:23-25,57-62; John 15:8,10,18-21
Success and the Christian, 140.

816. Obedience: need for

If we are alert enough to hear God's voice we must not content ourselves with merely "believing" it. . . . Commands are to be obeyed, and until we have obeyed them we have done exactly nothing at all about them. And to have heard them and not obeyed them is infinitely worse than never to have heard them at all.

John 14:21; James 1:22-25; 1 John 2:3-6
Keys to the Deeper Life, 26.

817. Obedience: need for

The Lord has spoken to us all and said, "If you are willing and obedient, you will eat the best from the land" (1:19).

Willing and obedient Christians—where are they? Why do we have so many spineless and shrinking Christians, apparently without any strength of character?

Why should we find a Christian man praying, "Oh Lord, help me to be honest." He knows well enough that if he is not honest he will go to jail.

I have heard people pray, "Oh Father, help me to quit lying." God never taught them to lie—He just says "Quit your lying.". . .

It is time that we Christians wake up and assume our spiritual responsibilities. Let us ask God to wind up our backbones; let us ask Him to give us the courage to pray, "Now, God, show me what to do!" and get out there and get active.

If we "are willing and obedient, [we] will eat the best from the land"—that is the promise of God. But if we refuse and rebel, nothing but judgment lies before us.

Deuteronomy 28:1-2; Isaiah 1:16-19; Jeremiah 42:3-6; Ephesians 4:25
Echoes from Eden, 81.

818. Obedience: need for; Gospel: moral implications; Faith: and works

The Church of our day has soft-pedaled the doctrine of obedience, either neglecting it altogether or mentioning it only apologetically and without urgency. This results from a fundamental confusion of obedience with works in the minds of preacher and people. To escape the error of salvation by works we have fallen into the opposite error of salvation without obedience. In our eagerness to get rid of the legalistic doctrine of works we have thrown out the baby with the bath and gotten rid of obedience as well.

Galatians 5:13; Ephesians 2:8-10; Titus 2:11-14
Paths to Power, 23, 24.

819. Obedience: need for; Holy Spirit: do not grieve

The Christian who gazes too long on the carnal pleasures of this world cannot escape a certain feeling of sympathy with them, and that feeling will inevitably lead to behavior that is worldly. And to expose our hearts to truth and consistently refuse or neglect to obey the impulses it arouses is to stymie the motions of life within us and, if persisted in, to grieve the Holy Spirit into silence.

The Scriptures and our own human constitution agree to teach us to love truth and to obey the sweet impulses of righteousness it raises within us. If we love our own souls we dare do nothing else.

John 14:21; Ephesians 4:30; 1 John 2:15-17
That Incredible Christian, 49.

820. Obedience: need for; Lordship of Christ

I am satisfied that when a man believes on Jesus Christ he must believe on the whole Lord Jesus Christ—not making any reservation! I am satisfied that it is wrong to look upon Jesus as a kind of divine nurse to whom we can go when sin has made us sick, and after He has helped us, to say "Goodbye"—and go on our own way.

Suppose I slip into a hospital and tell the staff I need a blood transfusion or perhaps an X-ray of my gall bladder. After they have ministered to me and given their services, do I just slip out of the hospital again with a cheery "Goodbye"—as though I owe them nothing and it was kind of them to help me in my time of need?

That may sound like a grotesque concept to you, but it does pretty well draw the picture of those who have been taught that they can use Jesus as a Savior in their time of need without owning Him as Sovereign and Lord and without owing Him obedience and allegiance.

Romans 10:8-10; Philippians 2:9-11; James 2:26
I Call It Heresy!, 7, 8.

821. Obedience: need for; Obedience: meaning of

To obey, in New Testament usage, means to give earnest attention to the Word, to submit to its authority, and to carry out its instructions.

Obedience in this sense is almost a dead letter in modern Christianity. It may be taught now and then in a languid sort of way, but it is not stressed sufficiently to give it power over the lives of the hearers. For, to become effective, a doctrine must not only be received and held by the Church, but must have behind it such pressure of moral conviction that the emphasis will fall like a blow upon a percussion cap, setting off the energy latent within.

The Church of our day has soft-pedaled the doctrine of obedience, either neglecting it altogether or mentioning it only apologetically and without urgency.

John 14:15-17; Romans 6:11-14; 1 John 5:3
Paths to Power, 23.

822. Obedience: need for; Submission; Faith: and works

A world of confusion and disappointment results from trying to believe without obeying. This puts us in the position of a bird trying to fly with one wing folded. We merely flap in a circle and seek to cheer our hearts with the hope that the whirling ball of feathers is proof that a revival is under way. . . .

A mere passive surrender may be no surrender at all. Any real submission to the will of God must include willingness to take orders from Him from that time on. When the heart is irrevocably committed to receiving and obeying orders from the Lord Himself, a specific work has been done, but not until then. We are not likely to see among us any remarkable transformations of individuals or churches until the Lord's ministers again give to obedience the place of prominence it occupies in the Scriptures.

Romans 12:1-2; Philippians 2:9-11; Colossians 3:5-11
This World: Playground or Battleground?, 71, 72.

823. Obedience: test of love

The Christian cannot be certain of the reality and depth of his love until he comes face to face with the commandments of Christ and is forced to decide what to do about them. Then he will know. "He that loveth me not keepeth not my sayings," said our Lord. "He that hath my commandments, and keepeth them, he it is that loveth me."

So the final test of love is obedience. Not sweet emotions, not willingness to sacrifice, not zeal, but obedience to the commandments of Christ. Our Lord drew a line plain and tight for everyone to see. On one side He placed those who keep His commandments and said, "These love Me." On the other side He put those who keep not His sayings, and said, "These love Me not."

John 14:21,24
That Incredible Christian, 134.

824. Obscurity; Unsung heroes

Unsung but singing: this is the short and simple story of many today whose names are not known beyond the small circle of their own small company. Their gifts are not many nor great, but their song is sweet and clear. . . . Well, the world is big and tangled and dark, and we are never sure where a true Christian may be found. One thing we do know: the more like Christ he is the less likely it will be that a newspaper reporter will be seeking him out. However much he may value the esteem of his fellow men, he may for the time be forced to stand under the shadow of their displeasure. Or the busy world may actually not even know he is there—except that they hear him singing.

2 Corinthians 4:5-7; Philippians 4:11-12; Colossians 3:16-18
Born after Midnight, 54, 55.

825. Old nature; Carnality

If the old man was something that could be lifted out, like an onion could be pulled out of a garden, then we'd all feel very proud of the fact that we'd been de-unionized and debunked. But the terrible part about crucifying the flesh is, the flesh is you. When the Lord says mortify the flesh, He doesn't mean abuse your body by starving it or lying on beds of nails. He means, put yourself on the cross. That is what people do not want to do. . . .

There are a lot of people trying to get away with the old man. What do I mean by the old man? I mean your pride, your bossiness, your nastiness, your temper, your mean disposition, your lustfulness and your quarrelsomeness. What do I mean, Reverend? I mean your study, your hunting for a bigger church, being dissatisfied with the offering and blaming the superintendent because you cannot get called. The reason you cannot get called is nobody wants you. That is what I mean, Reverend.

Deacons, what do I mean? I mean sitting around in board meetings wearing your poor pastor out, because you are too stubborn to humble yourself and admit you are wrong.

What do I mean, musicians? I mean that demeanor that makes you hate somebody that can sing a little better than you can. I mean that jealousy that makes you want to play the violin when everybody knows you can't, especially the choir director. You hate him, wish he were dead, and secretly pray that he would get called to Punxsutawney. That is what I mean. All of this may be under the guise of spirituality and we may have learned to put our head over on one side, fold our hands gently and put on a beatific smile like St. Francis of Assisi, and still be just as carnal as they come.

Romans 8:13; Ephesians 4:25-32; Colossians 3:5-11; Hebrews 13:17
Success and the Christian, 42, 43, 44.

826. Old nature; Spiritual warfare

The regenerate man often has a more difficult time of it than the unregenerate, for he is not one man but two. He feels within him a power that tends toward holiness and God, while at the same time he is still a child of Adam's flesh and a son of the red clay. This moral dualism is to him a source of distress and struggle wholly unknown to the once-born man. Of course the classic critique upon this is Paul's testimony in the seventh chapter of his Roman epistle.

The true Christian is a saint in embryo. The heavenly genes are in him and the Holy Spirit is working to bring him on into a spiritual development that accords with the nature of the Heavenly Father from whom he received the deposit of divine life. Yet he is here in this mortal body subject to weakness and temptation, and his warfare with the flesh sometimes leads him to do extreme things. "For the flesh lusteth against the Spirit, and the Spirit against the flesh: and these are contrary the one to the other: so that ye cannot do the things that ye would" (Gal. 5:17).

Romans 7:15-25; Galatians 5:17; 1 Peter 2:11-12
That Incredible Christian, 53, 54.

827. Old Testament; Bible: unity of

I do not mind telling you that I have always found Jesus Christ beckoning to me throughout the Scriptures. Do not be disturbed by those who say that Old Testament portions cannot be claimed by the Christian church. God has given us the Bible as a unit, and Jesus referred in His teachings to many Old Testament portions which foretold His person and His ministries.

For illustration, I would say that it would be very difficult for a man to live and function in a physical body that existed only from the waist up. He would be without some of the vital organs necessary for the sustenance of life.

Similarly, the Bible contains two parts of one organic revelation and it is divided so that the Old Testament is the Bible from the waist down and the New Testament is the Bible from the waist up. This may give an understanding to my expression that if we have one organic Bible and we cut it in two, we actually bleed it to death and we can, in effect, kill it by cutting it.

Let us read the Bible as the Word of God and never apologize for finding Jesus Christ throughout its pages, for Jesus Christ is what the Bible is all about!

Romans 15:4; 1 Corinthians 10:11-12;
2 Timothy 3:16-17
Who Put Jesus on the Cross?, 204, 205.

828. Old Testament; Bible: unity of

Imagine with me a capable housewife and cook preparing her dining room for guests. She has set the cloth-covered table with her best china and silverware, positioning everything precisely. She adds a centerpiece of cut flowers—a delicate floral complement to the food we suppose will soon be coming.

But instead of the platter of savory beef and the dishes of steaming mashed potatoes and other vegetables that we had anticipated, she brings a single loaf of bread into the dining room. This she upends on the buffet, placing a strong light behind it so that the loaf of bread casts its own distinct shadow over the table service beyond it. We would have further reason to question the woman's sanity if at that point she called family and guests to the table, announcing cheerily, "The shadow of the bread is ready. You may come!". . .

The Old Testament economy, the law of Moses, the priesthood

of imperfect men and the offering of sacrifices for sin—all of these were appointed of God for a time. They represented as a shadow the better things, the reality to come.

Acts 13:3839; Romans 8:3; Hebrews 10:1-2
Jesus, Our Man in Glory, 125, 126.

829. Opportunity

An opportunity may be defined as a providential circumstance which permits us to turn our time, our money and our talents to account. Of all gifts this is the most common, and it is the one which makes the other gifts of value to us and to mankind. The wise Christian will watch for opportunities to do good, to speak the life-bringing word to sinners, to pray the rescuing prayer of intercession.

The foe of opportunity is preoccupation. Just when God sends along a chance to turn a great victory for mankind, some of us are too busy puttering around to notice it. Or we notice it when it is too late. The old Greeks said that opportunity had a forelock but was close-shaven behind; if a man missed grabbing for her as she approached, he would reach for her in vain after she had passed.

Proverbs 3:27; Galatians 6:10; Ephesians 5:15-18; Colossians 4:5-6
We Travel an Appointed Way, 23.

830. Opposition; Church: religious game; Truth: necessity of response

Bible exposition without moral application raises no opposition. It is only when the hearer is made to understand that truth is in conflict with his heart that resistance sets in. As long as people can hear orthodox truth divorced from life they will attend and support churches and institutions without objection. The truth is a lovely song, become sweet by long and tender association; and since it asks nothing but a few dollars, and offers good music, pleasant friendships and a comfortable sense of well-being, it meets with no resistance from the faithful. Much that passes for New Testament Christianity is little more than objective truth sweetened with song and made palatable by religious entertainment.

Acts 4:16-17; 1 Corinthians 9:16; Philippians 1:27-28
Of God and Men, 27.

831. Organization; Church: organization

I am and have been for years much distressed about the tendency to over-organize the Christian community, and I have for that reason had it charged against me that I do not believe in organization. The truth is quite otherwise.

The man who would oppose organization in the church must needs be ignorant of the facts of life. Art is organized beauty; music is organized sound; philosophy is organized thought; science is organized knowledge; government is merely society organized. And what is the true church of Christ but organized mystery? . . .

Many church groups have perished from too much organization, even as others from too little. Wise church leaders will watch out for both extremes. A man may die as a result of having too low blood pressure as certainly as from having too high, and it matters little which takes him off. He is equally dead either way. The important thing in church organization is to discover the scriptural balance between two extremes and avoid both.

Exodus 18:19-23; Acts 6:3-7; 1 Corinthians 14:40; Titus 1:5
God Tells the Man Who Cares, 29, 31.

832. Organization; Church: organization

Another cause back of our top-heavy and ugly over organization is fear. Churches and societies founded by saintly men with courage, faith and sanctified imagination appear unable to propagate themselves on the same spiritual level beyond one or two generations. The spiritual fathers were not able to sire others with courage and faith equal to their own. The fathers had God and little else, but their descendants lose their vision and look to methods and constitutions for the power their hearts tell them they lack. Then rules and precedents harden into a protective shell where they can take refuge from trouble. It is always easier and safer to pull in our necks than to fight things out on the field of battle.

Psalm 73:25; Acts 26:13-19; 2 Timothy 2:2; Hebrews 11:1,2,8-10
God Tells the Man Who Cares, 32.

P

833. Para-church ministries

The highest expression of the will of God in this age is the church which He purchased with His own blood. To be scripturally valid any religious activity must be part of the church. Let it be clearly stated that there can be no service acceptable to God in this age that does not center in and spring out of the church. Bible schools, tract societies, Christian business men's committees, seminaries and the many independent groups working at one or another phase of religion need to check themselves reverently and courageously, for they have no true spiritual significance outside of or apart from the church.

Matthew 16:18; Acts 20:28-31
God Tells the Man Who Cares, 24.

834. Passive religion; Church: apathy

Most readers will remember (some with just a trace of nostalgia) his or her early struggles to learn the difference between the active and the passive voice in English grammar, and how it finally dawned that in the active voice, the subject *performs an act* ; in the passive voice, the subject *is acted upon*.

A good example of this distinction is to be found at the nearest mortuary. There the undertaker is active and the dead are passive. One acts while the others receive the action.

Now what is normal in a mortuary may be, and in this instance is, altogether abnormal in a church. Yet we have somehow gotten ourselves into a state where almost all church religion is passive. A limited number of professionals act, and the mass of religious people are content to receive the action. The minister, like the undertaker, performs his professional service while the members of the congregation relax and passively "enjoy" the service.

Romans 12:3-8; 1 Corinthians 12:18-27; Ephesians 4:11-13
We Travel an Appointed Way, 76.

835. Pastoral ministry: challenge; Church: boredom; Boredom: religious

That there is something gravely wrong with evangelical Christianity today is not likely to be denied by any serious-minded person acquainted with the facts.

Just what is wrong is not so easy to determine. . . .

One mark of the low state of affairs among us is religious boredom. Whether this is a thing in itself or merely a symptom of the thing, I do not know for sure, though I suspect that it is the latter. And that it is found to some degree almost everywhere among Christians is too evident to be denied.

Boredom is, of course, a state of mind resulting from trying to maintain an interest in something that holds no trace of interest for us. . . .

By this definition there is certainly much boredom in religion these days. The businessman on a Sunday morning whose mind is on golf can scarcely disguise his lack of interest in the sermon he is compelled to hear. The housewife who is unacquainted with the learned theological or philosophical jargon of the speaker; the young couple who feel a tingle of love for each other but who neither love nor know the One about whom the choir is singing—these cannot escape the lowgrade mental pain we call boredom while they struggle to keep their attention focused upon the service. All these are too courteous to admit to others that they are bored and possibly too timid to admit it even to themselves, but I believe that a bit of candid confession would do us all good.

Man: The Dwelling Place of God, 133, 134, 135.

836. Pastoral ministry: challenge; Preaching: awesome task

What a great responsibility God has laid upon us preachers of His gospel and teachers of His Word. In that future day when God's wrath is poured out, how are we going to answer? How am I going to answer? I fear there is much we are doing in the name of the Christian church that is wood, hay and stubble destined to be burned up in God's refining fire. A day is coming when I and my fellow ministers must give account of our stewardship:

What kind of a gospel did we preach?

Did we make it plain that men and women who are apart from Christ Jesus are lost?

Did we counsel them to repent and believe?

Did we tell them of the regenerating power of the Holy Spirit?

Did we warn them of the wrath of the Lamb—the crucified, resurrected, outraged Lamb of God?

With that kind of accounting yet to come, the question John hears from the human objects of God's wrath is especially significant: "Who can stand?" (6:17). Who indeed?

Acts 20:18-21; Romans 1:18; 1 Corinthians 3:12-14; Galatians 1:6-7; Ephesians 2:12-13; Revelation 6:12-17
Jesus Is Victor!, 108.

837. Pastoral ministry: competition; Humility; Pride: pastoral; Competition

Circumstances being what they are the Christian minister is the one most tempted to carry on competitive religious activity. Even where his self-respect and good taste will not allow him to engage in an obvious race for numbers or publicity or fame he may yet harbor the spirit of envy within his heart and so be as guilty as the coarser and less inhibited bellwether who openly seeks to excel. He can get deliverance from the spirit of religious rivalry by going straight to God and having an understanding about the whole thing. Let him humble himself in the presence of God and in all earnestness pray somewhat like this:

"Dear Lord, I refuse henceforth to compete with any of Thy servants. They have congregations larger than mine. So be it. I rejoice in their success. They have greater gifts. Very well. That is not in their power nor in mine. I am humbly grateful for their greater gifts and my smaller ones. I only pray that I may use to Thy glory such modest gifts as I possess. I will not compare myself with any, nor try to build up my self-esteem by noting where I may excel one or another in Thy holy work. I herewith make a blanket disavowal of all intrinsic worth. I am but an unprofitable servant. I gladly go to the foot of the class and own myself the least of Thy people. If I err in my self-judgment and actually underestimate myself I do not want to know it. I purpose to pray for others and to rejoice in their prosperity as if it were my own. And indeed it is my own if it is Thine own, for what is Thine is mine, and while one plants and another waters it is Thou alone that giveth the increase."

Romans 12:3-8; 1 Corinthians 3:5-9; 1 Peter 4:11
The Price of Neglect, 104, 105.

838. Pastoral ministry: dependence on God; Church: finances

We can learn important lessons by considering God's disciplines in dealing with Elijah. As Elijah fled to the wilderness following his first confrontation with King Ahab, God said to him, "Elijah, go to the brook Cherith, and I will feed you there." God sent big, black buzzards—ravens, scavenger birds—each morning and evening with Elijah's meals. What humiliation! All his life Elijah had been self-sufficient. Now he waited on scavenger birds to deliver him his daily bread....

Elijah was like so many faithful preachers of the Word who are too true and too uncompromising for their congregations.

"We don't have to take that," the people protest. And they stop contributing to the church. More than one pastor knows the meaning of economic strangulation. Preach the truth, and the brook dries up! But the Lord knows how to deal with each of us in our humiliations. He takes us from truth to truth.

1 Kings 17:3-6; Philippians 4:11-12;
1 Thessalonians 2:2-4
Men Who Met God, 96.

839. Pastoral ministry: dependence on God; Eloquence

One qualification everyone expects a preacher to have is the ability to discourse fluently on almost any religious or moral subject. Yet such ability is at best a doubtful asset and unless brought to Christ for cleansing may easily turn out to be the greatest enemy the preacher faces here below. The man who finds that he is able to preach on a moment's notice should accept his ability as an obstacle over which he must try to get victory before he is at his best for God and His kingdom.

Exodus 4:10-12; Jeremiah 9:23-24;
1 Corinthians 1:17
We Travel an Appointed Way, 91.

840. Pastoral ministry: dependence on God; Pastors: prophetic ministry; Boldness; Opposition

It is good for us to remember how strong He is—and how weak we are. I settled this issue a long time ago. I tell you I have talked to God more than I have talked to anyone else. I have reasoned more with God and had longer conferences with God than with anybody else.

And what did I tell Him? Among other things, I told Him, "Now, Lord, if I do the things I know I should do, and if I say what I know in my heart I should say, I will be in trouble with people and with groups—there is no other way!

"Not only will I be in trouble for taking my stand in faith and honesty, but I will certainly be in a situation where I will be seriously tempted of the devil!"

Then, after praying more and talking to the Lord, I have said, "Almighty Lord, I accept this with my eyes open! I know the facts and I know what may happen, but I accept it. I will not run. I will not hide. I will not crawl under a rug. I will dare to stand up and fight because I am on your side—and I know that when I am weak, then I am strong!"

2 Corinthians 12:9-10; Philippians 4:13;
1 Thessalonians 2:2-4
I Talk Back to the Devil, 146.

841. Pastoral ministry: dependence on God; Pastors: renewal

Will you pray for me as a minister of the gospel? I am not asking you to pray for the things people commonly pray for. Pray for me in light of the pressures of our times. Pray that I will not just come to a wearied end—an exhausted, tired, old preacher, interested only in hunting a place to roost. Pray that I will be willing to let my Christian experience and Christian standards cost me something right down to the last gasp!

Acts 20:24; 1 Corinthians 9:24-27; 2 Timothy 4:6-8
Who Put Jesus on the Cross?, 74.

842. Pastoral ministry: dependence on God; Pastors: stress

Attention has recently been focused upon the fact that ministers suffer a disproportionately high number of nervous breakdowns compared with other men. The reasons are many, and for the most part they reflect credit on the men of God. Still I wonder if it is all necessary. I wonder whether we who claim to be sons of the new creation are not allowing ourselves to be cheated out of our heritage. Surely it should not be necessary to do spiritual work in the strength of our natural talents. God has provided supernatural energies for supernatural tasks. The attempt to do the work of the Spirit without the Spirit's enabling may explain the propensity to nervous collapse on the part of Christian ministers.

John 15:1-7; 1 Corinthians 2:1-5;
2 Corinthians 4:5-7; 2 Corinthians 12:9-10
The Size of the Soul, 184, 185.

843. Pastoral ministry: dependence on God; Prayer: necessity of; Preaching: preparation for

It is written of Moses that he "went in before the Lord to speak with him. . . and he came out, and spake unto the children of Israel." This is the Biblical norm from which we depart to our own undoing and to the everlasting injury of the souls of men. No man has any moral right to go before the people who has not first been long before the Lord. No man has any right to speak to men about God who has not first spoken to God about men. And the prophet of God should spend more time in the secret place praying than he spends in the public place preaching.

Exodus 34:34; Galatians 1:13-17
The Root of the Righteous, 105, 106.

844. Pastoral ministry: dependence on God; Preaching: preparation for; Prayer: necessity of

Thomas a' Kempis wrote that the man of God ought to be more at home in his prayer chamber than before the public. . . .

No man should stand before an audience who has not first stood before God. Many hours of communion should precede one hour in the pulpit. The prayer chamber should be more familiar than the public platform.

Psalm 5:3; Daniel 1:10; Matthew 6:6
Renewed Day by Day, Volume 1, Jan. 10.

845. Pastoral ministry: expectations; Comparison; Church: pulpit committee

This problem of personal identity not infrequently troubles the faithful minister. The congregation has called him as their pastor and teacher, but the members have a hard time forgetting the saintly predecessor who died or who was called to another ministry. They find it hard to make room for the new minister—mainly because he is not enough like the former one. His voice is different. So are his gestures. His hair is not gray. His wife is not as friendly.

Be careful! God blesses people for their faith and obedience, not because they are old or young, bald or gray, pleasant voiced or raspy. God expects each one of us to let Him use us in helping people to a walk of spiritual blessing and victory. Not necessarily must we have had a long record as heroes in the faith to qualify.

1 Corinthians 4:2-3; 1 Corinthians 16:10-11;
1 Timothy 4:12
Jesus, Author of Our Faith, 70.

846. Pastoral ministry: need for spiritual reality; Humility

One of the greatest of the pre-reformation preachers in Germany was Johannes Tollar, certainly an evangelical before Luther's time. The story has been told that a devout layman, a farmer whose name was Nicholas, came down from the countryside, and implored Dr. Tollar to preach a sermon in the great church, dealing with the deeper Christian life based on spiritual union with Jesus Christ.

The following Sunday Dr. Tollar preached that sermon. It had 26 points, telling the people how to put away their sins and their selfishness in order to glorify Jesus Christ in their daily lives. It was a good sermon—actually, I have read it and I can underscore every line of it.

When the service was over and the crowd had dispersed, Nicholas came slowly down the aisle.

He said, "Pastor Tollar, that was a great sermon and I want to thank you for the truth which you presented. But I am troubled and I would like to make a comment, with your permission."

"Of course, and I would like to have your comment," the preacher said.

"Pastor, that was great spiritual truth that you brought to the people today, but I discern that you were preaching it to others as truth without having experienced the implications of deep spiritual principles in your own daily life," Nicholas told him. "You are not living in full identification with the death and resurrection of Jesus Christ. I could tell by the way you preached—I could tell!"

The learned and scholarly Dr. Tollar did not reply. But he was soon on his knees, seeking God in repentance and humiliation. . . .

After the long period of the dark sufferings in his soul, the day came when . . . he returned to his parish and to his pulpit to become one of the greatest and most fervent preachers of his generation . . . but Tollar first had to die.

Galatians 2:20; Philippians 3:10
Who Put Jesus on the Cross?, 174, 175, 176.

847. Pastoral ministry: need for spiritual reality; Law of the leader; Leaders: spiritual need

Cattle are driven; sheep are led; and our Lord compares His people to sheep, not to cattle.

It is especially important that Christian ministers know the law of the leader—that he can lead others only as far as he himself has gone. . . .

The minister must experience what he would teach or he will find himself in the impossible position of trying to drive sheep.

For this reason he should seek to cultivate his own heart before he attempts to preach to the hearts of others. . . .

If he tries to bring them into a heart knowledge of truth which he has not actually experienced he will surely fail. In his frustration he may attempt to drive them; and scarcely anything is so disheartening as the sight of a vexed and confused shepherd using the lash on his bewildered flock in a vain attempt to persuade them to go on beyond the point to which he himself has attained. . . .

The law of the leader tells us who are preachers that it is better to cultivate our souls than our voices. It is better to polish our hearts than our pulpit manners, though if the first has been done well and successfully it may be profitable for us to do the second. We cannot take our people beyond where we ourselves have been, and it thus becomes vitally important that we be men of God in the last and highest sense of that term.

Psalm 95:6-7; John 10:11-15; John 21:15-17; Acts 20:28-30; 1 Peter 5:1-4
The Price of Neglect, 151, 152, 153.

848. Pastoral ministry: need for spiritual reality; Pastors: call of God; Holiness: first need

"Your calling," said Meister Eckhart to the clergy of his day, "cannot make you holy; but you can make it holy. No matter how humble that calling may be, a holy man can make it a holy calling. A call to the ministry is not a call to be holy, as if the fact of his being a minister would sanctify a man; rather, the ministry is a calling for a holy man who has been made holy some other way than by the work he does. The true order is: God makes a man holy by blood and fire and sharp discipline. Then he calls the man to some special work, and the man being holy makes that work holy in turn. . . .

Every person should see to it that he is fully cleansed from all sin, entirely surrendered to the whole will of God and filled with the Holy Spirit. Then he will not be known as what he does, but as what he is. He will be a man of God first and anything else second. . . .

Ephesians 5:18-19; 2 Timothy 3:16-17; Hebrews 12:11
We Travel an Appointed Way, 59, 60.

849. Pastoral ministry: need for spiritual reality; Charm

It is true that much church activity is thrown back upon a shaky foundation of psychology and natural talents. It is sad but true that many a mother-in-law is actually praying that her handsome son-in-law may be called to preach because "he would have such a marvelous pulpit presence."

We live in a day when charm is supposed to cover almost the entire multitude of sins. Charm has taken a great place in religious expression. I am convinced that our Lord expects us to be tough enough and cynical enough to recognize all of this that pleases the unthinking in our churches: the charm stuff, the stage presence in the pulpit, the golden qualities of voice....

I feel sorry for the church that decides to call a pastor because "his personality simply sparkles!" I have watched quite a few of those sparklers through the years. In reality, as every kid knows at Fourth of July time, sparklers can be an excitement in the neighborhood—but only for about one minute! Then you are left holding a hot stick that quickly cools off in your hand.

Jeremiah 9:23-24; 1 Corinthians 2:1-5; 2 Corinthians 10:17-18
Tragedy in the Church: The Missing Gifts, 32, 33.

850. Pastoral ministry: prayer

Almost anything associated with the ministry may be learned with an average amount of intelligent application. It is not hard to preach or manage church affairs or pay a social call; weddings and funerals may be conducted smoothly with a little help from Emily Post and the Minister's Manual. Sermon making can be learned as easily as shoemaking—introduction, conclusion and all. And so with the whole work of the ministry as it is carried on in the average church today.

But prayer—that is another matter. There Mrs. Post is helpless and the Minister's Manual can offer no assistance. There the lonely man of God must wrestle it out alone, sometimes in fastings and tears and weariness untold. There every man must be an original, for true prayer cannot be imitated nor can it be learned from someone else....

Genesis 32:24; Psalm 126:5-6; 2 Corinthians 11:23-33
God Tells the Man Who Cares, 69.

851. Pastoral ministry: prayer; Prayer: hindrances

To pray successfully is the first lesson the preacher must learn if he is to preach fruitfully; yet prayer is the hardest thing he will ever be called upon to do and, being human, it is the one act he will be tempted to do less frequently than any other. He must set his heart to conquer by prayer, and that will mean that he must first conquer his own flesh, for it is the flesh that hinders prayer always.

Matthew 26:40-41; Romans 8:13;
1 Corinthians 9:24-27
God Tells the Man Who Cares, 69.

852. Pastoral ministry: prayer; Prayer: necessity of

Briefly, the way to escape religion as a front is to make it a fount. See to it that we pray more than we preach and we will never preach ourselves out. Stay with God in the secret place longer than we are with men in the public place and the fountain of our wisdom will never dry up. Keep our hearts open to the inflowing Spirit and we will not become exhausted by the outflow. Cultivate the acquaintance of God more than the friendship of men and we will always have abundance of bread to give to the hungry.

Our first responsibility is not to the public but to God and our own souls.

Matthew 6:6; Acts 6:3-7; 1 Timothy 4:13-16
God Tells the Man Who Cares, 115, 116.

853. Pastoral ministry: prayer; Prayer: necessity of

It is a high Christian privilege to pray for one another within each local church body and then for other believers throughout the world. As a Christian minister, I have no right to preach to people I have not prayed for. That is my strong conviction.

1 Samuel 12:23; Romans 1:9-10;
Colossians 1:9-11; 2 Timothy 1:3
Tragedy in the Church: The Missing Gifts, 51, 52.

854. Pastoral ministry: pride; Pastors: humility

Some young preacher will study until he has to get thick glasses to take care of his failing eyesight because he has an idea he wants to become a famous preacher. He wants to use Jesus Christ to make him a famous preacher. He's just a huckster buying and selling and getting gain. They will ordain him and he will be known as Reverend and if he writes a book, they will make him a doctor. And he will be known as Doctor; but he's still a huckster buying and selling and getting gain. And when the Lord comes back, He will drive him out of the temple along with the other cattle.

We can use the Lord for anything—or try to use Him. But what I'm preaching and what Paul taught and what was brought down through the years and what gave breath to the modern missionary movement that you and I know about and belong to was just the opposite: "O, God, we don't want anything You have, we want You." That's the cry of a soul on its way up.

Matthew 21:12-13; Galatians 6:14; Philippians 3:10; 1 Timothy 1:12-15
Success and the Christian, 29.

855. Pastoral ministry: shallowness; Preaching: awesome task

There is today no lack of Bible teachers to set forth correctly the principles of the doctrines of Christ, but too many of these seem satisfied to teach the fundamentals of the faith year after year, strangely unaware that there is in their ministry no manifest Presence, nor anything unusual in their personal lives. They minister constantly to believers who feel within their breasts a longing which their teaching simply does not satisfy.

The Pursuit of God, 8.

856. Pastoral ministry: shallowness; Reading: widely

All else being equal it is desirable that Christians, especially ministers of the gospel, should be widely read. It is a disagreeable experience to present oneself before a teacher for religious instruction and discover in less than three minutes that the said teacher should have changed places with his listeners and learned from them rather than they from him. If he is a humble man and sticks close to the small plot of ground with which he is familiar, he may, if he loves God and men, succeed in ministering to the spiritual needs of his flock. If, however, his ignorance is exceeded by his arrogance, then God help his hearers. If he boasts of his ignorance and scorns learning, show me the nearest exit! I can learn more from a child laughing on the lawn or a cloud passing overhead.

Proverbs 18:15; 1 Timothy 1:6-7; 2 Timothy 2:14-16
The Size of the Soul, 28, 29.

857. Pastoral ministry: spiritual impact; Preaching: awesome task; Prayer: intercession

To speak to God on behalf of men is probably the highest service any of us can render. The next is to speak to men in the name of God. Either is a privilege possible to us only through the grace of our Lord Jesus Christ.

1 Samuel 12:23; Acts 9:15-16; 1 Timothy 1:12-15
Born after Midnight, 3.

858. Pastors: burden for people

We cannot close our minds to everything that is happening around us. We dare not rest at ease in Zion when the church is so desperately in need of spiritually sensitive men and women who can see her faults and try to call her back to the path of righteousness. The prophets and apostles of Bible times carried in their hearts such crushing burdens for God's wayward people that they could say, "Tears have been my meat day and night," and "Oh that my head were waters, and mine eyes a fountain of tears, that I might weep day and night for the slain daughter of my people!" These men were heavy with a true burden.

Psalm 42:3; Jeremiah 9:1; Amos 6:1; Romans 9:1-3; 2 Corinthians 11:23-33
Man: The Dwelling Place of God, 68.

859. Pastors: call of God; Pastoral ministry: challenge

The true minister is one, not by his own choice, but by the sovereign commission of God.

From the study of the Scriptures, one might conclude that the man God calls seldom or never surrenders to the call without considerable reluctance.

The young man who rushes too eagerly into the pulpit at first glance seems to be unusually spiritual. But, he may, in fact, only be revealing his lack of understanding of the sacred nature of the ministry. . . .

I cannot recall, in any of my reading, of a single instance of a prophet who applied for the job!

The true minister simply surrenders to the inward pressure, and cries: "Woe is unto me, if I preach not the gospel"!

Jeremiah 1:5-8; Acts 9:15-16; 1 Corinthians 9:16
The Tozer Pulpit, Volume 1, Book 1, 76, 77.

860. Pastors: commitment; A.B. Simpson

By the time he [A. B. Simpson] was ten he already had a secret yearning to become a minister, and while still short of his teens he was struggling with the idea, desiring to be a minister, but unwilling to pay the price. The preachers he knew in those days must have been a dour and artificial lot, for the sum of his testimony is that he wrestled with himself over the question of whether to become a minister or to flee the service of the church and remain a human being.

Wingspread: A.B. Simpson, A Study in Spiritual Altitude, 18.

861. Pastors: commitment; Humble service; Prayers

Save me from the error of judging a church by its size, its popularity or the amount of its yearly offering. Help me to remember that I am a prophet—not a promoter, not a religious manager, but a prophet. Let me never become a slave to crowds. Heal my soul of carnal ambitions and deliver me from the itch for publicity. Save me from bondage to things. Let me not waste my days puttering around the house. Lay Thy terror upon me, O God, and drive me to the place of prayer where I may wrestle with principalities and powers and the rulers of the darkness of this world. Deliver me from overeating and late sleeping. Teach me self-discipline that I may be a good soldier of Jesus Christ. . . .

And now, O Lord of heaven and earth, I consecrate my remaining days to Thee; let them be many or few, as Thou wilt. Let me stand before the great or minister to the poor and lowly; that choice is not mine, and I would not influence it if I could. I am Thy servant to do Thy will, and that will is sweeter to me than position or riches or fame and I choose it above all things on earth or in heaven.

1 Corinthians 9:24-27; Ephesians 6:10-12; 2 Timothy 2:3-4
God Tells the Man Who Cares, 105, 106.

862. Pastors: humility; Pastors: commitment

Now, in confession, may I assure you that a Christian clergyman cannot follow any other route to spiritual victory and daily blessing than that which is prescribed so plainly in the Word of God. It is one thing for a minister to choose a powerful text, expound it and preach from it—it is quite something else for the minister to honestly and genuinely live forth the meaning of the Word from day to day. A clergyman is a man—and often he has a proud little kingdom of his own, a kingdom of position and often of pride and sometimes with power. Clergymen must wrestle with the spiritual implications of the crucified life just like everyone else, and to be thoroughgoing men of God and spiritual examples to the flock of God, they must die daily to the allurements of their own little kingdoms of position and prestige.

Romans 6:4-7; Galatians 2:20; 1 Timothy 4:12
Who Put Jesus on the Cross?, 174.

863. Pastors: integrity

The minister himself should simply carry into the pulpit on Sunday the same spirit that has characterized him all week long. He should not need to adopt another voice nor speak in a different tone. The subject matter would necessarily differ from that of his ordinary conversation, but the mood and attitude expressed in his sermons should be identical to his daily living.

2 Corinthians 1:12; 1 Thessalonians 2:10-12; 1 Timothy 4:13-16
This World: Playground or Battleground?, 61.

864. Pastors: integrity

I am afraid of the pastor that is another man when he enters the pulpit from what he was before. Reverend, you should never think a thought or do a deed or be caught in any situation that you couldn't carry into the pulpit with you without embarrassment. You should never have to be a different man or get a new voice and a new sense of solemnity when you enter the pulpit. You should be able to enter the pulpit with the same spirit and the same sense of reverence that you had just before when you were talking to someone about the common affairs of life.

2 Corinthians 1:12; 1 Thessalonians 2:10; 1 Timothy 3:1-7
Worship: The Missing Jewel, 25.

865. Pastors: integrity; False front; Pastoral ministry: need for spiritual reality

The tendency to make a mere front of religion is strongest among persons engaged in professional Christian service, such as pastors, evangelists, teachers, Sunday school workers and those who write, edit, publish and promote religion generally. The Christian worker must be always ready to lead in public prayer or to offer a "word of prayer" under all sorts of circumstances and in almost every imaginable situation. He must be ready with a spiritual epigram for all occasions and on a moment's notice must be able to come up with wise and devotional counsel for anyone who might ask for it. The necessity to say the godly thing at all times often forces him to display an enthusiasm he does not feel and to settle for others questions about which he is not too sure himself. His profession compels him to *seem* spiritual whether he is or not. Human nature being what it is, the man of God may soon adopt an air of constant piety and try to appear what the public thinks he is. The fixed smile and hollow tones of the professional cleric are too well known to require further mention.

2 Corinthians 1:12; Philippians 2:25-30;
1 Thessalonians 2:2-4
God Tells the Man Who Cares, 114.

866. Pastors: integrity; Honesty

I expect to so live and so preach that people can bring their friends to my church and assure them they can believe what they hear from my pulpit. I may be wrong sometimes, but I want always to be honest.

1 Samuel 12:3-4; 2 Corinthians 1:12;
2 Corinthians 7:2
Faith beyond Reason, 47.

867. Pastors: integrity; Pastoral ministry: need for spiritual reality

The tests for spiritual genuineness are two: First, the leader must be a good man and full of the Holy Ghost. Christianity is nothing if not moral. No tricks of theology, no demonstrations of supernatural wonders, no evidences of blind devotion on the part of the public can decide whether or not God is in the man or the movement. Every servant of Christ must be pure of heart and holy of life.... The man God honors will be humble, self-effacing, self-sacrificing, modest, clean living, free from the love of money, eager to promote the honor of God and just as eager to disclaim any credit or praise on his own part. His financial accounts will bear inspection, his ethical standards will be high and his personal life above reproach....

We must demand that every claimant for our confidence present a clean bill of health from the Holy Scriptures; that he do more than weave in a text occasionally, or hold up the Bible dramatically before the eyes of his hearers. His doctrines must be those of the Scriptures. The Bible must dominate his preaching. He must preach according to the Word of God.

The price of following a false guide on the desert may be death. The price of heeding wrong advice in business may be bankruptcy. The price of trusting to a quack doctor may be permanent loss of health. The price of putting confidence in a pseudo-prophet may be moral and spiritual tragedy. Let us take heed that no man deceive us.

Matthew 24:5,11,24; Acts 6:3-7; Ephesians 5:6; 1 John 3:7-8; 1 John 4:1
The Set of the Sail, 26, 27.

868. Pastors: laziness; Discipline: personal

Another trap into which the preacher is in danger of falling is that he may do what comes naturally and just take it easy. I know how ticklish this matter is and, while my writing this will not win me friends, I hope it may influence people in the right direction. It is easy for the minister to be turned into a privileged idler, a social parasite with an open palm and an expectant look. He has no boss within sight; he is not often required to keep regular hours, so he can work out a comfortable pattern of life that permits him to loaf, putter, play, doze and run about at his pleasure. And many do just that.

To avoid this danger the minister should voluntarily impose upon himself a life of labor as arduous as that of a farmer, a serious student or a scientist. No man has any right to a way of life less rugged than that of the workers who support him. No preacher has any right to die of old age if hard work will kill him.

Acts 20:28-31; 1 Corinthians 9:24-27; Colossians 3:23; 1 Timothy 4:13-16; 2 Timothy 2:3-4,14-16
God Tells the Man Who Cares, 94.

869. Pastors: ordination; Pastoral ministry: significance

But the aspiring prophet soon learns that a call from God is not sufficient; he must secure the approval of the senior prophets of the Presbytery before he can hope to make his voice heard in any Presbyterian pulpit in the land; and that approval is not an easy thing to obtain. The Presbyterian Church of that day had built a wall around its pulpit too high for any but the most heroic to leap over. . . .

After sitting in silence for several hours, during which time they were studiously ignored by the members of that August body, they are subjected to an examination that singes their pride and roots out any traces of conceit that might have survived that long siege of letting alone they had endured earlier in the day. The members of the examining board undoubtedly were one and all men of genuine Christian principles, and it is not hard to believe that they must have had good hearts about them somewhere, but this was no time to be soft, so they proceeded to take the boys apart piece by piece to see what made them run, and they examined the "parts" to see whether they were the stuff of which ministers are made.

We smile with sympathy for the country boy as he stands before his judges, and we could wish that they had been a bit less exacting in their demands, but in the light of the history of Protestant Christianity on the North American Continent over the last hundred years we cannot but admit the stern wisdom of their actions. If the men of that day erred it was on the side of right, and their error was inspired by a lofty conception of the sacredness and dignity of the Christian ministry. The wave of amateurism that swept over the American pulpit a generation ago with such tragic results would not have been possible if the Christian churches had maintained a higher standard of requirements for the ministers of the sanctuary.

1 Timothy 3:1-7; 1 Timothy 4:14-16; 1 Timothy 5:22; 2 Timothy 2:15
Wingspread: A. B. Simpson, A Study in Spiritual Altitude, 30, 31.

870. Pastors: prophetic ministry

We who preach the gospel must not think of ourselves as public relations agents sent to establish good will between Christ and the world. We must not imagine ourselves commissioned to make Christ acceptable to big business, the press, the world of sports or modern education. We are not diplomats but prophets, and our message is not a compromise but an ultimatum. . . .

Let us preach the old cross and we will know the old power.

Romans 1:14-16; 1 Corinthians 1:18,23-25
Man: The Dwelling Place of God, 44, 45.

871. Pastors: prophetic ministry

If there ever was an hour in which the church needed courageous men of prophetic vision, it is now. Preachers and pastors? They can be turned out in our schools like automobiles off the assembly line.

But prophets? Where are they?

The simple, humble, and courageous men who are willing to serve and wait on God in the long silences, who wait to hear what God says before they go to tell the world—these do not come along too often. When they do, they seek only to glorify their God, and His Christ!

Psalm 62:1; Psalm 63:1-2
Christ the Eternal Son, 135.

872. Pastors: prophetic ministry

Today the religious situation cries out for the skilled moral physician who can diagnose our ills and prescribe wisely for our cure. It is not enough simply to repeat correct doctrinal cliches. It is imperative right now that we have the benefit of the piercing discernment of the Spirit. We must not only know what God has said; *we must hear what God is now saying.*

1 Chronicles 12:32; Isaiah 1:3-4; Jeremiah 9:12
The Size of the Soul, 131.

873. Pastors: prophetic ministry; Boldness

I do not wish to draw too close a parallel between conditions under Ahaz and conditions in the churches today, but every enlightened soul can see how we languish for fearless leaders and bold reformers who will dare to pass holy judgment upon the unscriptural goings on that are being substituted for New Testament Christianity in the majority of our churches.

Somewhere there may be a freckle-faced stripling as yet unknown who will hear the call of God and go forth in dauntless love to become a conscience to the churches. Too many prophets of Jehovah these days are hiding in their caves, but somewhere there may be an Elijah. The bloodless softlings will say at first that he is uncharitable and harsh, but when he gets the prophets of Baal on the run they will tag along behind him, trying to look as if they had been on his side all the time.

Well, he can't come a day too soon.

1 Kings 18:18,40
The Size of the Soul, 190, 191.

874. Pastors: prophetic ministry; Boldness

Balaam's ass was used of God to rebuke a prophet. It would seem from this that God does not require perfection in the instrument He uses to warn and exhort His people.

When God's sheep are in danger the shepherd must not gaze at the stars and meditate on "inspirational" themes. He is morally obliged to grab his weapon and run to their defense. When the circumstances call for it, love can use the sword, though by her nature she would rather bind up the broken heart and minister to the wounded. It is time for the prophet and the seer to make themselves heard and felt again. For the last three decades timidity disguised as humility has crouched in her corner while the spiritual quality of evangelical Christianity has become progressively worse year by year. *How long, O Lord, how long?*

Numbers 22:28; 1 Kings 17:34-35;
Acts 20:28-31
Born after Midnight, 39.

875. Pastors: prophetic ministry; Boldness

Any man with fair pulpit gifts can get on with the average congregation if he just "feeds" them and lets them alone. Give them plenty of objective truth and never hint that they are wrong and should be set right, and they will be content.

On the other hand, the man who preaches truth and applies it to the lives of his hearers will feel the nails and the thorns. He will lead a hard life, but a glorious one. May God raise up many such prophets. The church needs them badly.

Acts 20:18-21; Philippians 1:29-30;
1 Thessalonians 2:2-4
Of God and Men, 28.

876. Pastors: prophetic ministry; Boldness; Motives

The Church at this moment needs men, the right kind of men—bold men. . . .

We languish for men who feel themselves expendable in the warfare of the soul, who cannot be frightened by threats of death because they have already died to the allurements of this world. Such men will be free from the compulsions that control weaker men. They will not be forced to do things by the squeeze of circumstances; their only compulsion will come from within—or from above.

This kind of freedom is necessary if we are to have prophets in our pulpits again instead of mascots. These free men will serve God and mankind from motives too high to be understood by the rank and file of religious retainers who today shuttle in and out of the sanctuary. They will make no decisions out of fear, take no course out of a desire to please, accept no service for financial considerations, perform no religious act out of mere custom; nor will they allow themselves to be influenced by the love of publicity or the desire for reputation. . . .

Yes, if evangelical Christianity is to stay alive she must have men again, the right kind of men. She must repudiate the weaklings who dare not speak out, and she must seek in prayer and much humility the coming again of men of the stuff prophets and martyrs are made of. God will hear the cries of His people as He heard the cries of Israel in Egypt. And He will send deliverance by sending deliverers. It is His way among men.

Exodus 3:7-10; Acts 20:18-21,33;
1 Corinthians 4:10-13
Of God and Men, 11, 12, 13.

877. Pastors: prophetic ministry; Cultural awareness

A prophet is one who knows his times and what God is trying to say to the people of his times. . . .

Religious leaders who continue mechanically to expound the Scriptures without regard to the current religious situation are no better than the scribes and lawyers of Jesus' day who faithfully parroted the Law without the remotest notion of what was going on around them spiritually. . . .

Today we need prophetic preachers; not preachers of prophecy merely, but preachers with a gift of prophecy. The word of wisdom is missing. We need the gift of discernment again in our pulpits. It is not ability to predict that we need, but the anointed eye, the power of spiritual penetration and interpretation, the ability to appraise the religious scene *as viewed from God's position*, and to tell us what is actually going on.

1 Chronicles 12:32; Romans 12:3-8;
1 Thessalonians 5:20-21
The Size of the Soul, 125, 126.

878. Pastors: prophetic ministry; Opposition

If not the greatest need, then surely one of the greatest is for the appearance of Christian leaders with prophetic vision. We desperately need seers who can see through the mist. Unless they come soon it will be too late for this generation. And if they do come we will no doubt crucify a few of them in the name of our worldly orthodoxy. But the cross is always the harbinger of the resurrection.

2 Chronicles 36:15-16; Matthew 5:10-12;
Acts 7:51-60
The Root of the Righteous, 110.

879. Pastors: prophetic ministry; Pastors: vision of God; Boldness

If Christianity is to receive a rejuvenation, it must be by other means than any now being used. If the Church in the second half of this century is to recover from the injuries she suffered in the first half, there must appear a new type of preacher. The proper, ruler-of-the-synagogue type will never do. Neither will the priestly type of man who carries out his duties, takes his pay and asks no questions, nor the smooth-talking pastoral type who knows how to make the Christian religion acceptable to everyone. All these have been tried and found wanting.

Another kind of religious leader must arise among us. He must be of the old prophet type, a man who has seen visions of God and has heard a voice from the Throne. When he comes (and I pray God there will be not one but many), he will stand in flat contradiction to everything our smirking, smooth civilization holds dear. He will contradict, denounce and protest in the name of God and will earn the hatred and opposition of a large segment of Christendom. Such a man is likely to be lean, rugged, blunt-spoken and a little bit angry with the world. He will love Christ and the souls of men to the point of willingness to die for the glory of the One and the salvation of the other. But he will fear nothing that breathes with mortal breath.

Isaiah 6:1-5; Matthew 14:3-4; John 1:20-23
The Size of the Soul, 128, 129.

880. Pastors: prophetic ministry; Pastors: vision of God; Cultural awareness

A prophet is one who knows his times and what God is trying to say to the people of his times. . . .

Today we need prophetic preachers—not preachers of prophecy merely, but preachers with a gift of prophecy. The word of wisdom is missing. We need the gift of discernment again in our pulpits. It is not ability to predict that we need, but the anointed eye, the power of spiritual penetration and interpretation, the ability to appraise the religious scene as viewed from God's position, and to tell us what is actually going on. . . .

Where is the man who can see through the ticker tape and confetti to discover which way the parade is headed, why it started in the first place and, particularly, who is riding up front in the seat of honor? . . .

What is needed desperately today is prophetic insight. Scholars can interpret the past; it takes prophets to interpret the present. Learning will enable a man to pass judgment on our yesterdays, but it requires a gift of clear seeing to pass sentence on our own day....

Another kind of religious leader must arise among us. He must be of the old prophet type, a man who has seen visions of God and has heard a voice from the Throne.

Isaiah 6:1-5; John 12:41; Acts 26:13-19
Of God and Men, 19, 20, 21, 22.

881. Pastors: prophetic ministry; Preaching: awesome task

The Christian minister, as someone has pointed out, is a descendant not of the Greek orator but of the Hebrew prophet.

The differences between the orator and the prophet are many and radical, the chief being that the orator speaks for himself while the prophet speaks for God. The orator originates his message and is responsible to himself for its content. The prophet originates nothing but delivers the message he has received from God who alone is responsible for it, the prophet being responsible to God for its delivery only. The prophet must hear the message clearly and deliver it faithfully, and that is indeed a grave responsibility; but it is to God alone, not to men.

Isaiah 51:16; Jeremiah 1:9-10; Ezekiel 2:7; Ezekiel 3:1-4
God Tells the Man Who Cares, 85.

882. Pastors: prophetic ministry; Preaching: awesome task

The true preacher is a man of God speaking to men; he is a man of heaven giving God's witness on earth. Because he is a man of God, he can speak from God. He can decode the message he receives from heaven and deliver it in the language of earth.

Jeremiah 1:7-9; John 1:6-7; 2 Timothy 4:1-5
God Tells the Man Who Cares, 86.

883. Pastors: renewal

Charles Finney, one of the greatest of all of God's men throughout the years, testified that in the midst of his labors and endeavors in bringing men to Christ, he would at times sense a coldness in his own heart.

Finney did not excuse it. In his writings he told of having to turn from all of his activities, seeking God's face and Spirit anew in fasting and prayer.

"I plowed up until I struck fire and met God," he wrote. What a helpful and blessed formula for the concerned children of God in every generation!

Psalm 5:3; Psalm 130:5-6
Who Put Jesus on the Cross?, 11.

884. Pastors: renewal

How frightful a thing it is for the preacher when he becomes accustomed to his work, when his sense of wonder departs, when he gets used to the unusual, when he loses his solemn fear in the presence of the High and Holy One; when, to put it bluntly, he gets a little bored with God and heavenly things.

Exodus 3:5-6; Joshua 5:15; Psalm 89:5-9; Isaiah 6:5, 8
God Tells the Man Who Cares, 92.

885. Pastors: Satan's opposition

Yet the ministry is one of the most perilous of professions. The devil hates the Spirit-filled minister with an intensity second only to that which he feels for Christ Himself. The source of this hatred is not difficult to discover. An effective, Christ-like minister is a constant embarrassment to the devil, a threat to his dominion, a rebuttal of his best arguments and a dogged reminder of his coming overthrow. No wonder he hates him.

Satan knows that the downfall of a prophet of God is a strategic victory for him, so he rests not day or night devising hidden snares and deadfalls for the ministry. Perhaps a better figure would be the poison dart that only paralyzes its victim, for I think that Satan has little interest in killing the preacher outright. An ineffective, half-alive minister is a better advertisement for hell than a good man dead. So the preacher's dangers are likely to be spiritual rather than physical, though sometimes the enemy works through bodily weaknesses to get to the preacher's soul.

Ephesians 6:10-12; James 4:7-10; 1 Peter 5:8-9
God Tells the Man Who Cares, 90.

886. Pastors: vision of God

The man whom God will use must be undone. He must be a man who has seen the King in His beauty.

Isaiah 6:1-8; 1 John 1:1-3; Revelation 4:1-8
Whatever Happened to Worship?, 78.

887. Pastors: vision of God; Pastors: prophetic ministry

We are overrun today with orthodox scribes, but the prophets, where are they? The hard voice of the scribe sounds over evangelicalism, but the church waits for the tender voice of the saint who has penetrated the veil and has gazed with inward eye upon the wonder that is God.

The Pursuit of God, 40.

888. Pastor's wife

The wife of a prophet has no easy road to travel. She cannot always see her husband's vision, yet as his wife she must go along with him wherever his vision takes him. She is compelled therefore to walk by faith a good part of the time—and her husband's faith at that.

Ruth 1:16; 2 Corinthians 5:1-8; Ephesians 5:22-33
Wingspread: A.B. Simpson, A Study in Spiritual Altitude, 87.

889. Peace: false; Christians: in the world

Peace of heart that is won by refusing to bear the common yoke of human sympathy is a peace unworthy of a Christian. To seek tranquility by stopping our ears to the cries of human pain is to make ourselves not Christians but a kind of degenerate stoic having no relation either to stoicism or Christianity.

We Christians should never try to escape from the burdens and woes of life among men. The hermit and the anchorite sound good in poetry, but stripped of their artificial romance, they are not good examples of what the followers of Christ should be. True peace comes not by a retreat from the world but by the overpowering presence of Christ in the heart. "Christ in you" is the answer to our cry for peace.

John 17:15-18; Romans 12:9-13,16-18; Colossians 1:27
The Next Chapter after the Last, 35.

890. Peace: inner

The world talks of peace, and by peace it means the absence of war. What it overlooks is that there is another meaning of the word, namely, tranquillity of heart, and without that kind of peace the peace of the world will continue to be but an unattainable dream. As long as peace between nations continues to depend upon the shifting moods of choleric old men filled with hatred and frustration at their approaching dissolution, and who are ready to pull the world down with them into the bottomless pit, just that long will there be no peace among nations. . . .

True peace is a gift of God and today it is found only in the minds of innocent children and in the hearts of trustful Christians.

John 14:27; Romans 5:1; Philippians 4:6-7; Colossians 3:15
Born after Midnight, 109, 110.

891. Peace: in trials; Fear; Trials: God's presence in

Surely Bible-reading Christians should be the last persons on earth to give way to hysteria. They are redeemed from their past offenses, kept in their present circumstances by the power of an all-powerful God, and their future is safe in His hands. God has promised to support them in the flood, protect them in the fire, feed them in famine, shield them against their enemies, hide them in His safe chambers until the indignation is past and receive them at last into eternal tabernacles.

If we are called upon to suffer, we may be perfectly sure that we shall be rewarded for every pain and blessed for every tear. Underneath will be the Everlasting Arms and within will be the deep assurance that all is well with our souls. Nothing can separate us from the love of God—not death, nor life, nor height, nor depth, nor any other creature.

This is a big old world, and it is full of the habitations of darkness, but nowhere in its vast expanse is there one thing of which a real Christian need be afraid. Surely a fear-ridden Christian has never examined his or her defenses.

Deuteronomy 33:27; Romans 8:35-39; Galatians 3:13; 2 Timothy 1:6-7; 1 Peter 1:3-5
This World: Playground or Battleground?, 7, 8.

892. Peace: in trials; Trials: attitude toward; God: His sovereignty

This idea was once expressed better by a simple-hearted man who was asked how he managed to live in such a state of constant tranquility even though surrounded by circumstances anything but pleasant. His answer was as profound as it was simple: "I have learned," he said, "to cooperate with the inevitable." . . .

Though we cannot control the universe, we can determine our attitude toward it. We can accept God's will wherever it is expressed and take toward it an attitude of worshipful resignation. If my will is to do God's will, then there will be no controversy with anything that comes in the course of my daily walk. Inclement weather, unpleasant neighbors, physical handicaps, adverse political conditions—all these will be accepted as God's will for the time and surrendered to provisionally, subject to such alterations as God may see fit to make, either by His own sovereign providence or in answer to believing prayer.

Psalm 143:10; Proverbs 3:1-2, 5-6; Philippians 4:11-12
Born after Midnight, 64, 65.

893. Permanence

Most of us do not see very much of permanence around us in our world. Some while ago, I was given a new definition for *permanent*. I picked up a flyer being distributed in my neighborhood advertising the opening of a new beauty shop. They were offering women a permanent wave, guaranteed to last three months!

So "permanent" is now something that will be around for three months. . . .

Men Who Met God, 92, 93.

894. Persecution

If we are serious about our Christian witness, the day may be near when we may be persecuted—even killed—for our faith. We should be stirred, as John was stirred, as we witness this vast company of God's saints in heaven who have come through earth's great tribulation.

I am not saying we are not Christians. I am only trying to find out why we are so far from revival and refreshing and renewal. I am only trying to determine why we are so far from recognizing the urgency of God's will laid upon us by the Holy Spirit.

If we belong to Jesus Christ, we should never compromise our spiritual decisions on the basis of "What is this going to cost me?" We ought only to ask, "What is my spiritual duty and my spiritual privilege before God?"

Luke 14:26,27,33; Acts 20:24; Revelation 7:9-14
Jesus Is Victor!, 115.

895. Persecution; Knowledge of God: divine encounter

There are people in our churches today who think they are being persecuted for their profession of faith in Jesus Christ. I have a word of encouragement and perspective for them.

Take a long look at Elijah the prophet! . . .

As a prophet in evil times, Elijah had reason to lean hard on his God. He had come often into the presence of Jehovah. His is one of the great examples of people born of the seed of Adam, yet willing and able to press into a deep knowledge of God through personal encounter with Him.

1 Kings 17:1,24; James 5:17-18
Men Who Met God, 89, 90.

896. Persecution; Opposition; Boldness

Yes, John could have taken the easier way. Just a little compromise and the important people would begin to say, "This man is really doing good things for the community." But John was a man of faith. He knew *what* he believed; he knew *in whom* he believed. He was willing to take the heat from those who hated the living God and His Christ.

If you are willing to lower the temperature of your testimony, the world will turn off the heat it has been applying. But if you are faithful to God and His Word, consistent and sincere in your testimony to what Christ means to you, you can expect both heat and pressure. John had a strong, uncompromising testimony. It evoked the opposition of the powers, who decided to silence his witness in Patmos's rocky isolation.

John 15:18-21; 2 Timothy 1:11-12; 2 Timothy 3:12; Revelation 1:9
Jesus Is Victor!, 58, 59.

897. Persecution; Tolerance/Intolerance; Church: ineffectiveness

People remark how favored the church is in this country. It does not have to face persecution and rejection. If the truth were known, our freedom from persecution is because we have taken the easy, the popular way. If we would love righteousness until it became an overpowering passion, if we would renounce everything that is evil, our day of popularity and pleasantness would quickly end. The world would soon turn on us.

We are too nice! We are too tolerant! We are too anxious to be popular! We are too quick to make excuses for sin in its many forms! If I could stir Christians around me to love God and hate sin, even to the point of being a bit of a nuisance, I would rejoice. If some Christian were to call me for counsel saying he or she is being persecuted for Jesus' sake, I would say with feeling, "Thank God!"

John 15:18-21; 1 Thessalonians 2:2-4; 2 Timothy 3:12
Jesus, Our Man in Glory, 66, 67.

898. Personal finances; Poverty

It is hard for a rich church to understand that her Lord was a poor man. Were He to appear today on our city streets as He appeared in Jerusalem, He would in all probability be picked up for vagrancy. Were He to teach here what He taught the multitudes about money, He would be blacklisted by churches, Bible conferences and missionary societies everywhere as unrealistic, fanatical and dangerous to organized religion.

Our Lord simply did not think about money the way His professed followers do today; and more particularly He did not give it the place our religious leaders give it. To them it is necessary; to Him it was not. He had nowhere to lay His head, and we have made poetry out of His poverty while being extremely careful not to share it.

Matthew 8:20; Matthew 19:24; Mark 6:8-9; Luke 6:20-38
The Warfare of the Spirit, 6.

899. Personal finances; Poverty; Stewardship

Again, he may be poor—and if he is a real Christian, he usually is—and yet he will always make others rich. Paul was a poor man in prison, but he immeasurably enriched the entire Christian world. John Bunyan was a poor man in Bedford jail, but he gave us *Pilgrim's Progress.*

You can go on down the scale throughout history and you will find that a rich Christian was generally poor and the poor Christian made everyone rich.

1 Corinthians 4:10-13; 2 Corinthians 9:6-14; Philippians 4:11-12
I Call It Heresy!, 161.

900. Personal finances; Stewardship

As sharers in a prosperous economy we Christians must not forget that ability involves responsibility. We have more than our fathers had, and are therefore able to do more for our fellow men than they could do. We are in danger of overlooking this. A larger income may be considered in either of two ways: (1) I earn more; therefore I can spend more and enjoy myself better. (2) I earn more; therefore I am able to do more good for more people and aid in the evangelization of more tribes and nations.

To use increased income to feed the flesh and enjoy greater luxuries is perfectly natural—and that is precisely why it is wrong; it accords with fallen human nature and is of the essence of selfishness and sin. To accept a larger income as a means whereby we may lay up treasures in heaven accords with the teachings of Christ. Every Christian who has this problem to face should prayerfully consider his larger responsibility in the light of his increased ability.

Matthew 6:19-21; Luke 12:33-34; 1 Timothy 6:17-19
The Warfare of the Spirit, 74, 75.

901. Personal testimony: Tozer

As a boy, I was not a Christian. I did not have the privilege of growing up in a home where Christ was known, loved and honored.

God spoke to me through a street preacher as he read Jesus' words . . . from Matthew 11:28: "Come unto me, all ye that labour and are heavy laden, and I will give you rest."

That invitation let me know that Jesus is still saying, "Come. Come now!" I went home and up into the attic, where I would be undisturbed. There in earnest prayer I gave my heart and life to Jesus Christ. I have been a Christian ever since.

My feet took me home and into the attic. But it was not my feet that went to Jesus. It was my heart. Within my heart I consented to go to Jesus. I made the determination, and I went!

Matthew 11:28-30; 2 Corinthians 6:1-2; Revelation 22:17
Men Who Met God, 10.

902. Personal testimony: Tozer

I was an ignorant 17-year-old boy when I first heard preaching on the street, and I was moved to wander into a church where I heard a man quoting a text: "Come unto me, all ye that labour and are heavy laden, and I will give you rest. Take my yoke upon you, and learn of me; for I am meek and lowly in heart: and ye shall find rest unto your souls" (Matthew 11:28-29, KJV).

Actually, I was little better than a pagan, but with only that kind of skimpy biblical background, I became greatly disturbed, for I began to feel and sense and acknowledge God's gracious presence. I heard His Voice—ever so faintly. I discerned that there was a Light—ever so dimly.

I was still lost, but thank God, I was getting closer. The Lord Jesus knows that there are such among us today, of whom He says: "Ye are not far from the kingdom of God."

Once again, walking on the street, I stopped to hear a man preaching at a corner, and he said to those listening: "If you do not know how to pray, go home and get down and ask, 'God, have mercy on me a sinner.'"

That is exactly what I did, and in spite of the dispensational teachers who tell me that I used the wrong text, I got into my Father's house. I got my feet under my Father's table. I got hold of a big spoon and I have been enjoying my Father's spiritual blessings ever since.

Matthew 11:28-30; Mark 12:34; Luke 18:9-14
Who Put Jesus on the Cross?, 135, 136.

903. Peter: affection for; Failure; Role models

For some queer reason, we seem to love people more when they are not too perfect.

In the presence of a faultless saint, the average one of us feels ill at ease. We are likely to be discouraged rather than inspired by the sight of a character too impeccable to be human. We draw more help from a man if we know that he is going through the fire along with the rest of us, and we may even take courage from the fact that he does not enjoy it any more than we do.

This may be the reason Christians have always felt a special affection for Simon Peter. . . .

Peter contained or has been accidentally associated with more contradictions than almost any other Bible character. He appeared to be a combination of courage and cowardice, reverence and disrespect, selfless devotion and dangerous self-love. Only Peter could solemnly swear that he would never desert Christ and then turn around and deny Him the first time he got in a tight place. Only Peter could fall at Jesus' feet and acknowledge his own sinfulness and then rebuke his Lord for suggesting something with which he did not agree. The two natures that strove within him made him say and do things that appeared to be in direct contradiction to each other—and all within a matter of hours. Peter was a "rock," yet he wavered, and so, I suppose, managed to become the only wavering rock in history. And he surely was the only man in the world who had faith enough to walk on water but not enough faith to continue to do so when the wind blew. . . .

Anyway, we are glad Peter lived, and we are glad Christ found him. He is so much like so many of us, at least in his weaknesses. It only remains for us to learn also the secret of his strength.

Matthew 14:22-33; Matthew 16:18; Matthew 16:22; Matthew 26:33,69-75; Luke 5:8
We Travel an Appointed Way, 103, 104, 106.

904. Pharisees; Communion with God; Concept of God

To a Pharisee, the service of God was a bondage which he did not love but from which he could not escape without a loss too great to bear. God, as the Pharisees saw Him, was not a God easy to live with. So their daily religion became grim and hard, with no trace of true love in it.

It can be said about us, as humans, that we try to be like our God. If He is conceived to be stern and exacting and harsh, so will we be!

The blessed and inviting truth is that God is the most winsome of all beings, and in our worship of Him we should find unspeakable pleasure. . . .

Unbeknown to the understanding of a Pharisee, God communes with His redeemed ones in an easy, uninhibited fellowship that is restful and healing to the soul.

Matthew 23:4; Luke 11:46; Acts 15:10
Whatever Happened to Worship?, 28.

905. Philosophy

Philosophy has tried to give us answers. But the philosophical concepts concerning God have always been contradictory. The philosopher is like a blind person trying to paint someone's portrait. The blind person can feel the face of his subject and try to put some brush strokes on canvas. But the project is doomed before it is begun. The best that philosophy can do is to feel the face of the universe in some ways, then try to paint God as philosophy sees Him.

Most philosophers confess belief in a "presence" somewhere in the universe. Some call it a "law"—or "energy" or "mind" or "essential virtue." Thomas Edison said if he lived long enough, he thought he could invent an instrument so sensitive that it could find God. Edison was an acknowledged inventor. He had a great mind and he may have been a philosopher. But Edison knew no more about God or what God is like than the boy or girl who delivers the morning newspaper.

Proverbs 14:12-13; 2 Corinthians 10:5; Colossians 2:8-9; 1 Timothy 6:20-21
Jesus, Our Man in Glory, 41, 42.

906. Philosophy; Science; Knowledge: inadequacy of

Philosophy tries to find out the reason for things and to get at the riddle of existence. And they try it by searching—philosophers try it by searching into their own heads. There really isn't too much in our heads, and since philosophers are compelled to stay within the confines of their own craniums, the result is, of course, disappointing. They never get at the real reason for existence because they're hunting around in their little dark skulls with a flashlight and they don't find very much. So philosophy has never been able to give us the real answer to life's questions.

Science, in our day, has taken over and displaced philosophy—and theology, for that matter—and science is reason's search for knowledge in nature. Philosophy searches for knowledge in the philosophers' own heads and science searches in nature. And knowledge there is obtained by observation and experiment. But neither can the scientist understand life. The key is in God. And hence, the godly man is the true sage. The man who knows God knows the Fountain and Source of everything; he has the key that unlocks everything.

Proverbs 1:7; 1 Timothy 2:1-8; 2 Timothy 3:1-7
Success and the Christian, 113.

907. Philosophy of life; Eternal perspective

Actually, the wisest person in the world is the person who knows the most about God. The only real sage worthy of the name is the one who realizes that the answer to creation and life and eternity is a theological answer—not a scientific answer. . . .

If we are to have any satisfying and lasting understanding of life, it must be divinely given. It begins with the confession that it is indeed the God who has revealed Himself to us who is the great central pillar bearing up the universe.

Believing that, we then go on to acknowledge that we have thus discovered His great eternal purpose. God made us as men and women in His own image. He has now redeemed and restored us through His plan of salvation to love Him and worship Him forever.

Genesis 1:26-27; Jeremiah 9:23-24;
1 Corinthians 3:16-23
Whatever Happened to Worship?, 62, 64.

908. Pilgrims; Heaven: longing for

If we are genuine, committed Christians, intent upon walking by faith with our Lord Jesus Christ, then we are continually confessing that we are pilgrims and that we are strangers!

The Holy Spirit, who is the real author of this Letter to the Hebrews, uses the terms *pilgrims* and *strangers* to remind the early

Christians that they were not yet at their final home.

The message still reads the same today. Christian pilgrims are journeying by faith from an old city that is cursed and under threat of judgment to a blessed and celestial city where dwells Immanuel!

Hebrews 11:13-16; 1 Peter 2:11-12; Revelation 21:2
Jesus, Author of Our Faith, 59.

909. Politics; America: greatness; Accountability

It was the belief in the accountability of man to his maker that made America a great nation. Among those earlier leaders was Daniel Webster whose blazing eyes and fiery oratory often held the Senate spellbound. In those days the Congress was composed of strong, noble statesmen who carried the weight of the nation in their hearts and minds.

Someone asked: "Mr. Webster, what do you consider the most serious thought that has ever entered your mind?"

"The most solemn thought that has ever entered my mind is my accountability to my maker," he replied.

Men like that cannot be corrupted and bought. They do not have to worry if someone listens to their telephone calls. What they are in character and in deportment results from their belief that they will finally be accountable to God.

2 Corinthians 5:10; Hebrews 9:27; 1 John 4:17
Echoes from Eden, 130.

910. Politics; Eternal perspective

Any form of human government, however lofty, deals with the citizen only as long as he lives. At the graveside it bids him adieu. It may have made his journey a little easier, and, if so, all lovers of the human race will thank God for that. But in the cool earth, slaves and free men lie down together. Then what matter the talk and the turmoil? Who was right and who was wrong in this or that political squabble doesn't matter to the dead. Judgment and sin and heaven and hell are all that matter then.

Psalm 39:4-6; Matthew 16:24-26; James 4:13-14
The Next Chapter after the Last, 46.

911. Politics; Predictions

Even the so-called diplomats and statesmen have little knowledge and even less control over the day-to-day incidents that bring tension and violence among the nations. The story has been told of one of our own State Department officials saying to another as they arrived at the Washington offices in the morning. "Well, what is our long-range, unchanging foreign policy going to be today?"...

I have only heard one prediction made by a world statesman in recent years that was absolutely foolproof, and that was a remark that the next war will be fought in the future!

Proverbs 27:1; Luke 12:19-21; James 4:13-14
Who Put Jesus on the Cross?, 80, 81.

912. Popular beliefs

The human heart is heretical by nature. Popular religious beliefs should be checked carefully against the Word of God, for they are almost certain to be wrong.

Ecclesiastes 9:3; Jeremiah 17:9; Mark 7:21-22
That Incredible Christian, 98.

913. Potential; Man: self-centeredness of

The widest thing in the universe is not space; it the potential capacity of the human heart. Being made in the image of God, it is capable of almost unlimited extension in all directions. And one of the world's worst tragedies is that we allow our hearts to shrink until there is room in them for little beside ourselves.

Genesis 1:26-27; Proverbs 4:23; Matthew 12:34-37
The Root of the Righteous, 112, 113.

914. Poverty

No one in this world has ever been saved and gone to heaven because he was poor. You can be as poor as a church mouse and still be as bad as a church rat.

Echoes from Eden, 100.

915. Power: high price of

Emerson once said to a young man with political aspirations: "Young man, you want to be president? You want to go to the White House? Ah, if you only knew how much of his manhood that man had to sell out to get there, you wouldn't want it. If you only knew how he must obey those who stand erect behind the throne and tell him what to do, you wouldn't want it!"

I do not make this as a political comment. No matter which party is in office or what man is in office, it is true that everything is defiled all over the world. . . .

My point is this: because of humanity's lost and defiled condition, money and influence and power generally bear the taint and touch of defilement upon them. This is in contrast to the believer's divine inheritance, pure and unsoiled.

Matthew 6:19-21,24-33; 1 Peter 1:3-5
I Call It Heresy!, 101, 102.

916. Power of God

Anyone can do the possible; add a bit of courage and zeal and some may do the phenomenal; only Christians are obliged to do the impossible.

2 Corinthians 12:9-10; Ephesians 3:20-21; Philippians 4:13
The Warfare of the Spirit, 12.

917. Power of God; Obedience: need for; Spiritual victory

What does all this add up to? What are its practical implications for us today? Just that the power of God is at our disposal, waiting for us to call it into action by meeting the conditions which are plainly laid down. God is ready to send down floods of blessing upon us as we begin to obey His plain instructions. We need no new doctrine, no new movement, no "key," no imported evangelist or expensive "course" to show us the way. It is before us as clear as a four-lane highway.

To any inquirer I would say, "Just do the next thing you know you should do to carry out the will of the Lord. If there is sin in your life, quit it instantly. Put away lying, gossiping, dishonesty, or whatever your sin may be. . . .

Look to no cost and fear no consequences. Study the Bible to learn the will of God and then do His will as you understand it. Start now by doing the next thing, and then go on from there."

Romans 12:1-2; Ephesians 4:25-32; Ephesians 5:15-18; 1 Thessalonians 4:3-7
Paths to Power, 29, 30.

918. Pragmatism; Church: current condition

Pragmatism has a number of facets and can mean various things to various people, but basically it is the doctrine of the utility of truth. For the pragmatist there are no absolutes; nothing is absolutely good or absolutely true. Truth and morality float on a sea of human experience. If an exhausted swimmer can lay hold of a belief or an ethic, well and good; it may keep him afloat till he can get to shore; then it only encumbers him, so he tosses it away. He feels no responsibility to cherish truth for its own sake. It is there to serve him; he has no obligation to serve it.

Truth is to use. Whatever is useful is true for the user, though for someone else it may not be useful, so not true. The truth of any idea is its ability to produce desirable results. If it can show no such results it is false. That is pragmatism stripped of its jargon. . . .

As one fairly familiar with the contemporary religious scene, I say without hesitation that a part, a very large part, of the activities carried on today in evangelical circles are not only influenced by pragmatism but almost completely controlled by it. Religious methodology is geared to it; it appears large in our youth meetings; magazines and books constantly glorify it; conventions are dominated by it; and the whole religious atmosphere is alive with it.

What shall we do to break its power over us? The answer is simple. *We must acknowledge the right of Jesus Christ to control the activities of His church.*

John 17:15-18; Ephesians 1:22,23;
Colossians 1:18
God Tells the Man Who Cares, 80, 81, 83.

919. Prayer: boldness in

When entering the prayer chamber, we must come filled with faith and armed with courage. Nowhere else in the whole field of religious thought and activity is courage so necessary as in prayer. The successful prayer must be one without condition. We must believe that God is love and that, being love, He cannot harm us but must ever do us good. Then we must throw ourselves before Him and pray with boldness for whatever we know our good and His glory require, and the cost is no object! Whatever He in His love and wisdom would assess against us, we will accept with delight because it pleased Him. Prayers like that cannot go unanswered. The character and reputation of God guarantee their fulfillment.

We should always keep in mind the infinite loving kindness of God. No one need fear to put his life in His hands. His yoke is easy; His burden is light.

Matthew 7:7-11; Matthew 11:28-30;
Matthew 21:21; James 1:5-6
We Travel an Appointed Way, 48.

920. Prayer: conditions

When we go to God with a request that He modify the existing situation for us, that is, that He answer prayer, there are two conditions that we must meet: (1) We must pray in the will of God and (2) we must be on what old-fashioned Christians often call "praying ground"; that is, we must be living lives pleasing to God.

It is futile to beg God to act contrary to His revealed purposes. To pray with confidence the petitioner must be certain that his request falls within the broad will of God for His people.

The second condition is also vitally important. God has not placed Himself under obligation to honor the requests of worldly, carnal or disobedient Christians. He hears and answers the prayers only of those who walk in His way.

Matthew 7:7-11; John 14:13-14; John 15:1-7,14-16; 1 John 3:21-22 ; 1 John 5:14-15
Man the Dwelling Place of God, 86.

921. Prayer: conditions

Prayer is usually recommended as the panacea for all ills and the key to open every prison door, and it would indeed be difficult to overstate the advantages and privilege of Spirit-inspired prayer. But we must not forget that unless we are wise and watchful prayer itself may become a source of self-deception. There are as many kinds of prayer as there are problems and some kinds are not acceptable to God. The prophets of the Old Testament denounced Israel for trying to hide their iniquities behind their prayers. Christ flatly rejected the prayers of hypocrites and James declared that some religious persons ask and receive not because they ask amiss.

Matthew 23:14; James 4:3-4
Man the Dwelling Place of God, 89, 90.

922. Prayer: expectation

There must be expectation. We've got to point up our prayers. I have said it before and repeat it, that one of the greatest snares in praying is to pray vaguely. I used to go out rifle shooting in the state of Pennsylvania. I still like to when I get out that way. I used to enjoy using a big gun, like an eight millimeter or a 30-30, because the thing would go "Boom!" and the smoke would fly and I'd almost fall over and I felt really big. But if I'd been shooting at something, I was red-faced because I'd usually miss it.

And when a man prays vaguely, he makes a big boom and others say, "Oh, he is a praying man." But what is he praying about? Has God heard his prayer, or is he just shooting at a cloud? How do you know if he hits it or not? He is shooting at the side of a barn.

Success and the Christian, 98.

923. Prayer: expectation; Faith: confidence in God

You can have this confidence in God, and you can have this respect for His will. Do not expect God to perform miracles for you so you can write books about them. Do not ever be caught asking God to send you toys like that to play around with.

But if you are in trouble and concerned about your situation and willing to be honest with God, you can have confidence in Him. You can go to Him in the merit of His Son, claiming His promises, and He will not let you down. God will help you, and you will find the way of deliverance.

God will move heaven and earth for you if you will trust Him.

Psalm 3:3-6; Matthew 6:1-6;
Hebrews 4:14-16; 1 Peter 5:7
Faith beyond Reason, 49.

924. Prayer: expectation; Faith: confidence in God

What profit is there in prayer? "Much every way." Whatever God can do faith can do, and whatever faith can do prayer can do when it is offered in faith. An invitation to prayer is, therefore, an invitation to omnipotence, for prayer engages the Omnipotent God and brings Him into our human affairs. Nothing is impossible to the man who prays in faith, just as nothing is impossible with God. This generation has yet to prove all that prayer can do for believing men and women.

Genesis 18:14; Jeremiah 32:17,27;
Mark 9:23; James 5:15
The Set of the Sail, 33.

925. Prayer: fellowship with God

Years ago, Max Reich, who spoke in our church a number of times, was asked to describe his prayer life. "If you are asking me about getting by myself and spending long periods alone on my knees in prayer, then I would have to say that I am relatively a prayerless man," Dr. Reich told us. "But if you accept praying without ceasing as a continual, humble communion with God, day and night, under all circumstances—the pouring out of my heart to God in continual, unbroken fellowship—then I can say I pray without ceasing."

Psalm 63:6-8; Ephesians 6:18;
1 Thessalonians 5:16-17
Faith beyond Reason, 151.

926. Prayer: fellowship with God; Prayer: lifestyle

It is the privilege of every Christian to live so fully in God that he never gets out of the experienced Presence for one moment....

A life lived in Christ becomes in the true sense a life of unceasing prayer. The whole life becomes a prayer: words are verbal prayers, thoughts become mental prayers, deeds become prayers in action and even sleep may be but unconscious prayer.

1 Thessalonians 5:16-17
The Next Chapter after the Last, 90.

927. Prayer: fellowship with God; Prayer: wrong use of; Communion with God

Prayer among evangelical Christians is always in danger of degenerating into a glorified gold rush. Almost every book on prayer deals with the "get" element mainly. How to get things we want from God occupies most of the space. Now, we gladly admit that we may ask for and receive specific gifts and benefits in answer to prayer, but we must never forget that the highest kind of prayer is never the making of requests. Prayer at its holiest moment is the entering into God to a place of such blessed union as makes miracles seem tame and remarkable answers to prayer appear something very far short of wonderful by comparison.

Psalm 27:4,8; Psalm 139:17-18;
John 17:20-24; Revelation 3:20
The Set of the Sail, 14.

928. Prayer: intercession; Women

If prayer is (as we believe it is) an integral part of the total divine scheme of things and must be done if the will of God is to be done, then the prayers of the thousands of women who meet each week in our churches is of inestimable value to the kingdom of God. More power to them, and may their number increase tenfold.

Acts 2:42-44; Acts 16:13; Philippians 4:3
We Travel an Appointed Way, 15.

929. Prayer: lifestyle

Prayer at its best is the expression of the total life....

All things else being equal, our prayers are only as powerful as our lives....

Most of us in moments of stress have wished that we had lived so that prayer would not be so unnatural to us and have regretted that we had not cultivated prayer to the point where it would be as easy and as natural as breathing....

Undoubtedly the redemption in Christ Jesus has sufficient moral power to enable us to live in a state of purity and love where our whole life will be a prayer. Individual acts of prayer that spring out of that kind of total living will have about them a wondrous power not known to the careless or the worldly Christian.

John 15:1-7
The Root of the Righteous, 81, 82, 83.

930. Prayer: mere ritual

When religion loses its sovereign character and becomes mere form, this spontaneity is lost also, and in its place come precedent, propriety, system—and the file-card mentality....

The slave to the file card soon finds that his prayers lose their freedom and become less spontaneous, less effective. He finds himself concerned over matters that should give him no concern whatever—how much time he spent in prayer yesterday, whether he did or did not cover his prayer list for the day, whether he gets up as early as he used to or stays up in prayer as late at night. Inevitably the calendar crowds out the Spirit and the face of the clock hides the face of God. Prayer ceases to be the free breath of a ransomed soul and becomes a duty to be fulfilled. And even if under such circumstances he succeeds in making his prayer amount to something, still he is suffering tragic losses and binding upon his soul a yoke from which Christ died to set him free.

Psalm 1:1-3; Psalm 5:3; Psalm 119:147-148
Of God and Men, 79, 81.

931. Prayer: necessity of; Bible: reading of

I am reminded that one old saint was asked, "Which is the more important: reading God's Word or praying?" To which he replied, "Which is more important to a bird: the right wing or the left?"

Acts 6:3-7
Jesus, Our Man in Glory, 104.

932. Prayer: necessity of; Church: spiritual condition; Revival: need for

For some years I have had a growing conviction that the world situation as God sees it presents two major goals to be reached by praying people, two objects at which to aim our prayers.

One is *that the glory of God be seen again among men, and the other that the church be delivered from her present Babylonian captivity....*

I believe we are under positive spiritual obligation to pray effectively till the present veil is torn away and the face of God is seen again by believing men.

The second object at which our prayers should be aimed is the restoration of the spiritual life of the church. We must continue to pray that she should cease her disgraceful fornication with the world and return to her first love and her true Lord. Her living has degenerated, her tastes have declined, her standards have sunk to the bottom. Nothing short of a radical reformation can save her. Only those with anointed eyes are able to see her plight and only those with Spirit-filled hearts can intercede for her effectively.

Exodus 40:34-35; Matthew 24:10-12;
2 Timothy 3:13-17; Revelation 2:4-5
Keys to the Deeper Life, 62, 63.

933. Prayer: necessity of; Pastoral ministry: prayer

I knew of an able preacher greatly used of the Lord in evangelism and Bible conferences. He was a busy, busy man. There came the occasion when someone frankly asked him, "Doctor, tell us about your prayer life. How do you pray? How much do you pray?"

The man was embarrassed as he replied, "I must confess to you something I have not confessed before. I do not have the time to pray as I used to. My time alone with God has been neglected."

Not too long afterward, that preacher sustained a serious failure. It brought his ministry to an abrupt end, and he was put on the shelf.

If we want to be honest with God, we will take solemnly the admonition to pray without ceasing. God's work on this earth languishes when God's people give up their ministries of prayer and supplication. I cannot tell you why this is true, but it is true.

Acts 6:3-7; 1 Corinthians 9:24-27;
1 Thessalonians 5:16-17
Men Who Met God, 46, 47.

934. Prayer: necessity of; Pastoral ministry: prayer

It is significant that the schools teach everything about preaching except the important part, praying. For this weakness the schools are not to be blamed, for the reason that prayer cannot be taught; it can only be done. The best any school or any book (or any article) can do is to recommend prayer and exhort to its practice. Praying itself must be the work of the individual. That it is the one religious work which gets done with the least enthusiasm cannot but be one of the tragedies of our times.

Luke 18:1-8; Ephesians 6:18; Philippians 4:6-7
God Tells the Man Who Cares, 70.

935. Prayer: patience in

Dr. Moody Stuart, a great praying man of a past generation, once drew up a set of rules to guide him in his prayers. Among these rules is this one: "Pray till you pray.". . .

The habit of breaking off our prayers before we have truly prayed is as common as it is unfortunate. Often the last 10 minutes may mean more to us than the first half hour, because we must spend a long time getting into the proper mood to pray effectively. We may need to struggle with our thoughts to draw them in from where they have been scattered through the multitude of distractions that result from the task of living in a disordered world. . . .

If when we come to prayer our hearts feel dull and unspiritual, we should not try to argue ourselves out of it. Rather, we should admit it frankly and pray our way through. Some Christians smile at the thought of "praying through," but something of the same idea is found in the writings of practically every great praying saint from Daniel to the present day. We cannot afford to stop praying till we have actually prayed.

Luke 18:1-8; Acts 1:12-14; Romans 12:9-13; Colossians 4:2
This World: Playground or Battleground?, 69, 70.

936. Prayer: patience in

Think of the kernels of grain, the seed, that the farmer plants in the ground in the fall of the year. How patient the farmer must be! Throughout the long, cold winter the seed is dormant. There is no evidence at all that it is there—covered by the cold earth itself. The snows come and go. The ground freezes and thaws. Does the farmer lie awake at night worrying that those seeds he placed in the ground may be ineffective? He does not. He knows that spring will come!

And in due course, the sunshine of March or April warms the air. Spring rains water the ground. The farmer knows then that it will not be long until green shoots suddenly break out from their covering of earth. And in their own time, great waving fields of grain are ready for the harvest. The farmer's faith in the seed he planted is fully justified.

Likewise, God wants us to be patient with every prayer and petition we sincerely send up to that heavenly altar. Our praying done in the Spirit cannot be ineffective. It is as though God is saying to us: "You have planted the seed. You have prayed for My will to be done and for My kingdom to come on earth. . . . The effective prayers of my Son, Jesus, will join with the effective prayers of righteous men and women. Be patient and put your trust in Me, day by day!"

Matthew 6:10; Romans 8:25-27; James 5:16
Jesus Is Victor!, 122.

937. Prayer: privilege of; Faith: confidence in God

Most of us go through life praying a little, planning a little, jockeying for position, hoping but never being quite certain of anything, and always secretly afraid that we will miss the way. This is a tragic waste of truth and never gives rest to the heart.

There is a better way. It is to repudiate our own wisdom and take instead the infinite wisdom of God. Our insistence upon seeing ahead is natural enough, but it is a real hindrance to our spiritual progress. God has charged Himself with full responsibility for our eternal happiness and stands ready to take over the management of our lives the moment we turn in faith to Him. . . .

With the goodness of God to desire our highest welfare, the wisdom of God to plan it, and the power of God to achieve it, what do we lack? Surely we are the most favored of all creatures.

Job 23:8-10; Proverbs 3:1-2, 5-6; James 1:5-6
The Knowledge of the Holy, 97, 99.

938. Prayer: privilege of; Spiritual victory

It is characteristic of human nature to turn to God only after every other avenue of help has been explored and been found useless. This is one of the many evils which sin has visited upon us—the bent to look everywhere for aid but in the right place, and if we do look in the right place, to look there last. . . .

God should come first. If in our sinful ignorance we once knew no better, there is no reason for our continuing in the same rut now that we are children of the kingdom. It cheats us out of many a victory and leaves us for long periods in a state of perplexity and distress when we might be walking in freedom without a care in the world.

Psalm 121:2; Psalm 124:8; Romans 7:24-25; 2 Corinthians 2:14
The Next Chapter after the Last, 48, 49.

939. Prayer: unanswered; Unbelief

If unanswered prayer continues in a congregation over an extended period of time, the chill of discouragement will settle over the praying people. If we continue to ask and ask and ask, like petulant children, never expecting to get what we ask for but continuing to whine for it, we will become chilled within our beings.

If we continue in our prayers and never get answers, the lack of results will tend to confirm the natural unbelief of our hearts. Remember this: the human heart by nature is filled with unbelief....

Perhaps worst of all is the fact that our failures in prayer leave the enemy in possession of the field. The worst part about the failure of a military drive is not the loss of men or the loss of face but the fact that the enemy is left in possession of the field. In the spiritual sense, this is both a tragedy and a disaster. The devil ought to be on the run, always fighting a rear guard action. Instead, this blasphemous enemy smugly and scornfully holds his position, and the people of God let him have it. No wonder the work of the Lord is greatly retarded. Little wonder the work of God stands still!

Isaiah 55:8,9; John 14:13,14; James 4:3-4
Faith beyond Reason, 36, 37.

940. Prayer: unanswered; Revival: conditions for; Obedience: need for

Intensity of prayer is no criterion of its effectiveness. A man may throw himself on his face and sob out his troubles to the Lord and yet have no intention to obey the commandments of Christ. Strong emotion and tears may be no more than the outcropping of a vexed spirit, evidence of stubborn resistance to God's known will....

No matter what I write here, thousands of pastors will continue to call their people to prayer in the forlorn hope that God will finally relent and send revival if only His people wear themselves out in intercession. To such people God must indeed appear to be a hard taskmaster, for the years pass and the young get old and the aged die and still no help comes. The prayer meeting room becomes a wailing wall and the lights burn long, and still the rains tarry.

Has God forgotten to be gracious? Let any reader begin to obey and he will have the answer. "Whoever has my commands and obeys them, he is the one who loves me. He who loves me will be loved by my Father, and I too will love him and show myself to him" (John 14:21).

Isn't that what we want after all?

2 Chronicles 7:14; John 14:21; 1 John 3:21-22
The Size of the Soul, 20, 21.

941. Prayer: wrong use of

Many prayer meetings are being called these days. And no wonder, for the need is great. But if my observation is correct much effort is wasted; very little comes of them.

The reason is that motives are not sound.

Too many praying persons seek to use prayer as a means to ends that are not wholly pure. Prayer is often conceived to be little more than a technique for self-advancement, a heavenly method of achieving earthly success. . . .

To pray effectively we must want what God wants—that and only that is to pray in the will of God.

John 14:3-4; James 4:3; 1 John 5:14-15
Keys to the Deeper Life, 59, 61.

942. Prayer: wrong use of

There is an idea abroad that wrestling in prayer is always a good thing, but that is by no means true. Extreme religious exercises may be undergone with no higher motive than to get our own way.

The spiritual quality of a prayer is determined not by its intensity but by its origin. In evaluating prayer we should inquire who is doing the praying—our determined hearts or the Holy Spirit? If the prayer originates with the Holy Spirit, then the wrestling can be beautiful and wonderful; but if we are the victims of our own overheated desires, our praying can be as carnal as any other act.

Genesis 32:24; Romans 8:25-27;
2 Corinthians 12:8-9
This World: Playground or Battleground?, 16.

943. Prayer: wrong use of; Evangelism: wrong emphasis

We go to God as we send a boy to a grocery store with a long written list, "God, give me this, give me this, and give me this," and our gracious God often does give us what we want. But I think God is disappointed because we make Him to be no more than a source of what we want. Even our Lord Jesus is presented too often much as "Someone who will meet your need." That's the throbbing heart of modern evangelism. You're in need and Jesus will meet your need. He's the Need-meeter. Well, He is that indeed; but, ah, He's infinitely more than that.

Psalm 106:14-15; Philippians 4:11-12; Hebrews 12:1-2
Worship: The Missing Jewel, 24, 25.

944. Prayer: wrong use of; God: His sovereignty

In all our praying, however, it is important that we keep in mind that God will not alter His eternal purposes at the word of a man. We do not pray in order to persuade God to change His mind. Prayer is not an assault upon the reluctance of God, nor an effort to secure a suspension of His will for us or for those for whom we pray. Prayer is not intended to overcome God and "move His arm." God will never be other than Himself, no matter how many people pray, nor how long nor how earnestly.

God's love desires the best for all of us, and He desires to give us the best at any cost. He will open rivers in desert places, still turbulent waves, quiet the wind, bring water from the rock, send an angel to release an apostle from prison, feed an orphanage, open a land long closed to the gospel. All these things and a thousand others He has done and will do in answer to prayer, but only because it had been His will to do it from the beginning. No one persuades Him.

What the praying man does is to bring his will into line with the will of God so God can do what He has all along been willing to do. Thus prayer changes the man and enables God to change things in answer to man's prayer.

Exodus 17:6; Isaiah 41:18; Matthew 8:26; Matthew 14:22-33; Acts 12:7
The Price of Neglect, 51, 52.

945. Prayer: wrong use of; Self-interest; Pride: spiritual

The problem is self. Selfishness is never so exquisitely selfish as when it is on its knees....

Self turns what would otherwise be a pure and powerful prayer into a weak and ineffective one.

I may, for instance, pray earnestly for the glory of God to be manifested to this generation of men, and spoil the whole thing by my secret hope that I may be the one through whom He manifests the glory.

I may cry loudly to God that the church be restored to her New Testament splendor, and secretly dream that I may be the one to lead her in; thus I block the work of the Spirit by my impure motive. My hidden desire for a share of the glory prevents God from hearing me. So self, all bold and shameless, follows me to the altar, kneels with me in prayer and destroys my prayer before it is uttered....

Too often we pray for right things but desire the answer for wrong reasons, one reason being a desire to gain a reputation among the saints. Long after every hope of getting on the cover of Time magazine has ebbed away from our hearts we may still harbor the unconfessed desire to get on the cover of Christian Life. That is, if the world will not appreciate our sterling worth, then the church will!

Isaiah 42:8; Matthew 6:1-5; James 4:3-4
Keys to the Deeper Life, 63, 64, 65.

946. Prayers; Finishing well

Out of my own experience at this point I wrote a few words years ago which have long been my constant prayer:

"O God, let me die right, rather than letting me live wrong.

"Keep me, Lord, from ever hardening down into the state of being just another average Christian.

"Lord, I would rather reach a high point and turn off the light than to live a poor, useless life on a low level."

Acts 20:24; 1 Corinthians 9:24-27; 2 Timothy 4:6-8
I Talk Back to the Devil, 99.

947. Prayers; Finishing well

For years I have made a practice of writing many of my earnest prayers to God in a little book—a book now well worn. I still turn often to the petitions I recorded in that book. I remind God often of what my prayers have been.

One prayer in the book—and God knows it well by this time, for I pray it often—goes like this:
Oh God,

> Let me die rather than to go on day by day living wrong. I do not want to become a careless, fleshly old man. I want to be right so that I can die right. Lord, I do not want my life to be extended if it would mean that I should cease to live right and fail in my mission to glorify You all of my days!...

As you will recall from Second Kings 20, the Lord gave Hezekiah a 15-year extension of life. Restored to health and vigor, Hezekiah disgraced himself and dishonored God before he died and was buried.

I would not want an extra 15 years in which to backslide and dishonor my Lord. I would rather go home right now than to live on—if living on was to be a waste of God's time and my own!

2 Kings 20; Psalm 139:23-24; 2 Timothy 4:6-8
Jesus Is Victor!, 141, 142.

948. Prayers; Knowledge of God: supreme value of

Our Heavenly Father: Let us see Thy glory, if it must be from the shelter of the cleft rock and from beneath the protection of Thy covering hand. Whatever the cost to us in loss of friends or goods or length of days let us know Thee as Thou art, that we may adore Thee as we should. Through Jesus Christ our Lord. *Amen.*

Exodus 33:18-23; Isaiah 6:1-5; John 1:18
The Knowledge of the Holy, 67.

949. Prayers; Pride: spiritual; Wisdom

Thou, O Christ, who wert tempted in all points like as we are, yet without sin, make us strong to overcome the desire to be wise and to be reputed wise by others as ignorant as ourselves. We turn from our wisdom as well as from our folly and flee to Thee, the wisdom of God and the power of God. Amen.

1 Corinthians 1:23-25; Hebrews 4:14-16; James 1:5-6
The Knowledge of the Holy, 91.

950. Preaching: awesome task; Pastoral ministry: challenge

Because we are the kind of persons we are and because we live in a world such as we do, the shepherd of souls is often forced to work at what would appear to be cross purposes with himself.

For instance, he must encourage the timid and warn the self-confident; and these may at any given time be present in his congregation in almost equal numbers. . . .

Another problem he faces is the presence in the normal Christian assembly of believers in every stage of development, from the newly converted who knows almost nothing about the Christian life to the wise and experienced Christian who seems to know almost everything.

Again, the Christian minister must have a word from God for the teen-aged, the middle-aged and the very aged. He must speak to the scholar as well as to the ignorant; he must bring the living Word to the cultured man and woman and to the vulgarian who reads nothing but the sports page and the comic strip. He must speak to the sad and to the happy, to the tender-minded and to the tough-minded, to those eager to live and to some who secretly wish they could die. And he must do this all in one sermon and in a period of time not exceeding 45 minutes. Surely this requires a Daniel, and Daniels are as scarce in the United States today as in Babylon in 600 B.C.

1 Thessalonians 5:13-15; 2 Timothy 3:16-17;
Hebrews 4:12; 2 Peter 3:18
The Set of the Sail, 82, 83.

951. Preaching: awesome task; Spiritual warfare; Pastors: Satan's opposition

I have never given more time and more pain and more prayer to any other series of sermons in my ministry.

Because of their importance, I have literally felt Satan attempting to thwart the purpose of God. I have felt I was in raw contact with hell.

There are so many in the Church who are spiritually blind that I tell God that I want to be able to see—I want to be a lower-case "seer." I want to penetrate and understand and have discernment concerning the whole plan of God. I want to appraise the situation and see it as God sees it—to know the role of God in this day of religious confusion.

Now, that doesn't make a man easy to live with. It doesn't make him popular and it doesn't create any problem for police taking care of the crowd.

This course has forced me frequently to follow the trail of opposition and temptation straight to the foe! But I would rather have it this way than to have to admit—as some will have to admit—to having spent a lifetime preaching the Word of God and yet never having met the devil once in open combat! ...

But, I will tell you something—it is a delightful thing when you know that you are close enough to the adversary that you can hear him roar! Too many Christians never get into "lion country" at all!

Daniel 10:12-13; 2 Corinthians 4:4; 2
Corinthians 12:7; 2 Timothy 4:17; 1 Peter 5:8-9
I Talk Back to the Devil, 1, 2.

952. Preaching: experiencing God; Jesus Christ: intimacy with

I insist that the effective preaching of Jesus Christ, rightly understood, will produce spiritual experience in Christian believers. Moreover, if Christian preaching does *not* produce spiritual experience and maturing in the believer, the preaching is not being faithful to the Christ revealed in the Scriptures!

Let me say it again another way. The Christ of the Bible is not rightly known until there is an experience of Him within the believer, for our Savior and Lord offers Himself to human experience....

Jesus Christ, truly known and loved and followed, becomes a spiritual experience for seeking men and women.

Matthew 7:7-11; Ephesians 4:11-13; Colossians 1:28,29
Men Who Met God, 9, 10.

953. Preaching: experiencing God; Knowledge of God: personal, intimate

Sound Bible exposition is an imperative *must* in the Church of the Living God. Without it no church can be a New Testament church in any strict meaning of that term. But exposition may be carried on in such a way as to leave the hearers devoid of any true spiritual nourishment whatever. For it is not mere words that nourish the soul, but God Himself, and unless and until the hearers find God in personal experience they are not the better for having heard the truth. The Bible is not an end in itself, but a means to bring men to an intimate and satisfying knowledge of God, that they may enter into Him, that they may delight in His Presence, may taste and know the inner sweetness of the very God Himself in the core and center of their hearts.

Psalm 1:1-3; Psalm 119:9-11; Psalm 119:38-40; Psalm 119:111-112
The Pursuit of God, 9.

954. Preaching: illustrations in

Many of the stories brought forward to justify the ways of God to men actually prove nothing except the unsoundness of the speaker's intellectual fiber. Yet if all chimney-corner Scripture and old wives' tales were forbidden, many a preacher would have to get out of the ministry. It is a deep pity that the Christian public must be forced to listen to so much nonsense and be helpless to do anything about it.

The point is, the Word of God needs no support from men. It stands alone, strong and majestic as the Matterhorn. When we call in the aid of childish stories and shaky illustrations to prove its truth, we do no more than to reveal our hidden unbelief and air our weak credulity.

Nehemiah 8:8
We Travel an Appointed Way, 6.

955. Preaching: inadequacy for

None of us can approach a serious study and consideration of the eternal nature and person of Jesus Christ without sensing and confessing our complete inadequacy in the face of the divine revelation. . . .

What should we do, then?

All we can hope to do is to toddle along on our short legs and gaze heavenward, like a goose whose wings have been clipped but whose heart is in the sky. Those wings just will not take her there.

Now, I have said all of this because my best faith and my loftiest expectation do not allow me to believe that I can do justice to a text that begins: "And the Word became flesh, and made his dwelling among us" (John 1:14) and concludes: "No man hath seen God at any time; the only begotten Son, which is in the bosom of the Father, he hath declared him" (John 1:18).

This is what we will attempt to do: we will walk along the broad seashore of God and pick up a shell here and a shell there, holding each up to the light to admire its beauty. While we may ultimately have a small store of shells to take with us, they can but remind us of the truth and the fact that there stretches the vastness of the seashore around the great lips of the oceans—and that still buried there is far more than we can ever hope to find or see!

John 1:14,18; 2 Corinthians 3:5-6
Christ the Eternal Son, 9, 10, 11.

956. Preaching: inadequacy for; John: Gospel of

I believe I had anticipated that it was going to be a pleasure to expound this beautiful and high-soaring Gospel of John. However, I must confess that in my preparation and study a sense of inadequacy has come over me—a feeling of inadequacy so stunning, so almost paralyzing that I am not at this juncture able to call it a pleasure to preach.

Perhaps this will be God's way of reducing the flesh to a minimum and giving the Holy Spirit the best possible opportunity to do His eternal work.

Romans 15:18-19; 1 Corinthians 2:1-5;
2 Corinthians 3:5-6; 2 Corinthians 4:5-7
Christ the Eternal Son, 3.

957. Preaching: manipulation

When they want to get blessed, some people try getting worked up psychologically. There are some who, while they have not studied psychology, are master psychologists. They know how to manipulate audiences, knowing when to lower their voices and when to raise them, when to make them sound very sad and all the rest. They know how to get people all worked up.

I sat listening to a preacher one time, and right across from me was a young woman, maybe 22 or 23 years old. The only reason I noticed her was that she had on a pair of glass shoes. The preacher went on preaching, and he never, as far as I remember, said anything about the Lord. But he did tell us all about his father and his mother and how his father left home and the whole story. I watched this woman, then I would watch the preacher and then look at her again. At first she could not have cared less, but slowly he got hold of her. When it came to the point where the evangelist said in a tremulous voice that every time he faced an audience he hoped that his old father might be there, the girl broke down and went to pieces. From that moment she was eating out of his hand. He knew how to handle her psychologically. He got her, and she would have done anything for him.

2 Corinthians 1:12; 2 Corinthians 2:17;
2 Corinthians 4:2; 1 Thessalonians 2:13
Rut, Rot or Revival: The Condition of the Church, 50, 51.

958. Preaching: need for application

God's Word says that a faithful and wise steward gives the people their meat in due season. Some people preach the Bible all right, and you cannot deny that. But they go to the Bible as you would to a medical book to find out what you should prescribe. But instead of prescribing to suit each patient, they just prescribe for everybody at one time.

When a preacher is not preaching to a given situation, it is like giving medicine to people indiscriminately. That approach is not particularly fitted for teaching the Word of God. Even though it may be faithful and true, without any regard to the current situation, it is like teaching the multiplication table.

Matthew 24:45; Hebrews 4:12
Rut, Rot or Revival: The Condition of the Church, 90, 91.

959. Preaching: need for application; Bible: teaching of

The great American evangelist, Charles Finney, went so far as to declare bluntly that it is sinful to teach the Bible without moral application. He asked what good is accomplished merely to study a course in the Bible to find out what it says, if there is to be no obligation to do anything as a result of what has been learned?

There can be a right and a wrong emphasis in conducting Bible classes. I am convinced that some Bible classes are nothing more than a means whereby men become even more settled in their religious prejudices.

Only when we have moral application are we in the Bible method! . . .

"This is what God did, and this is what God did. Therefore, this is what you ought to do!" That is always the Bible way.

Titus 2:11-14; James 1:22-25; 1 Peter 1:6-9, 13; 1 John 3:1
I Call It Heresy!, 137.

960. Preaching: need for application; Pastors: prophetic ministry

A church can wither as surely under the ministry of soulless Bible exposition as it can where no Bible is given at all. To be effective, the preacher's message must be alive—it must alarm, arouse, challenge; it must be God's present voice to a particular people. Then, and not until then, is it the prophetic word and the man himself, a prophet.

To perfectly fulfill his calling, the prophet must be under the constant sway of the Holy Spirit. Further, he must be alert to moral and spiritual conditions. All spiritual teaching should relate to life. It should intrude into the daily and private living of the hearers. Without being personal, the true prophet will nevertheless pierce the conscience of each listener as if the message had been directed to him or her alone.

1 Chronicles 12:32; 1 Thessalonians 1:5; 2 Timothy 4:1-5
This World: Playground or Battleground?, 85, 86.

961. Preaching: need for application; Truth: necessity of response; Obedience: need for

There is scarcely anything so dull and meaningless as Bible doctrine taught for its own sake. Truth divorced from life is not truth in its biblical sense, but something else and something less. . . .

By far the greater portion of the book is devoted to an urgent effort to persuade people to alter their ways and bring their lives into harmony with the will of God as set forth in its pages.

No man is better for knowing that God in the beginning created the heaven and the earth. The devil knows that, and so did Ahab and Judas Iscariot. No man is better for knowing that God so loved the world of men that He gave His only begotten Son to die for their redemption. In hell there are millions who know that. Theological truth is useless until it is obeyed. The purpose behind all doctrine is to secure moral action.

Genesis 1:1; Matthew 7:24-27; John 3:16; Romans 2:13; James 1:22-25; James 2:19-20
Of God and Men, 25, 26.

962. Preaching: need for freshness

It would probably be an oversimplification to name any single cause as being alone responsible for the dullness of our preaching, but I nevertheless venture to suggest that one very important factor is our habit of laboring the obvious. . . .

This engrossment in first principles has an adverse effect upon the evangelical church. It is as if an intelligent child should be forced to stay in the third grade five or six years. The monotony is just too great. . . .

Our tendency to repeat endlessly a half dozen basic doctrines is the result of our lack of prophetic insight and our failure to meet God in living encounter. The knowledge of God presents a million facets, each one shining with a new ravishing light. The teacher who lives in the heart of God, reads Scriptures with warm devotion, undergoes the discipline and chastisement of the Holy Spirit and presses on toward perfection is sure every now and again to come upon fresh and blessed vistas of truth, old indeed as the Word itself, but bright as the dew on the grass in the morning. The heart that has seen the far glimpses of advanced truth will never be able to keep quiet about them. His experiences will get into his sermons one way or another, and his messages will carry an element of surprise and delight altogether absent from the ordinary Bible talks heard everywhere these days.

Romans 11:33-36; Ephesians 3:8; Ephesians 4:11-13; Hebrews 6:1
The Warfare of the Spirit, 68, 69, 70.

963. Preaching: need for freshness

You may say, "I believe all that. You surely don't think you are telling us anything new!" I don't hope to tell you very much that is new; I only hope to set the table for you, arranging the dishes a little better and a little more attractively so that you will be tempted to partake.

How to Be Filled with the Holy Spirit, 12.

964. Preaching: originality in

Some preachers have such a phobia for repetition and such an unnatural fear of the familiar that they are forever straining after the odd and the startling. The church page of the newspaper almost any Saturday will be sure to announce at least one or two sermon topics so far astray as to be positively grotesque; only by the most daring flight of uncontrolled imagination can any relation be established between the topic and the religion of Christ. We dare not impugn the honesty or the sincerity of the men who thus flap their short wings so rapidly in an effort to take off into the wild blue yonder, but we do deplore their attitudes. No one should try to be more original than an apostle.

God Tells the Man Who Cares, 144.

965. Preaching: preach the Word

I heard of one graduate of a theological school who determined to follow his old professor's advice and preach the Word only. His crowds were average. Then one day a cyclone hit the little town and he yielded to the temptation to preach on the topic "Why God Sent the Cyclone to Centerville." The church was packed. This shook the young preacher and he went back to ask his professor for further advice in the light of what had happened. Should he continue to preach the Word to smaller crowds or try to fill his church by preaching sermons a bit more sensational? The old man did not change his mind. "If you preach the

Word," he told the inquirer, "you will always have a text. But if you wait for cyclones you will not have enough to go around."

2 Timothy 4:1-5
God Tells the Man Who Cares, 86.

966. Preaching: preach the Word; Church: current condition; Pastors: prophetic ministry

We must face up to what is going on in the churches and meet it as men and women of God. It is not enough just to show a smiling countenance and insist that we are hoping for the best. Where we see there is wrong, we must face up to it, show why it is wrong and dismiss it; and then plant truth in its place. A builder dares not erect any structure until he has cleared the sand and debris away in order to place the foundation squarely down on rock.

As Christian believers, we must stand together against some things. So, if you hear anyone saying that A.W. Tozer preaches a good deal that is negative, just smile and agree. "That is because he preaches the Bible!"

Galatians 2:11; Ephesians 5:11; 1 Timothy 5:20-21; 2 Timothy 4:1-5
Jesus, Author of Our Faith, 114, 115.

967. Preaching: preach the Word; Dialogue

Frankly, I am too busy serving Jesus to spend my time and energy engaging in contemporary dialogue.

I think I know what "contemporary dialogue" means. It means that all of those intellectual preachers are busy reading the news magazines so they will be able to comment on the world situation from their pulpits on Sunday mornings. But that is not what God called me to do. He called me to preach the glories of Christ. He commissioned me to tell my people there is a kingdom of God and a throne in the heavens. And that we have One of our own representing us there.

That is what the early church was excited about. And I think our Lord may have reason to ask why we are no longer very excited about it.

Ephesians 3:8; Hebrews 8:1-2; Revelation 4:2-3
Jesus, Our Man in Glory, 5, 6.

968. Preaching: preparation for; Preaching: need for skill

Among the countless gifts of God, one of the most precious to us is our beautiful, expressive English tongue. That such a gift should be neglected by busy men and women in their wild race to make a living is at least understandable, if unfortunate; but that it should be neglected as well by the ministers of the sanctuary is not only impossible to understand but completely inexcusable.

For the very reason that God has committed His saving truth to the receptacle of human language, the man who preaches that truth should be more than ordinarily skillful in the use of language. It is necessary that every artist master his medium, every musician his instrument. For a man calling himself a concert pianist to appear before an audience with but a beginner's acquaintance with the keyboard would be no more absurd than for a minister of the gospel to appear before his congregation without a thorough knowledge of the language in which he expects to preach.

There have been extraordinary situations where God has blessed a halting and broken message to the edification of the hearers, but these must be recognized as instances of providential overrulings and not as the operation of the highest will of God. Under an abnormal set of circumstances God moved Balaam's ass to speak with enough eloquence to convict a renegade prophet and rate being quoted in the Bible. But surely no one would cite this as proof that religious teachers should not concern themselves about their skill in the use of language.

Numbers 22:28; Colossians 3:23; 1 Timothy 4:13-16; 2 Timothy 2:14-16
The Size of the Soul, 41, 42.

969. Preaching: problem texts; Boldness

There is a problem in this passage, but I may die tomorrow and I would not want to die knowing that only a day before I had been too cowardly and timid to deal with a text of Scripture!

Acts 2:20,27,30; 1 Timothy 4:6; 1 Peter 3:1-7
I Call It Heresy!, 126.

970. Preaching: response to; Church: boredom

Every one who has come to the years of responsibility seems to have gone on the defensive. Even some of you who have known me for years are surely on the defensive—you have your guard up all the time!

I know that you are not afraid of me, but you are afraid, nevertheless, of what I am going to say. Probably every faithful preacher today is fencing with masters as he faces his congregation. The guard is always up. The quick parry is always ready.

It is very hard for me to accept the fact that it is now very rare for anyone to come into the house of God with guard completely down, head bowed and with the silent confession: "Dear Lord, I am ready and willing to hear what You will speak to my heart today!"

We have become so learned and so worldly and so sophisticated and so blasé and so bored and so religiously tired that the clouds of glory seem to have gone from us.

1 Samuel 3:10; 1 Timothy 1:6-7; 2 Timothy 4:1-5
Christ the Eternal Son, 108, 109.

971. Preaching: response to; Church: spiritual condition

The difference between a wooden leg and a good leg is that if you prick a wooden leg the person would never notice. The difference between a church that has dry rot and a church that is alive is that if you prick the live church it will respond. If you prick the other kind, it is already dead. The tree that stands alive has lush, green leaves. Take a knife, scar the bark deeply and the tree will bleed. It is alive. The old dead tree just stands there, a watchtower for old sentinel crows. Take your knife and dig in as far as you want to, and nothing will happen because the tree is dead.

So it is with my message. If you will get neither mad nor glad nor sad under my preaching, I know nothing can be done. But there are some who are alive, and I believe it is the majority.

Acts 2:37-38; Acts 4:1-2; 1 Corinthians 1:23-25; 1 Corinthians 2:12-16; Ephesians 2:1-7; 1 Thessalonians 1:9
Rut, Rot or Revival: The Condition of the Church, 12.

972. Preaching: response to; Listening to God

It is carelessly assumed by most persons that when a preacher pronounces a message of truth and his words fall upon the ears of his listeners there has been a bona fide act of hearing on their part. They are assumed to have been instructed because they have listened to the Word of God. But it does not follow.

If we would be truly instructed we must be worthy to hear; or more accurately, we must hear in a worthy manner. In listening to a sermon, reading a good book or even reading the Bible itself, much may be lost to us because we are not worthy to hear the truth. That is, we have not met the moral terms required to hear the truth rightly. . . .

God will speak to the hearts of those who prepare themselves to hear; and conversely, those who do not so prepare themselves will hear nothing even though the Word of God is falling upon their outer ears every Sunday.

Good hearers are as important as good preachers. We need more of both.

Psalm 139:23-24; John 5:36-40; 2 Timothy 4:1-5
The Root of the Righteous, 19, 20, 22.

973. Preaching: too deep

Many a preacher would like to challenge the intellectual and thinking capacity of his congregation, but he has been warned about preaching over the people's heads.

I ask, "What are people's heads for? God Almighty gave them those heads and I think they ought to use them!"

As a preacher, I deny that any of the truths of God which I teach and expound are over the heads of the people. I deny it!

My preaching may go right through their heads if there is nothing in there to stop it, but I do not preach truths which are too much for them to comprehend. We ought to begin using our heads. Brother, you ought to take that head of yours, oil it and rub the rust off and begin to use it as God has always expected you would. God expects you to understand and have a grasp of His truth because you need it from day to day.

1 Corinthians 3:1-3; 1 Corinthians 14:20; Hebrews 5:11-12; 1 Peter 2:1-2
I Call It Heresy!, 145.

974. Preaching: watered down

I have listened to certain speakers and have recognized the ingredients that went to make up their teachings. A bit of Freud, a dash of Émile Coué, a lot of watered-down humanism, tender chunks of Emersonian transcendentalism, auto-suggestion à la Dale Carnegie, plenty of hopefulness and religious sentimentality, but nothing hard and sharp and specific. Nothing of the either/or of Christ and Peter and Paul. None of the "Who is on the LORD's side" (Exodus 32:26, KJV) of Moses, or the "Choose for yourselves this day whom you will serve" (Joshua 24:15) of Joshua: just tender pleading to "take Jesus and let Him solve your problems.". . .

The notion is now pretty well disseminated throughout the ranks of current evangelicalism that love is really all that matters and for that reason we ought to receive everyone whose intention is right, regardless of his doctrinal position, granted of course that he is ready to read the Scriptures, trust Jesus and pray.

Exodus 32:26; Deuteronomy 10:12;
Joshua 24:14-15; 1 Kings 18:21
God Tells the Man Who Cares, 66, 67.

975. Preaching: watered down; Boldness; Discipleship

The contemporary moral climate does not favor a faith as tough and fibrous as that taught by our Lord and His apostles. The delicate, brittle saints being produced in our religious hothouses today are hardly to be compared with the committed, expendable believers who once gave their witness among men. And the fault lies with our leaders. They are too timid to tell the people all the truth. They are now asking men to give to God that which costs them nothing.

Our churches these days are filled (or one-quarter filled) with a soft breed of Christian that must be fed on a diet of harmless fun to keep them interested. About theology they know little. Scarcely any of them have read even one of the great Christian classics, but most of them are familiar with religious fiction and spine tingling films. No wonder their moral and spiritual constitution is so frail. Such can only be called weak adherents of a faith they never really understood.

Luke 9:23-25; Acts 20:27-30; Ephesians 4:11-16
That Incredible Christian, 76.

976. Preaching: watered down; Pastoral ministry: shallowness

Admittedly, this is not an easy concept for us to grasp. We are not used to stretching our minds! The preachers of our generation are failing us. They are not forcing us to crank up our minds and to exercise our souls in the contemplation of God's eternal themes.

Too many preachers are satisfied to dwell primarily on the escape element in Christianity. I acknowledge that the escape element is real. No one is more sure of it than I. I am going to escape a much-deserved hell because of Christ's death on the cross and His resurrection from the grave. But if we continue to emphasize that truth to the exclusion of all else, Christian believers will never fully grasp what the Scriptures are teaching us about all of the eternal purposes of God.

John 3:16; Acts 20:20,24-27; Ephesians 4:14-16; 1 Peter 2:1-2
Jesus, Our Man in Glory, 26.

977. Preaching: watered down; Preaching: preach the Word; Pastors: vision of God

If some watcher or holy one who has spent his glad centuries by the sea of fire were to come to earth, how meaningless to him would be the ceaseless chatter of the busy tribes of men. How strange to him and how empty would sound the flat, stale, and profitless words heard in the average pulpit from week to week. And were such a one to speak on earth would he not speak of God? Would he not charm and fascinate his hearers with rapturous descriptions of the Godhead? And after hearing him could we ever again consent to listen to anything less than theology, the doctrine of God? Would we not thereafter demand of those who would presume to teach us that they speak to us from the mount of divine vision or remain silent altogether?

Colossians 4:3-4; 1 Thessalonians 2:10-12; 2 Timothy 4:1-5
The Knowledge of the Holy, 110.

978. Preaching: watered down; Religious language; Pastors: integrity

Religious people are psychologically conditioned to the trite phrase and the hackneyed expression. True, the stereotyped pattern varies slightly between different groups, but there would seem to be no reason why a clever speaker could not preach tonight to Calvinists, tomorrow to Arminians, the next day to Pentecostals, the next to Holiness people, and successively to Separatists and Adventists, and preach acceptably to each one by the simple expedient of finding out what they were conditioned to expect and giving it to them. A clever man could do this, I say, but an honest man would not. And the reason the clever man could do it is that the ability to create a specific pattern of words is all that is demanded of the speaker. That he may be talking about something he has never experienced to people who do not understand him seems not to occur to anyone. The reassuring drone of safe and familiar religious phrases is enough to give the listeners an enjoyable sense of well-being. The absence of reality is not even noticed. . . .

We have reared a temple of religious words comfortably disassociated from reality. And we will soon stand before that just and gentle Monarch who told us that we should give an account of every idle word. God have mercy on us.

Matthew 12:34-37; 1 Corinthians 1:17;
1 Thessalonians 2:4-6
The Size of the Soul, 60, 61, 63.

979. Preaching: with authority

You will notice that throughout the four Gospels the disciples were asking questions—while in the book of Acts and after Pentecost they were answering questions. That is the difference between the man who is Spirit-filled and the man who is not. The preacher who is not filled with the Spirit uses many phrases like, "And now, let us ask ourselves this question." I know you have heard that from the pulpit—"Now let us ask ourselves . . ." I have often wondered why the reverend wanted to ask himself a question. Why didn't he settle that in his study before he came into the pulpit? "What shall we say?" and "What should we think?" God never puts a preacher in the pulpit to ask questions. He puts the preacher in the pulpit to answer questions. He puts him there with authority to stand up in the name of God and speak and answer questions.

Haggai 1:5,7; Acts 2:14; 1 Thessalonians 2:2-4
The Counselor, 149.

980. Preaching: with authority

I don't want to be unkind, but I am sure there ought to be a lot more authority in the pulpit than there is now. A preacher should reign from his pulpit as a king from his throne. He should not reign by law nor by regulations and not by board meetings or man's authority. He ought to reign by moral ascendance.

When a man of God stands to speak, he ought to have the authority of God on him so that he makes the people responsible to listen to him. When they will not listen to him, they are accountable to God for turning away from the divine Word. In place of that needed authority, we have tabby cats with their claws carefully trimmed in the seminary, so they can paw over the congregations and never scratch them at all. They have had their claws trimmed and are just as soft and sweet as can be. . . .

I believe in the authority of God, and I believe if a man doesn't have it, he should go away and pray and wait until he gets the authority and then stand up to speak even if he has to begin by preaching on a soapbox on a street corner. Go to a rescue mission and preach with authority! They had it in those days—when they stood up, there was authority!

1 Thessalonians 2:2-4; 2 Timothy 4:1-5;
1 Peter 4:11
The Counselor, 150, 151.

981. Preaching: with authority; Boldness

I was not brought up in a Christian home and so was not accustomed to the conventional language of religion, and when I chanced occasionally to hear a sermon I listened with an ear undulled by familiarity. How strange the preachers sounded to me, how artificial their tones and how unnatural their demeanor.

They were men, obviously, but they lacked completely the candor and downrightness I knew so well in other men. The bold, man-to-man approach was missing. They seemed to be afraid of something, though I could not tell what, for certainly the tame, patient, almost indifferent persons who listened to them were harmless enough. No one paid much attention to what they said anyway. I am sure that if one of them had slyly interspersed into his sermon stray bits of the Gettysburg Address repeated backwards few of those present would have noticed or cared. Yet they spoke so gingerly and apologetically that one got the impression that they would rather remain silent forever than to offend anyone. After listening to some of them now and again, I knew the meaning of the French saying (though I did not hear it till many years later), "There are three sexes: men, women and preachers.". . .

It is true that the church has suffered from pugnacious men who would rather fight than pray, but she has suffered more from timid preachers who would rather be nice than be right. The latter have done more harm if for no other reason than that there are so many more of them. I do not think, however, that we must make our choice between the two. It is altogether possible to have love and courage at the same time, to be both true and faithful. . . .

Every man who stands to proclaim the Word should speak with something of the bold authority of the Word itself.

Jeremiah 1:7-9; Acts 20:20,24,27
God Tells the Man Who Cares, 130, 131, 133.

982. Preaching: with authority; Boldness; Pastors: commitment

To escape the snare of artificiality it is necessary that a man enjoy a satisfying personal experience with God. He must be totally committed to Christ and deeply anointed with the Holy Spirit. Further, he must be delivered from the fear of man. The focus of his attention must be God and not men. He must let everything dear to him ride out on each sermon. He must so preach as to jeopardize his future, his ministry, even his life itself. He must make God responsible for the consequences and speak as one who will not have long to speak before he is called to judgment. Then the people will know they are hearing a voice instead of a mere echo.

Psalm 118:6; Acts 4:20; Acts 20:24;
1 Thessalonians 2:2-4
God Tells the Man Who Cares, 133, 134.

983. Preaching: with authority; Pastors: prophetic ministry

I preach to my congregation week after week. And I pray that I may be able to preach with such convicting power that my people will sweat! I do not want them to leave my services feeling good. The last thing I want to do is to give them some kind of religious tranquilizer—and let them go to hell in their relaxation.

The Christian church was designed to make sinners sweat. I have always believed that, and I still believe it. The messages preached in our churches should make backslidden Christians sweat. And if I achieve that objective when I preach, I thank God with all of my heart, no matter what people think of me.

John 16:8; Acts 2:37-38; Acts 5:33; Acts 7:54
Jesus Is Victor!, 61, 62.

984. Pretense; Love: genuine; Evangelism: concern for lost

Kierkegaard wisely said that there is nothing in the Holy Scriptures about loving man in the mass, only about loving our neighbor as ourself. Yet there is among us much evidence of love for mankind and little evidence of love for the individual. The idea of love for our brother is a beautiful thing as long as it does not demand that we put it into practice on some particular person; then it becomes a nuisance.

Many Christians love foreign missions who cannot bring themselves to love foreigners. They pray tenderly for the colored man in Africa but they cannot stand him in

America. They love the Chinese in Hong Kong and are willing to give generously to send someone to convert him, but they never try to convert him when he is in a laundry on Main Street. They wear a flower to honor mother on her day, but she is too much of an inconvenience to be welcome in the home, so she is shunted from place to place till she is so sick and weary that she can be sent at last to a nursing home to await the end.

Matthew 5:43-44; Matthew 22:37-39; Romans 12:9-13; 1 Timothy 1:5-6
The Warfare of the Spirit, 79.

985. Pride: human

Humans try to ignore God, continuing to make their own ambitious, selfish plans. In the years before World War I, German's Kaiser Wilhelm, largely blamed for the beginning of that first world conflict, was exceedingly headstrong. At a chapel service attended by the kaiser, a faithful German minister preached on the coming again of Jesus Christ to establish God's kingdom of righteousness and peace throughout the earth. Wilhelm was greatly offended and spoke to the minister at the close of the service.

"I never want to hear that kind of a sermon again," he warned the preacher. "Such an event is not at all in keeping with the plans we have for the future and the glory of our Fatherland!"

But Kaiser Wilhelm and, a generation later, Adolph Hitler are merely fading memories—illustrations of that vain human propensity to make ourselves big and God small.

Psalm 2:1-4; Proverbs 16:18; Isaiah 40:12-15; Jeremiah 10:10
Jesus Is Victor!, 18.

986. Pride: human; God: His sovereignty; Man: rebellion against God

Yet in their pride men assert their will and claim ownership of the earth. Well, for a time it is true, this is man's world. God is admitted only by man's sufferance. He is treated as visiting royalty in a democratic country. Everyone takes His name upon his lips and (especially at certain seasons) He is feted and celebrated and hymned. But behind all this flattery men hold firmly to their right of self-determination. As long as man is allowed to play host he will honor God with his attention, but always He must remain a guest and never seek to be Lord. Man will have it understood that this is his world; he will make its laws and decide how it shall be run. God is permitted to decide nothing. Man bows to Him and as he bows, manages with difficulty to conceal the crown upon his own head.

Psalm 2:1-4; Psalm 9:19-20; Ezekiel 28:2; Daniel 4:17
The Divine Conquest, 45, 46.

987. Pride: human; Self

Boasting is particularly offensive when it is heard among the children of God, the one place above all others where it should never be found. Yet it is quite common among Christians, though disguised somewhat by the use of the stock expression, "I say this to the glory of God."...

Another habit not quite so odious is belittling ourselves. This might seem to be the exact opposite of boasting, but actually it is the same old sin traveling under a nom de plume. It is simply egoism trying to act spiritual....

Self-derogation is bad for the reason that self must be there to derogate. Self, whether swaggering or groveling, can never be anything but hateful to God.

Boasting is an evidence that we are pleased with self; belittling, that we are disappointed in it. Either way we reveal that we have a high opinion of ourselves....

The victorious Christian neither exalts nor downgrades himself. His interests have shifted from self to Christ. What he is or is not no longer concerns him. He believes that he has been crucified with Christ and is not willing either to praise or deprecate such a man.

Galatians 2:20; Galatians 5:24; Philippians 2:3-4; Colossians 3:12-14
Man: The Dwelling Place of God, 70, 71, 72.

988. Pride: human; Self-interest

I think that we ought to be mature enough to confess that many have been converted to Christ and have come into the church without wrestling with that basic human desire for honor and praise. As a result, some have actually spent a lifetime in religious work doing little more than getting glory for themselves!

Brethren, the glory can belong only to God! If we take the glory, God is being frustrated in the church....

You can write it down as a fact: no matter what a man does, no matter how successful he seems to be, if the Holy Spirit is not the chief energizer of his activity, it will all fall apart when he dies!

Jeremiah 9:23-24; 1 Corinthians 10:31; Galatians 6:14
Renewed Day by Day, Volume 1, Jan. 22.

989. Pride: human; Self-love; Criticism

The labor of self-love is a heavy one indeed. Think for yourself whether much of your sorrow has not arisen from someone speaking slightingly of you. As long as you set yourself up as a little god to which you must be loyal there will be those who will delight to offer affront to your idol. How then can you hope to have inward peace? The heart's fierce effort to protect itself from every slight, to shield its touchy honor from the bad opinion of friend and enemy, will never let the mind have rest. Continue this fight through the years and the burden will become intolerable. Yet the sons of earth are carrying this burden continually, challenging every word spoken against them, cringing under every criticism, smarting under each fancied slight, tossing sleepless if another is preferred before them.

1 Corinthians 4:3-5; 2 Corinthians 4:5-7; Galatians 1:9-10; Philippians 2:3-4
The Pursuit of God, 103, 104.

990. Pride: pastoral; Church: success; Correction: unwillingness to hear

Churches and Christian organizations have shown a tendency to fall into the same error that destroyed Israel: inability to receive admonition. After a time of growth and successful labor comes the deadly psychology of self-congratulation. Success itself becomes the cause of later failure. The leaders come to accept themselves as the very chosen of God. They are special objects of the divine favor; their success is proof enough that this is so. They must therefore be right, and anyone who tries to call them to account is instantly written off as an unauthorized meddler who should be ashamed to dare to reprove his betters.

Proverbs 8:33-36; Proverbs 15:10; Ecclesiastes 4:13; Jeremiah 5:3
The Root of the Righteous, 28, 29.

991. Pride: pastoral; Holy Spirit: need for

The Biblical teaching that God's work through the church can be accomplished only by the energizing of the Holy Spirit is very hard for us humans to accept. It is a fact that frustrates our carnal desire for honor and praise, for glory and recognition. . . .

Even though God faithfully reminds us that a ministry of the Holy Spirit is to hide the Christian worker in the work, the true humility He seeks among us is still too often the exception and not the rule. We might as well confess that many have been converted to Christ and have come into the church without renouncing that human desire for honor and praise. As a result, some have actually spent lifetimes in religious work doing little more than getting glory for themselves.

But the glory can belong only to God. If we take the glory, God is being frustrated in the church.

Zechariah 4:6; 1 Corinthians 3:5-9;
1 Corinthians 3:12-14
Tragedy in the Church: The Missing Gifts, 3, 4.

992. Pride: pastoral; Humility

Some time ago we heard a short address by a young preacher during which he quoted the following, "If you are too big for a little place, you are too little for a big place."

This World: Playground or Battleground?, 34.

993. Pride: spiritual; Humility

I have met two classes of Christians: the proud who imagine they are humble and the humble who are afraid they are proud. There should be another class: the self-forgetful who leave the whole thing in the hands of Christ and refuse to waste any time trying to make themselves good. They will reach the goal far ahead of the rest.

Romans 12:3-8; 1 Corinthians 15:9-10;
Philippians 2:3-4
God Tells the Man Who Cares, 174, 175.

994. Pride: spiritual; Prayer: wrong use of

Nothing is so vital as prayer, yet a reputation for being a mighty prayer warrior is probably the most perilous of all reputations to have. No form of selfishness is so deeply and dangerously sinful as that which glories in being a man of prayer. It comes near to being self-worship; and that while in the very act of worshiping God.

Matthew 6:1-6; Matthew 23:5
Keys to the Deeper Life, 65.

995. Pride: spiritual; Self-righteousness

When self whispers an assurance to you that you are different—look out! "You are different," self whispers, and then adds the proof. "You have given up enough things to make you a separated Christian. You love the old hymns, and you can't stand the modern nonsense. You have a good standard—none of those movies and none of this modern stuff for you!"

You don't really know what is happening to you, but you are feeling pretty good about everything by this time. But the good feeling is strictly from being coddled and comforted and scratched by a self that has refused to die. Self-trust is still there—and you thought it had gone!

Romans 7:18; 1 Corinthians 15:9-10;
2 Corinthians 4:5-7; 1 Timothy 1:12-15
I Talk Back to the Devil, 125.

996. Priorities; Bible: reading of; Entertainment

Do you want God to bless you? You say, "We want God to bless us. We believe the Lord is coming." Did you read the Bible or watch TV more this week? Think of the time you have spent. How many half-hour periods did you spend with your Bible, and how many did you spend with amusements? We do not take our faith seriously enough.

Joshua 1:7-8; Psalm 1:1-3; Psalm 119:97
Rut, Rot or Revival: The Condition of the Church, 143.

997. Priorities; Choices

Our break with the world will be the direct outcome of our changed relation to God. For the world of fallen men does not honor God. Millions call themselves by His name, it is true, and pay some token respect to Him, but a simple test will show how little He is really honored among them. Let the average man be put to the proof on the question of who or what is *above*, and his true position will be exposed. Let him be forced into making a choice between God and money, between God and men, between God and personal ambition, God and self, God and human love, and God will take second place every time. Those other things will be exalted above. However the man may protest, the proof is in the choices he makes day after day throughout his life.

Joshua 24:14-15; Matthew 6:24, 33;
Colossians 1:18; 1 John 2:15-17
The Pursuit of God, 94, 95.

998. Priorities; Earthly things; Worship: supremacy of

Before the Lord God made man upon the earth He first prepared for him a world of useful and pleasant things for his sustenance and delight. In the Genesis account of the creation these are called simply "things." They were made for man's use, but they were meant always to be external to the man and subservient to him. In the deep heart of the man was a shrine where none but God was worthy to come. . . .

Our woes began when God was forced out of His central shrine and things were allowed to enter. Within the human heart things have taken over. Men have now by nature no peace within their hearts, for God is crowned there no longer, but there in the moral dusk, stubborn and aggressive usurpers fight among themselves for first place on the throne.

Genesis 1:24-26; Matthew 16:24-26; Luke 16:10-13; 1 Timothy 6:17-19
The Pursuit of God, 21, 22.

999. Priorities; Life purpose; Commitment

It is my judgment that every one of us should be sure we have had that all-important encounter with God. It is an experience that leaves us delighted in our love for Him. Like Abraham, we become satisfied with the revelation that only God matters.

If you are living only to buy and sell and get gain, that is not enough. If you are living only to sleep and work, that is not enough. If you are living only to prosper and marry and raise a family, that is not enough.

If you live only to get old and die, and never find forgiveness and the daily sense of God's presence in your life, you have missed God's great purpose for you.

Matthew 16:24-26; Luke 21:34-36; Hebrews 11:8-10
Men Who Met God, 32.

1000. Problems; Philosophy of life

. . . because we are the handiwork of God, it follows that *all our problems and their solutions are theological.* Some knowledge of what kind of God it is that operates the universe is indispensable to a sound philosophy of life and a sane outlook on the world scene.

Isaiah 45:11-12; Colossians 1:15-17
The Knowledge of the Holy, 43.

1001. Problems; Trials: attitude toward; Pessimism

I have always felt compassion for Christian men and women who seem to major in pessimism, looking on the dark and gloomy side and never able to do anything with life's problems but grumble about them!

I meet them often, and when I do I wonder: "Can these people be reading the same Bible that I have been reading? . . ."

Peter states it as a paradox: the obedient Christian greatly rejoices even in the midst of great heaviness, trials and suffering. God's people know that things here are not all they ought to be, but they are not spending any time in worrying about it. They are too busy rejoicing in the gracious prospect of all that will take place when God fulfills all of His promises to His redeemed children!

Romans 8:18-19; Titus 2:11-14;
Hebrews 11:13-16; 1 Peter 1:6-7
I Call It Heresy!, 151, 159.

1002. Promises of God; Faith: foundation of; Knowledge of God: basis for faith

I must confess that in my ministry I keep repeating some of the things I know about God and His faithful promises. Why do I insist that all Christians should know for themselves the kind of God they love and serve? It is because all the promises of God rest completely upon His character.

Why do I insist that all Christians should search the Scriptures and learn as much as they can about this God who is dealing with them? It is because their faith will only spring up naturally and joyfully as they find that our God is trustworthy and fully able to perform every promise He has made.

Jeremiah 32:17,27; John 5:36-40; Romans 4:19-21; 1 Thessalonians 5:23-24
Jesus, Our Man in Glory, 81, 82.

1003. Prophecy

Let me warn you that many preachers and Bible teachers will answer to God some day for encouraging curious speculations about the return of Christ and failing to stress the necessity for "loving His appearing"!

The Bible does not approve of this modern curiosity that plays with the Scriptures and which seeks only to impress credulous and gullible audiences with the "amazing" prophetic knowledge possessed by the brother who is preaching or teaching!

I cannot think of even one lonely passage in the New Testament which speaks of Christ's revelation, manifestation, appearing or coming that is not directly linked with moral conduct, faith and spiritual holiness.

Titus 2:11-14; 1 Peter 1:6-7; 1 John 3:2-3
I Call It Heresy!, 166, 167.

1004. Prophecy

Perhaps, after all, the greatest prophetic problem facing us is one of readiness rather than one of knowledge. We may not always be sure we have every detail right, but we need never be uncertain about our moral and spiritual preparation for the great day of our Lord's coming. "You too, be patient and stand firm, because the Lord's coming is near."

Romans 13:11-14; James 5:8; 1 Peter 4:7
This World: Playground or Battleground?, 30.

1005. Prophecy; Judgment of God: future

We may have differing opinions about the symbols and details of prophetic warnings, but God's truth is here. We cannot get around it. Into history, into our world, the horsemen of the Apocalypse will come riding forth in God's time. Dare we imagine we can live in pampered opulence—not even remembering to pray for this dying world—and still believe we will be ready for that hour when our Lord will call His people home?

As a minister of God's Word, I add my caution to every caution and warning God has given us. If we are wasting our time and money and energy in foolish play, it will be tragic for us in that awful, coming hour.

I pray for myself. I pray that I may be more detached from this world and from its evils and its selfish systems. I pray that I may recognize that soft, silky, deceptive voice that is opposed to our Lord Jesus Christ. I pray that I will be able to stand with the overcomers, even if it means that everyone around me is an enemy, even if it means martyrdom.

Matthew 24:29-30; 1 Thessalonians 5:1-8; Revelation 6:1-8; Revelation 21:6-7
Jesus Is Victor!, 102.

1006. Prophecy; Judgment of God: future; Satanism

Everything I read these days tells me we are experiencing a great new wave of interest in spiritism and devil worship. I take this as one of the signs that God's age of grace and mercy is approaching the end point. It is evidence that the time may be near when He proclaims: "I have seen enough of mankind's sin, rebellion and perversion. It is time for the trumpets of judgment to sound!". . .

In our day, we have seen the vision dimly, and we can only confess that we do not understand it all. I have said it before. Let us not get involved in trying to decipher all the minute details of God's plans. The great central truth is what matters: When God gets enough of this world's sin and violence and rebellion, He will do something about it!

God intends to restore the unity of His creation. He will sort out good from bad. He will halt the infection of evil. He will balance the scales of justice.

Psalm 2:2-6; Philippians 2:9-11; 2 Thessalonians 2:3-4; Revelation 8:2,6
Jesus Is Victor!, 133, 138.

1007. Public reading of Scripture

Of course we of this generation cannot know by firsthand experience how the Word of God was read in other times. But it would be hard to conceive of our fathers having done a poorer job than we do when it comes to the public reading of the Scriptures. Most of us read the Scriptures so badly that a good performance draws attention by its rarity.

It could be argued that since everyone these days owns his own copy of the Scriptures, the need for the public reading of the Word is not as great as formerly. If that is true, then let us not bother to read the Scriptures at all in our churches. But if we are going to read the Word publicly, then it is incumbent upon us to read it well. A mumbled, badly articulated and unintelligent reading of the Sacred Scriptures will do more than we think to give the listeners the idea that the Word is not important. . . .

We should by all means read it, and we should make the reading a memorable experience for those who hear.

1 Timothy 4:13-16
The Next Chapter after the Last, 27.

1008. Public reading of Scripture

Every man who is honored with the leadership of public worship should learn to read well. And do not imagine that anyone who can read at all can read well. . . .

To read the Bible well in public we must first love it. The voice, if it is free, unconsciously follows the emotional tone. Reverence cannot be simulated. No one who does not *feel* the deep solemnity of the Holy Word can properly express it. . . .

Probably the hardest part of learning to read well is eliminating ourselves. We read best when we get ourselves out of the transaction and let God talk through the imperfect medium of our voice.

Psalm 119:97,111,131,162
The Next Chapter after the Last, 27, 28.

1009. Punctuality

Now, this is probably the place to consider punctuality in the work of God, also.

Isn't it strange that the very fault that would wreck a business, sink a ship, ruin a railroad, is tolerated at the very altar of God?

Why is it that in the church of God so few are concerned about lack of punctuality? The carelessness they show about the work of God would wreck a business or upset the economy, or if done in our bodies would ruin our health. . . .

I have been around a long time and I am convinced that generally people are not spiritual at all if they are not punctual. If they are so lacking in self-discipline and so selfish and so inconsiderate of others and their time that they will not be punctual in the service of God and His church, they are fooling nobody! I repeat it again—if you are not punctual, you are not spiritual!

Everyone can be excused for the emergencies of life—there are accidents that will at times keep any of us from meeting our appointments. But I am trying to show my concern about those who practice the art of not being punctual until it has become a habit in their life.

There isn't anyone important enough to justify that kind of behavior, and anybody that is not punctual, habitually, is guilty of deception and falsehood. He says he will be there—then he fails to appear!

Who Put Jesus on the Cross?, 30, 31.

R

1010. Rationalism; Lordship of Christ

People prefer their logic, their powers of reason. Even when God speaks, they refuse to recognize His voice. They will not confess that God has spoken through Jesus Christ, the eternal Son. When He confronts them with their sin, they consult a psychiatrist and hope they can get their personalities "properly adjusted." But in a coming day, every knee will bow and every tongue will confess that Jesus Christ is Lord of all.

Isaiah 45:23; Philippians 2:9-11; Hebrews 11:1-2
Jesus Is Victor!, 120.

1011. Rationalism; Textualism; Holy Spirit: illumination

But *revelation is not enough!* There must be illumination before revelation can get to a person's soul. It is not enough that I hold an inspired book in my hands. I must have an inspired heart. There is the difference, in spite of the evangelical rationalist who insists that revelation is enough. . . .

In His day, Christ's conflict was with the theological rationalist. It revealed itself in the Sermon on the Mount and in the whole book of John. Just as Colossians argues against Manichaeism and Galatians argues against Jewish legalism, so the book of John is a long, inspired, passionately outpoured book trying to save us from evangelical rationalism—the doctrine that says the text is enough. Textualism is as deadly as liberalism.

John 4:23-24; John 8:31-32; John 14:26; John 16:13-15; 1 John 2:20
Faith beyond Reason, 23, 24.

1012. Reading: classics

I suggest also that we try to acquaint ourselves as far as possible with the good and saintly souls who lived before our times and now belong to the company of the redeemed in heaven. How sad to limit our sympathies to those of our own day, when God in His providence has made it possible for us to enjoy the rich treasures of the minds and hearts of so many holy and gifted saints of other days. To confine our reading to the works of a few favorite authors of today or last week is to restrict our horizons and to pinch our souls dangerously.

I have no doubt that the prayerful reading of some of the great spiritual classics of the centuries would destroy in us forever that constriction of soul which seems to be the earmark of modern evangelicalism.

Man: The Dwelling Place of God, 79.

1013. Reading: classics; Current conditions: shallowness

So powerful is the effect of the printed page on human character that the reading of good books is not only a privilege but an obligation, and the habitual reading of poor ones a positive tragedy. . . .

Why does the gospel Christian of today find the reading of great books almost beyond him? . . .

The major cause of the decline in the quality of current Christian literature is not intellectual; it is spiritual. To enjoy a great religious work requires a degree of consecration to God and detachment from the world that few modern Christians have experienced. The early Christian Fathers, the mystics, the Puritans, are not hard to understand, but they inhabit the highlands where the air is crisp and rarefied and none but the God-enamored can come.

Rather than climb the mountain we choose to dig our shallow caves a few feet above the floor of the valley. Our spiritual moods and emotions are degraded. We eat and drink and rise up to play. We take our religious instruction in the form of stories, and anything that requires meditation bores us. And writers and publishers contribute to our delinquency by providing us with plenty of religious nothing to satisfy our carnal appetite.

The Warfare of the Spirit, 125, 128, 129.

1014. Reading: hymnal; Bible: reading of

Since what we read in a real sense enters the soul, it is vitally important that we read the best and nothing but the best. I cannot but feel that Christians were better off before there was so much reading matter to choose from. Today we must practice sharp discipline in our reading habits. Every Christian should master the Bible, or at least spend hours and days and years trying. And always he should read his Bible, as George Müller said, "with meditation."

After the Bible the next most valuable book for the Christian is a good hymnal. Let any young Christian spend a year prayerfully meditating on the hymns of Watts and Wesley alone and he will become a fine theologian. Then let him read a balanced diet of the Puritans and the Christian mystics. The results will be more wonderful than he could have dreamed.

Joshua 1:7-8; Psalm 1:1-3; Psalm 119; Ecclesiastes 12:12
Man: The Dwelling Place of God, 150, 151.

1015. Reading: limitations of; Thinking: need for; Meditation

When the noted scholar Dr. Samuel Johnson visited the king, the two sat for a while before the fire in silence. Then the king said, "I suppose, Dr. Johnson, that you read a great deal." "Yes, Sire," replied Johnson, "but I *think* a great deal more."

Joshua 1:7-8; Psalm 1:1-3; Psalm 119:14-16; Proverbs 4:5-9
The Size of the Soul, 27, 28.

1016. Reading: limitations of; Thinking: need for; Meditation

The book that informs us without inspiring us may be indispensable to the scientist, the lawyer, the physician, but mere information is not enough for the minister. If knowledge about things constituted learning, the encyclopedia would be all the library one needed for a fruitful ministry. The successful Christian, however, must know God, himself and his fellow men. Such knowledge is not gained by assembling data but by sympathetic contact, by intuition, by meditation, by silence, by inspiration, by prayer and long communion. I therefore recommend reading, not for diversion, nor for information alone, but for communion with great minds. The book that leads the soul out into the sunlight, points upward and bows out is always the best book. . . .

The book that serves as a ramp from which my mind can take off is the best book for me. The book that follows me into the pulpit and intrudes itself into my sermon is my enemy and an enemy to my hearers. The book that frees me to think my own inspired thoughts is my friend.

The Size of the Soul, 29, 30.

1017. Reading: newspaper

It hardly need be said that most of us are not selective enough in our reading. I have often wondered how many square yards of newsprint passes in front of the eyes of the average civilized man in the course of a year. Surely it must run into several acres; and I am afraid our average reader does not realize a very large crop on his acreage. The best advice I have heard on this topic was given by a Methodist minister. He said, "Always read your newspaper standing up." Henry David Thoreau also had a low view of the daily press. Just before leaving the city for his now-celebrated sojourn on the banks of Walden Pond a friend asked him if he would like to have a newspaper delivered to his cottage. "No," replied Thoreau, "I have already seen a newspaper."

Man: The Dwelling Place of God, 148.

1018. Reading: secular

When a very young minister, I asked the famous holiness preacher, Joseph H. Smith, whether he would recommend that I read widely in the secular field. He replied, "Young man, a bee can find nectar in the weed as well as in the flower." I took his advice (or, to be frank, I sought confirmation of my own instincts rather than advice) and I am not sorry that I did.

John Wesley told the young ministers of the Wesleyan Societies to read or get out of the ministry, and he himself read science and history with a book propped against his saddle pommel as he rode from one engagement to another. Andy Dolbow, the American Indian preacher of considerable note, was a man of little education, but I once heard him exhort his hearers to improve their minds for the honor of God. "When you are chopping wood," he explained, "and you have a dull axe you must work all the harder to cut the log. A sharp axe makes easy work. So sharpen your axe all you can."

Proverbs 1:5; Proverbs 9:9; Ecclesiastes 12:11; 2 Timothy 4:13
The Size of the Soul, 33.

1019. Reading: widely; Meditation

Lastly reading. To think without a proper amount of good reading is to limit our thinking to our own tiny plot of ground. The crop cannot be large. To observe only and neglect reading is to deny ourselves the immense value of other people's observations; and since the better books are written by trained observers the loss is sure to be enormous. Extensive reading without the discipline of practical observation will lead to bookishness and artificiality. Reading and observing without a great deal of meditating will fill the mind with learned lumber that will always remain alien to us. Knowledge to be our own must be digested by thinking.

Proverbs 4:7; Proverbs 16:16; Proverbs 23:23
Man: The Dwelling Place of God, 147.

1020. Realism; Death: certainty of; Unsaved

I must charge it back upon the worldling, the unsaved man, that he is really the unrealistic person because he must spend his whole life pretending. If I were to invent a title to cover the *genus homo*, the human being, unsaved and out of Christ, I would have to call him "the great pretender."

For instance, he must pretend all of his lifetime that he is not going to die. He must put on that act day after day, month after month. That is not realism—it is the fuzziest kind of fantasy in which humans can indulge.

What is it with us?—humans continually acting in a pretense that we are never going to die yet knowing all the time that we must and that we will!

But the Christian has become a realist.

He is already prepared for that next chapter. He has packed his suitcase and he is ready to go. In fact, you may see him somewhere sitting on his suitcase, with the pair of steel rails close by. He knows for a certainty that the train is on the way and that it is not going to pass him by. He is the realist and it is the other fellow who is the dreamer of deadly and fateful dreams.

Philippians 1:21-24; 2 Timothy 4:6-8; Hebrews 9:27
Echoes from Eden, 71.

1021. Realism; Unsaved

Some shallow thinkers dismiss the Christian as an unrealistic person who lives in a make-believe world. . . .

If realism is the recognition of things as they actually are, the Christian is of all persons the most realistic. He of all intelligent thinkers is the one most concerned with reality. He insists that his beliefs correspond with facts. He pares things down to their stark essentials and squeezes out of his mind everything that inflates his thinking. He demands to know the whole truth about God, sin, life, death, moral accountability and the world to come. He wants to know the worst about himself in order that he may do something about it. Something in him refuses to be cheated, however pleasant the deception might be to his self-esteem. He takes into account the undeniable fact that he has sinned. He recognizes the shortness of time and the certainty of death. These he does not try to avoid or alter to his own liking. They are facts and he faces them full on. He is a realist.

We of the Christian faith need not go onto the defensive. The man of the world is the dreamer, not the Christian. The sinner can never be quite himself. All his life he must pretend. He must act as if he were never going to die, and yet he knows too well that he is. He must act as if he had not sinned, when in his deep heart he knows very well that he has. He must act unconcerned about God and judgment and the future life, and all the time his heart is deeply disturbed about his precarious condition. He must keep up a front of nonchalance while shrinking from facts and wincing under the lash of conscience. The news of a friend's sudden death leaves him shaken with the suggestion that he may be next, but he dare not show this; he must cover his terror the best he can and continue to act his part. All his adult life he must dodge and hide and conceal. When he finally drops the act he either loses his mind or tries suicide.

Matthew 16:24-26; Romans 3:23; 2 Corinthians 5:10; Hebrews 9:27; James 4:13-14
Of God and Men, 131, 132.

1022. Reason; Apologetics

Now, if you have done any serious reading you have no doubt discovered the charge made by some critics that reason says one thing and religion says something else.

I dare say that whoever says that is still wet behind his intellectual ears, for religion is on the side of reason, always. Whatever is irreligious and unbelieving is on the side of unreason and not on the side of reason.

Psalm 14:1-3; Psalm 36:1-9; Jeremiah 10:8,14; Jeremiah 51:17-18; Romans 1:20-23
Echoes from Eden, 73.

1023. Reconciliation; Church: unity

Many a congregation has been renewed and blessed when believers have been willing to reopen the Bible wells of reconciliation and confession. When Christians are harboring hard feelings against each other, they need to be reconciled. They need to confess and ask forgiveness.

I refer here to actual sins and faults. There are people in continual bondage to mere trifles and inconsequential matters. God has given us the Holy Spirit to be our prompter and our guide. And He has given us good sense as well to go along with our consciences.

In sincere and honest confession, two areas are involved. If you have sinned and wronged someone, you need to take the matter to the Lord first and receive His forgiveness. Then you need to go to the person you have wronged and ask his or her forgiveness.

Matthew 5:23-24; Ephesians 4:1-6; Ephesians 4:31-32; Colossians 3:12-14
Men Who Met God, 42.

1024. Redemption; Happiness

So remember, redemption does a lot of things for us. You and I are inclined to take the kindergarten attitude toward salvation—we think its purpose is to make us happy. That attitude is abroad everywhere; people are writing books about how to be happy—just take Jesus and you'll feel good inside. But the whole purpose of redemption is not to give you a tickle inside your heart, but to reverse the inverted order of things. Redemption puts God where He belongs—exalted to the throne—and man where he belongs—down in the dust—in order that God may, from the dust, raise man to the throne. But never, never does God raise a man to the throne except from the dust. Never does He lift him to His right hand except from the low place of humiliation.

Luke 9:23-25; Colossians 1:19-22; Titus 2:11-14
Success and the Christian, 137, 138.

1025. Redemption; Salvation: God's plan

If you get nothing else from this chapter, it is essential that you understand and retain this truth: *the world's redemption is not in mankind's hands.* I cannot tell you how glad I am that there is at least one thing that we humans cannot bungle. The plan of salvation is God's plan. The power in redemption is God's power. Only the Lamb of God could die in our place. This is God's way of doing things, not ours. . . .

Our redemption was not by muscle, but by love. It was not wrought by vengeance, but by forgiveness. It was not by sword, but by sacrifice.

We are Christians because Jesus destroyed His enemies by dying for them. He conquered death by letting death conquer Him, and then He turned death inside out as He burst forth from the tomb as victor! This whole work of redemption had to be accomplished in the way things are done in heaven.

Romans 3:24; Ephesians 1:7; Titus 3:4-7; 1 Peter 1:18-19
Jesus Is Victor!, 86, 87.

1026. Redemption; Salvation: God's plan

Seen from our human standpoint redemption must rank first among all the acts of God. No other achievement of the Godhead required such vast and precise knowledge, such perfection of wisdom or such fullness of moral power. To bring man into communion with Himself God must deal effectively with the whole matter of justice and righteousness; He must dispose of sin, reconcile an enemy and make a rebel willingly obedient. And this He must do without compromising His holiness or coercing the race He would save.

Ephesians 2:4-10; Colossians 1:13-14
Titus 2:11-14
That Incredible Christian, 83, 84.

1027. Reformation; Revival: conditions for; Obedience: need for

We urgently need a new kind of reformation throughout our Christian churches—a reformation that will cause us not only to accept the will of God but to actively seek it and adore it! . . .

The reformation we need now can best be described in terms of spiritual perfection—which reduced to its simplest form is no more and no less than doing the will of God! This would expose us all at the point of our need, no matter how sound we think we are in doctrine and no matter how great our reputations.

I long for the positive and genuine renewal which would come if the will of God could be totally accomplished in our lives. Everything that is unspiritual would flee, and all that is not Christlike would vanish, and all that is not according to the New Testament would be rejected. . . .

Do we voluntarily and actively observe God's commandments, making positive changes in our lives as God may indicate in order to bring the entire life into accord with the New Testament?

That is the active aspect of the will of God that I would own as reformation in the church, and it would surely result in revival.

Joshua 1:7-8; Psalm 119:14-16;
John 14:15-17; 1 John 5:3
I Talk Back to the Devil, 89, 90.

1028. Regret; Self-love; Forgiveness

Regret is a kind of frustrated repentance that has not been quite consummated. Once the soul has turned from all sin and committed itself wholly to God there is no longer any legitimate place for regret. When moral innocence has been restored by the forgiving love of God the guilt may be remembered, but the sting is gone from the memory. The forgiven man knows that he has sinned, but he no longer feels it. . . .

Regret may be no more than a form of self-love. A man may have such a high regard for himself that any failure to live up to his own image of himself disappoints him deeply. He feels that he has betrayed his better self by his act of wrongdoing, and even if God is willing to forgive him he will not forgive himself. Sin brings to such a man a painful loss of face that is not soon forgotten. He becomes permanently angry with himself and tries to punish himself by going to God frequently with petulant self-accusations. This state of mind crystallizes finally into a feeling of chronic regret which appears to be a proof of deep penitence but is actually proof of deep self-love.

Psalm 32:1-2; Romans 8:1;
Hebrews 10:19-23
That Incredible Christian, 99, 100.

1029. Rejection; Unsaved

The reason many do not want to hear what God is saying through Jesus to our generation is not hard to guess. God's message in Jesus is a moral pronouncement. It brings to light such elements as faith and conscience and conduct, obedience and loyalty. Men and women reject this message for the same reason they have rejected all of the Bible. They do not wish to be under the authority of the moral Word of God.

John 3:19-21; John 7:7; Romans 1:18-32
Jesus, Our Man in Glory, 22.

1030. Rejection; Unsaved; Apologetics

Israel did not reject the Lord because of philosophical reasons. Israel's rejection was for moral reasons. . . .

I'm telling you this, and it's a statement that I need not modify. I do not believe there is anybody that ever rejects Jesus Christ on philosophical grounds.

The man who continues in his rejection of Christ has a pet sin somewhere—he's in love with iniquity.

He rejects Jesus on moral grounds, and then hides behind false philosophy—philosophical grounds. . . .

I believe that every one of these who are having intellectual difficulties is hiding because he is morally reprobate. When we fall in love with our sin, we can imagine and manufacture 10,000 syllogisms to keep us away from the cross.

John 3:19; Romans 1:20-23; 2 Corinthians 3:14-15; Ephesians 4:17-24
The Tozer Pulpit, Volume 1, Book 1, 27, 28.

1031. Religion: emptiness of

Oh, it is amazing how many things religious people want to do to you. They can start when you are eight days old with circumcision and end up with the last rites when you are 108 years old—and all of that time they will be rubbing something on you, or putting something around your neck, or making you eat something or insisting that you should not eat something. They will manipulate you, maul you, and sweety massage your soul all the time—and when it is all done you are just what you were. You are just a decorated and massaged sinner—a sinner who did not eat meat or on the other hand, a sinner who did eat fish.

When religion has done all it can, you are still a sinner who either went to the temple or did not go to the temple. If you attended church you are still a sinner who attended church. If you did not go to church you are still a sinner who did not go to church.

Measured in any direction and approached from any point of view, we are still sinners if all we have is that which religion has offered and tried to do for us. Religion can put us on the roll and educate us and train us and instruct us and discipline us; and when it is all over there is still something within our being that cries, "Eternity is in my heart and I have not found anything to satisfy it."

Romans 3:28; Ephesians 2:8-10; 2 Timothy 1:9; Titus 3:4-7
Christ the Eternal Son, 149, 150.

1032. Religion: emptiness of

Religion is one of the heaviest burdens that has ever been laid upon the human race. People have been forever using it as a kind of self-medication. Conscious of their own moral and spiritual disorders, they try a dose of religion, hoping to get better by their own treatment.

I often wonder if there is any kind of self-cure or human medication that people have not tried in their efforts to restore themselves and gain merit. In India, millions of pilgrims may be seen prostrate on the ground, crawling like inchworms toward the Ganges River, hoping that a dip in the sacred waters will release them from the burden of guilt.

Countless numbers have tried to deal with guilt by abstaining from food and drink and by other forms of self-denial. People have tortured themselves, wearing hair shirts, walking on spikes, running over hot coals. Others have shunned society—hiding in caves, living in monasteries—hoping to gain some merit that would compensate for their sinful natures and bring them closer to God. Even in our own day and in our own land, the attempts at self-medication still go on. People fail to recognize that the Cure for what ails them has already come. . . .

So, I repeat, it is Jesus Christ Himself whom Christianity offers. And He is enough! A person's relation to Jesus Christ is the all-important matter in this life.

Romans 10:1-3; Ephesians 2:8-10; Titus 3:4-7
Tragedy in the Church: The Missing Gifts, 60, 61.

1033. Religion: emptiness of; Hypocrisy

I have not said that religion without power makes no changes in a man's life, only that it makes no fundamental difference. . . . *The changes are in form only, they are not in kind.* Behind the activities of the non-religious man and the man who has received the gospel without power lie the very same motives. An unblessed ego lies at the bottom of both lives, the difference being that the religious man has learned better to disguise his vice. His sins are refined and less offensive than before he took up religion, but the man himself is not a better man in the sight of God. He may indeed be a worse one, for always God hates artificiality and pretense. Selfishness still throbs like an engine at the center of the man's life. True he may learn to "redirect" his selfish impulses, but his woe is that self still lives unrebuked and even unsuspected within his deep heart. He is a victim of religion without power.

Ephesians 1:15-23; Hebrews 6:1; 3 John 9
The Pursuit of Man, 19-20.

1034. Religion: in life

"Things have come to a pretty pass," said a famous Englishman testily, "when religion is permitted to interfere with our private lives."

To which we may reply that things have come to a worse pass when an intelligent man living in a Protestant country could make such a remark. Had this man never read the New Testament?

Of God and Men, 39.

1035. Religion: in life; Church: religious game

The comfortable drone of the Gloria Patri or the Lord's Prayer repeated in unison has a marvelously tranquilizing effect upon such a man. He may sleep through the sermon, or if he remains alert enough to hear it he will never apply it to his own life in a practical way; yet the sonorous sound of the benediction followed by the sweet choral response gives him the feeling that he has profited immeasurably by his attendance at church. On the way out he will smile, shake hands, congratulate the preacher and go his way completely unchanged. Tomorrow he will drive just as hard a bargain in his business, tell the same shady stories, cheat on his income tax, shout at the driver ahead of him, bark at his wife, overeat and otherwise live like the son of this world that he in fact is.

The next Sunday he will go to church again and for a few moments experience the same radiant feeling of well-being and good will toward men that he has enjoyed once a week for years. He simply cannot relate religion to life. To him Christianity has no necessary bearing upon present conduct. It is only a pleasant thing like, say, a sunset or a Swedish massage, and it is nothing more.

1 Samuel 15:22; Psalm 51:15-17;
Isaiah 1:11-20
The Warfare of the Spirit, 78.

1036. Religion: in the news

Greater publicity for religion may be well and I have no fault to find with it. Surely religion should be the most newsworthy thing on earth, and there may be some small encouragement in the thought that vast numbers of persons want to read about it. What disturbs me is that, amidst all the religious hubbub, hardly a voice is raised to tell us what God thinks about the whole thing.

Where is the man who can see through the ticker tape and confetti to discover which way the parade is headed, why it started in the first place and, particularly, who is riding up front in the seat of honor?

Colossians 1:18
The Size of the Soul, 127.

1037. Religion: popular; Celebrities

The present flair for religion has not made people heavenly minded; rather it has secularized religion and put its approval upon the carnal values of fallen men. It glorifies success and eagerly prints religious testimonials from big corporation tycoons, actors, athletes, politicians and very important persons of every kind regardless of their reputation or lack of one. Religion is promoted by the identical techniques used to sell cigarettes. You pray to soothe your nerves just as you smoke to regain your composure after a sharp business transaction or a tight athletic contest. Books are written by the scores to show that Jesus is a Regular Fellow and Christianity a wise use of the highest psychological laws. All the holy principles of the Sermon on the Mount are present in reverse. Not the meek are blessed, but the self-important; not they that mourn but they that smile and smile and smile. Not the poor in spirit are dear to God, but they who are accounted somebody by the secular press. Not they that hunger and thirst after righteousness are filled, but they that hunger for publicity.

Matthew 5:3-12; 1 Corinthians 3:1-3; Philippians 2:25-30; Colossians 3:1-4
The Price of Neglect, 100.

1038. Religious entertainment; Church: entertainment

Religious entertainment has so corrupted the Church of Christ that millions don't know that it's a heresy. Millions of evangelicals throughout the world have devoted themselves to religious entertainment. They don't know that it's as much a heresy as the counting of beads or the splashing of holy water or something else. To expose this, of course, raises a storm of angry protest among the people. . . .

One man wrote an article as an exposé of me. He said that I claimed that religious entertainment was wrong and he said, "Don't you know that every time you sing a hymn, it's entertainment?" Every time you sing a hymn? I don't know how that fellow ever finds his way home at night. He ought to have a seeing eye dog and a man with a white cane to take him home!

When you raise your eyes to God and sing, "Break Thou the bread of life, dear Lord, to me," is that entertainment—or is it worship? Isn't there a difference between worship and entertainment? The church that can't worship must be entertained. And men who can't lead a church to worship must provide the entertainment. That is why we have the great evangelical heresy here today—the heresy of religious entertainment.

Psalm 92:1-4; Psalm 95:1-7; Psalm 96:1-6; Psalm 100; Psalm 150
Success and the Christian, 6, 7.

1039. Repentance

There are many peculiar ideas about biblical repentance. I have talked with people who tried to tell me that repentance is necessary because "it makes you fit so that God can save you." The Bible does not teach that, and it never did. No man or woman has changed the character and goodness of God by an act of repentance. All the repentance in the universe cannot make God any more loving, any more gracious. Repentance is not a meritorious act. God is eternally good, and He welcomes us into His love, grace and mercy when we meet His condition of an about-face so that we are aware of His smile.

Repentance means turning around from our evil ways in order to look to Jesus. The person who will not repent still has his or her back turned on God.

Repentance is a condition we meet in order that God, already wanting to be good to us, can be good to us, forgiving and cleansing us. In that sense, then, the man who loves his sin and hangs on to it cannot reasonably expect the goodness and the grace of God.

Mark 1:15; Luke 13:3,5; Acts 2:37-38; Acts 26:20
Men Who Met God, 45.

1040. Repentance

C.H. Spurgeon preached on repentance week after week, and somebody came to him and said, "When are you going to quit preaching on repentance, pastor?" Spurgeon replied, "When you repent." When we talk about confession and repentance, we keep right on talking about it until either it has had its effect or we know it will have none.

Acts 3:19; Revelation 2:4-5
Rut, Rot or Revival: The Condition of the Church, 64.

1041. Repentance

A man who truly comes to God in repentance and contrition of heart does not work up a defense on the basis that he has not broken every law and every commandment. . . .

Remember, an outlaw is not a man who has broken all the laws of his country—he may actually have ignored and flouted and violated only a few. The bandit Jesse

James may have broken only a couple of laws—those that say "You shall not kill" and "You shall not steal." But he was a notorious outlaw with a price on his head, even though there were thousands of other laws on the books which he had not violated.

Friend, when I come before my God as an outlaw, returning home as the prodigal, returning from the pig pen, I will not be dickering and bargaining with God about the sins that I did not commit. I will not even be conscious of those—for the fact that I have broken any of God's laws or committed any sins will so overwhelm me that I will go before God as though I were the worst sinner in all the wide world.

Psalm 32:3-5; Psalm 51:3-4; Luke 15:20-24
Who Put Jesus on the Cross?, 61.

1042. Repentance; Church: concept of God; God: His awesomeness

Why is it we no longer find any sorrow, any tears of repentance in our church life? It is because we do not get the right start as Christians. We do not begin with a vision of the awesome God.

We do not start right because we are jockeyed, cajoled, coaxed, kidded and sometimes pushed into the kingdom of God. We do not have tears because we do not have true repentance. We do not have a higher spirituality because we did not begin right. . . .

All of our Christian church denominations that have had great ministries for Christ began with the recognition of God's greatness. God's might and His wise sovereignty were the bedrock upon which their effective Christian witness was founded. Humbled by that concept, they became great.

1 Chronicles 16:25-29; Psalm 145:3-5;
Isaiah 6:1-5; Acts 2:37-38; Acts 9:3-5
Men Who Met God, 81, 83.

1043. Repentance; Salvation: transformation

A story has been told about a governor of one of the states. He was concerned about the plight of many in the prison system, and he visited one of the prisons, going incognito. The prisoners did not know who he was.

Having opportunity to talk to a young man, he asked why he was there and for how long.

"I suppose you would like to get outside again," the governor said in conversation.

"I would sure like to be out," was the reply. "But I doubt it. They threw the book at me."

Then the governor asked: "Tell me, if you were free again, what would be the first thing you would do?"

The face of the inmate changed to a grim scowl and he almost growled as he said: "The first thing I would do would be to cut the throat of that blankety-blank judge that sent me here!"

The governor, the man with the power of pardon and release, had not expected to hear that kind of snarl. He was hoping for an indication of remorse and repentance and reform. He was hoping he might hear a prisoner's desire to be a good man again, desiring to try and straighten out the wrongs that had put him in that place.

He stayed in there, you see, because pardons are conditioned upon intention to reform. You cannot save a man who insists upon continuing in the thing that caused him to be unsaved.

Isaiah 1:16-19; Isaiah 55:6-8;
Colossians 3:5-11; 1 Thessalonians 1:9
Echoes from Eden, 78, 79.

1044. Resentment; Bitterness

I have been around religious circles quite a long time and I have never heard the word resent used by a victorious man. Or at least if he used the word it was not to express any feelings within his own heart.

In the course of scores of conferences and hundreds of conversations, I have many times heard people say, "I resent that." But I repeat: I have never heard the words used by a victorious man. Resentment simply cannot dwell in a loving heart. Before resentfulness can enter, love must take its flight and bitterness take over. . . .

The worst feature about this whole thing is that it does no good to call attention to it. The bitter heart is not likely to recognize its own condition, and if the resentful man reads this he will smile smugly and think I mean someone else. In the meantime he will grow smaller and smaller trying to get bigger, and he will become more and more obscure trying to become known. As he pushes on toward his selfish goal his very prayers will be surly accusations against the Almighty and his whole relationship toward other Christians will be one of suspicion and distrust.

Ephesians 4:31-32; Colossians 3:5-11;
Hebrews 12:15
Of God and Men, 105, 108.

1045. Revelation: book of

Have you ever heard of a person eagerly reading an interesting book, then suddenly deciding to abandon it without reading the last chapter? The last chapter ties together the threads of the narrative; it summarizes the arguments; it climaxes the action. You and I would agree that to close a book without reading the final chapter would be to read without purpose and without satisfaction.

I have had people tell me that although they read the Bible, they stop short of Revelation—the final "chapter." Imagine! That particular Bible book announces itself as the Revelation of Jesus Christ. It forecasts the consummation of all things and introduces the new order. How can readers form a balanced understanding of God, sin, unbelief and divine judgment if they ignore so important a book? In these crisis days of world government, no Christian can afford to ignore the climactic Revelation. . . .

There is vastly more in the Revelation than you or I will ever know while we are on this earth. But just God's urging that we be ready for the announced coming events should be sufficient to keep us expectant, interested—and praying!

Revelation 1:1,19; Revelation 22:6-7,20
Jesus Is Victor!, 13, 18.

1046. Revelation: book of

Those who ignore Revelation take their place with the many who believe a humanistic view of life is sufficient: that men and women are responsible captains of their own souls. They take their place with the defiant multitude who shout the age-old refrain: "We will not have this Man to rule over us!"

Those who take Revelation seriously are convinced of an actual heavenly realm as real as the world we now inhabit. They are persuaded that the day of consummation nears when "the kingdom of the world" becomes "the kingdom of our Lord and of his Christ," who "will reign for ever and ever" (Revelation 11:15).

Daniel 7:14; Philippians 2:9-11; Revelation 11:15
Jesus Is Victor!, 14.

1047. Revelation: book of; Eternal perspective

God's message in Revelation, viewed as a whole, is a prognosis of events affecting the entire created universe—"the things that must soon take place" (22:6). Those who give themselves to its reading will sense they are on a fast-moving guided tour, discerning a variety of scenes and events in John's panoramic view of the heavens and earth. In quick succession he takes us from the highest heaven to the deepest hell. We hear the trumpets sounding in heaven and see the woes and judgments that follow upon the earth and its seas. Instead of repenting, people harden their hearts against the God who created them and loved them. . . .

We have in the Scriptures many appeals to be ready for that day. We are not to live just for now and for this world. We are to live each day with a view of the world above!

Titus 2:11-14; 1 John 3:2-3; Revelation 22:6
Jesus Is Victor!, 21, 24.

1048. Revival: conditions for

Christian leaders can help to bring about revival by refusing to pander to the carnal tastes of the religious public and going on a holy crusade for a purified church. If leaders have the courage to follow Christ all the way, they can be a powerful instrument of the Holy Ghost to bring about real revival. . . .

If enough influential Christians will rethink this whole thing and turn to the New Testament for guidance, there may yet come a new birth of revival among us. These leaders must see that the believer's true ambition should not be success but saintliness. They must see that they are not called to imitate the world, but to renounce it, and that publicity is no substitute for the power of the Holy Ghost.

Romans 12:1-2; Ephesians 5:15-18; Titus 2:11-14; 1 John 3:2-3
Keys to the Deeper Life, 90, 91.

1049. Revival: conditions for

There seems to be a notion abroad that if we talk enough and pray enough, revival will set in like a stock market boom or a winning streak on a baseball club. We appear to be waiting for some sweet chariot to swing low and carry us into the Big Rock Candy Mountain of religious experience.

Well, it is a pretty good rule that if everyone is saying something it is not likely to be true; or, if it has truth at the bottom, it has been so distorted by wrong emphasis as to have the effect of error in its practical outworking. And such, I believe, is much of the revival talk we hear today. . . .

Our mistake is that we want God to send revival on our terms. We want to get the power of God into our hands, to call it to us that it may work for us in promoting and furthering our kind of Christianity. We want still to be in charge, guiding the chariot through the religious sky in the direction we want it to go, shouting "Glory to God," it is true, but modestly accepting a share of the glory for ourselves in a nice inoffensive sort of way. We are calling on God to send fire on our altars, completely ignoring the fact that they are *our* altars and not God's.

Isaiah 42:8; Isaiah 55:6-8; Acts 8:18-21
The Size of the Soul, 8, 9.

1050. Revival: conditions for

Revival may occur in the local church, too. When a fair percentage of the members of any local church begin to pray more, lead holier lives, love each other more fervently, serve God and their fellow men with greater zeal, and seek to be holy and Christlike, then you have revival on the church level. I am happy to say this does occur sometimes.

And revival may occur in the individual believer's life. Wherever a careless, fleshly Christian suddenly pulls his life together, turns on himself and seeks the face of God in penitence and tears, you have the beginning of a personal revival. . . .

Christian leaders can help to bring about revival by refusing to pander to the carnal tastes of the religious public and going on a holy crusade for a purified church. If leaders have the courage to follow Christ all the way, they can be a powerful instrument of the Holy Ghost to bring about real revival.

Psalm 85:6; Ephesians 6:18; Philippians 1:9-11; 1 Thessalonians 4:3-7
Keys to the Deeper Life, 90.

1051. Revival: conditions for

If a song could be worn out, we have worn out the same old song: "Revive us again, fill each heart with Thy love." We have sung that one and nobody means it—nobody will pay the price.

Rut, Rot or Revival: The Condition of the Church, 15.

1052. Revival: conditions for; Church: activities; Church: focus

No matter how sincere they may be, ministers without discernment are sure to err. Their conclusions are inevitably false because their reasoning is mechanical and without inspiration. I hear their error in our pulpits and read it in our religious periodicals; and it all sounds alike: revived churches engage in foreign missions; hence let us plunge into missionary activity and spiritual refreshing is sure to follow. The healthy church wins souls; let us begin to win souls and we will surely be revived. The early Church enjoyed miracles, so let's begin to expect mighty signs and wonders and we will soon be like the early Church. We have neglected the "social implications" of the gospel; let us engage in political activities and charitable endeavors and all will be well again.

Miserable counselors these, and physicians of no value. Their advice is not only poor; it is spiritually damaging.

What doctor in his right mind would tell a patient dying of tuberculosis, "Healthy men play football; go out and play ball and you will regain your health"? Such advice given under such circumstances would reveal only that effect was being mistaken for cause; and that is exactly what is happening these days in religious circles. *The effects of revival are being mistaken for the causes of revival.* . . .

The critical need in this hour of the church's history is not what it is so often said to be: soul-winning, foreign missions, miracles. These are effects, not causes. . . .

Real repentance will result in purified hearts and sanctified lives. A hard and determined return to the pattern shown us in the mount will bring the smile of God upon our efforts.

2 Corinthians 7:1; James 4:7-10; 1 John 3:2-3
The Size of the Soul, 131, 132, 133.

1053. Revival: conditions for; Church: presence of Christ; Lordship of Christ

Many adherents of Christianity are beginning to admit that their attachment is to little more than a pallid "world religion." If they think about it at all, they may wonder where the moral and spiritual dynamic of the early church has gone. . . .

We hear much discussion about revival and renewal. People talk about spiritual power in the churches. I think this fact—this truth—that Jesus Christ wants to be known in His church as the ever-living, never-changing Lord of all could bring back again the power and the testimony of the early church.

I wonder if you feel like me when I survey much of Christendom in today's world: "They have taken away my Lord and I do not know what they have done with Him!" If we would only seek and welcome our Lord's presence in our midst, we would have the assurance that He is the same Lord He has always been!

Malachi 3:6; John 20:13; Hebrews 7:25; Hebrews 13:8
Jesus, Author of Our Faith, 137, 141.

1054. Revival: conditions for; Church: unity

God always works where His people meet His conditions, but only when and as they do. Any spiritual visitation will be limited or extensive, depending how well and how widely conditions are met.

The first condition is oneness of mind among the persons who are seeking the visitation....

Historically, revivals have been mainly the achieving of a oneness of mind among a number of Christian believers....

Every church should strive for unity among its members, not languidly, but earnestly and optimistically. Every pastor should show his people the possibilities for power that lie in this fusion of many souls into one.

Psalm 133; 1 Corinthians 1:10-12; Ephesians 4:3-6; Philippians 2:1-4, Philippians 4:3
Paths to Power, 59, 61, 64.

1055. Revival: conditions for; Knowledge of God: church's need; Church: presence of God

In what I have to say I may not be joined by any ground swell of public opinion, but I have a charge to make against the church. We are not consciously aware of God in our midst. We do not seem to sense the tragedy of having almost completely lost the awareness of His presence....

Revival and blessing come to the church when we stop looking at a picture of God and look at God Himself. Revival comes when, no longer satisfied just to know about a God in history, we meet the conditions of finding Him in living, personal experience....

Modern mankind can go everywhere, do everything and be completely curious about the universe. But only a rare person now and then is curious enough to want to know God.

Exodus 33:14-16; Psalm 42:1-2; Psalm 63:1-2
Men Who Met God, 121, 122, 127.

1056. Revival: conditions for; Obedience: need for

Prayer for revival will prevail when it is accompanied by radical amendment of life; not before.

All-night prayer meetings that are not preceded by practical repentance may actually be displeasing to God. "To obey is better than sacrifice."

We must return to New Testament Christianity, not in creed only but in complete manner of life as well. Separation, obedience, humility, simplicity, gravity, self-control, modesty, cross-bearing: these all must again be made a living part of the total Christian concept and be carried out in everyday conduct. We must cleanse the temple of the hucksters and the money changers and come fully under the authority of our risen Lord once more. And this applies to this writer as well as to everyone that names the name of Jesus. Then we can pray with confidence and expect true revival to follow.

1 Samuel 15:22; Isaiah 1:11-20; Matthew 21:12-13; Luke 9:23-25; 2 Corinthians 6:17-18
Keys to the Deeper Life, 25.

1057. Revival: conditions for; Obedience: need for

It is my conviction that much, very much, prayer for and talk about revival these days is wasted energy. Ignoring the confusion of figures, I might say that it is hunger that appears to have no object; it is dreamy wishing that is too weak to produce moral action. It is fanaticism on a high level for, according to John Wesley, "a fanatic is one who seeks desired ends while ignoring the constituted means to reach those ends.". . .

The correction of this error is extremely difficult for it entails more than a mere adjustment of our doctrinal beliefs; it strikes at the whole Adam-life and requires self-abnegation, humility and cross-carrying. In short it requires *obedience.* And that we will do anything to escape.

It is almost unbelievable how far we will go to avoid obeying God. We call Jesus "Lord" and beg Him to rejuvenate our souls, but we are careful to do not the things He says. When faced with a sin, a confession or a moral alteration in our life, we find it much easier to pray half a night than to obey God.

Matthew 5:6; Matthew 7:21-23; Luke 6:46
The Size of the Soul, 18, 19.

1058. Revival: conditions for; Obedience: need for; Church: current condition

Of this we may be certain: We cannot continue to ignore God's will as expressed in the Scriptures and expect to secure the aid of

God's Spirit. God has given us a complete blueprint for the Church and He requires that we adhere to it 100 percent. Message, morals and methods are there, and we are under strict obligation to be faithful to all three. Today we have the strange phenomenon of a company of Christians solemnly protesting to heaven and earth the purity of their Bible creed, and at the same time following the unregenerate world in their methods and managing only with difficulty to keep their moral standards from sinking out of sight. Coldness, worldliness, pride, boasting, lying, misrepresenting, love of money, exhibitionism—all these things are practiced by professedly orthodox Christians, not in secret but in plain sight and often as a necessary part of the whole religious show.

It will take more than talk and prayer to bring revival. There must be a return to the Lord in practice before our prayers will be heard in heaven. We dare not continue to trouble God's way if we want Him to bless ours. . . .

If we are foolish enough to do it, we may spend the new year vainly begging God to send revival, while we blindly overlook His requirements and continue to break His laws. Or we can begin now to obey and learn the blessedness of obedience. The Word of God is before us. We have only to read and do what is written there and revival is assured. It will come as naturally as the harvest comes after the plowing and the planting.

Yes, this could be the year the revival comes. It's strictly up to us.

Joshua 1:7-8; Joshua 7:10-12; Colossians 3:5-11
The Size of the Soul, 10, 11.

1059. Revival: conditions for; Prayer: diligence in

Among revival-minded Christians I have heard the saying, "Revivals are born after midnight."

This is one of those proverbs which, while not quite literally true, yet points to something very true.

If we understand the saying to mean that God does not hear our prayer for revival made in the daytime, it is of course not true. If we take it to mean that prayer offered when we are tired and worn-out has greater power than prayer made when we are rested and fresh, again it is not true. . . .

Yet there is considerable truth in the idea that revivals are born after midnight, for revivals (or any other spiritual gifts and graces) come only to those who want them badly enough. . . .

No, there is no merit in late hour prayers, but it requires a serious mind and a determined heart to pray past the ordinary into the unusual. Most Christians never do. And it is more than possible that the rare soul who presses on into the unusual experience reaches there after midnight.

Matthew 5:6
Born after Midnight, 7, 8, 10.

1060. Revival: conditions for; Prayer: unanswered; Obedience: need for

Have you noticed how much praying for revival has been going on of late—and how little revival has resulted?

Considering the volume of prayer that is ascending these days, rivers of revival should be flowing in blessing throughout the land. That no such results are in evidence should not discourage us; rather it should stir us to find out why our prayers are not answered. . . .

I believe our problem is that we have been trying to substitute praying for obeying; and it simply will not work. . . .

Prayer is never an acceptable substitute for obedience. The sovereign Lord accepts no offering from His creatures that is not accompanied by obedience. To pray for revival while ignoring or actually flouting the plain precept laid down in the Scriptures is to waste a lot of words and get nothing for our trouble.

1 Samuel 15:22; 2 Chronicles 7:14; James 4:3-4
Of God and Men, 55, 56.

1061. Revival: conditions for; Reformation; Christians: in the world; Church: current condition

I believe that the imperative need of the day is not simply revival, but a radical reformation that will go to the root of our moral and spiritual maladies and deal with causes rather than with consequences, with the disease rather than with symptoms.

It is my considered opinion that under the present circumstances we do not want revival at all. A widespread revival of the kind of Christianity we know today in America might prove to be a moral tragedy from which we would not recover in a hundred years. . . .

The radical element in testimony and life that once made Christians hated by the world is missing from present-day evangelicalism. Christians were once revolutionists—moral, not political—but we have lost our revolutionary character. It is no longer either dangerous or costly to be a Christian. Grace has become not free, but cheap. We are busy these days proving to the world that they can have all the benefits of the gospel without any inconvenience to their customary way of life. It's "all this, and heaven too."

This description of modern Christianity, while not universally applicable, is yet true of an overwhelming majority of present-day Christians. For this reason it is useless for large companies of believers to spend long hours begging God to send revival. Unless we intend to reform we may as well not pray. Unless praying men have the insight and faith to amend their whole way of life to conform to the New Testament pattern there can be no true revival.

John 15:18-21; Acts 17:6; 2 Timothy 3:12
Keys to the Deeper Life, 18, 22, 23.

1062. Revival: God's work

So we sit down to have a board meeting. What are we going to do to stir ourselves up? Who can we get? Where will we look? We forget that all the time Jehovah is present. "I am *Jehovah-shammah*; I am in the midst of you. Why don't you talk to me?" No, we don't ask Him.

"I am your banner of victory." But we say, "I just wonder how much it will cost?" How much does a revival cost? Absolutely nothing and absolutely everything—that is how much it will cost. It will cost not one dime, and it will cost everything we have. You cannot import it by flying someone in from New Zealand. How many of these blessed preachers have come in from Ireland and England? They did some big things over there, we heard, so we flew them in and they never got anywhere. I never saw anything result from trying to import God. He does not fly over in a jet. He says, "I am Jehovah; I am with you. I am where you are; I am here now. Call on me."

Leviticus 26:11-12; Jeremiah 33:3; Matthew 18:20
Rut, Rot or Revival: The Condition of the Church, 158, 159.

1063. Revival: God's work; God: His work

They did not program this woman. They could not. She had too much bounce in her soul! She was not involved in anything formal. She just went as fast as she could. No one planned her testimony for her (and thank God for that!). Sometimes I have been asked to meet with one group or another to "plan a revival." You might as well try to plan a lightning bolt as to plan a revival. No one has ever done it yet, and no one will ever really "plan" or "program" a true revival.

The Lord God Almighty makes a world, and nobody "plans" it. When He raises the dead, no one "plans" it. And—let me tell you this—when God raises the dead it never comes as the fifth item on the "program." Of that you can be sure!

1 Kings 17:22-23; Luke 7:15; John 4; Hebrews 11:32-40
Faith beyond Reason, 108.

1064. Revival: meaning of

Revivals, as they have appeared at various times among the churches of the past, have been essentially a quickening of the spiritual life of persons already orthodox. The revivalist, as long as he exercised his ministry as a revivalist, did not try to teach doctrine. His one object was to bring about a quickening of the churches which while orthodox in creed were devoid of spiritual life. When he went beyond this he was something else than a revivalist. Revival can come only to those who know truth. When the inner meaning of familiar doctrines suddenly flashes in upon the heart of a Christian the revival for him has already begun. It may go on to be much more than this but it can never be less.

Psalm 85:6; Psalm 98:1-6; Psalm 119:38-40; Revelation 3:1-3
That Incredible Christian, 58.

1065. Revival: meaning of

A genuine revival would raise the moral standards of society; instead, those standards are at a dismally low level everywhere. A genuine revival would check the divorce rate and bring back the sanctity of the home; instead, the divorce rate is higher than ever and the home is becoming little more than a place to sleep and watch television. A revival of true religion would discourage crime and juvenile delinquency; instead, the crime rate is higher than at any time in our history and youthful gang wars have become major police problems in our large cities.

Were the faith of our fathers exercising a major influence in society there would be a revolution in moral values among all Christians and a change in the outlook of multitudes who, while not themselves Christians, would nevertheless feel the strong pressure of Christian ethics and ideals around them. . . .

But in America no such change is found.

Proverbs 14:34; Romans 13:11-14;
2 Timothy 3:13-17
The Price of Neglect, 99, 100.

1066. Revival: need for; Church: numbers; Church: spiritual condition

Our most pressing obligation today is to do all in our power to obtain a revival that will result in a reformed, revitalized, purified church. It is of far greater importance that we have better Christians than that we have more of them. Each generation of Christians is the seed of the next, and degenerate seed is sure to produce a degenerate harvest not a little better than but a little worse than the seed from which it sprang. Thus the direction will be down until vigorous, effective means are taken to improve the seed. . . .

To carry on these activities [evangelism, missions] scripturally the church should be walking in fullness of power, separated, purified and ready at any moment to give up everything, even life itself, for the greater glory of Christ. For a worldly, weak, decadent church to make converts is but to bring forth after her own kind and extend her weakness and decadence a bit further out. . . .

So vitally important is spiritual quality that it is hardly too much to suggest that attempts to grow larger might well be suspended until we have become better.

Acts 20:28-31; 2 Corinthians 6:17-18;
Philippians 3:6-8
The Set of the Sail, 154, 155, 156.

1067. Revival: need for; Church: spiritual condition; Celebrities

The real peril today arises from within the fold of orthodox believers. It consists of an acceptance of the world's values, a belief that the kingdoms of the world and the glory of them are valid prizes to be pursued by believing men and women. Blind leaders of blind souls are admitting that there is something to be said in favor of the world-glory after all; they insist that Christians should not cut themselves off from the pleasures of the world, except, of course, from those that are too degraded for respectable society. Everything else goes, and the very values that

Christ scorned are now being used to attract people to the gospel.

Christ now stands in need of a patron, a celebrity who will sponsor Him before the world. He looks weakly about for some well-known figure upon whose inside popularity He can ride forth as He once rode into Jerusalem on the back of an ass's colt. His ability to draw men unto Him is frankly doubted, so He is provided with a gimmick to do the trick for Him. The cheap and tawdry glory which He once rejected is placed around His head as a crown. The crown they give Him is studded with paste imitations, all borrowed from the world: middle class prosperity, success, fame, publicity, money, crowds, social acceptance, pomp, display, earthly honor. The lust of the flesh, the lust of the eyes and the pride of life have all been Christianized (not by the liberal, mind you, but by the evangelicals) and are now offered along with Christ to everyone who will "believe."

And on top of this we still pray for revival, with no awareness of our dark betrayal and no intention to repent.

Matthew 4:8-10; 1 Peter 2:11-12;
1 John 2:15-17
God Tells the Man Who Cares, 22.

1068. Revival: personal

No church is any better or worse than the individual Christians who compose it. . . .

One consequence of our failure to see clearly the true nature of revival is that we wait for years for some supernatural manifestation that never comes, overlooking completely our own individual place in the desired awakening. Whatever God may do for a church must be done in the single unit, the one certain man or woman. Some things can happen only to the isolated, single person; they cannot be experienced en masse. Statistics show, for instance, that 100 babies are born in a certain city on a given day. Yet the birth of each baby is for the baby a unique experience, an isolated, personal thing. Fifty people die in a plane crash; while they die together they die separately, one at a time, each one undergoing the act of death in a loneliness of soul as utter as if he alone had died. Both birth and death are experienced by the individual in a loneness as complete as if only that one person had even known them.

Three thousand persons were converted at Pentecost, but each one met his sin and his Savior alone. The spiritual birth, like the natural one, is for each one a unique, separate experience shared in by no one. And so with that up-rush of resurgent life we call revival. It can come to the individual only.

John 3:3; Acts 2:41; Romans 12:3-8
The Size of the Soul, 14, 15.

1069. Revival: personal

It will require a determined heart and more than a little courage to wrench ourselves loose from the grip of our times and return to biblical ways. But it can be done. Every now and then in the past Christians have had to do it. History has recorded several large-scale returns led by such men as St. Francis, Martin Luther and George Fox. Unfortunately, there seems to be no Luther or Fox on the horizon at present. Whether or not another such return may be expected before the coming of Christ is a question upon which Christians are not fully agreed, but that is not of too great importance to us now.

What God in His sovereignty may yet do on a world-scale I do not claim to know. But what He will do for the plain man or woman who seeks His face I believe I do know and can tell others. Let any man turn to God in earnest, let him begin to exercise himself unto godliness, let him seek to develop his powers of spiritual receptivity by trust and obedience and humility, and the results will exceed anything he may have hoped in his leaner and weaker days.

Hosea 10:12; 1 Timothy 4:7-8; Revelation 2:15-16
The Pursuit of God, 63, 64.

1070. Revival: personal

Nothing can prevent the spiritual rejuvenation of the soul that insists upon having it. Though that solitary man must live and walk among persons religiously dead, he may experience the great transformation as certainly and as quickly as if he were in the most spiritual church in the world.

The man that *will* have God's best becomes at once the object of the personal attention of the Holy Spirit. Such a man will not be required to wait for the rest of the church to come alive. He will not be penalized for the failures of his fellow Christians, nor be asked to forego the blessing till his sleepy brethren catch up. God deals with the individual heart as exclusively as if only one existed. . . .

Every prophet, every reformer, every revivalist had to meet God alone before he could help the multitudes. The great leaders who went on to turn thousands to Christ had to begin with God and their own soul. The plain Christian of today must experience personal revival before he can hope to bring renewed spiritual life to his church.

Isaiah 6:1-5; Jeremiah 1:9-10; Matthew 6:6; Galatians 1:13-17
The Size of the Soul, 15, 16.

1071. Revival: personal; Commitment

It is easy to learn the doctrine of personal revival and victorious living; it is quite another thing to take our cross and plod on to the dark and bitter hill of self-renunciation. Here many are called and few are chosen. For every one that actually crosses over into the Promised Land there are many who stand for a while and look longingly across the river and then turn sadly back to the comparative safety of the sandy wastes of the old life.

No, there is no merit in late hour prayers, but it requires a serious mind and a determined heart to pray past the ordinary into the unusual. Most Christians never do.

Matthew 22:14; Matthew 26:40-41
 Luke 9:23-25
Born after Midnight, 10.

1072. Revival: personal; Discipleship; Spiritual growth

Well, here are some suggestions which anyone can follow and which, I am convinced, will result in a wonderfully improved Christian life.

1. Get thoroughly dissatisfied with yourself. Complacency is the deadly enemy of spiritual progress. The contented soul is the stagnant soul. . . .

2. Set your face like a flint toward a sweeping transformation of your life. . . .

3. Put yourself in the way of blessing. . . . There are plainly marked paths which lead straight to the green pastures; let us walk in them. To desire revival, for instance, and at the same time to neglect prayer and devotion is to wish one way and walk another.

4. Do a thorough job of repenting. . . . Until we allow the consciousness of sin to wound us, we will never develop a fear of evil. It is our wretched habit of tolerating sin that keeps us in our half-dead condition.

5. Make restitution whenever possible. . . .

6. Bring your life into accord with the Sermon on the Mount and such other New Testament

Scriptures as are designed to instruct us in the way of righteousness. An honest man with an open Bible and a pad and pencil is sure to find out what is wrong with him very quickly. . . .

7. Be serious-minded. You can well afford to see fewer comedy shows on TV. Unless you break away from the funny boys, every spiritual impression will continue to be lost to your heart, and that right in your own living room. . . .

8. Deliberately narrow your interests. . . .

9. Begin to witness. . . .

10. Have faith in God. Begin to expect. Look up toward the throne where your Advocate sits at the right hand of God. All heaven is on your side. God will not disappoint you.

Psalm 1:1-3; Isaiah 6:5-8; Acts 1:8; Romans 7:24-25; Philippians 3:13-14; 2 Timothy 1:6-7;1 John 2:1-2
The Size of the Soul, 22, 23, 24, 25, 26.

1073. Riches in Christ

What has Christ to offer to us that is sound, genuine and desirable? He offers forgiveness of sins, inward cleansing, peace with God, eternal life, the gift of the Holy Spirit, victory over temptation, resurrection from the dead, a glorified body, immortality and a dwelling place in the house of the Lord forever. These are a few benefits that come to us as a result of faith in Christ and total committal to Him. Add to these the expanding wonders and increasing glories that shall be ours through the long, long reaches of eternity, and we get an imperfect idea of what Paul called "the unsearchable riches of Christ."

Psalm 23:6; Acts 13:38-39; Romans 5:1; 1 Corinthians 10:13; Ephesians 3:18;1 John 5:11-12
That Incredible Christian, 117, 118.

1074. Riches in Christ; Experiencing God

The experience of God within the believer ought to result from the text, but it is possible to have the text and not have the experience!

This can be simply but plainly illustrated. Suppose a very rich man dies and leaves a will, the text of which passes on all of his millions to his only son. So the son and heir borrows the text of his father's will from the attorney and carries it around with him. He becomes ragged and hungry, begging on the street for a crust of bread.

But when someone says, "Poor fellow, you are in bad shape, weak and pale and sickly," the heir to the fortune reacts strongly.

"Don't talk to me like that," he says. "I have much more than I will ever be able to use!"

To prove it, he opens the will and reads: "Unto my dear son, Charles, I bequeath my property, my stocks and bonds, my bank accounts, my entire estate."

You see, Charles is completely satisfied with the text of the will. He has it and he holds it—but he has never had it executed, never had it filed for probate, never presented his legitimate claims to the inheritance. In actual experience, he has received nothing. He simply holds the text of the will.

In the same sense, a Christian may go around clutching the book of Ephesians and not realize that he is spiritually lean and hungry, pallid and weak, and ragged as well. . . .

It is one thing to have the text of the will—it is another thing to come into possession of the riches.

Ephesians 1:3; Ephesians 3:8
I Talk Back to the Devil, 103, 104.

1075. Righteous/Wicked

There will always be "evildoers" and "workers of iniquity," and for the most part they will appear to succeed while the forces of righteousness will seem to fail. The wicked will always have the money and the talent and the publicity and the numbers, while the righteous will be few and poor and unknown. The prayerless Christian will surely misread the signs and fret against the circumstances. That is what the Spirit warns us against.

Let us look out calmly upon the world; or better yet, let us look down upon it from above where Christ is seated and we are seated in Him. Though the wicked spread himself like "a green bay tree" it is only for a moment. Soon he passes away and is not. "But the salvation of the righteous is of the Lord: he is their strength in the time of trouble." This knowledge should cure the fretting spirit.

Psalm 37:1,35,39; Psalm 92:7; Colossians 3:1-4
Man: The Dwelling Place of God, 69.

1076. Righteousness

I claim nothing and my testimony is the same as Martin Luther's prayer: "Oh, Lord Jesus, Thou art my righteousness—I am Thy sin!"

The only sin Jesus had was mine, Luther's and yours—and the only righteousness we can ever have is His.

Romans 3:25; 2 Corinthians 5:19-21; Ephesians 2:14-16
I Talk Back to the Devil, 135.

1077. Role models; Christlikeness

It is a law of the human soul that people tend to become like that which they admire most intensely. Deep and long continued admiration can alter the whole texture of the mind and heart and turn the devotee into something quite other than he was before.

For this reason it is critically important that we Christians should have right models. It is not enough to say that our model should be Christ. While that is true, it is also true that Christ is known mostly through the lives of His professed followers, and the more prominent and vocal these followers are the more powerful will be their influence upon the rank and file of Christians. If the models are imperfect the whole standard of Christian living must suffer as a result.

A sacred obligation lies upon each of us to be Christlike. This generation of Christians must have models it can safely admire. That is not the primary reason for seeking to be holy, but it is a powerful one.

Romans 8:28-30; 1 Corinthians 11:1; Philippians 3:17
The Warfare of the Spirit, 177, 178.

1078. Role models; World: imitation of; Celebrities

Popular evangelicalism has been selling out to the worldly spirit and worldly methods to a point where Hollywood now has more influence than Jerusalem ever had. Youth take for their examples not the saints of old but the stars of today. The chaste dignity and sparkling purity of true Christianity has been displaced by a cheap hillbillyism wholly unworthy of our Lord Jesus Christ.

Romans 12:1-2; 2 Corinthians 6:17-18; Hebrews 12:1-2
Keys to the Deeper Life, 89.

S

1079. Sacrifice; Giving

Our Lord knew that in these times there would be those in our churches who are just highly-groomed show pieces of Christianity—middle class and well-to-do, satisfied with a religious life that costs them nothing.

Oh, yes, we do tithe! But the nine-tenths that we keep is still a hundred times more than our mothers and fathers used to have. It is right that we should tithe because it is God's work, but it does not really cost us anything—it does not bring us to the point of sacrificial giving. An old prophet of God long ago said something for us all: "Shall I offer God something that costs me nothing?"

Friend, what has your Christian faith and witness cost you this week? . . .

I realize that this message will not win any popularity prizes in the Christian ranks, but I must add this based on my observations on the current state of the church: Christianity to the average evangelical church member is simply an avenue to a good and pleasant time, with a little biblical devotional material thrown in for good measure!

It is time that we begin to search our hearts and ask ourselves: "What is my Christian faith costing me? Am I offering to God something that has cost me absolutely nothing in terms of blood or sweat or tears?"

2 Samuel 24:24; Malachi 1:13-14; Matthew 24:10-12
Who Put Jesus on the Cross?, 88, 89, 90.

1080. Sacrifice; Riches in Christ; Personal testimony: Tozer

I have been asked more than once what I gave up when I was converted and became a believing child of God. I was a young man, and I well remember that I gave up the hot and smelly rubber factory. I was making tires for an hourly wage, and I gave that up to follow Christ's call into Christian ministry and service.

As a youth I was scared of life and I was scared of death—and I gave that up. I was miserable and glum and unfulfilled—and I gave that up. I had selfish earthly and material ambitions that I could never have achieved—and I gave them up.

That forms the outline of the worthless things that I gave up. And I soon discovered that in Jesus Christ, God had given me everything that is worthwhile.

If God takes away from us the old, wrinkled, beat-up dollar bill we have clutched so desperately, it is only because He wants to exchange it for the whole Federal mint, the entire treasury! He is saying to us, "I have in store for you all the resources of heaven. Help yourself!"

2 Corinthians 5:17; Ephesians 1; Philippians 3:6-8; Hebrews 11:8-10
Jesus, Author of Our Faith, 49, 50.

1081. Salvation: from/to; Worship: for eternity

The evangelical church today is in the awkward position of being wrong while it is right, and a little preposition makes the difference. . . .

One place where we are wrong while we are right is in the relative stress we lay upon the prepositions *to* and *from* when they follow the word *saved*. For a long generation we have been holding the letter of truth while at the same time we have been moving away from it in spirit because we have been preoccupied with what we are saved *from* rather than what we have been saved *to*. . . .

We have not learned where to lay our emphasis. Particularly we have not understood that we are saved to know God, to enter His wonder-filled Presence through the new and living way and remain in that Presence forever. We are called to an everlasting preoccupation with God. The Triune God with all of His mystery and majesty is ours and we are His, and eternity will not be long enough to experience all that He is of goodness, holiness and truth.

In heaven they rest not day or night in their ecstatic worship of the Godhead. We profess to be headed for that place; shall we not begin now to worship on earth as we shall do in heaven?

1 Thessalonians 1:9; Hebrews 10:19-23; Revelation 4:1-8
That Incredible Christian, 44, 46.

1082. Salvation: invitation to

Sometimes preachers get carried away and start sermonizing on the great calamities posed by communism and secularism and materialism. But our greatest calamity is the closed heaven, the silent heaven. God meant for us to be in fellowship with Him. When the heavens are closed, men are left to themselves. They are without God. . . .

But in the Christian faith it is imperative that the individual meet God. We are not talking about just the possibility of meeting God. We are not saying just that it would be a good thing to meet God. *Meeting God is imperative!*

Thankfully, the gospel of Christ tells us how to find God, to respond to Him, to love Him. The gospel tells us that there is a door—only one door. Jesus Christ is that door, and through Him we meet God.

Ezekiel 1:1-5; John 10:7,9; John 14:6;
Ephesians 2:12-13
Men Who Met God, 119, 120.

1083. Salvation: invitation to

This is so desperately a matter of importance for every human being who comes into the world that I first become indignant, and then I become sad, when I try to give spiritual counsel to a person who looks me in the eye and tells me: "Well, I am trying to make up my mind if I should accept Christ or not."

Such a person gives absolutely no indication that he realizes he is talking about the most important decision he can make in his lifetime—a decision to get right with God, to believe in the eternal Son, the Savior, to become a disciple, an obedient witness to Jesus Christ as Lord.

How can any man or woman, lost and undone, sinful and wretched, alienated from God, stand there and intimate that the death and Resurrection of Jesus Christ and God's revealed plan of salvation do not take priority over some of life's other decisions?

John 1:11-13; John 3:14-15; Acts 4:12;
2 Corinthians 6:1-2
Christ the Eternal Son, 156.

1084. Salvation: preparation for eternity; Earthly things

It has been suggested here before that life, for all its apparent complexities, is at bottom very simple indeed if we could only realize it. Thank God, only a few things matter. The rest are incidental and unimportant. . . .

What really matters after all? My personal relation to God matters. That takes priority over everything else. A man may be born in a sanitary hospital, receive his education in progressive schools, ride in an air-conditioned car, sleep on a foam rubber mattress, wear synthetic clothing, eat vitamin-enriched food, read by flourescent lights, speak across 12,000 miles of empty space to a friend on the other side of the world, lose his anxieties by taking tranquilizing pills, die without pain by the aid of some new drug and be laid to rest in a memorial park as lovely as a country garden; yet what will all this profit him if he must later rise to face in judgment a God who knows him not and whom he does not know? To come at last before the bar of eternal justice with no one to plead his cause and to be banished forever from the presence of the great Judge—is that man any better off than if he had died a naked savage in the hinterlands of Borneo? . . .

Where can a man find security? Can philosophy help him? or psychology? or science? or "progress"? or atoms or wonder drugs or vitamins? No. Only Christ can help him, and His aid is as old as man's sin and man's need. The naked aborigine is as near to God (and as far from Him) as the Ph.D. Nothing new can save my soul; neither can saving grace be modernized. We must each come as Abel came, by atoning blood and faith demonstrated in repentance. No new way has been discovered. The old way is the true way and there is no new way. The Lamb of God was slain "before the foundation of the world."

Genesis 4:4; Mark 8:36-37; 2 Corinthians 5:10; Hebrews 11:4; 1 Peter 1:19-20
Born after Midnight, 88, 90, 91.

1085. Salvation: sovereign calling; Evangelism: wrong emphasis; Gospel: accept Christ

There is another and worse evil which springs from this basic failure to grasp the radical difference between the natures of the two worlds. It is the habit of languidly "accepting" salvation as if it were a small matter and one wholly in our hands. Men are exhorted to think things over and "decide" for Christ, and in some places one day each year is set aside as "Decision Day," at which time people are expected to condescend to grant Christ the right to save them, a right which they have obviously refused Him up to that time. Christ is thus made to stand again before men's judgment seat; He is made to wait upon the pleasure of the individual, and after long and humble waiting is either turned away or patronizingly admitted. By a complete misunderstanding of the noble and true doctrine of the freedom of the human will salvation is made to depend perilously upon the will of man instead of upon the will of God.

However deep the mystery, however many the paradoxes involved, it is still true that men become saints not at their own whim but by sovereign calling.

John 6:35,37,44,63-65; Romans 8:28-30;
1 Corinthians 1:1-2
The Pursuit of Man, 37-38.

1086. Salvation: transformation

Let us get it straight. Jesus Christ does not just offer us salvation as though it is a decoration or a bouquet or some addition to our garb. He says plainly: "Throw off your old rags; strip to the skin! Let me dress you in the fine clean robes of My righteousness—all Mine. Then, if it means loss of money, lose it! If it means loss of job, lose it! If it means persecution, take it! If it brings the stiff winds of opposition, bow your head into the wind and take it—for My sake!"

Luke 14:26-27; John 1:11-13; Philippians 3:6-8
Faith beyond Reason, 14.

1087. Salvation: transformation

. . . I mean spiritual energy of sufficient voltage to produce great saints once again. That breed of mild, harmless Christian grown in our generation is but a poor sample of what the grace of God can do when it operates in power in a human heart. The emotionless act of "accepting the Lord" practiced among us bears little resemblance to the whirlwind conversions of the past. We need the power that transforms, that fills the soul with a sweet intoxication, that will make a former persecutor to be "beside himself" with the love of Christ. We have today theological saints who can (and must) be proved to be saints by an appeal to the Greek original. We need saints whose lives proclaim their sainthood, and who need not run to the concordance for authentication.

1 Corinthians 15:9-10; 2 Corinthians 5:13-17;
2 Corinthians 11-12
Paths to Power, 10.

1088. Salvation: transformation

In the light of what God is willing to do and wants to do, consider how we try to "get them in" in modern Christianity.

We get them in any way we can. Then we try to work on them—to adjust them and to reform them.

I may be misunderstood when I say this, but we even have two works of grace because the first was so apologetically meaningless that we try to have two.

I do not speak against the second work of grace; but I am pleading for the work that ought to be done in a man's heart when he first meets God. What I am asking is this: Why should we be forced to invent some second or third or fourth experience somewhere along the line to obtain what we should have received the first time we met God?

Psalm 51:10; 2 Corinthians 5:17; 1 Peter 1:3-5
I Call It Heresy!, 31.

1089. Satan

Oh, what a cheat the devil is! What a deceiver and what a confidence man he is!

I think of the cheating devil when I think of the sly confidence men who have sold the Brooklyn Bridge to poor people, grinning as they have taken their last dollar, leaving them to find out too late that the Brooklyn Bridge was never on the market.

The devil is a liar, I say, and a deceiver. He is busy leading people to spend the best years of their lives laying up treasures for themselves, which even before they die will begin to rust and rot and decay.

Matthew 6:19-21; John 8:44-47; 1 Peter 1:3-5
I Call It Heresy!, 96.

1090. Satan

There is an amazing provision for Christian believers in our daily encounters and conflicts with Satan, the enemy of our souls. I cannot agree with those optimistic people who try to dismiss Satan as a figment of the imagination. They are wrong. There is a real devil. But we do not have to be afraid of him if we know and exercise the dominion and authority of the saints of God. . . .

God holds no mental reservations about any of us when we become His children by faith. When He forgives us, He trusts us as though we had never sinned. When Satan comes around to taunt me about my past sins, I remind him that everything that had been charged against me came from him, and now everything I have—forgiveness and peace and freedom—I have freely received from my Lord Jesus Christ!

As long as you remain on this earth, God has not completed His work in you. The Spirit of God will help you discern when the chastening hand of God is upon you. But if it is the devil trying to tamper with your Christian life and testimony, dare to resist him in the victorious power of the living Christ.

Psalm 103:10-12; Hebrews 4:14-16; Hebrews 8:12; Revelation 1:5-6
Jesus Is Victor!, 49, 50.

1091. Satan; Discouragement; Spiritual warfare

It is part of the devil's business to keep the Christian's spirit imprisoned. He knows that the believing and justified Christian has been raised up out of the grave of his sins and trespasses. From that point on, Satan works that much harder to keep us bound and gagged, actually imprisoned in our own grave clothes!

He knows that if we continue in this kind of bondage we will never be able to claim our rightful spiritual heritage. He knows also that while we continue bound in this kind of enslavement we are not much better off than when we were spiritually dead.

Romans 6:4-7; Galatians 5:1; 1 John 3:7-8
Renewed Day by Day, Volume 1, Jan. 12.

1092. Satan; Guilt; Forgiveness

God knows that sin is a terrible thing—and the devil knows it, too. So he follows us around and as long as we will permit it, he will taunt us about our past sins.

As for myself, I have learned to talk back to him on this score. I say, "Yes, Devil, sin is terrible—but I remind you that I got it from you! And I remind you, Devil, that everything good—forgiveness and cleansing and blessing—everything that is good I have freely received from Jesus Christ!"

Everything that is bad and that is against me I got from the devil—so why should he have the effrontery and the brass to argue with me about it? Yet he will do it because he is the devil, and he is committed to keeping God's children shut up in a little cage, their wings clipped so that they can never fly!

Psalm 32:1-2; Psalm 103:10-12; Romans 8:1
I Talk Back to the Devil, 6.

1093. Satan; Jesus Christ: intimacy with

The best way to keep the enemy out is to keep Christ in. The sheep need not be terrified by the wolf; they have but to stay close to the shepherd. It is not the praying sheep Satan fears but the presence of the shepherd.

Isaiah 40:11; John 10:11-15,27-29; Revelation 7:14-17
Born after Midnight, 43.

1094. Satan; Opposition

Is Satan giving you a hard time in your life of faith—in the Christian race you are running? Expect it if you are a believing child of God!

Satan hates your God. He hates Jesus Christ. He hates your faith. You should be aware of the devil's evil intentions. He wants you to lose the victor's crown in the race you have entered by faith through grace.

1 Corinthians 9:24-27; 2 Timothy 4:6-8; Hebrews 12:1-2
Jesus, Author of Our Faith, 75.

1095. Satan; Spiritual warfare

A proof of this propensity to extremes is seen in the attitude of the average Christian toward the devil. I have observed among spiritual persons a tendency either to ignore him altogether or to make too much of him. Both are wrong. . . .

Satan hates God for His own sake, and everything that is dear to God he hates for the very reason that God loves it. Because man was made in God's image the hatred with which Satan regards him is particularly malevolent, and since the Christian is doubly dear to God he is hated by the powers of darkness with an aggravated fury probably not equaled anywhere else in the moral universe.

In view of this it cannot be less than folly for us Christians to disregard the reality and presence of the enemy. To live in a world under siege is to live in constant peril; to live there and be wholly unaware of the peril is to increase it a hundredfold and to turn the world into a paradise for fools.

While we must not underestimate the strength of the foe, we must at the same time be careful not to fall under his evil spell and live in constant fear of him. "We are not ignorant of his devices." If he cannot make skeptics of us he will make us devil-conscious and thus throw a permanent shadow across our lives. There is but a hairline between truth and superstition. We should learn the truth about the enemy, but we must stand bravely against every superstitious notion he would introduce about himself. . . . .

The Scriptural way to see things is to set the Lord always before us, put Christ in the center of our vision, and if Satan is lurking around he will appear on the margin only and be seen as but a shadow on the edge of the brightness. It is always wrong to reverse this—to set Satan in the focus of our vision and push God out to the margin. Nothing but tragedy can come of such inversion.

2 Corinthians 2:11; James 4:7-10 ; 1 Peter 5:8-9
Born after Midnight, 40, 41, 42, 43.

1096. Satan; Spiritual warfare

As we move farther on and mount higher up in the Christian life we may expect to encounter greater difficulties in the way and meet increased hostility from the enemy of our souls. . . .

Satan hates the true Christian for several reasons. One is that God loves him, and whatever is loved by God is sure to be hated by the devil. Another is that the Christian, being a child of God, bears a family resemblance to the Father and to the household of faith. Satan's ancient jealousy has not abated nor his hatred for God diminished in the slightest. Whatever reminds him of God is without other reason the object of his malignant hate.

A third reason is that a true Christian is a former slave who has escaped from the galley, and Satan cannot forgive him for this affront. A fourth reason is that a praying Christian is a constant threat to the stability of Satan's government. The Christian is a holy rebel loose in the world with access to the throne of God. Satan never knows from what direction the danger will come.

Romans 6:16-18; Ephesians 6:18; 1 John 4:10
That Incredible Christian, 71.

1097. Saving faith; Faith: intellectual only; Evangelism: true conversion

There are some frank things that need to be expressed about saving faith in our day, for even in our evangelical Christian circles there is a basic misunderstanding of faith.

It is a simple matter to get people to come forward when the invitation is given. It is a simple matter to get them on their knees. Then what happens?

Someone rushes in with a marked New Testament, sticks a text under their nose, and demands, "Now, who said that?"

The kneeling person says, "God?"

"Do you believe God?"

"Yes."

"Well, then, do you believe the text?"

"Yes. I must believe it because I believe God."

"Well, then, get right up and testify."

In so many cases, he gets up with an intellectual faith that has no saving quality.

Matthew 7:21-23; John 16:8; Romans 10:8-10; 1 John 2:19
Echoes from Eden, 34.

1098. Saving faith; Salvation: transformation

The faith of Paul and Luther was a revolutionizing thing. It upset the whole life of the individual and made him into another person altogether. It laid hold on the life and brought it under obedience to Christ. It took up its cross and followed along after Jesus with no intention of going back. It said goodbye to its old friends as certainly as Elijah when he stepped into the fiery chariot and went away in the whirlwind. It had a finality about it. It snapped shut on a man's heart like a trap; it captured the man and made him from that moment forward a happy love-servant of his Lord. It turned earth into a desert and drew heaven within sight of the believing soul. It realigned all life's actions and brought them into accord with the will of God. It set its possessor on a pinnacle of truth from which spiritual vantage point he viewed everything that came into his field of experience. It made him little and God big and Christ unspeakably dear. All this and more happened to a man when he received the faith that justifies.

2 Kings 2:11; Luke 9:23-25; Romans 6:4-7; 2 Corinthians 5:17
The Root of the Righteous, 46.

1099. Saving faith; Salvation: transformation; Lordship of Christ

This generation of Christians must hear again the doctrine of the perturbing quality of faith. People must be told that the Christian religion is not something they can trifle with. The faith of Christ will command or it will have nothing to do with a man. It will not yield to experimentation. Its power cannot reach any man who is secretly keeping an escape route open in case things get too tough for him. The only man who can be sure he has true Bible faith is the one who has put himself in a position where he cannot go back. His faith has resulted in an everlasting and irrevocable committal, and however strongly he may be tempted he always replies, "Lord, to whom shall we go? thou hast the words of eternal life."

John 6:68
The Root of the Righteous, 48.

1100. Science

When God spoke out of heaven to our Lord, self-centered men who heard it explained it by natural causes, saying, "It thundered." This habit of explaining the Voice by appeals to natural law is at the very root of modern science. In the living, breathing cosmos there is a mysterious Something, too wonderful, too awful for any mind to understand. The believing man does not claim to understand. He falls to his knees and whispers, "God." The man of earth kneels also, but not to worship. He kneels to examine, to search, to find the cause and the how of things. Just now we happen to be living in a secular age. Our thought habits are those of the scientist, not those of the worshiper. We are more likely to explain than to adore. "It thundered," we exclaim, and go our earthly way. But still the Voice sounds and searches. The order and life of the world depend upon that Voice, but men are mostly too busy or too stubborn to give attention.

Genesis 1:9; Psalm 33:6-9; John 1:1
John 6:63-65
The Pursuit of God, 71, 72.

1101. Science

Science and philosophy are more arrogant and bigoted than religion could ever possibly be. They try to brand evangelical Christians as bigots.

But I have never taken my Bible and gone into the laboratory and tried to tell the scientist how to conduct his experiments, and I would thank him if he didn't bring his test tube into the holy place and tell me how to conduct mine!

Colossians 2:8-9; 1 Timothy 6:20-21
The Tozer Pulpit, Volume 1, Book 1, 36.

1102. Science; Creation

Consider why we think like we do in today's society. We are participants in a new age—a scientific age, an atomic age, a space age. We have been conditioned by our sciences. No longer have we any great sense of wonder or appreciation for what God continues to do in His creation. Amid our complex engineering and technological accomplishments, it is difficult for us to look out on God's world as we should.

As believers in God and in His plan for mankind, we must not yield to the philosophies that surround us. We have a God-given message to proclaim to our generation: *The world was made by Almighty God.* It bears the stamp of deity upon it and within it.

An architect leaves his stamp upon the great buildings he has designed. A notable artist leaves his mark and personality on his paintings. The same principle applies to the visible and invisible worlds.

Genesis 1:1; Psalm 19:1-6; Hebrews 1:6-8
Jesus, Our Man in Glory, 50.

1103. Science; Creation

I have leafed through a book entitled *Earth's Earliest Ages*. I will not say that I have actually read it because I quickly concluded that the author seems to believe that he knows more about the antediluvian period than Moses did. When I discover a man who claims to know more than Moses on a subject in which Moses is a specialist, I shy away from his book.

Christ the Eternal Son, 16.

1104. Science; Miracles: belief in

I receive a lot of magazines, most of which I dutifully and joyously never read. I looked at one recently after I came home in the evening, and it had a question and answer department in it.

One question was: "Dear Doctor So and So: What about the whale swallowing Jonah? Do you believe that?"

And the good doctor replied: "Yes, I believe it. Science proves that there are whales big enough to swallow men."

I folded the magazine, and laid it down, for that man had come up to bat, but he had struck out beautifully.

For I believe that Jonah was swallowed by a whale, not because a scientist has crawled in and measured a whale's belly, and come out and said, "Yes, God can do that."

If God said that Jonah was swallowed by a whale, then the whale swallowed Jonah, and we do not need a scientist to measure the gullet of the whale. . . .

Whenever I find men running to science to find support for the Bible, I know they are rationalists and not true believers!

Grant me God and miracles take care of themselves.

Jeremiah 32:17-27; Jonah 1:17; Matthew 19:26
The Tozer Pulpit, Volume 1, Book 1, 33, 34.

1105. Science; Philosophy; Reason; Skeptics

Philosophy and science have not always been friendly toward the idea of God, the reason being that they are dedicated to the task of accounting for things and are impatient with anything that refuses to give an account of itself. The philosopher and the scientist will admit that there is much that they do not know; but that is quite another thing from admitting that there is something which they can *never* know, which indeed they have no technique for discovering. To admit that there is One who lies beyond us, who exists outside of all our categories, who will not be dismissed with a name, who will not appear before the bar of our reason, nor submit to our curious inquiries: this requires a great deal of humility, more than most of us possess, so we save face by thinking God down to our level, or at least down to where we can manage Him.

Romans 1:18-32; Colossians 2:8-9;
1 Timothy 6:20-21
The Knowledge of the Holy, 41, 42.

1106. Science; Skeptics; Miracles: denial of

You may have heard of the two scientists who reported that the story of Balaam's ass speaking to the prophet is false because "the larynx of a donkey could not possibly articulate human speech."

A thoughtful Scotchman overheard them and he walked up to them and said, "Man, you make a donkey and I'll make him talk."

There you have it, brother. If God can make a donkey, God can make him talk.

Numbers 22:28
The Counselor, 32.

1107. Seasons of life; Unsaved; Death: certainty of

We are not much given to moralizing on natural objects, but who can fail to notice the parallel between God's great lovely world and the little tribes of flesh and blood who inhabit it? Is it not plain that every human being runs through the same stages as the seasons? Spring, the time of childhood and youth when all the world is big with promise, a promise which the later years invariably fail to keep. Summer, the period of full power when life multiplies and it is hard to believe that it can ever end. Autumn, with its repose after toil, a gracious tapering off of our fuller powers, a kindly preparation for our longer rest. Winter, when the leaves have dropped away and the last sign of life has disappeared. Then only faith remains to assure us that there will be for us a bright tomorrow.

To the man out of Christ, the fall of the year, in spite of its many charms, must surely bring with it a deep and hidden terror. For it speaks of the approaching end, the time when it may be said, "The summer is ended, and we are not saved." It would be good indeed if the autumn winds could preach to the lost soul of the brevity of life and the long winter ahead.

Psalm 39:4-6; Jeremiah 8:20; James 4:13-14
We Travel an Appointed Way, 11, 12.

1108. Second coming: hope for

This is the kind of age and hour when the Lord's people should be so alert to the hope and promise of His coming that they should get up every morning just like a child on Christmas morning—eager and believing that it should be today!

1 Corinthians 15:51-57; 1 Thessalonians 4:13-18
Who Put Jesus on the Cross?, 191.

1109. Second coming: hope for

In summary, I think we must note that there is a vast difference between the doctrine of Christ's coming and the hope of His coming. It surely is possible to hold the doctrine without feeling a trace of the blessed hope. Indeed, there are multitudes of Christians today who hold the doctrine. What I have tried to center on here is that overwhelming sense of anticipation that lifts the life upward to a new plane and fills the heart with rapturous optimism. This is largely lacking among us now.

Acts 1:9-11; Titus 2:11-14; Revelation 22:20
Tragedy in the Church: The Missing Gifts, 137.

1110. Second coming: hope for

Shortly after the close of the first World War, I heard a great Southern preacher say that he feared the intense interest in prophecy current at that time would result in a dying out of the blessed hope when events had proved the excited interpreters wrong. The man was a prophet, or at least a remarkably shrewd student of human nature, for exactly what he predicted has come to pass. The hope of Christ's coming is today all but dead among evangelicals. . . .

The truth touching the second advent, where it is presented today, is for the most part either academic or political. The joyful personal element is altogether missing. . . .

The longing to see Christ that burned in the breasts of those first Christians seems to have burned itself out. All we have left are the ashes.

1 Corinthians 15:51-57; 1 Corinthians 16:22; Titus 2:11-14; Revelation 22:20
Born after Midnight, 131, 132.

1111. Second coming: hope for

So, for many there is no emotional yearning for the return of Jesus. The best hope they know is a kind of intellectual, theological hope. But an intellectual knowledge of what the New Testament teaches about the return of Christ is surely a poor substitute for a love-inflamed desire to look on His face! . . .

The crux of the whole matter is this: our wonderful, created world will be restored to its rightful Owner. I for one look forward to that day. I want to live here when Jesus Christ owns and rules the world. Until that hour, there will be conflict, distress and war among the nations. We will hear of suffering and terror and fear and failure. But the God who has promised a better world is the God who cannot lie. He will shake loose Satan's hold on this world and its society and systems. Our heavenly Father will put this world into the hands that were once nailed to a cross for our race of proud and alienated sinners.

It is a fact. Jesus Christ is returning to earth. . . .

I bow my head and continue to pray with the humble writer of the Revelation: "Amen! Come, Lord Jesus!"

Matthew 24:30-36; Philippians 2:9-11;
1 Thessalonians 5:1-8; Revelation 22:20
Jesus Is Victor!, 30, 31, 35, 36, 37.

1112. Second coming: lack of interest in; Christians: other-worldly; World: contentment with

It is safe to say that the pleasurable anticipation of the better things to come has almost died out in the church of Christ. It is a great temptation to take the shallow view that we do not need any heaven promised for tomorrow because we are so well situated here and now.

This is the emphasis of our day: "We don't need to hope—we have it now!"

But the modern emphasis is wretched and it is wrong. When we do talk about the future we talk about eschatology instead of heaven. When I find any Christian who can live and work and serve here and snuggle down into the world like your hand fits into an old and familiar glove, I worry about him. I must wonder if he has ever truly been born again.

Brethren, we are still living in a wicked and adulterous generation and I must confess that the Christians I meet who really amount to something for the Saviour are very much out of key and out of tune with their generation.

Matthew 6:19-21; Hebrews 11:13-16;
1 Peter 1:3-5
I Call It Heresy!, 39, 40.

1113. Second coming: lack of interest in; Evangelism: urgency of; Complacency

Christians are never to be caught unawares. They are never to put on their smoking jacket or the lounging robe while it is dark and the call of the trumpet is expected. The only safety for anyone is the blood. While the call of God may come at any minute to take us out of this Egypt we call the world, you and I cannot afford to be careless.

Instead of letting the cross keep us always on the alert and ready to go, we have painted the cross and reshaped it, and geared it in with the better element of the world. The people of God are asleep doing their little labors, while we wait for the call of the trumpet that will take us out of this world.

Oh, that we might again have that sense of immediacy and urgency that was upon the early church!

Exodus 12:11; 1 Thessalonians 4:13-18; 1 Peter 1:6-9, 13
The Tozer Pulpit, Volume 1, Book 1, 128.

1114. Second coming: lack of interest in; Persecution; Suffering

Again, in these times religion has become jolly good fun right here in this present world, and what's the hurry about heaven anyway? Christianity, contrary to what some had thought, is another and higher form of entertainment. Christ has done all the suffering. He has shed all the tears and carried all the crosses; we have but to enjoy the benefits of His heartbreak in the form of religious pleasures modeled after the world but carried on in the name of Jesus. . . .

History reveals that times of suffering for the Church have also been times of looking upward. Tribulation has always sobered God's people and encouraged them to look for and yearn after the return of their Lord. Our present preoccupation with this world may be a warning of bitter days to come. God will wean us from the earth some way—the easy way if possible, the hard way if necessary. It is up to us.

Romans 8:18-19; Colossians 3:1-4; 1 Peter 1:6-9,13; 1 Peter 4:12-13; 2 Peter 3:12
Born after Midnight, 134.

1115. Second coming: lack of interest in; World: contentment with

Another reason for the absence of real yearning for Christ's return is that Christians are so comfortable in this world that they have little desire to leave it. For those leaders who set the pace of religion and determine its content and quality, Christianity has become of late remarkably lucrative. The streets of gold do not have too great an appeal for those who find it so easy to pile up gold and silver in the service of the Lord here on earth. We all want to reserve the hope of heaven as a kind of insurance against the day of death, but as long as we are healthy and comfortable, why change a familiar good for something about which we know very little actually? . . .

Again, in these times religion has become jolly good fun right here in this present world, and what's the hurry about heaven anyway? Christianity, contrary to what some had thought, is another and higher form of entertainment. Christ has done all the suffering. He has shed all the tears and carried all the crosses; we have but to enjoy the benefits of His heartbreak in the form of religious pleasures modeled after the world but carried on in the name of Jesus. So say the same people who claim to believe in Christ's second coming.

Matthew 6:19-21; Hebrews 11:13-16; Revelation 21:21
The Price of Neglect, 120, 121.

1116. Second coming: patient waiting for

When Jesus was on earth 2,000 years ago, He told His hearers that the "day of the Lord" was coming. He said no one except the Father in heaven knew the day or the hour. It is our understanding that God's patience and His time of grace will endure until the world's cup of iniquity overflows. According to the Scriptures, patience—the ability to wait—is one of the fruits of the Holy Spirit. The human, natural part of us does not like to wait for anything. But the great God Almighty, who has all of eternity to accomplish His purposes, can afford to wait. In our creature impatience we are prone to cry out, "Oh God, how long? How long?" And God replies, in effect, "Why are you in such a hurry? We have an eternity stretching before us. Why get excited and irritated?"

Matthew 24:36-39; Galatians 5:22-23; Revelation 6:1-8
Jesus Is Victor!, 94.

1117. Second coming: preparation for

"I have read that John Wesley was asked at one time how he would react if he knew that Christ was coming that very night. His instant reply was 'I don't think I would change any of my plans.'"

Whatever Happened to Worship?, 7.

1118. Second coming: preparation for; Christlikeness

The promise to us is this: what Jesus is, we will be. Not in a sense of deity, certainly, but in all the rights and privileges. In standing we will be equal to Jesus and like Him, for we shall see Him as He is....

Why do we not actually believe that? We do not half believe it! If we did, we would begin to act like it, in preparation for the great day. I cannot understand why we do not begin to act like children of God if we believe that we have a special higher right to be children of God. We have a right to be sick inside when we see children of heaven acting like the sons of earth, acting like children of the world and the flesh, living like Adam and yet saying they believe in a new birth by God's Spirit.

John 1:11-13; Titus 2:11-14; 1 John 3:2-3
Faith beyond Reason, 9, 10.

1119. Second coming: preparation for; Eternal perspective

It is amazing that segments in the Christian church that deny the possibility of the imminent return of the Lord Jesus accuse those who do believe in His soon coming of sitting around, twiddling their thumbs, looking at the sky and blankly hoping for the best!

Nothing could be further from the truth. We live in the interim between His two appearances, but we do not live in a vacuum. We have much to do and little time in which to get it done!

Stretch your mind and consider some very apparent facts of our day.

Who are the Christians leaving all to staff the missionary posts around the world? Who are the Christians staying at home and sacrificing in order to support the great evangelical thrust of the Christian gospel everywhere? Those who fervently believe that Christ is coming.

What kind of churches are busy praying and teaching and giving, preparing their young people for the ministry and for missionary work? Churches that are responding to Christ's appeal to "Occupy until I come!" (Luke 19:13, KJV).

Luke 19:13; 1 Corinthians 15:58; Titus 2:11-14
Who Put Jesus on the Cross?, 177, 178.

1120. Second coming: preparation for; Eternal perspective

Enoch reminds us that the quality and boldness of our faith will be the measure of our preparation for the return of Jesus Christ to this earth. . . .

All of us surely have moments when we wonder if we are seriously living in preparation for the coming of our Lord and for the eternity when we will be at home with Him. In our faith and trust, we know that God in His grace owns us and calls us His believing children, His saints. Yet, we do have times of discouragement concerning our shortcomings and failures.

The faith of Enoch continues to be an encouragement to walk with the King of heaven while we live down here. Then we know we will feel comfortable and at home when we get to heaven! . . .

I think we may draw the certain conclusion that when Enoch arrived in God's presence—raptured, translated, changed—he was completely at home, completely satisfied.

Genesis 5:24; Matthew 24:36-39; Hebrews 11:5
Jesus, Author of Our Faith, 21, 26.

1121. Second coming: preparation for; Second coming: contrary views about

The devil is smart enough not to waste his attacks on minor and non-vital aspects of Christian truth and teaching. . . .

But the believing Christian lives in joyful anticipation of the return of Jesus Christ and that is such an important segment of truth that the devil has always been geared up to fight it and ridicule it. One of his big successes is being able to get people to argue and get mad about the second coming—rather than looking and waiting for it.

Suppose a man has been overseas two or three years, away from his family. Suddenly a cable arrives for the family with the message, "My work completed here; I will be home today."

After some hours he arrives at the front door and finds the members of his family in turmoil. There had been a great argument as to whether he would arrive in the afternoon or evening. There had been arguments about what transportation he would be using. As a result, there were no little noses pushing against the window glass, no one looking to be able to catch the first glimpse of returning Daddy.

You may say, "That is only an illustration." But what is the situation in the various segments of the Christian community?

They are fighting with one another and glaring at each other. They are debating whether He is coming and how He is coming and they are busy using what they consider to be proof texts about the fall of Rome and the identification of the antichrist.

That is the work of the devil—to make Christian people argue about the details of His coming so they will forget the most important thing.

Matthew 24:36-39; 1 Timothy 6:13-16; Titus 2:11-14
Who Put Jesus on the Cross?, 185, 186.

1122. Secularism

One cannot long read the Scriptures sympathetically without noticing the radical disparity between the outlook of men of the Bible and that of modern men. We are today suffering from a secularized mentality. Where the sacred writers saw God, we see the laws of nature. Their world was fully populated; ours is all but empty. Their world was alive and personal; ours is impersonal and dead. God ruled their world; ours is ruled by the laws of nature and we are always once removed from the presence of God.

Genesis 17:1-5; Revelation 1:12-18; Revelation 19:6
The Knowledge of the Holy, 103.

1123. Seeking God; Knowledge of God: supreme value of

God being who He is must always be sought for Himself, never as a means toward something else. . . .

Whoever seeks God as a means toward desired ends will not find God. The mighty God, the maker of heaven and earth, will not be one of many treasures, not even the chief of all treasures. He will be all in all or He will be nothing. God will not be used. His mercy and grace are infinite and His patient understanding is beyond measure, but He will not aid men in their selfish striving after personal gain. He will not help men to attain ends which, when attained, usurp the place He by every right should hold in their interest and affection. . . .

God wills that we should love Him for Himself alone with no hidden reasons, trusting Him to be to us all our natures require. Our Lord said all this much better: "Seek ye first the kingdom of God, and his righteousness; and all these things shall be added unto you." (Matt. 6:33)

Jeremiah 29:13; Matthew 6:33; Colossians 1:18
Man: The Dwelling Place of God, 56, 57, 59.

1124. Seeking God; Knowledge of God: supreme value of

... so many professing Christians just want to get things from God. Anyone can write a book now that will sell—just give it a title like, *Seventeen Ways to Get Things from God!* You will have immediate sales. Or, write a book called, *Fourteen Ways to Have Peace of Mind*—and away they go by the ton. Many people seem to be interested in knowing God for what they can get out of Him.

They do not seem to know that God wants to give Himself. He wants to impart Himself with His gifts. Any gift that He would give us would be incomplete if it were separate from the knowledge of God Himself. ...

I feel that we must repudiate this great, modern wave of seeking God for His benefits. The sovereign God wants to be loved for Himself and honored for Himself, but that is only part of what He wants. The other part is that He wants us to know that when we have Him, we have everything—we have all the rest. Jesus made that plain when He said, "But seek first his kingdom and his righteousness, and all these things will be given to you as well" (Matthew 6:33).

Matthew 6:33; Mark 10:29-30
I Talk Back to the Devil, 24, 25.

1125. Self; Repentance

Self is the opaque veil that hides the face of God from us. It can be removed only in spiritual experience, never by mere instruction. We may as well try to instruct leprosy out of our system. There must be a work of God in destruction before we are free. We must invite the cross to do its deadly work within us. We must bring our self-sins to the cross for judgement.

Romans 6:4-7; Galatians 2:20; Galatians 5:24
The Pursuit of God, 43.

1126. Self-denial; Discipleship; Cross: personal

Where we have failed is in the practical application of the teaching concerning the crucified life. Too many have been content to be armchair Christians, satisfied with the theology of the cross. Plainly Christ never intended that we should rest in a mere theory of self-denial. His teaching identified

His disciples with Himself so intimately that they would have had to be extremely dull not to have understood that they were expected to experience very much the same pain and loss as He Himself did.

Luke 9:23-25; Galatians 2:20; Philippians 3:10
Man: The Dwelling Place of God, 72, 73.

1127. Self-image; Individual importance

I believe many Christians are tempted to downgrade themselves too much. I am not arguing against true humility and my word to you is this: Think as little of yourself as you want to, but always remember that our Lord Jesus Christ thought very highly of you—enough to give Himself for you in death and sacrifice.

If the devil does come to you and whispers that you are no good, don't argue with him. In fact, you may as well admit it, but then remind the devil: "Regardless of what you say about me, I must tell you how the Lord feels about me. He tells me that I am so valuable to Him that He gave Himself for me on the cross!"

So, the value is set by the price paid—and, in our case, the price paid was our Lord Himself!

Romans 5:8; Titus 2:11-14; 1 John 4:19
Who Put Jesus on the Cross?, 179, 180.

1128. Self-interest; Pride: human

We are willing to join heartily in singing, "To God Be the Glory," but we are strangely ingenius in figuring out ways and means by which we keep some of the glory for ourselves. In this matter of perpetually seeking our own interests, we can only say that people who want to live for God often arrange to do very subtly what the worldly souls do crudely and openly....

Yes, we have it among professing Christians—this strange ingenuity to seek our own interest under the guise of seeking the interests of God. I am not afraid to say what I fear—that there are thousands of people who are using the deeper life and Bible prophecy, foreign missions and physical healing for no other purpose than to promote their own private interests secretly. They continue to let their apparent interest in these things to serve as a screen so that they don't have to take a look at how ugly they are on the inside.

Isaiah 42:8; Philippians 3:10;
1 Timothy 1:15-16
I Talk Back to the Devil, 83.

1129. Self-knowledge

It remains for us to know ourselves as accurately as possible. For this reason I offer some rules for self-discovery; and if the results are not all we could desire they may be at least better than none at all. We may be known by the following:

1. *What we want most.* We have but to get quiet, recollect our thoughts, wait for the mild excitement within us to subside, and then listen closely for the faint cry of desire. Ask your heart, What would you rather have than anything else in the world? Reject the conventional answer. Insist on the true one, and when you have heard it you will know the kind of person you are.

2. *What we think about most.* The necessities of life compel us to think about many things, but the true test is what we think about voluntarily. . . .

3. *How we use our money.* . . .

4. *What we do with our leisure time.* A large share of our time is already spoken for by the exigencies of civilized living, but we do have some free time. What we do with it is vital. Most people waste it staring at the television, listening to the radio, reading the cheap output of the press or engaging in idle chatter. What I do with mine reveals the kind of man I am.

5. *The company we enjoy.* . . .

6. *Whom and what we admire.* I have long suspected that the great majority of evangelical Christians, while kept somewhat in line by the pressure of group opinion, nevertheless have a boundless, if perforce secret, admiration for the world. We can learn the true state of our minds by examining our unexpressed admirations. . . .

7. *What we laugh at.* . . .

These are a few tests. The wise Christian will find others.

Psalm 90:12; Proverbs 23:7; Ephesians 5:15-18; Philippians 4:8; Colossians 3:1-4; 1 Timothy 6:17-19
That Incredible Christian, 102, 103.

1130. Self-knowledge; Discipline: personal

The philosopher Socrates said, "An unexamined life is not worth living." If a common philosopher could think that, how much more we Christians ought to listen to the Holy Spirit when He says, "Examine yourself." An unexamined Christian lies like an unattended garden. Let your garden go unattended for a few months, and you will not have roses and tomatoes but weeds. An unexamined Christian life is like an unkempt house. Lock your house up as tight as you will and leave it long enough, and when you come back you will not believe the dirt that got in from somewhere. An unexamined Christian is like an untaught child. A child that is not taught will be a little savage. It takes examination, teaching, instruction, discipline, caring, tending, weeding and cultivating to keep the life right.

1 Corinthians 10:11-12; 1 Corinthians 11:23-29; 2 Corinthians 13:5; Galatians 6:4
Rut, Rot or Revival: The Condition of the Church, 43.

1131. Self-knowledge; Pride: human

Hardly anything else reveals so well the fear and uncertainty among men as the length to which they will go to hide their true selves from each other and even from their own eyes. . . .

Self-knowledge is so critically important to us in our pursuit of God and His righteousness that we lie under heavy obligation to do immediately whatever is necessary to remove the disguise and permit our real selves to be known. It is one of the supreme tragedies in religion that so many of us think so highly of ourselves when the evidence is all on the other side; and our self-admiration effectively blocks out any possible effort to discover a remedy for our condition. Only the man who knows he is sick will go to a physician.

Psalm 139:23-24; Romans 12:3-8; 1 Corinthians 11:31-32
That Incredible Christian, 101.

1132. Self-righteousness; Judgmentalism; Complacency

Self-righteousness is terrible among God's people. If we feel that we are what we ought to be, then we will remain what we are. We will not look for any change or improvement in our lives. This will quite naturally lead us to judge everyone by what we are. This is the judgment of which we must be careful. To judge others by ourselves is to create havoc in the local assembly.

Self-righteousness also leads to complacency. Complacency is a great sin. . . . Some have the attitude, "Lord, I'm satisfied with my spiritual condition. I hope one of these days You will come, I will be taken up to meet You in the air and I will rule over five cities." These people cannot rule over their own houses and families, but they expect to rule over five cities. They pray spottily and sparsely, rarely attending prayer meeting, but they read their Bibles and expect to go zooming off into the blue yonder and join the Lord in the triumph of the victorious saints.

Luke 19:19; Philippians 3:12-14; 1 Timothy 3:5
Rut, Rot or Revival: The Condition of the Church, 10, 11.

1133. Self-sufficiency; Judgment of God: future; Pride: spiritual

A Muslim falls down on the ground five times a day in reverence to God in heaven—and a lot of people laugh at him. The Hindu measures himself painfully on the way to the Ganges River to bathe himself—and a lot of people comment, "How foolish can you get?"

But I would rather be a Muslim or a Hindu or a primitive tribesman living in a hut in Africa, kneeling before bones and feathers and mumbling some kind of homemade prayer, than to come into judgment as a self-sufficient American businessman who ruled God out of his life and out of his business and out of his home.

Many an unthinking, secular-minded American would reply: "I'm willing to take my chances!"

What foolish talk from a mortal man!

Men do not have the luxury of taking their chances—either they are saved or they are lost. Surely this is the great curse that lies upon mankind today—men are so wrapped up in their own godless world that they refuse the Light that shines, the Voice that speaks, and the Presence that pervades. . . .

The Spirit of God tries to speak to this modern man of the great curse that lies upon his heart and life—he has become so absorbed with money and bank accounts and profit and loss and markets and loans and interest that any thought of God and salvation and eternity has been crowded out. There are dollar signs before his eyes and he would rather close another deal and make a neat profit than to make his way into the kingdom of God.

Psalm 14:1-3; Mark 8:36-37; John 1:10; John 3:19-21
Who Put Jesus on the Cross?, 131, 132.

1134. Self-sufficiency; Pride: human; Dependence on God

Only God is self-sufficient. When men boast of being self-sufficient, they are indulging a fiction that can be proven fictitious just by taking a quick look around. . . .

The human body cannot live on itself. To live it must have constant help from the outside. Though filled with pride and overflowing with self-assurance, men and women must humble themselves to receive aid from the lower creation. Every monarch must trust the common cow for food. Every strutting lord of the manor must beg his dinner from the barnyard hen. The cold prima donna manages to stay alive only by the grace of pigs and fish. The genius must look to bees, shrubs, seeds and berries. From these things come the energy without which all people would die, the great as well as the lowly. . . .

The tragic history of the world is, at the bottom line, the record of sinning men trying to live on their own resources and never succeeding, because they are ignoring the most simple law of creation—*no living thing is self-sufficient.* God made us dependent upon Him. Either we recognize our need of Him, or we adopt the false philosophy of independence and go on our stubborn way to die at last and everlastingly.

Isaiah 45:22; Habakkuk 2:4; John 6:35
This World: Playground or Battleground?, 107, 108, 109.

1135. Separation; World: love not

Whether or not the Christian should separate himself from the world is not open to debate. The question has been settled for him by the Sacred Scriptures, an authority from which there can be no appeal.

The New Testament is very plain: "They are not of the world," said our Lord, "even as I am not of the world." James wrote, "Ye adulterers and adulteresses, know ye not that the friendship of the world is enmity with God? Whosoever therefore will be a friend of the world is the enemy of God." John said, "Love not the world, neither the things that are in the world. If any man love the world, the love of the Father is not in him."

Such teaching as this would appear to be plain enough, and there should be no doubt about what is intended. But we must never underestimate the ability of the human mind to get itself lost on a paved highway in broad daylight.

John 17:14-16; James 4:3-4; 1 John 2:15-17
The Next Chapter after the Last, 34.

1136. Servanthood; Humility; Celebrities

In this day when shimmering personalities carry on the Lord's work after the methods of the entertainment world, it is refreshing to associate for a moment even in the pages of a book with a sincere and humble man who keeps his own personality out of sight and places the emphasis upon the inner working of God. It is our belief that the evangelical movement will continue to drift farther and farther from the New Testament position unless its leadership passes from the modern religious star to the self-effacing saint who asks for no praise and seeks no place, happy only when the glory is attributed to God and himself forgotten.

Philippians 1:12-18; Philippians 2:19-22; 3 John 9
Of God and Men, 16.

1137. Servanthood; Suffering; Cross: personal

When God needs a person for His service—a good person, an effective person, a humble person—why does He most often turn to a person in deep trouble? Why does He seek out a person deep in the crucible of suffering, a person who is not the jovial, "happy-happy" kind? I can only say that this is the way of God with His human creation....

Ezekiel did not come out of pleasant and favorable circumstances. The light had gone out in his heart. He probably thought that God takes a long time to work out His will.

Does not this same view surface in much of our Christian fellowship? We do not want to take the time to plow and to cultivate. We want the fruit and the harvest right away! We do not want to be engaged in any spiritual battle that takes us into the long night. We want the morning light right now! We do not want to go through the processes of planning and preparation and labor pains. We want the baby this instant!

We do not want the cross. We are more interested in the crown.

The condition is not peculiar to our century. Thomas à Kempis wrote long ago, "The Lord has many lovers of His crown but few lovers of His cross."

Ezekiel 1:1-5; Philippians 2:9-11; Hebrews 2:9
Men Who Met God, 114, 115.

1138. Servanthood; Unsung heroes; Celebrities

We have but to become acquainted with, or even listen to, the big names of our times to discover how wretchedly inferior most of them are. Many appear to have arrived at their present eminence by pull, brass, nerve, gall and lucky accident. We turn away from them sick to our stomach and wonder for a discouraged moment if this is the best the human race can produce. But we gain our self-possession again by the simple expedient of recalling some of the plain men we know, who live unheralded and unsung, and who are made of stuff infinitely finer than the hoarse-voiced braggarts who occupy too many of the highest offices in the land. . . .

. . . the church also suffers from this evil notion. Christians have fallen into the habit of accepting the noisiest and most notorious among them as the best and the greatest. They too have learned to equate popularity with excellence, and in open defiance of the Sermon on the Mount they have given their approval not to the meek but to the self-assertive; not to the mourner but to the self-assured; not to the pure in heart who see God but to the publicity hunter who seeks headlines.

Matthew 5:3-12; Matthew 6:1-5; Colossians 1:24; 1 Thessalonians 2:8-9
Man: The Dwelling Place of God, 96, 97.

1139. Service: insufficiency for

Every Christian should be looking to the Lord for something to do in the kingdom of God, and everyone ought to be asking God to honor him with a job too big for him. . . .

I think it may be safely said that God is still looking for men who know their own insufficiencies so well that He can perform the miraculous through them. . . .

This is a principle so true of us all in our human experiences. Whenever I think I can stand up and say, "I am now strong enough, sufficient enough—I can do it!" then God fades out, and there comes only grief and woe and sterility and fruitlessness and finally, eclipse.

Exodus 3:11; 1 Corinthians 10:11-12; 1 Corinthians 15:9-10; 2 Corinthians 3:5-6; 2 Corinthians 4:5-7
The Tozer Pulpit, Volume 1, Book 1, 66, 67.

1140. Service: motives for; Judgment seat of Christ

Any serious-minded Christian may at some time find himself wondering whether the service he is giving to God is the best it could be. He may even have times of doubting, and fear that his toil is fruitless and his life empty. . . .

The church has marked out certain work and approved it as service acceptable to God, and for the most part the church has been right. But it should be kept in mind that it is not the kind or quantity of work that makes it true service—it is the *quality*.

Before the judgment seat of Christ, very little will be heard of numbers or size; moral quality is about all that will matter then....

In Christian service motive is everything, for it is motive that gives to every moral act its final quality.

1 Corinthians 4:3-5; 1 Corinthians 15:58; Colossians 3:16-1823
The Next Chapter after the Last, 69, 70.

1141. Service: motives for; Missions: motives for

Christians, and especially very active ones, should take time out frequently to search their souls to be sure of their motives. Many a solo is sung to show off; many a sermon is preached as an exhibition of talent; many a church is founded as a slap at some other church. Even missionary activity may become competitive, and soul winning may degenerate into a sort of brush-salesman project to satisfy the flesh. Do not forget, the Pharisees were great missionaries and would compass sea and land to make a convert.

Psalm 139:23-24; Matthew 23:15; 1 Corinthians 4:3-5; Colossians 3:16-18,23
The Root of the Righteous, 90, 91.

1142. Service: possibilities for

There is no limit to what God can do through us if we are His yielded and purified people, worshiping and showing forth His glory and His faithfulness.

Romans 6:19; Ephesians 2:8-10; 1 Peter 1:22; 1 John 3:2-3
Whatever Happened to Worship?, 101.

1143. Service: privilege of; Call of God

I hope our young people never forget the true estimate of honors and of values. Young man, the president of the United States could call you to Washington, commission you as an ambassador of your country and send you off on important missions to other nations—but how much greater for you to be owned and commissioned and empowered and sent from God on His business and for His glory.

No king and no president has authority and power enough to bestow that greatest of all honors—to be owned and honored and sent from God!

John 1:6-7; 2 Corinthians 5:19-21; 1 Timothy 1:12-15
Christ the Eternal Son, 129.

1144. Service: privilege of; God: His self-sufficiency; Missions: motives for

I do not think I could ever worship a God who was suddenly caught unaware of circumstances in His world around me. I do not think that I could bow my knees before a God that I had to apologize for.

I could never offer myself to a God that needed me, brethren. If He needed me, I could not respect Him, and if I could not respect Him, I could not worship Him.

I could never get down and say: "Father, I know that things are going tough for You these days. I know that modernism is making it tough for the saints and I know that communism is a serious threat to the kingdom. God, I know You really need my help, so I offer myself to You."

Some of our missionary appeals are getting close to that same error: that we should engage in missionary work because God needs us so badly.

The fact is that God is riding above this world and the clouds are the dust of His feet and if you do not follow Him, you will lose all and God will lose nothing. He will still be glorified in His saints and admired of all those who fear Him. To bring ourselves into a place where God will be eternally pleased with us should be the first responsible act of every man!

Psalm 104:3-4; Nahum 1:3; Matthew 16:24-26
Christ the Eternal Son, 46.

1145. Service: sacrificial; Giving; Judgment seat of Christ

Before the judgment seat of Christ my service will be judged not by how much I have done but by how much I could have done. In God's sight my giving is measured not by how much I have given but by how much I could have given and how much I had left after I made my gift. The needs of the world and my total ability to minister to those needs decide the worth of my service.

Not by its size is my gift judged, but by how much of me there is in it. No man gives at all until he has given all. No man gives anything acceptable to God until he has first given himself in love and sacrifice. . . .

In the work of the church the amount one man must do to accomplish a given task is determined by how much or how little the rest of the company is willing to do. It is a rare church whose members all put their shoulder to the wheel. The typical church is composed of the few whose shoulders are bruised by their faithful labors and the many who are unwilling to raise a blister in the service of God and their fellow men. There may be a bit of wry humor in all this, but it is quite certain that there will be no laughter when each of us gives account to God of the deeds done in the body.

Matthew 10:42; Mark 12:42-44;
2 Corinthians 5:10; 2 Corinthians 8:2-5
That Incredible Christian, 105.

1146. Service: worship first

Another example of our wrong thinking about God is the attitude of so many that God is now a charity case. He is a kind of frustrated foreman who cannot find enough help. He stands at the wayside asking how many will come to His rescue and begin to do His work.

Oh, if we would only remember who He is! God has never actually needed any of us—not one. But we pretend that He does and we make it a big thing when someone agrees "to work for the Lord."

We all should be willing to work for the Lord, but it is a matter of grace on God's part. I am of the opinion that we should not be concerned about working for God until we have learned the meaning and the delight of worshiping Him.

A worshiper can work with eternal quality in his work. But a worker who does not worship is only piling up wood, hay and stubble for the time when God sets the world on fire. . . .

God is trying to call us back to that for which He created us—to worship Him and to enjoy Him forever!

It is then, out of our deep worship, that we do His work.

1 Corinthians 3:12-14; 1 Corinthians 10:31;
Revelation 4:8-11
Whatever Happened to Worship?, 11, 12.

1147. Service: worship first

Recall what happened when Jesus said to the disciples, "Go into all the world and preach the good news to all creation" (Mark 16:15).

Peter jumped up right away, grabbed his hat and would have been on his way, but Jesus stopped him, and said, "Not yet, Peter! Don't go like that. Tarry until you are endued with power from on high, and then go!"

I believe that our Lord wants us to learn more of Him in worship before we become busy for Him. He wants us to have a gift of the Spirit, an inner experience of the heart, as our first service, and out of that will grow the profound and deep and divine activities which are necessary.

Mark 16:15; Acts 1:4
I Talk Back to the Devil, 139.

1148. Sharing; Evangelism: concern for lost

Spiritual experiences must be shared. It is not possible for very long to enjoy them alone. The very attempt to do so will destroy them.

The reason for this is obvious. The nearer our souls draw to God the larger our love will grow, and the greater our love the more unselfish we shall become and the greater our care for the souls of others. Hence increased spiritual experience, so far as it is genuine, brings with it a strong desire that others may know the same grace that we ourselves enjoy. This leads quite naturally to an increased effort to lead others to a closer and more satisfying fellowship with God....

The impulse to share, to impart, normally accompanies any true encounter with God and spiritual things. The woman at the well, after her soul-inspiring meeting with Jesus, left her waterpots, hurried into the city and tried to persuade her friends to come out and meet Him. "Come, see a man," she said, "which told me all things that ever I did: is not this the Christ?" Her spiritual excitement could not be contained within her own heart. She had to tell someone.

John 4:28-29; Acts 17:26; 1 Corinthians 12:20
The Set of the Sail, 50, 51.

1149. Silence

The Bible and Christian biography make a great deal of silence, but we of today make of it exactly nothing....

At the risk of being written off as an extremist or a borderline fanatic we offer it as our mature opinion that more spiritual progress can be made in one short moment of speechless silence in the awesome presence of God than in years of mere study. While our mental powers are in command there is always the veil of nature between us and the face of God. It is only when our vaunted wisdom has been met and defeated in a breathless encounter with Omniscience that we are permitted really to know, when prostrate and wordless the soul receives divine knowledge like a flash of light on a sensitized plate. The exposure may be brief, but the results are permanent.

Psalm 4:4; Psalm 62:1,5
The Root of the Righteous, 145, 146.

1150. Silence; Church: services

The Bible and Christian biography emphasize silence, but today we use silence in exactly nothing. The average service in gospel circles these days is kept alive by noise. By making a religious din we assure our faltering hearts that everything is well. Conversely, we suspect silence and regard it as proof that the meeting is "dead." Even the most devout seem to think they must storm heaven with loud outcries and mighty bellowing or their prayers are of no avail.

This World: Playground or Battleground?, 41.

1151. Silence; Prayer: fellowship with God

Some of the most wonderful meetings in the world are where God is there in such awful power people are afraid to speak. Some of the most wonderful meetings I've ever been in have been meetings where nobody would even whisper. The mighty power of God was there and nobody dared open his mouth. When I am praying the most eloquently, I am getting the least accomplished in my prayer life. But when I stop getting eloquent and give God less theology and shut up and just gaze upward and wait for God to speak to my heart He speaks with such power that I have to grab a pencil and a notebook and take notes on what God is saying to my heart.

Psalm 4:4; Psalm 46:10; Psalm 77:6
Success and the Christian, 46, 47.

1152. Silence; Solitude

Very few of us know the secret of bathing our souls in silence. It was a secret our Lord Jesus Christ knew very well. There were times when He had to send the multitudes away so He could retire alone into the silence of the mountainside. There He would turn the God-ward side of His soul toward heaven and for a long time expose Himself to the face of His Father in heaven. . . .

My eyes and ears and spirit are aware of the immaturities in the so-called evangelicalism of our time. The more noise we make, the more we advertise, the more bells we jingle, the happier we seem to be. All of the signs of immaturity are among us.

We are seeing a general abhorrence of being alone, of being silent before the Lord. We shrink from allowing our souls to be bathed in the healing silences.

Matthew 14:22-33; Mark 6:46; Luke 6:12; Luke 9:28; John 6:15
Men Who Met God, 103, 104.

1153. Silence; Solitude; Meditation; Self-knowledge

Then, too, Moses had a most unusual but highly effective postgraduate course. God took him out of the activity and the noise of Egypt and placed him in the silence of the open spaces. He kept the flock of Jethro, his father-in-law. Tending the sheep, he learned lessons of meditation and observation that he could only have learned in the silence.

Probably more important than anything else, Moses learned to know himself. That knowledge was a part of God's preparation of the man for his future tasks. We, today, know everything but ourselves. We never really come to know ourselves because we cannot get quiet enough.

Exodus 3:1; Exodus 33:11
Men Who Met God, 70.

1154. Silent Christians

We have all heard at some time about persons who were supposed to be "secret" or "silent" Christians.

I have heard men say we will be surprised when we get to heaven and find people there who were secret Christians but who never talked about it.

It is my opinion, brethren, that the silent Christian has something wrong with him. . . .

Someone describing the Quakers said they don't talk about their religion—they live it. Oh, how foolish can we get? The things that are closest to our hearts are the things we talk about, and if God is close to your heart, you will talk about Him! . . .

You say, "Well, I worship God in my heart."

I wonder if you do. I wonder if you are simply just excusing the fact that you haven't generated enough spiritual heat to get your mouth open!

Romans 1:14-16; 1 Corinthians 9:16
The Tozer Pulpit, Volume 1, Book 1, 30, 31, 32.

1155. Simplicity

We have too many gods. We have too many irons in the fire. And we have too much theology that we don't understand. We have too much religion and too much "churchianity" and too much institutionalism and too much, too much. The result is, God isn't in there by Himself. He says, "If I'm not in your heart by Myself, I won't work." When Jesus Christ has everything cleansed from the temple and dwells there alone, He will work.

Exodus 20:3; Jeremiah 35:15;
Matthew 21:12-13
Success and the Christian, 23.

1156. Simplicity; Earthly things

Start by simplifying your life. Practically everyone has too much, knows too much, sees too much, hears too much, goes to too many places and comes back from too many places. We must simplify our lives or we are going to lose terribly. . . .

Socrates was in Athens and somebody took him around Athens' 10-cent stores. After half a day of paddling around in his old bare feet, they let him sit down and rest. Then they said, "Socrates, what do you think of it?"

He replied, "I never knew before how many things there are in Athens that I do not want."

Philippians 4:11-12; 1 Timothy 6:6-8;
Hebrews 13:5
Success and the Christian, 46, 47.

1157. Simplicity; Jesus Christ: intimacy with

If you will narrow your interests, God will enlarge your heart. "Jesus only" seems to the unconverted man to be the motto of death, but a great company of happy men and women can testify that it became to them a way into a world infinitely wider and richer than anything they had ever known before. Christ is the essence of all wisdom, beauty and virtue. To know Him in growing intimacy is to increase in appreciation of all things good and beautiful. The mansions of the heart will become larger when their doors are thrown open to Christ and closed against the world and sin. Try it.

John 17:3; Philippians 3:10; Hebrews 12:1-2;
2 Peter 1:3
The Size of the Soul, 25.

1158. Sin: consequences of

Paul was speaking about the presence of God in the universe—a Presence that becomes the living, vibrant voice of God causing the human heart to reach out after Him. Alas! Man has not known where to reach because of sin. Sin has blinded his eyes, dulled his hearing and made his heart unresponsive.

Sin has made man like a bird without a tongue. It has within itself the instinct and the desire to sing, but not the ability. The poet Keats expressed beautifully, even brilliantly, the fantasy of the nightingale that had lost its tongue. Not being able to express the deep instinct to sing, the bird died of an overpowering suffocation within.

Matthew 13:15; Acts 17:27-28;
Acts 28:25-27; 2 Corinthians 4:4
Jesus, Our Man in Glory, 40, 41.

1159. Sin: consequences of

Sin, I repeat, in addition to anything else it may be, is always an act of wrong judgment. To commit a sin a man must for the moment believe that things are different from what they really are; he must confound values; he must see the moral universe out of focus; he must accept a lie as truth and see truth as a lie; he must ignore the signs on the highway and drive with his eyes shut; he must act as if he had no soul and was not accountable for his moral choices.

Sin is never a thing to be proud of. No act is wise that ignores remote consequences, and sin always does.

Psalm 14:1-3; Psalm 36:1-9; Jeremiah 4:22;
Romans 3:10-18
Man: The Dwelling Place of God, 47.

1160. Sin: consequences of

In the western United States there grows a plant called the locoweed. It looks like a fern and bears the horrendous botanical name of *astragalus mollissimus*.

This plant is poisonous to cattle and when eaten by a steer has the effect of shorting his equilibrium, destroying his muscular coordination and throwing his eyes out of focus so that he may shy away from the smallest object or misjudge the size of a large object and walk right into the side of a cliff.

I am reliably informed; but since the locoweed is quite obviously outside my field of interest, or at least my sphere of responsibility, I would just skip the whole thing except that it points straight to another and more serious matter which is certainly of critical interest to me. I refer to sin and its effect upon people....

While the life of the ordinary person is not so dramatic and violent as those of the persons cited here, his conduct is nevertheless fully as contradictory. He blows hot and cold from day to day; he is kind and cruel, chaste and lustful, honest and deceitful, generous and covetous; he longs to be good and chooses to be evil, yearns to know God and turns his back upon Him, hopes for heaven and heads toward hell. He is morally loco.

Sin is a poisonous weed that throws the whole nature out of order. The inner life disintegrates; the flesh lusts after forbidden pleasures; the moral judgment is destroyed so that often good appears evil and evil good; time is chosen over eternity, earth over heaven and death over life.

Isaiah 1:5-6; Romans 7:15-25; Galatians 5:17
The Warfare of the Spirit, 49, 50, 51.

1161. Sin: consequences of; Man: rebellion against God

You see, in our time we have over-emphasized the psychology of the sinner's condition. We spend much time describing the woe of the sinner, the grief of the sinner and the great burden he carries. He does have all of these, but we have over-emphasized them until we forget the principal fact—that the sinner is actually a rebel against properly-constituted authority! ...

By way of illustration, suppose a man escapes from prison. Certainly he will have grief. He is going to be in pain after bumping logs and stones and fences as he crawls and hides away in the dark. He is going to be hungry and cold and weary. His beard will grow long and he will be tired and cramped and cold—all of these will happen, but they are incidental to the fact that he is a fugitive from justice and a rebel against law.

So it is with sinners. Certainly they are heartbroken and they carry a heavy load. Certainly they labor and are heavy-laden. The Bible takes full account of these things; but they are incidental to the fact that the reason the sinner is what he is, is because he has rebelled against the laws of God and he is a fugitive from divine judgment.

Psalm 107:10-11; Isaiah 53:6; Romans 1:18,20-25; 1 John 3:4
I Call It Heresy!, 9, 10.

1162. Sin: folly of; World: contempt for Christians

The world has divided men into two classes, the stupid good people and the clever wicked ones. ...

In the Holy Scriptures things are quite the opposite. There righteousness is always associated with wisdom and evil with folly. Whatever other factors may be present in an act of wrongdoing, folly is one that is never absent. To do a wrong act a man must for the moment think wrong; he must exercise bad judgment. ...

The notion that the careless sinner is the smart fellow and the serious-minded Christian, though well-intentioned, is a stupid dolt altogether out of touch with life will not stand up under scrutiny. Sin is basically an act of moral folly, and the greater the folly the greater the fool.

Psalm 14:1-3; Proverbs 1:7; Proverbs 24:24; Isaiah 5:20-23; Romans 1:22
Man: The Dwelling Place of God, 46, 48.

1163. Sin: folly of; Worldliness

Of all the calamities that have been visited upon the world, the surrender of the human spirit to this present world and its ways is the worst—without doubt! . . .

That we who were made to communicate with angels and archangels and seraphim and with the God who made them all—that we should settle down here as a wild eagle of the air come down to scratch in the barnyard with the common hens— this I say is the worst of anything that has ever come to the world!

Colossians 3:1-4; 1 John 2:15-17
Renewed Day by Day, Volume 1, Jan. 11.

1164. Sin: folly of; Youth

It is time the young people of this generation learned that there is nothing smart about wrongdoing and nothing stupid about righteousness. We must stop negotiating with evil. We Christians must stop apologizing for our moral position and start making our voices heard, exposing sin for the enemy of the human race which it surely is, and setting forth righteousness and true holiness as the only worthy pursuits for moral beings.

Proverbs 21:21; Ecclesiastes 12:1-8; Matthew 5:6; Ephesians 4:22-24
Man: The Dwelling Place of God, 48.

1165. Sin: hatred of

When Jesus was on earth, He was not the passive, colorless, spineless person He is sometimes made out to be in paintings and literature. He was a strong man, a man of iron will. He was able to love with an intensity of love that burned Him up. He was able to hate with the strongest degree of hatred against everything that was wrong and evil and selfish and sinful.

Invariably someone will object when I make a statement like that. "I cannot believe such things about Jesus. I always thought it was a sin to hate!"

Study long and well the record and the teachings of Jesus while He was on earth. In them lies the answer. It is a sin for the children of God not to hate what ought to be hated. Our Lord Jesus loved righteousness, but He hated iniquity. I think we can say He hated sin and wrong and evil perfectly!

Amos 5:15; Matthew 21:12-13;
John 2:14-17; Romans 12:9-13
Jesus, Our Man in Glory, 64.

1166. Sin: hatred of; Conviction; Zeal; Tolerance/Intolerance

Jesus hated the devil and He hated those evil spirits that He challenged and drove out. We present-day Christians have been misled and brain-washed, at least in a general way, by a generation of soft, pussycat preachers. They would have us believe that to be good Christians we must be able to purr softly and accept everything that comes along with Christian tolerance and understanding. Such ministers never mention words like *zeal* and *conviction* and *commitment*. They avoid phrases like "standing for the truth."

I am convinced that a committed Christian will show a zealous concern for the cause of Christ. He or she will live daily with a set of spiritual convictions taken from the Bible. He or she will be one of the toughest to move—along with a God-given humility—in his or her stand for Christ. Why, then, have Christian ministers so largely departed from exhortations to love righteousness with a great, overwhelming love, and to hate iniquity with a deep, compelling revulsion?

John 2:14-17; Acts 20:20, 24, 27;
1 Thessalonians 5:21-22
Jesus, Our Man in Glory, 65, 66.

1167. Sin: leads to death

God terminates sin in death! I lived in Chicago when the notorious killer gangster, John Dillinger, was being hunted. The police printed pictures of Dillinger with warnings about his violence with guns. Always he was shown with a cynical, sarcastic smile on his face. But the final picture indicated that he had stopped sinning. He was lying on his back, toes up. He was covered with a sheet. Dillinger was dead.

Sin ends at death. When a person dies, he or she will sin no more. That is God's way of ending sin. He lets death terminate it.

Romans 5:12; Romans 6:23; James 1:13-15
Jesus, Our Man in Glory, 120.

1168. Sin: never private; Sin: consequences of

No sin is private. It may be secret but it is not private. . . .

Coming still closer, we Christians should know that our unchristian conduct cannot be kept in our own back yard. The evil birds of sin fly far and influence many to their everlasting loss. The sin committed in the privacy of the home will have its effect in the assembly of the saints. The minister, the deacon, the teacher who yields to temptation in secret becomes a carrier of moral disease whether he knows it or not. The church will be worse because one member sins. The polluted stream flows out and on, growing wider and darker as it affects more and more persons day after day and year after year.

1 Corinthians 5:6-7; James 3:1; 1 John 1:6-9
The Size of the Soul, 74, 77.

1169. Sin: personal responsibility for; Repentance

The day when it is once more understood that God will not be responsible for our sin and unbelief will be a glad one for the Church of Christ. The realization that we are personally responsible for our individual sins may be a shock to our hearts, but it will clear the air and remove the uncertainty. Returning sinners waste their time begging God to perform the very acts He has sternly commanded them to do. He will not argue with them; He will simply leave them to their disappointment. Unbelief is a great sin; or more accurately stated, *it is an evidence of sins unconfessed.* Repent and believe is the order. Faith will follow repentance, and salvation will be the outcome.

Mark 1:15; Luke 24:47; Acts 2:37-38; Acts 3:19
Paths to Power, 20, 21.

1170. Sin: prevalence of; America: sinfulness

I have only the voice and opinion of one man—but I do fear for the future of our great nations on this continent where our laws are taking little account of sin and authorities are letting crime on crime pile up with soft sentiment taking over in so many areas.

There are members of organized crime and killers who boast about their many crimes, and authorities arrest one of the offenders and tell him: "You are a bad boy—you did not pay your income tax!" Meanwhile, the eloquent voice of shed blood cries out to God Almighty! . . .

I have little fear that any nation or combination of nations could bring down the United States and Canada by military action from without. But this I do fear—we sin and sin and do nothing about it. There is so little sense of the need of repentance—so little burden for the will of God to be wrought in our national life. I fear that the voice of blood will become so eloquent that God Almighty will have no choice but to speak the word that will bring us down.

Genesis 4:10; 2 Chronicles 7:14;
Isaiah 5:20-23
Echoes from Eden, 43, 44.

1171. Sin: refined; Salvation: transformation

We Christians must look sharp that our Christianity does not simply refine our sins without removing them. . . .

The gossip and troublemaker sometimes at conversion turns into a "spiritual counselor," but often a closer look will reveal the same restless, inquisitive spirit at work that made her a nuisance before her conversion. The whole thing has been refined and given a religious appearance, but actually nothing radical has happened. She is still running the same stand, only on the other side of the street. There has been a certain refinement of the sin, but definitely not a removal of it. This is Satan's most successful way of getting into the church to cause weakness, backsliding and division.

2 Corinthians 12:20-21; Ephesians 4:20-32;
Colossians 3:5-11; 1 Peter 2:1-2
Born after Midnight, 80, 82.

1172. Sin: seared conscience; Judgment of God: future; Man: sinfulness of

Noah decided to find out from the bird if there was dry ground below. He wanted to know if the waters of judgment had abated. He opened the window and pushed the raven out. . . .

The evidence of death and judgment should have been a repulsive and horrible sight, but the raven was built for it. Something in his dark heart loved it, because he lived on it. He immediately sailed down and lighted on a near and likely corpse. He began to tear hunks of half-rotten flesh with his strong claws and beak. He tore away and ate until he was stuffed and sleepy with overeating. Then, fastening his claws down into the floating thing, happy and restful, he went to sleep croaking a goodnight word. The happiness that he had found was what his heart wanted. Corruption and desolation, silt and dirt, rotten flesh and dead things—all fitted his disposition and his temperament. He fed on the floating dead. . . .

The great judgment of God is upon mankind, all the stock of mankind—red, yellow, black, white, educated and uneducated, cultured and uncultured, cave men and learned men around the world. Yet it does not seem to bother people because man has in him that thing we call sin. It does not bother him at all, because he is just as the raven was—at home in the desolation. His dark heart had an affinity for judgment and desolation. Man also finds himself at home in a world under the judgment of God.

Genesis 8:6; Romans 1:20-23; Hebrews 9:27
The Counselor, 161, 162, 163.

1173. Sin problem

Others are insisting that it is not the "sin" problem but the "Son" problem that is troubling mankind.

This statement has been credited to a preacher in our day: "Sin has no more meaning to God. On Calvary sin beat itself to death and perished. And now sin has no meaning to God, since Calvary."

He may have been a good man but he was talking like a blooming idiot when he said that.

John 16:8; Romans 7:15-25; 1 John 1:6-9
Echoes from Eden, 35.

1174. Sin problem; Jesus Christ: response to; Claims of Christ

Two questions are embraced within the one problem: What shall I do with my sin? and what shall I do with Jesus which is called Christ? In spite of every effort of the pseudo-learned world to dispose of the sin question, it remains still, a perennial heartache to the sons and daughters of Adam and Eve. It is one of those persistent pains that lies deep in the soul and never quite stops hurting. It just won't go away. The devil and the busy sons of men have sought throughout the centuries for something to make this problem go away. They have invented how many thousands of amusements, they have created innumerable pleasures to take the mind off its central woe; but nothing works. Sin is still the world's first problem.

The second question, What shall I do with Jesus? is the answer to the first one, because Jesus came to save men from their sins. Let us answer the second one rightly and the first one will be solved automatically. If we but come to Jesus with our sin upon us and without any hope except His mercy, we shall surely be delivered from the ancient curse. But remember, sin demands an answer. It won't just go away. It must be carried away by redeeming blood, and redeeming blood was never shed by any other lamb except the Lamb of God.

Matthew 27:22; Romans 3:10-18;
Ephesians 2:8-10; 1 Peter 1:18-19
The Next Chapter after the Last, 66.

1175. Solitude; Devotional life; Distractions

Modern civilization is so complex as to make the devotional life all but impossible. It wears us out by multiplying distractions and beats us down by destroying our solitude, where otherwise we might drink and renew our strength before going out to face the world again.

"The thoughtful soul to solitude retires," said the poet of other and quieter times; but where is the solitude to which we can retire today? Science, which has provided men with certain material comforts, has robbed them of their souls by surrounding them with a world hostile to their existence. "Commune with your own heart upon your bed and be still" is a wise and healing counsel, but how can it be followed in this day of the newspaper, the telephone, the radio and the television? These modern playthings, like pet tiger cubs, have grown so large and dangerous that they threaten to devour us all. What was intended to be a blessing has become a positive curse. No spot is now safe from the world's intrusion.

Psalm 4:4; Psalm 62:1; Matthew 14:22-23
Of God and Men, 125, 126.

1176. Solitude; Devotional life; Simplicity

Retire from the world each day to some private spot, even if it is only the bedroom (for a while I retreated to the furnace room for want of a better place). Stay in the secret place till the surrounding noises begin to fade out of your heart and a sense of God's presence envelops you. Deliberately tune out the unpleasant sounds and come out of your closet determined not to hear them. Listen for the inward Voice till you learn to recognize it. Stop trying to compete with others. Give yourself to God, and then be what and who you are without regard to what others think. Reduce your interests to a few. Don't try to know what will be of no service to you. Avoid the digest type of mind—short bits of unrelated facts, cute stories and bright sayings. Learn to pray inwardly every moment. After a while you can do this even while you work. Practice candor, child-like honesty, humility. Pray for a single eye. Read less, but read more of what is important to your inner life. Never let your mind remain scattered for very long. Call home your roving thoughts. Gaze on Christ with the eyes of your soul. Practice spiritual concentration.

Psalm 5:3; Matthew 6:6; 1 Thessalonians 5:16-17; Hebrews 12:1-2
Of God and Men, 128.

1177. Solitude; Pastoral ministry: prayer

Just prior to this miraculous multiplying of the bread and fish, Jesus "went up on a mountainside and sat down with his disciples"(6:3). That fact is noteworthy. It seems plain that Jesus withdrew purposely from the great press of people who had been pursuing Him.

There are some things that you and I will never learn when others are present. I believe in church and I love the fellowship of the assembly. There is much we can learn when we come together on Sundays and sit among the saints. But there are certain things that you and I will never learn in the presence of other people.

Unquestionably, part of our failure today is religious activity that is not preceded by aloneness, by inactivity. I mean getting alone with God and waiting in silence and quietness until we are charged with God's Spirit. Then, when we act, our activity really amounts to something because we have been prepared by God for it. . . .

Now, in the case of our Lord, the people came to Him, John reports, and He was ready for them. He had been quiet and silent. He had sat alone with His disciples and meditated. Looking upward, He waited until the whole hiatus of divine life moved down from the throne of God into His own soul. He was a violin tuned. He was a battery recharged. He was poised and prepared for the people when they came.

Luke 10:38-42; Luke 24:49; John 6:3
Faith beyond Reason, 130, 133.

1178. Solitude; Silence; John the Baptist

Let me give you some reasons why I believe God could honor John the Baptist in that day in which he lived.

First, John had the ability to live and meditate in solitude. He knew the meaning of quietness. He was in the desert until the time of his showing forth unto Israel as a prophet. He came out of his lonely solitude to break the silence like a drumbeat or as the trumpet sounds. The crowds came—all gathered to hear this man who had been with God and who had come from God.

In our day we just cannot get quiet enough and serene enough to wait on God. Somebody has to be talking. Somebody has to be making noise. But John had gone into the silence and had matured in a kind of special school with God and the stars and the wind and the sand. . . .

I do not believe it is stretching a point at all to say that we will most often hear from God in those times when we are silent.

Psalm 62:1; Psalm 63:1-2; Matthew 3:4-5; Luke 7:28; John 1:6-7
Christ the Eternal Son, 130, 131.

1179. Sowing and reaping

Every man sows what he will later reap and reaps what he has previously sown. This is a law of life, says Paul, and we may as well know that we cannot beat it. God will not be mocked. . . .

Our today is bound to all our yesterdays, and our tomorrow will be the sum of our present and our past. . . .

We may sow to the flesh if we will. There will be no interference from above. Thus to sow is our privilege—if we want to reap the harvest of corruption which must inevitably follow, a harvest no man in his right mind could deliberately choose. No, the snare lies in choosing the pleasures of sowing with the secret hope that in some way we can escape the sorrows of the reaping; but never since the beginning of the world has it been possible to separate the one from the other.

Job 4:8; Proverbs 22:8; 2 Corinthians 9:6-14; Galatians 6:7-8
The Next Chapter after the Last, 86, 87.

1180. Spiritual depth

One marked difference between the faith of our fathers as conceived by the fathers and the same faith as understood and lived by their children is that the fathers were concerned with the root of the matter, while their present-day descendants seem concerned only with the fruit. . . .

"The root of the righteous yieldeth fruit," said the wise man in the Proverbs. Our fathers looked well to the root of the tree and were willing to wait with patience for the fruit to appear. We demand the fruit immediately even though the root may be weak and knobby or missing altogether.

Proverbs 12:12
The Root of the Righteous, 7.

1181. Spiritual growth; Current conditions: shallowness; Church: current condition

Failure to see this is the cause of a very serious breakdown in modern evangelicalism. The idea of cultivation and exercise, so dear to the saints of old, has now no place in our total religious picture. It is too slow, too common. We now demand glamour and fast flowing dramatic action. A generation of Christians reared among push buttons and automatic machines is impatient of slower and less direct methods of reaching their goals. We have been trying to apply machine-age methods to our relations with God. We read our chapter, have our short devotions and rush away, hoping to make up for our deep inward bankruptcy by attending another gospel meeting or listening to another thrilling story told by a religious adventurer lately returned from afar.

The tragic results of this spirit are all about us: Shallow lives, hollow religious philosophies, the preponderance of the element of fun in gospel meetings, the glorification of men, trust in religious externalities, quasi-religious fellowships, salesmanship methods, the mistaking of dynamic personality for the power of the Spirit. These and such as these are the symptoms of an evil disease, a deep and serious malady of the soul.

Psalm 1:1-3; Psalm 27:8; 1 Corinthians 9:24-27
The Pursuit of God, 62, 63.

1182. Spiritual growth; Discipleship

Once while walking among the hills of a southeastern state I noticed a piece of white paper lying by the roadside.

Its presence there was, under the circumstances, so unexpected that it aroused my curiosity. I picked it up and found written on it in a clear, legible hand these words: "In all the world there are only two creatures that are larger when they are born than when they get their growth; one is a wasp and the other is a church member.". . .

Not being an apiarist I am unable to judge the truth of the statement that a baby wasp is larger than an adult one; but that part about the church member I find too true to be amusing or even comfortable. . . .

Now I do not insist that my description applies to all Christians. In fact I think our epigrammatist was covering too much territory when he gave the impression that all church members get smaller as they get older. I do not think they all do, but the fact that some do is enough to disturb one who loves the church and carries the welfare of the saints on his heart; and the fact that any do calls for prayer and careful investigation.

Ephesians 4:14-16; 1 Peter 2:1-2; 2 Peter 3:18
God Tells the Man Who Cares, 125, 126, 127.

1183. Spiritual growth; Discipleship; Bible: neglect of

Every farmer knows the hunger of the wilderness, that hunger which no modern farm machinery, no improved agricultural methods, can ever quite destroy. No matter how well prepared the soil, how well kept the fences, how carefully painted the buildings, let the owner neglect for a while his prized and valued acres and they will revert again to the wild and be swallowed up by the jungle or the wasteland. The bias of nature is toward the wilderness, never toward the fruitful field. That, we repeat, every farmer knows....

We cannot escape the law that would persuade all things to remain wild or to return to a wild state after a period of cultivation. What is true of the field is true also of the soul, if we are but wise enough to see it.

Psalm 119:9-11; 1 Timothy 4:13-16
The Root of the Righteous, 100, 101.

1184. Spiritual growth; Longing for God; Christlikeness

At the root of all true spiritual growth is a set of right and sanctified desires. The whole Bible teaches that we can have whatever we want badly enough if, it hardly need be said, our desire is according to the will of God. The desire after God and holiness is back of all real spirituality, and when that desire becomes dominant in the life nothing can prevent us from having what we want. The longing cry of the God-hungry soul can be expressed in the five words of the song, "Oh, to be like Thee!" While this longing persists there will be steady growth in grace and a constant progress toward Christlikeness.

Romans 8:5-7; Romans 8:28-30; Colossians 3:1-4
The Root of the Righteous, 116, 117.

1185. Spiritual growth; New believer; Choices

The new birth does not produce the finished product. The new thing that is born of God is as far from completeness as the new baby born an hour ago. That new human being, the moment he is born, is placed in the hands of powerful molding forces that go far to determine whether he shall be an upright citizen or a criminal. The one hope for him is that he can later choose which forces shall shape him, and by the exercise of his own power of choice he can place himself in the right hands. In that sense he shapes himself and is responsible at last for the outcome.

It is not otherwise with the Christian. He can fashion himself by placing himself in the hands first of the supreme Artist, God, and then by subjecting himself to such holy influences and such formative powers as shall make him into a man of God. Or he may foolishly trust himself to unworthy hands and become at last a misshapen and inartistic vessel, of little use to mankind and a poor example of the skill of the heavenly Potter.

Jeremiah 18:6; 1 Peter 2:1-2; 2 Peter 3:18
Born after Midnight, 127, 128.

1186. Spiritual growth; Pride: spiritual; Penitence

The rapidity with which improvement is made in the life will depend altogether upon the degree of self-criticism we bring to our prayers and to the school of daily living. Let a man fall under the delusion that he has arrived, and all progress is stopped until he has seen his error and forsaken it. Paul said, "Not that I have already obtained all this, or have already been made perfect, but I press on to take hold of that for which Christ Jesus took hold of me" (Philippians 3:12)....

All this is to say that a growing Christian must have at his roots the life-giving waters of penitence. The cultivation of a penitential spirit is absolutely essential to spiritual progress....

Let the public accept a man as unusual, and he is soon tempted to accept himself as being above reproof. Soon a hard shell of impenitence covers his heart and chokes his spiritual life almost out of existence. The cure, if there is to be a cure, would be simple, of course. Let him look to his past and to the cross where Jesus died. If he can still defend himself after that, then let him look into his own heart and tell what he finds there. If after that he can still boast, close the coffin lid.

1 Corinthians 11:31-32; Philippians 3:12; 1 John 1:6-9
We Travel an Appointed Way, 66, 67, 68.

1187. Spiritual growth; Spiritual disciplines; Fruit of the Spirit

I would like to be able to ask every Christian in the world this question: Are you really interested in God's producing in you the beautiful fruits and fragrances of the Holy Spirit?

For every affirmative answer, I would quickly recommend: Then look to your own willingness to be regular in the habits of a holy life—for flowers and fruit do not grow in thin air! They grow and come up out of a root and "the root of the righteous flourishes" (Proverbs 12:12).

For every beautiful garden that you see, whose fragrance comes out to welcome you, has its roots down into the hard earth. The beautiful flowers and blooms will grow and appear and flourish only when there are deep roots and strong stalks. If you take the roots away, the blossom and flower will endure perhaps one day. The sun will scorch them and they will be gone. . . .

According to my Bible, there should be a people of God—they do not all have to belong to one church—but there should be a people called out by the Lord God and subjected to a spiritual experience given by God. Then they are to learn to walk in the way of the Truth and the way of the Scripture, producing the righteous fruit of the child of God whatever world conditions may be. . . .

So, this is the answer. Every flower and every fruit has a stalk and every stalk has a root, and long before there is any bloom there must be a careful tending of the root and the stalk. This is where the misunderstanding lies—we think that we get the flower and the fragrance and the fruit by some kind of magic, instead of by cultivation.

Proverbs 12:12; Song of Solomon 4:16; Galatians 5:22-23
Who Put Jesus on the Cross?, 15, 16, 17, 20.

1188. Spiritual growth; Spiritual victory

A lifetime of observation, Bible reading and prayer has led to the conclusion that the only thing that can hinder a Christian's progress is the Christian himself. . . .

God has so ordered things that His children may grow as successfully in the middle of a desert as in the most fruitful land. It is necessary that this should be so, seeing that the very world itself is a field where nothing good can grow except by some kind of miracle. The old hymn asks the rhetorical question, "Is this vile world a friend to grace, to help me on to God?" And the implied answer is no. Grace operates without the help of the world....

Attitude is all-important. Let the soul take a quiet attitude of faith and love toward God, and from there on the responsibility is God's. He will make good on His commitments. There is not on earth a lonely spot where a Christian cannot live and be spiritually victorious if God sends him there. He carries his own climate with him or has it supplied supernaturally when he arrives. Since he is not dependent for his spiritual health upon local moral standards or current religious beliefs, he lives through a thousand earthly changes, unaffected by any of them. He has a private supply from above and is in reality a little world within a world and very much of a wonder to the rest of creation.

1 Kings 17:3-6; Colossians 4:5-6
We Travel an Appointed Way, 31, 32.

1189. Spiritual leadership;
Pastoral ministry: need for spiritual reality

A number of factors contribute to bad spiritual leadership....

Absence of true spiritual experience. No one can lead another farther than he himself has gone. For many ministers this explains their failure to lead. They simply do not know where to go.

God Tells the Man Who Cares, 61, 62.

1190. Spiritual leadership;
Pastors: ambition;
Pastoral ministry: pride

A number of factors contribute to bad spiritual leadership....

Ambition. When Christ is not all in all to the minister he is tempted to seek place for himself, and pleasing the crowds is a time-proved way to get on in church circles. Instead of leading his people where they ought to go he skillfully leads them where he knows they want to go. In this way he gives the appearance of being a bold leader of men, but avoids offending anyone, and thus assures ecclesiastical preferment when the big church or the high office is open.

2 Corinthians 1:12; Galatians 1:9-10;
Colossians 1:18; 1 Thessalonians 2:2-4
God Tells the Man Who Cares, 61, 62.

1191. Spiritual leadership;
Pastors: stress; Church:
finances

A number of factors contribute to bad spiritual leadership....
The economic squeeze. The Protestant ministry is notoriously underpaid and the pastor's family is often large. Put these two facts together and you have a situation ready-made to bring trouble and temptation to the man of God. The ability of the congregation to turn off the flow of money to the church when the man in the pulpit gets on their toes is well known. The average pastor lives from year to year barely making ends meet. To give vigorous moral leadership to the church is often to invite economic strangulation, so such leadership is withheld. But the evil thing is that *leadership withheld is in fact a kind of inverted leadership.* The man who will not lead his flock up the mountainside leads it down without knowing it.

2 Corinthians 4:2; 1 Timothy 5:20-21;
2 Timothy 4:1-5
God Tells the Man Who Cares, 61, 62.

1192. Spiritual neglect; Church:
spiritual condition

The neglected heart will soon be a heart overrun with worldly thoughts; the neglected life will soon become a moral chaos; the church that is not jealously protected by mighty intercession and sacrificial labors will before long become the abode of every evil bird and the hiding place for unsuspected corruption. The creeping wilderness will soon take over that church that trusts in its own strength and forgets to watch and pray.

Matthew 26:40-41; Acts 20:28-31;
1 Timothy 4:13-16
The Root of the Righteous, 102.

1193. Spiritual philosophy

You know that I preached some time ago in Dr. A. B. Simpson's old tabernacle church at Times Square in New York City. The pastor was a learned brother with a delightful southern drawl.

After I had preached several days, we were walking together in the midst of those hurrying throngs when he turned to me and said, "Brother Tozer, I think I have figured you out."

I asked him what he had discovered.

"I believe I have found your basic spiritual philosophy," he said. "I think it boils down to this: 'Everything is wrong until Jesus sets it right!'"

I replied, "Thank you, brother. That is it. I would say you have summed it up."

I had not thought about it in that way but I think he had it right, and that is where I stand, ladies and gentlemen. Everything is wrong until Jesus sets it right.

Ecclesiastes 3:11; John 1:4; Colossians 1:19-22
Christ the Eternal Son, 59.

1194. Spiritual reality

The world of sense intrudes upon our attention day and night for the whole of our lifetime. It is clamorous, insistent and self-demonstrating. It does not appeal to our faith; it is here, assaulting our five senses, demanding to be accepted as real and final. But sin has so clouded the lenses of our hearts that we cannot see that other reality, the City of God, shining around us. The world of sense triumphs. The visible becomes the enemy of the invisible, the temporal, of the eternal. That is the curse inherited by every member of Adam's tragic race.

John 17:20-24; Philippians 1:21-24; Hebrews 11:6,16,39-40
The Pursuit of God, 51.

1195. Spiritual reality; Faith: defective

But why do the very ransomed children of God themselves know so little of that habitual, conscious communion with God which Scripture offers? The answer is because of our chronic unbelief. Faith enables our spiritual sense to function. Where faith is defective the result will be inward insensibility and numbness toward spiritual things. This is the condition of vast numbers of Christians today. No proof is necessary to support that statement. We have but to converse with the first Christian we meet or enter the first church we find open to acquire all the proof we need.

A spiritual kingdom lies all about us, enclosing us, embracing us, altogether within reach of our inner selves, waiting for us to recognize it. God Himself is here waiting our response to His presence. This eternal world will come alive to us the moment we begin to reckon upon its reality.

Matthew 5:8; Hebrews 11:6, 16, 39-40
The Pursuit of God, 47, 48.

1196. Spiritual victory

Remember, we are compared with what we *could* be, not just what we *should* be. God being who He is, and Jesus Christ being His risen and all-powerful Son, anything we ought to be we can be. Anything that God has declared that we should be we can be.

Romans 7:24-25; Galatians 5:22-23; Ephesians 4:26-5:2
Rut, Rot or Revival: The Condition of the Church, 19, 20.

1197. Spiritual victory

Everyone has a private battle going on, a private fight. You are in the midst of a wicked and adulterous generation, but you have got to overcome. He who overcame indicates that you also can overcome, but He indicates that not all do. You can overcome your own flesh, which will be the hardest. You can overcome tradition and custom, which will be the second hardest. You can overcome all things. "To him who overcomes, I will give the right to eat from the tree of life, which is in the paradise of God" ([Revelation] 2:7b).

The world is waiting to hear an authentic voice, a voice from God—not an echo of what others are doing and saying, but an authentic voice.

Romans 6:11-14; 2 Corinthians 2:14; Revelation 2:7, 11
Rut, Rot or Revival: The Condition of the Church, 177, 178.

1198. Spiritual victory

The whole Bible and all past history unite to teach that battles are always won before the armies take the field. The critical moment for any army is not the day it engages the foe in actual combat; it is the day before or the month before or the year before. . . .

Preparation is vital. The rule is, prepare or fail. Luck and bluster will do for a while, but the law will catch up with us sooner or later, usually sooner. . . .

It did not take Moses long to lead the children of Israel out through the Red Sea to deliverance and freedom; but his fittedness to lead them out was the result of years of hard discipline. It took David only a few minutes to dispose of Goliath; but he had beaten the giant long before in the person of the lion and the bear. Elijah faced a sulking King Ahab and stared him down in the name of Jehovah, but we must remember that his courage to stand before kings was the result of years spent in standing before the King of kings. Christ stood silent in the presence of Pilate and for our sake went calmly out to die. He could endure the anguish of the cross because He had suffered the pains of Gethsemane the night before; there was a direct relationship between the two experiences. One served as a preparation for the other....

Preparation is vital. Let this be noted by everyone. We can seek God today and get prepared to meet temptation tomorrow; but if we meet the enemy without first having met God, the outcome is not conjectural; the issue is already decided. We can only lose.

Exodus 3:1; 1 Samuel 17:34-36; 1 Kings 18:18-19; Matthew 26:36; Ephesians 6:18
The Next Chapter after the Last, 77, 78, 79.

1199. Spiritual warfare; Holy Spirit: need for

Someday the church can relax her guard, call her watchmen down from the wall and live in safety and peace; but not yet, not yet....

The church lives in a hostile world. Within and around her are enemies that not only could destroy her, but are meant to and will unless she resists force with yet greater force. The Christian would collapse from sheer external pressure were there not within him a counterpressure sufficiently great to prevent it. The power of the Holy Spirit is, therefore, not optional but necessary. Without it the children of God simply cannot live the life of heaven on earth. The hindrances are too many and too effective.

Amos 6:1; Luke 6:20-38; Revelation 3:14-22
That Incredible Christian, 86, 87.

1200. Spiritual warfare; Satan; Christian life

If Satan opposes the new convert he opposes still more bitterly the Christian who is pressing on toward a higher life in Christ. The Spirit-filled life is not, as many suppose, a life of peace and quiet pleasure. It is likely to be something quite the opposite.

Viewed one way it is a pilgrimage through a robber-infested forest; viewed another, it is a grim warfare with the devil. Always there is struggle, and sometimes there is a pitched battle with our own nature where the lines are so confused that it is all but impossible to locate the enemy or to tell which impulse is of the Spirit and which of the flesh....

My point here is that if we want to escape the struggle we have but to draw back and accept the currently accepted low-keyed Christian life as the normal one. That is all Satan wants. That will ground our power, stunt our growth and render us harmless to the kingdom of darkness.

Compromise will take the pressure off. Satan will not bother a man who has quit fighting. But the cost of quitting will be a life of peaceful stagnation. We sons of eternity just cannot afford such a thing.

Romans 7:15-25; Galatians 5:17; Ephesians 6:10-18; 1 Peter 1:6-9, 13; 1 Peter 5:8-9
That Incredible Christian, 73.

1201. Spiritual warfare; Satan; Christians: in the world

There are two spirits in the earth, the Spirit of God and the spirit of Satan, and these are at eternal enmity. The ostensible cause of religious hatred may be almost anything; the true cause is nearly always the same: the ancient animosity which Satan, since the time of his inglorious fall, has ever felt toward God and His kingdom. Satan is aflame with desire for unlimited dominion over the human family; and whenever that evil ambition is challenged by the Spirit of God, he invariably retaliates with savage fury. . . .

It is possible within the provisions of redemptive grace to enter into a state of union with Christ so perfect that the world will instinctively react toward us exactly as it did toward Him in the days of His flesh. . . .

It is the Spirit of Christ in us that will draw Satan's fire. The people of the world will not much care what we believe and they will stare vacantly at our religious forms, but there is one thing they will never forgive us—the presence of God's Spirit in our hearts. They may not know the cause of that strange feeling of antagonism which rises within them, but it will be nonetheless real and dangerous. Satan will never cease to make war on the Man-child, and the soul in which dwells the Spirit of Christ will continue to be the target for his attacks.

John 15:18-21; John 17:14-16; 2 Corinthians 12:7; 1 Peter 5:8-9; 1 John 3:13
The Warfare of the Spirit, 3, 4.

1202. Spiritual warfare; Timidity; Boldness

Now I do not think that Satan much cares to destroy us Christians physically. The soldier dead in battle who died performing some deed of heroism is not a great loss to the army but may rather be an object of pride to his country. On the other hand the soldier who cannot or will not fight but runs away at the sound of the first enemy gun is a shame to his family and a disgrace to his nation. So a Christian who dies in the faith represents no irreparable loss to the forces of righteousness on earth and certainly no victory for the devil. But when whole regiments of professed believers are too timid to fight and too smug to be ashamed, surely it must bring an astringent smile to the face of the enemy; and it should bring a blush to the cheeks of the whole Church of Christ.

The devil's master strategy for us Christians then is not to kill us physically (though there may be some special situations where physical death fits into his plan better), but to destroy our power to wage spiritual warfare. And how well he has succeeded. The average Christian these days is a harmless enough thing, God knows. He is a child wearing with considerable self-consciousness the harness of the warrior; he is a sick eaglet that can never mount up with wings; he is a spent pilgrim who has given up the journey and sits with a waxy smile trying to get what pleasure he can from sniffing the wilted flowers he has plucked by the way.

Psalm 78:9; Isaiah 40:29-31; 2 Timothy 1:6-7
That Incredible Christian, 72.

1203. Staleness; Fatigue

Periods of staleness in the life are not inevitable but they are common. He is a rare Christian who has not experienced times of spiritual dullness when the relish has gone out of his heart and the enjoyment of living has diminished greatly or departed altogether....

One often-unsuspected cause of staleness is fatigue. Shakespeare said something to the effect that no man could be a philosopher when he had a toothache, and while it is possible to be a weary saint, it is scarcely possible to be weary and *feel* saintly; and it is our want of feeling that we are considering here. The Christian who gets tired in the work of the Lord and stays tired without relief beyond a reasonable time will go stale. The fact that he grew weary by toiling in the Lord's vineyard will not make his weariness any less real. Our Lord knew this and occasionally took His disciples aside for a rest.

Isaiah 40:29-31; Matthew 11:28-30; Galatians 6:9
That Incredible Christian, 107, 108.

1204. Standards; Church: separation

I must confess as a pastor and minister that I have had to say "Goodbye" to people in some instances when they have said, "We cannot worship here. You are too strict. Your standards are too strict for this day and age. Your message is too strict!"

My only apology is that I am still not as strict as the Bible is. I have to confess that I am still not up to the standard of the Scriptures. I am trying, but I am not that strict.

But, occasionally, we have to say farewell to someone who says they have to find a different kind of church, an easy-going church, a church that majors in relaxation.

What did Jesus say to us? He said that unless we are ready to turn from everything and follow Him with devotion, we are not yet ready to be His disciples, and unless we are ready to die for Him, we are not ready to live for Him. The whistle is going to blow for us one of these days and then we will have to appear and tell God how we carried on His work, how we conducted ourselves in the light of what Jesus said.

So we cannot afford to let down our Christian standards just to hold the interest of people who want to go to hell and still belong to a church.

Luke 9:23-25; Luke 14:26-27
Who Put Jesus on the Cross?, 46, 47.

1205. Standing firm

Shall we surrender to the world? No! Shall we surrender to liberalism? No! Shall we surrender to apostate Protestantism? The answer is no! Shall we surrender to the brainwashed churches whose preachers are afraid to stand up and talk as I am? The answer again is no!

Our church is going to go the way of the gospel. We are not radicals nor fools. We do not fast 40 days. We dress like other people, drive vehicles and have modern homes. We are human and like to laugh. But we believe that God Almighty has not changed and that Jesus Christ is the same. He is victorious, and we do not have to apologize for Him. We do not have to modify, adjust, edit or amend. He stands as the glorious Lord, and nobody needs to apologize for Him. . . .

We are not going to be sheep running over the precipice because other dumb sheep are running over it. We see the precipice—we know it is there. We are listening to the voice of the shepherd, not the voice of terrified sheep. The terrified, intimidated sheep are going everywhere.

Malachi 3:6; Hebrews 13:8; Revelation 2:7,11; Revelation 3:21
Rut, Rot or Revival: The Condition of the Church, 106, 107.

1206. Standing firm; Eternal perspective

Vance Havner used to remark that too many are running for something when they ought to be standing for something. God's people should be willing to stand! We have become so brainwashed in so many ways that Christians are afraid to speak out against uncleanness in any form. The enemy of our souls has persuaded us that Christianity should be a rather casual thing—certainly not something to get excited about.

Fellow Christian, we only have a little time. We are not going to be here very long. Our triune God demands that we engage in those things that will remain when the world is on fire, for fire determines the value and quality of every person's work.

1 Corinthians 3:12-14; Ephesians 6:10-12; 1 Thessalonians 2:2-4
Jesus, Our Man in Glory, 67.

1207. Stillness; Meditation

Our fathers had much to say about stillness, and by stillness they meant the absence of motion or the absence of noise or both.

They felt that they must be still for at least a part of the day, or that day would be wasted. God can be known in the tumult of the world if His providence has for the time placed us there, but He is known best in the silence. So they held, and so the sacred Scriptures declare. Inward assurance comes out of the stillness. We must be still to know.

Psalm 46:10
God Tells the Man Who Cares, 12.

1208. Submission

Whenever and wherever there is a controversy between God and a man, God is always right and the man always wrong. "So that you may be proved right in your words and prevail in your judging" (Psalm 51:4).

The only way any man can be right is to come over onto God's side. Whoever sticks to his own side is forever wrong. . . .

Our desire for moral self-preservation should dictate that we come over immediately onto God's side and stay there even if (as is likely) it may result in our being out of accord with man's philosophies and man's moral codes. We cannot win when we work against God, and we cannot lose when we work with Him.

Psalm 51:3-4; John 17:15-18; Romans 3:4
We Travel an Appointed Way, 44, 46.

1209. Submission

The experiences of men who walked with God in olden times agree to teach that the Lord cannot fully bless a man until He has first conquered him. The degree of blessing enjoyed by any man will correspond exactly with the completeness of God's victory over him.

Genesis 32:28; Galatians 2:20
The Pursuit of Man, 45, 46.

1210. Submission; Old nature

We might well pray for God to invade and conquer us, for until He does, we remain in peril from a thousand foes. We bear within us the seeds of our own disintegration. . . . Deliverance can come to us only by the defeat of our old life. Safety and peace come only after we have been forced to our knees. God rescues us by breaking us, by shattering our strength and wiping out our resistance. Then He invades our natures with that ancient and eternal life which is from the beginning. So He conquers us and by that benign conquest saves us for Himself.

Romans 6:4-7; 2 Corinthians 5:17; Galatians 5:24; Galatians 6:14
The Pursuit of Man, 50.

1211. Success/Failure

God may allow His servant to succeed when He has disciplined him to a point where he does not need to succeed to be happy. The man who is elated by success and cast down by failure is still a carnal man. At best his fruit will have a worm in it.

God will allow His servant to succeed when he has learned that success does not make him dearer to God nor more valuable in the total scheme of things. We cannot buy God's favor with crowds or converts or new missionaries sent out or Bibles distributed. All these things can be accomplished without the help of the Holy Spirit. A good personality and a shrewd knowledge of human nature is all that any man needs to be a success in religious circles today. . . .

We can afford to follow Him to failure. Faith dares to fail. The resurrection and the judgment will demonstrate before all worlds who won and who lost. We can wait.

Born after Midnight, 59.

1212. Success/Failure; Pastoral ministry: pride

Our Lord died an apparent failure, discredited by the leaders of established religion, rejected by society and forsaken by His friends. The man who ordered Him to the cross was the successful statesman whose hand the ambitious hack politician kissed. It took the resurrection to demonstrate how gloriously Christ had triumphed and how tragically the governor had failed.

Yet today the professed church seems to have learned nothing. We are still seeing as men see and judging after the manner of man's judgment. How much eager-beaver religious work is done out of a carnal desire to make good. How many hours of prayer are wasted beseeching God to bless projects that are geared to the glorification of little men. How much sacred money is poured out upon men who, in spite of their tear-in-the-voice appeals, nevertheless seek only to make a fair show in the flesh.

The true Christian should turn away from all this. Especially should ministers of the gospel search their own hearts and look deep into their inner motives. No man is worthy to succeed until he is willing to fail. No man is morally worthy of success in religious activities until he is willing that the honor of succeeding should go to another if God so wills.

Matthew 26:56; Matthew 27:26;
1 Corinthians 3:5-9; 2 Corinthians 4:5-7
Born after Midnight, 58.

1213. Success; Happiness

In this world men are judged by their ability to do.

They are rated according to the distance they have come up the hill of achievement. At the bottom is utter failure; at the top complete success, and between these two extremes the majority of civilized men sweat and struggle from youth to old age.

A few give up, slide to the bottom and become inhabitants of Skid Row. There, with ambition gone and will broken, they subsist on handouts till nature forecloses on them and death takes them away.

At the top are the few who by a combination of talent, hard work and good fortune manage to reach the peak and all the luxury, fame and power that are found there.

But in all of this there is no happiness. . . .

The man who reaches the pinnacle is seldom happy for very long. He soon becomes eaten by fears that he may slip back a peg and be forced to surrender his place to another. Examples of this are found in the feverish way the TV star watches his rating and the politician his mail. . . .

This mania to succeed is a good thing perverted. The desire to fulfill the purpose for which we were created is of course a gift from God, but sin has twisted this impulse about and turned it into a selfish lust for first place and top honors. By this lust the whole world of mankind is driven as by a demon, and there is no escape.

Matthew 16:24-26; Luke 10:20;
Luke 12:15-21; 1 Corinthians 9:24-27
Born after Midnight, 56, 57.

1214. Success; Sacrifice; Discipline: personal

Success in any field is costly, but the man who will pay the price can have it.

The concert pianist must become a slave to his instrument; four hours, five hours each day he must sit at the keyboard. The scientist must live for his work. The philosopher must devote himself to thought, the scholar to his books. The price may seem excessively heavy, but there are some who consider the reward worthwhile.

The laws of success operate also in the higher field of the soul—spiritual greatness has its price. Eminence in the things of the Spirit demands a devotion to these things more complete than most of us are willing to give. But the law cannot be escaped. If we would be holy we know the way; the law of holy living is before us. The prophets of the Old Testament, the apostles of the New and, more than all, the sublime teachings of Christ are there to tell us how to succeed. . . .

The amount of loafing practiced by the average Christian in spiritual things would ruin a concert pianist if he allowed himself to do the same thing in the field of music. The idle puttering around that we see in church circles would end the career of a big league pitcher in one week. No scientist could solve his exacting problem if he took as little interest in it as the rank and file of Christians take in the art of being holy. The nation whose soldiers were as soft and undisciplined as the soldiers of the churches would be conquered by the first enemy that attacked it. Triumphs are not won by men in easy chairs. Success is costly.

If we would progress spiritually, we must separate ourselves unto the things of God and concentrate upon them to the exclusion of a thousand things the worldly man considers important. We must cultivate God in the solitudes and the silence; we must make the kingdom of God the sphere of our activity and labor in it like a farmer in his field, like a miner in the earth.

Proverbs 4:23; Colossians 3:23; 1 Timothy 4:7,8,13-16; 2 Timothy 2:3-4
We Travel an Appointed Way, 25, 26, 27.

1215. Success; Servanthood; Pastors: humility

No man is worthy to succeed until he is willing to fail. No man is morally worthy of success in religious activities until he is willing that the honor of succeeding should go to another if God so wills.

God may allow His servant to succeed when He has disciplined him to a point where he does not need to succeed to be happy.

Matthew 23:10-12; James 4:7-10; 1 Peter 5:6
Renewed Day by Day, Volume 1, Mar. 24.

1216. Suffering; Cross: personal; Trials: necessity of

Willingness to suffer for Jesus' sake—this is what we have lost from the Christian church. We want our Easter to come without the necessity of a Good Friday. We forget that before the Redeemer could rise and sing among His brethren He must first bow His head and suffer among His brethren!

We forget so easily that in the spiritual life there must be the darkness of the night before there can be the radiance of the dawn. Before the life of resurrection can be known, there must be the death that ends the dominion of self. It is a serious but a blessed decision, this willingness to say, "I will follow Him no matter what the cost. I will take the cross no matter how it comes!"

Psalm 30:5; Luke 9:23-25; Galatians 2:20; Philippians 2:9-11
I Talk Back to the Devil, 98, 99.

1217. Suffering; Self-assurance; Humility

All great Christians have been wounded souls. It is strange what a wound will do to a man. Here's a soldier who goes out to the battlefield. He is full of jokes and strength and self-assurance; then one day a piece of shrapnel tears through him and he falls, a whimpering, beaten, defeated man. Suddenly his whole world collapses around him and this man, instead of being the great, strong, broad-chested fellow that he thought he was, suddenly becomes a whimpering boy again. And such have even been known, I am told, to cry for their mothers when they lie bleeding and suffering on the field of battle. There is nothing like a wound to take the self-assurance out of us, to reduce us to childhood again and make us small and helpless in our own sight.

Job 5:17-18; Proverbs 27:6; James 1:2-4;
1 Peter 4:12-13
Man: The Dwelling Place of God, 101.

1218. Suffering; Trials: inevitability of

The Bible has a great deal to say about suffering and most of it is encouraging. . . .

We cannot afford to neglect it, for whether we understand it or not we are going to experience some suffering. As human beings we cannot escape it.

From the first cold shock that brings a howl of protest from the newborn infant down to the last anguished gasp of the aged man, pain and suffering dog our footsteps as we journey here below. It will pay us to learn what God says about it so that we may know how to act and what to expect when it comes. . . .

There is a kind of suffering which profits no one: it is the bitter and defiant suffering of the lost. . . . To such there is not much that we can say. . . .

As long as we remain in the body we shall be subject to a certain amount of that common suffering which we must share with all the sons of men—loss, bereavement, nameless heartaches, disappointments, partings, betrayals and griefs of a thousand sorts. . . . We should be watchful lest we lose any blessing which such suffering might bring.

But there is another kind of suffering, known only to the Christian: it is voluntary suffering deliberately and knowingly incurred for the sake of Christ. Such is a luxury, a treasure of fabulous value, a source of riches beyond the power of the mind to conceive. And it is rare as well as precious, for there are few in this decadent age who will of their own choice go down into this dark mine looking for jewels. . . . Such as these have said good-bye to the world's toys; they have chosen to suffer affliction with the people of God; they have accepted toil and suffering as their earthy portion. The marks of the cross are upon them and they are known in heaven and in hell.

Romans 5:3-5; 2 Corinthians 9:9-10;
Philippians 3:7-16; Hebrews 11:24-26
The Root of the Righteous, 131, 132, 133, 134.

1219. Sunday Christians; Big shots

When we have a revival and the blessing of God comes to us and we do get the help we need from God, those who make religion merely a Sunday garment won't like it very well—in fact, they will be disturbed. From the biblical side, we will insist that they live right on Monday morning, and they don't want to do that. They want to keep their religion disengaged from practical living. Their religion is here and their living is over there. On Sunday they go in and polish their religion, but about 11 p.m. in the evening they put it on the shelf. On Monday they go out and live the way they want to live. I refuse to surrender to that kind of thing and to that kind of people. We are to be a church of the living God, and not a gathering of the influential and the big shots. The big shots can come if they get on their knees—a big shot on his knees isn't any taller than anyone else, you know.

Matthew 6:1-5,14-16; Matthew 23:5; 1 Peter 5:6
The Counselor, 11.

T

1220. Teachers; Pastoral ministry: need for spiritual reality

Toward anything like thorough scholarship I make no claim. I am not an authority on any man's teaching; I have never tried to be. I take my help where I find it and set my heart to graze where the pastures are greenest. Only one stipulation do I make: my teacher must know God, as Carlyle said, "otherwise than by hearsay," and Christ must be all in all to him. If a man have only correct doctrine to offer me I am sure to slip out at the first intermission to seek the company of someone who has seen for himself how lovely is the face of Him who is the Rose of Sharon and the Lily of the Valleys. Such a man can help me, and no one else can.

Song of Solomon 2:1; John 12:21;
Hebrews 12:1-2
The Pursuit of Man, xiv.

1221. Tears; Pastors: burden for people

The Bible was written in tears and to tears it will yield its best treasures. God has nothing to say to the frivolous man. . . .

The psalmists often wrote in tears, the prophets could hardly conceal their heavyheartedness, and the apostle Paul in his otherwise joyous epistle to the Philippians broke into tears when he thought of the many who were enemies of the cross of Christ and whose end was destruction. Those Christian leaders who shook the world were one and all men of sorrows whose witness to mankind welled out of heavy hearts. There is no power in tears per se, but tears and power ever lie close together in the Church of the First-born. . . .

The whole Christian family stands desperately in need of a restoration of penitence, humility and tears. May God send them soon.

Psalm 126:5-6; Jeremiah 9:1; Jeremiah 13:17;
Luke 19:41; Philippians 3:18-21
God Tells the Man Who Cares, 2, 3, 6.

1222. Temper: attempts to excuse

We are always finding a new stratagem to cover up that devil—temper! You never read anywhere that a man lost his temper. Instead, he "got upset." You never read that a woman lost her temper. Instead, she "was aggravated." But those expressions usually mean the person lost his or her temper—"flew off the handle," "got mad." It is a spiritual, heart condition, not an emotional condition.

When people smile and nod their heads as I preach, that is not the real them. Those are more than likely conditioned reflexes. But when the same people have a temper upset, that is the real them. What they do out of their inner beings, out of their appetites, out of the explosions of their natures—that is really what they are.

John 8:44-47; Ephesians 4:31-32; Colossians 3:5-11
Faith beyond Reason, 91, 92.

1223. Temper: attempts to excuse; Temper: provocation

We have all noticed how quick many people are to excuse themselves for some outburst by pleading that they were provoked to it. Thus their own wrongdoing is laid to others. What is overlooked in this neat trick of self-exoneration is that provocation cannot stir up what is not there. It never adds anything to the human heart; it merely brings out what is already present. It does not change the character; it simply reveals it.

What a man does under provocation is what he is. The mud must be at the bottom of the pool or it cannot be stirred up. You cannot roil pure water. Provocation does not create the moral muck; it brings it to the surface. . . .

It may bring some kind of cheap consolation to the man who has just lost his temper or let himself go in a display of bad disposition to consider that he was provoked to it by the act of another, but if he values his soul he will not thus excuse himself. Honesty will compel him to admit that he had a bad disposition to start with and the provocation merely brought it to the surface. The fault is his own, not that of the one who exposed it.

Genesis 3:12; Matthew 15:18-19; James 1:13-15
The Price of Neglect, 71, 72.

1224. Temper: loss of control; Violence

The bull out there in the farmyard is a domesticated animal, but once in a while he goes berserk. Unexpectedly, something will make him mad and he will explode. He will lower his head and roar and bellow. Anyone unfortunate enough to be in the field when that happens may have to climb a tree or jump over a bull-proof fence to keep from getting mauled! What has happened? That bull has simply risen in his anger and thrown off centuries of domestication. Underneath the domestication, he is really the same old wild beast, his nature unchanged.

Once the bull is over his tantrum, he probably will be ashamed of himself and meekly follow his owner back to the barnyard. But the farmer does not know when the bull will go on another rampage, for he is dealing with a bull—an animal tamed through a long process of conditioning, but by nature wild.

And we humans are not much different. I read of a man with six years of graduate and professional training beyond college. But one day he blew up, lost his temper and killed his wife. Do not ever think that it is only the poor, the uneducated and the underprivileged who commit crimes of violence. It is happening in the top brackets of society, too. It takes more than education to change people's nature. Education may bring about certain restraints and some degree of control, but just let those people act freely from within, and you will find out what they really are.

Romans 3:10-18; Ephesians 2:1-3;
2 Peter 2:12-15
Faith beyond Reason, 92, 93.

1225. Temptation; Spiritual victory

To want a thing, or feel that we want it, and then to turn from it because we see that it is contrary to the will of God is to win a great battle on a field larger than Gettysburg or Bunker Hill. To bring our desires to the cross and allow them to be nailed there with Christ is a good and a beautiful thing. To be tempted and yet to glorify God in the midst of it is to honor Him where it counts.

Romans 7:24-25; 1 Corinthians 10:13;
2 Corinthians 2:14
The Root of the Righteous, 117, 118.

1226. Temptation; Spiritual victory; Youth

Young people are beset by dirty talk and irreverence and every kind of temptation in their schools. I know of Christian young people who have found a way to turn those things to personal spiritual blessing. Hearing an obscenity, they have an instant reaction and a compensation within: "Oh, God, I hate that kind of talk so much that I want You to make my own mind and speech cleaner than it ever was before!" Seeing an injurious, wicked habit in others, they breathe a silent prayer: "Oh, God,

You are able to keep me and shield me from that bad habit!"

It is possible, even in this sensual world with its emphasis on violence and immorality to turn those very influences in the direction of God's promised victory. We are assured in the Word of God that we do not have to yield in weakness to the pull that would drag us down. When we see something that we know is wrong and therefore displeasing to God, we can react to it with a positive assurance as we say, "God helping me, I will be different from that!" In that sense, the very sight of evil can drive us farther into the kingdom of God.

Romans 6:11-14; 1 Corinthians 10:13;
2 Corinthians 10:5; Ephesians 2:1-3
Tragedy in the Church: The Missing Gifts, 124, 125.

1227. Ten Commandments; Law

I will only remind you, for you surely know it well, that many people have declared the Ten Commandments no longer valid, no longer relevant in our society. I watch the papers to check on the sermon topics of my fellow ministers, and it is apparent that Christian churches are not paying attention to the Ten Commandments.

Dwight L. Moody preached often on the Commandments. John Wesley said he preached the commands of the Law in order to prepare the way for the gospel. R.A. Torrey told ministers if they did not preach the Law they would have no response to the preaching of the gospel. It is the Law that prepares us for the gospel. It is the Law that shows us our need for the gospel of salvation and forgiveness.

Romans 3:19-20; Galatians 3:24;
Hebrews 12:29
Jesus, Author of Our Faith, 127.

1228. Textualism; Fundamentalism; Worldliness

Then came the revolt. The human mind can endure textualism just so long before it seeks a way of escape. So, quietly and quite unaware that any revolt was taking place, the masses of Fundamentalism reacted, not from the teaching of the Bible but from the mental tyranny of the scribes. With the recklessness of drowning men they fought their way up for air and struck out blindly for greater freedom of thought and for the emotional satisfaction their natures demanded and their teachers denied them.

The result over the last 20 years has been a religious debauch hardly equaled since Israel worshiped the golden calf. Of us Bible Christians it may truthfully be said that we "sat down to eat and to drink, and rose up to play." The separating line between the church and the world has been all but obliterated.

Exodus 32:1-6; John 8:44-47; 1 Corinthians 10:6-11; Galatians 5:13
Keys to the Deeper Life, 21, 22.

1229. Textualism; Joy; God: His love

I cannot help but believe that in our generation there is a great, concealing cloud over much of the fundamental, gospel church which has practically shut off our consciousness of the smiling face of God.

Textualism, a system of rigid adherence to words, has largely captured the church, with the language of the New Testament still being used but with the Spirit of the New Testament grieved.

The doctrine of verbal inspiration of the Scriptures, for instance, is still held, but in such a way that its illumination and life are gone and rigor mortis has set in. As a result religious yearning is choked down, religious imagination has been stultified and religious aspiration smothered. . . .

It is glorious knowledge indeed that the smiling face of God is turned toward us. Why, then, do we not capture the wondrous, divine illumination of our Savior, Jesus Christ? Why do we not know the divine fire in our own souls? Why do we not strive to sense and experience the knowledge of exhilaration of reconciliation with God?

Let me tell you why—it is because there is between us and the smiling face of God a cloud of concealment. . . .

I believe the smiling face of God is always turned toward us—but the cloud of concealment is of our own making. . . .

What is the answer to this growing list of cloud-forming attitudes? I think it is the willingness to put the cloud which is above us under our feet by faith and through grace!

Romans 5:20; 2 Corinthians 3:15-18; 2 Corinthians 5:10-21
I Talk Back to the Devil, 111, 113, 117.

1230. Thanksgiving; Jesus Christ: intimacy with

Lastly, because most precious of all, is the friendship and communion of Jesus. He is the friend that sticketh closer than a brother and He has assured us that He will never leave us nor forsake us. Let this knowledge keep us ever thankful. We dare not take Jesus for granted. His love alone should keep the flame of our gratitude at white heat until that day when we shall be presented to the Father with exceeding joy.

Joshua 1:5; Proverbs 18:24; Hebrews 13:5; Jude 24-25
The Price of Neglect, 43.

1231. Theology; Knowledge of God: neglected

It is precisely because God *is*, and because man is made in His image and is accountable to Him, that theology is so critically important. Christian revelation alone has the answer to life's unanswered questions about God and human destiny. To let these authoritative answers lie neglected while we search everywhere else for answers and find none is, it seems to me, nothing less than folly.

No motorist would be excused if he neglected to consult his road map and tried instead to find his way across the country by looking for moss on logs, or by observing the flight of wild bees or watching the movements of the heavenly bodies. If there were no map a man might find his way by the stars; but for a traveler trying to get home the stars would be a poor substitute for a map.

Psalm 19:7-11; Isaiah 30:21; 2 Timothy 3:13-17
That Incredible Christian, 81.

1232. Theology; Knowledge of God: personal, intimate; Prayer: mere ritual

To be articulate at certain times we are compelled to fall back upon "Oh!" or "O!"—a primitive exclamatory sound that is hardly a word at all and that scarcely admits of a definition. . . .

In theology there is no "Oh!" and this is a significant if not ominous thing. Theology seeks to reduce what may be known of God to intellectual terms, and as long as the intellect can comprehend it can find words to express itself. When God Himself appears before the mind, awesome, vast and incomprehensible, then the mind sinks into silence and the heart cries out "O Lord God!" There is the difference between theological knowledge and spiritual experience, the difference between knowing God by hearsay and knowing Him by acquaintance. And the difference is not verbal merely; it is real and serious and vital.

We Christians should watch lest we lose the "Oh!" from our hearts....

When we become too glib in prayer we are most surely talking to ourselves. When the calm listing of requests and the courteous giving of proper thanks take the place of the burdened prayer that finds utterance difficult we should beware the next step, for our direction is surely down whether we know it or not.

Psalm 8:1,9; Psalm 95:6-7; Psalm 105:1-5; Psalm 106:1-2; Jeremiah 1:5-8; Ezekiel 37:3
Born after Midnight, 85, 86, 87.

1233. Theology; Man: alienation from God

We being what we are and all things else being what they are, the most important and profitable study any of us can engage in is without question the study of theology.

That theology probably receives less attention than any other subject tells us nothing about its importance or lack of it. It indicates rather that men are still hiding from the presence of God among the trees of the garden and feel acutely uncomfortable when the matter of their relation to God is brought up. They sense their deep alienation from God and only manage to live at peace with themselves by forgetting that they are not at peace with God.

Genesis 3:8; Ephesians 3:12; Colossians 1:19-22
That Incredible Christian, 80.

1234. Thinking: avoidance of; Solitude

I knew of a young man who was hospitalized and forced to lie quietly for a time. He implored his father, "Dad, bring my record player or something to keep me busy. Otherwise I just have to lie here and think." Then he added his own commentary on the nature of his personal life, "And it is hell to think."

Psalm 4:4; Psalm 77:6
Jesus, Author of Our Faith, 47.

1235. Thinking: need for; Fundamentalism

The church today is anguishing for men who can bring to the problems of religion reverent, courageous minds intent upon a solution.

Unfortunately Fundamentalism has never produced a great thinker....

Let it be understood by everyone that I am now and have always been an evangelical.... Yet it is my painful duty to record not only that I have not been challenged by the intellectual output of the evangelicals of this generation, but that I have found evidence of genuine religious thinking almost exclusively on the side of those who for one or another reason are in revolt against Fundamentalism. We of the gospel churches have sat quietly by and allowed those on the other side to do all the thinking. We have been content to echo the words of other men and to repeat religious cliches *ad nauseam*. . . .

Modern gospel Christians are parrots, not eagles, and rather than sail out and up to explore the illimitable ranges of the kingdom of God they are content to sit safe on their familiar perches and repeat in a bright falsetto religious words and phrases the meaning of which they scarcely understand at all.

The Set of the Sail, 61, 62, 63.

1236. Thoughts

Every person is really what he or she secretly admires. If I can learn what you admire, I will know what you are, for people are what they think about when they are free to think about what they will.

Now, there are times when we are forced to think about things that we do not care to think about at all. All of us have to think about income taxes, but income taxes are not what we want to think about. The law makes us think about them every April. You may find me humped over Form 1040, just like everyone else, but that is not the real me. It is really the man with the tall hat and the spangled stars in Washington who says, "You can't let it go any longer!" I assure you it is not consentingly done! But if you can find what I think about when I am free to think about whatever I will, you will find the real me. That is true of every one of us.

Your baptism and your confirmation and your name on the church roll and the big Bible you carry—these are not the things that are important to God. You can train a chimpanzee to carry a Bible. Every one of us is the sum of what we secretly admire, what we think about and what we would like to do most if we became free to do what we wanted to do.

Proverbs 4:23; Proverbs 23:7; Matthew 12:34-37; John 8:44-47
Faith beyond Reason, 96.

1237. Thoughts

What we think about when we are free to think about what we will—that is what we are or will soon become. . . .

Anyone who wishes to check on his true spiritual condition may do so by noting what his voluntary thoughts have been over the last hours or days. What has he thought about when free to think of what he pleased? Toward what has his inner heart turned when it was free to turn where it would? When the bird of thought was let go did it fly out like the raven to settle upon floating carcasses or did it like the dove circle and return again to the ark of God? Such a test is easy to run, and if we are honest with ourselves we can discover not only what we are but what we are going to become. We'll soon be the sum of our voluntary thoughts. . . .

The best way to control our thoughts is to offer the mind to God in complete surrender. The Holy Spirit will accept it and take control of it immediately. Then it will be relatively easy to think on spiritual things, especially if we train our thought by long periods of daily prayer. Long practice in the art of mental prayer (that is, talking to God inwardly as we work or travel) will help to form the habit of holy thought.

Proverbs 4:23; 2 Corinthians 10:5; Philippians 4:8
Born after Midnight, 44, 46, 47.

1238. Thoughts

It is doubtful whether any sin is ever committed until it first incubates in the thoughts long enough to stir the feelings and predispose the will toward it favorably. . . .

All our acts are born out of our minds and will be what the mind is at last. This is clearly taught in the Word: "Keep thy heart with all diligence; for out of it are the issues of life."

Genesis 6:5; Proverbs 4:23; Matthew 15:18-19; 2 Corinthians 5:10; Philippians 4:8
The Set of the Sail, 72, 73.

1239. Thoughts

To think God's thoughts requires much prayer. If you do not pray much, you are not thinking God's thoughts. If you do not read your Bible much and often and reverently, you are not thinking God's thoughts. Those thoughts you are having—and your head buzzes with them all day long and into the night—are earthly thoughts—thoughts of a fallen race. They are the thoughts of a lost society. They should not be our thoughts. . . .

Your thoughts will one day come up before God's judgment. We are responsible for our premeditative thoughts. They make our mind a temple where God can dwell with pleasure, or they make our mind a stable where Christ is angry, ties a rope and drives out the cattle. It is all up to us.

Psalm 119:9-11; Matthew 12:34-37;
1 Corinthians 6:19-20; Philippians 2:5
Rut, Rot or Revival: The Condition of the Church, 42, 43.

1240. Thoughts; Perspective

We all live in two environments, the one being the world around us, the other our thoughts about that world. The larger world cannot affect us directly; it must be mediated to us by our thoughts, and will be to us at last only what we allow it to be.

Three men walking side by side may yet be inhabiting three different worlds. Imagine a poet, a naturalist and a lumberman traveling together through a forest. The poet's mind races back over the centuries to the time when the mighty trees now towering above him were but beginning to appear as tiny green shoots out of the gray earth. He dreams of the mighty of the world who then wore crowns and swayed empires, but who have long ago passed from this earthly scene and been forgotten by everyone but a few historians.

The naturalist's world is smaller and more detailed. He hears the sweet, hardly audible bird song that floats among the branches and seeks to discover the hidden singer; he knows what kind of moss it is that clings to the base of the centuries-old trees; he sees what the others miss, the fresh claw marks on the bark of a tree, and knows that a bear has recently passed that way.

The lumberman's world is smaller still. He is concerned neither with history nor nature but with lumber. He judges the diameter and height of the tree, and by quick calculation determines how much it will bring on the market. His world is the dull world of commerce. He sees nothing beyond it.

It is obvious that one external world has been turned into three internal worlds by the thinking of the three men. External things and events are the raw material only; the finished product is whatever the mind makes of these.

2 Corinthians 10:5; Philippians 2:5
That Incredible Christian, 95, 96.

1241. Thoughts; Values

As the needle of the compass has an affinity for the north magnetic pole, so the heart can keep true to its secret love though separated from it by miles and years. What that loved object is may be discovered by observing which direction our thoughts turn when they are released from the hard restraints of work or study. Of what do we think when we are free to think of what we will? What object gives us inward pleasure as we brood over it? Over what do we muse in our free moments? To what does our imagination return again and again?

When we have answered these questions honestly we will know what kind of persons we are; and when we have discovered what kind of persons we are we may deduce the kind of fruit we will bear.

Psalm 4:4; Proverbs 4:23; Matthew 15:18-19
The Root of the Righteous, 104, 105.

1242. Thoughts; Wonder

It is not a cheerful thought that millions of us who live in a land of Bibles, who belong to churches and labor to promote the Christian religion, may yet pass our whole life on this earth without once having thought or tried to think seriously about the being of God. Few of us have let our hearts gaze in wonder at the I AM, the self-existent Self back of which no creature can think. Such thoughts are too painful for us. We prefer to think where it will do more good—about how to build a better mousetrap, for instance, or how to make two blades of grass grow where one grew before. And for this we are now paying a too heavy price in the secularization of our religion and the decay of our inner lives.

Exodus 3:14
The Knowledge of the Holy, 42, 43.

1243. Today; God: His grace

To each one it is given to occupy his own spot in history. He must, like David, do the will of God by serving his own generation. It is in his own day that he must meet God in satisfying encounter. It is in his today, not in some pensive yesterday, that he must explore the riches of divine grace, do his allotted work and win his crown. . . .

Today is our day. No one at any time has ever had any spiritual graces that we at this time cannot enjoy if we will meet the terms on which they are given. If these times are morally darker, they but provide a background against which we can shine the brighter. Our God is the God of today as well as of yesterday, and we may be sure that wherever our tomorrows may carry us, our faithful God will be with us as He was with Abraham and David and Paul.

Acts 13:36; 1 Thessalonians 5:23-24; 2 Thessalonians 3:3; Hebrews 13:8
The Next Chapter after the Last, 23, 24.

1244. Tolerance/Intolerance

Christians have quite a reputation for being among the great denouncers. The odd thing about it is this: they often denounce the ones whom the Lord receives with open arms and receive the ones the Lord denounces! That is how some carnal rascals get into our churches.

John 4:9-10; James 2:1-5
Faith beyond Reason, 104.

1245. Tolerance/Intolerance

There is a great hue and cry throughout the world today on behalf of tolerance and much of it comes from a rising spirit of godlessness in the nations. . . .

This is the situation of the people of God; the most intolerant book in all the wide world is the Bible, the inspired Word of God, and the most intolerant Teacher that ever addressed Himself to an audience was the Lord Jesus Christ Himself.

On the other hand, Jesus Christ demonstrated the vast difference between being charitable and being tolerant. Jesus Christ was so charitable that in His great heart He took in all the people in the world and was willing to die even for those who hated Him.

But even with that kind of love and charity crowning His being, Jesus was so intolerant that He taught: "If you do not believe that I am the one I claim to be, you will indeed die in your sins" (John 8:24). He did not leave any middle ground to accommodate the neutral who preach tolerance. There is no "twilight zone" in the teachings of Jesus—no place in between.

Charity is one thing but tolerance is quite another matter.

Matthew 12:30; Luke 11:30; Romans 5:8; Galatians 2:20
Who Put Jesus on the Cross?, 160, 161.

1246. Tolerance/Intolerance; Absolutes

Immediately someone is bound to protest. "What arrogance! What intolerance! I do not believe Christians should be intolerant!" Well, I can startle such a person a little more. I believe in Christian charity, but I do not believe at all in Christian tolerance. The person who hates the name of Jesus, who believes that He was not the Son of God but an imposter, deserves charity on our part. I think if I lived next door to such a person, I would not put a fence between us. If I worked with him or her, I would not refuse to be friendly. I believe in Christian charity, but I do not believe in the weak tolerance that we hear preached so often now—the idea that Jesus must tolerate everyone and that the Christian must tolerate every kind of doctrine. I do not believe it for one minute, for there are not a dozen "rights." There is only one "right." There is but one Jesus and one God and one Bible.

When we become so tolerant that we lead people into mental fog and spiritual darkness, we are not acting like Christians. We are acting like cowards! We cannot do better than to remember that when Jesus Christ has spoken, that is it!

John 8:31-32; John 14:6; Acts 4:12
Faith beyond Reason, 53, 54.

1247. Tolerance/Intolerance; Christians: in the world

To teach that the spirit of the once-born is at enmity with the Spirit of the twice-born is to bring down upon one's head every kind of violent abuse. No language is too bitter to hurl against the conceited bigot who would dare to draw such a line of distinction between men. Such malignant ideas are at odds with the brotherhood of man, says the once-born, and are held only by the apostles of disunity and hate. This mighty rage against the twice-born only serves to confirm the truth they teach. But this no one seems to notice.

John 3:6-8; John 14:19; Galatians 4:29
Man: The Dwelling Place of God, 21.

1248. Tolerance/Intolerance; Religion: emptiness of; Dialogue

"We will talk to you about religion" is the seemingly kindly offer people give us today. But then they add the disclaimer: "Just do not make religion personal."

"Christianity is all right," they assure us, "if you are willing to be tolerant and not try to make something exclusive of your Christian faith." Most people seem to have come to terms with an acceptance of religion if it does not have the cross of Christ within it.

But as soon as you begin to quote the words of Jesus and the Scriptures that declare there is only one mediator between God and mankind, as soon as you insist that Christ has given us the only way to God through His death and atonement, you are dead!

"That is bigoted, narrow dogmatism," they shout. "No more dialogue with you! You have no place on a panel where we are cooperatively interested in intellectual ferment!"

John 14:6; Acts 4:12; 1 Timothy 2:1-8
Jesus, Author of Our Faith, 47, 48.

1249. Tolerance/Intolerance; Spiritual warfare; Satan

To capture a city an enemy must first weaken or destroy its resistance, and so it is with the evangelical forces at any given time or place. It is impossible for Satan to storm the citadel of God as long as faithful watchmen stand on the walls to rouse her soldiers to action. The church will never fall as long as she resists. This the devil knows; consequently he uses any stratagem to neutralize her resistance. . . .

He first creates a maudlin and wholly inaccurate concept of Christ as soft, smiling and tolerant. He reminds us that Christ was "brought as a lamb to the slaughter, and as a sheep before her shearers is dumb, so he openeth not his mouth," and suggests that we go and do likewise. Then if we notice his foot in the door and rise to oppose him he appeals to our desire to be Christlike. "You must not practice negative thinking," he tells us. "Jesus said, 'He that is not against Me is for Me.' Also He said 'Judge not,' and how can you be a good Christian and pass adverse judgment on any religious talk or activity? Controversy divides the Body of Christ. Love is of God, little children, so love everybody and all will be well."

Thus speaks the devil, using Holy Scripture falsely for his evil purpose; and it is nothing short of tragic how many of God's people are taken in by his sweet talk. The shepherd becomes afraid to use his club and the wolf gets the sheep. The watchman is charmed into believing that there is no danger, and the city falls to the enemy without a shot.

Isaiah 53:7; Ezekiel 3:17; Matthew 12:30; Acts 20:28-31; 1 Peter 5:8-9
The Set of the Sail, 114, 115.

1250. Total depravity

One of the great German poets of 200 years ago, von Goethe, summed it up for us all, when he wrote: "I have never heard of a sin being committed without knowing full well that I had the seed of it within myself."

We are on the most blessed ground with our forgiving Savior when we dare to be honest, telling Him, "O dear Lord, I have the potential of all those sins within me. I did not get them done but I have had the seed within me. Forgive me and cleanse me and keep me, for Thy glory!"

Psalm 51:5; 1 Corinthians 10:11-12; 2 Peter 3:17
Echoes from Eden, 46.

1251. Tranquility; Peace: inner

There are two kinds of tranquility among us—not counting the tranquilizers a person can buy in bottles. There is the tranquility that people find in just taking themselves and everything around them for granted. They tend to believe all kinds of good things about themselves—which are not really true. That is dangerous.

Then there is the true tranquility that God has promised when the soul has been shaken to its foundation. There is little preaching about this kind of tranquility in our day. Too often men and women get referred to psychiatrists rather than to God. If they would do what the Bible directs, they would take their disturbances and their alarms to God and to an open Bible. If the Holy Spirit is allowed to illuminate the Word of God, the Word will first do its surgery, but then it will mend what it has cut. The result is true tranquility of soul, spirit and mind.

Jeremiah 15:16; Romans 5:1; 1 John 5:3-10; Revelation 10:8-11
Jesus Is Victor!, 167.

1252. Transiency; Permanence

A beauty salon ad recently defined a term which has long needed clarification. It read: "Permanent Waves. Guaranteed to last three months." So, permanence is the quality of lasting three months! These may be extreme cases, but they illustrate the transiency of men's hopes and the brevity of their dreams apart from God.

James 4:13-14
The Next Chapter after the Last, 7.

1253. Trials: attitude toward; Faith: confidence in God

Ten thousand enemies cannot stop a Christian, cannot even slow him down, if he meets them in an attitude of complete trust in God. They will become to him like the atmosphere that resists the airplane, but which because the plane's designer knew how to take advantage of that resistance, actually lifts the plane aloft and holds it there for a journey of 2,000 miles. What would have been an enemy to the plane becomes a helpful servant to aid it on its way. . . .

If this should seem like a bit of theorizing, remember that always the greatest Christians have come out of hard times and tough situations. Tribulations actually worked for their spiritual perfection in that they taught them to trust not in themselves but in the Lord who raised the dead. They learned that the enemy could not block their progress unless they surrendered to the urgings of the flesh and began to complain. And slowly, they learned to stop complaining and start praising. It is that simple—and it works!

Romans 5:3-5; James 1:2-4
We Travel an Appointed Way, 32, 33.

1254. Trials: attitude toward; God: His inscrutability; Faith: confidence in God

A determination to know what cannot be known always works harm to the Christian heart.

Ignorance in matters on our human level is never to be excused if there has been opportunity to correct it. But there are matters which are obviously "too high for us." These we should meet in trusting faith and say as Jesus said, "Even so, Father: for so it seemed good in thy sight." . . .

Human curiosity and pride often combine to drive us to try to understand acts of God which are plainly outside the field of human understanding. We dislike to admit that we do not know what is going on, so we torture our minds trying to fathom the mysterious ways of the Omniscient One. It's hard to conceive of a more fruitless task. . . .

Under such circumstances the Christian thing to do is to say, "That thou mightest be justified when thou speakest, and be clear when thou judgest . . . Even so, Father: for so it seemed good in thy sight." A blind confidence which trusts without seeing is far dearer to God than any fancied knowledge that can explain everything. . . .

To the adoring heart, the best and most satisfying explanation for anything always will be, "It seemed good in thy sight."

1 Samuel 3:18; Job 2:10; Psalm 51:3-4;
Matthew 11:26; Romans 11:33-36;
1 Corinthians 2:12-16
The Next Chapter after the Last, 54, 55.

1255. Trials: attitude toward; Patience: God's timing; Humility

In this call to His people for true humility, God adds the promise that He will exalt us in due time! "Due time." I think that means a time that is proper to all of the circumstances. It will be the time that God knows is best suited to perfect us and a time that will bring honor to God and the most good to men. That is "due time."

It may be that in God's will He will expect us to wait a long time before He can honor us or exalt us. He may let us labor in humility and subjection for a long period because it is not yet His time—due time.

Brethren, God knows what is best for each of us in His desire to make us the kind of saints that will glorify and honor Him in all things! . . .

God has said He will exalt you in due time, but remember, He is referring to His time and not yours!

Some of you are actually in a fiery furnace right now. You are in a special kind of spiritual testing. The pastor may not know it and others may not know it, but you have been praying and asking the Lord: "Why don't you get me out of this?"

In God's plan it is not yet "due time." When you have come through the fire, God will get you out and there will not be any smell of smoke on your garment and you will not have been harmed.

The only harm that can come will be from your insistence that God must get you out sooner than He plans.

The Lord has promised to exalt you in due time and He has always kept His promises to His people.

Job 23:8-10; Ecclesiastes 3:11; Daniel 3:27; Galatians 6:9; 1 Peter 5:6
I Call It Heresy!, 114, 115, 116, 117.

1256. Trials: difficulty of; Spiritual victory

Some of you know something of that which has been called "the dark night of the soul." Some of you have spiritual desire and deep longing for victory but it seems to you that your efforts to go on with God have only brought you more bumps and more testings and more discouragement. You are tempted to ask, "How long can this go on?" . . .

Yes, there is a dark night of the soul. There are few Christians willing to go into this dark night and that is why there are so few who enter into the light. It is impossible for them ever to know the morning because they will not endure the night.

Psalm 13:1-2; Habakkuk 1:2; Revelation 6:9-10
I Talk Back to the Devil, 80, 81.

1257. Trials: difficulty of; Spiritual victory; Happiness

I remind you that we live in a spiritually troubled time in history. Christianity has gone over to the jingle-bell crowd. Everyone is just delighted that Jesus has done all of the sorrowing, all of the suffering, all of the dying.

Christian believers are emphasizing happiness. They no longer want to hear what the Bible says about death to self and the life of spiritual victory through identification with Christ in His death and resurrection. The number is great of those who will no longer admit that spiritual victory often comes through wrestling in a long, dark night of the soul.

Genesis 32:24; Galatians 2:20
Men Who Met God, 67, 68.

1258. Trials: inevitability of

Let us not be shocked by the suggestion that there are disadvantages to the life in Christ. . . . Everyone who has lived for Christ in a Christless world has suffered some losses and endured some pains that he could have avoided by the simple expedient of laying down his cross.

However, the pains are short and the losses inconsequential compared with the glory that will follow, "for our light affliction, which is but for a moment, worketh for us a far more exceeding and eternal weight of glory." But while we are here among men with our sensitive hearts exposed to the chilly blasts of the unbelieving and uncomprehending world it is imperative that we take a realistic view of things and learn how to deal with disadvantages.

Romans 8:18-19; 2 Corinthians 4:16-18; Hebrews 11:32-40
That Incredible Christian, 74, 75.

1259. Trials: inevitability of

We are all idealists. We picture to ourselves a life on earth completely free from every hindrance, a kind of spiritual Utopia where we can always control events, where we can move about as favorites of heaven, adjusting circumstances to suit ourselves. This we feel would be quite compatible with the life of faith and in keeping with the privileged place we hold as children of God.

In thinking thus we simply misplace ourselves; we mistake earth for heaven and expect conditions here below which can never be realized till we reach the better world above. While we live we may expect troubles, and plenty of them. We are never promised a life without problems as long as we remain among fallen men.

Job 5:7; John 16:33; Acts 14:22; Philippians 1:21-24; 1 Thessalonians 3:3; 2 Timothy 3:12
Of God and Men, 121, 122.

1260. Trials: necessity of

Religious contentment is the enemy of the spiritual life always. The biographies of the saints teach that the way to spiritual greatness has always been through much suffering and inward pain. . . .

The value of the stripping experience lies in its power to detach us from life's passing interests and to throw us back upon eternity. It serves to empty our earthly vessels and prepare us for the inpouring of the Holy Spirit.

Matthew 5:3; 2 Corinthians 12:9-10;
Ephesians 5:18-19
The Pursuit of Man, 133, 135.

1261. Trials: necessity of

The devil, things and people being what they are, it is necessary for God to use the hammer, the file and the furnace in His holy work of preparing a saint for true sainthood. It is doubtful whether God can bless a man greatly until He has hurt him deeply.

Job 23:8-10; Hebrews 12:5-11; James 1:2-4
The Root of the Righteous, 137.

1262. Trials: necessity of; Complacency; Spiritual growth

The fallow field is smug, contented, protected from the shock of the plow and the agitation of the harrow. Such a field, as it lies year after year, becomes a familiar landmark to the crow and the blue jay. Had it intelligence, it might take a lot of satisfaction in its reputation; it has stability; nature has adopted it; it can be counted upon to remain always the same while the fields around it change from brown to green and back to brown again. Safe and undisturbed, it sprawls lazily in the sunshine, the picture of sleepy contentment. But it is paying a terrible price for its tranquility: Never does it see the miracle of growth; never does it feel the motions of mounting life nor see the wonders of bursting seed nor the beauty of ripening grain. Fruit it can never know because it is afraid of the plow and the harrow.

In direct opposite to this, the cultivated field has yielded itself to the adventure of living. The protecting fence has opened to admit the plow, and the plow has come as plows always come, practical, cruel, business-like and in a hurry. Peace has been shattered by the shouting farmer and the rattle of machinery. The field has felt the travail of change; it has been upset, turned over, bruised and broken, but its rewards come hard upon its labors.

The seed shoots up into the daylight its miracle of life, curious, exploring the new world above it. All over the field the hand of God is at work in the age-old and ever renewed service of creation. New things are born, to grow, mature, and consummate the grand prophecy latent in the seed when it entered the ground. Nature's wonders follow the plow.

Jeremiah 4:3-4; Hosea 10:12
Paths to Power, 31, 32.

1263. Trials: necessity of; Discipline: corrective; Scourging

Another way in which we may have to learn this lesson from God is with harsh scourgings. Perhaps this makes me appear to belong to the 17th century for it does not have a popular sound in our day. We are more likely to bring in the cow bells and try to give everyone a little bit of pleasure than to faithfully declare that our dear heavenly Father may use harsh scourgings to teach His children distrust of self.

Actually, I would prefer to preach from the 23rd Psalm every Sunday for a year. Then I would take up the 53rd chapter of Isaiah and after a long time I would come to the 13th chapter of First Corinthians.

But if I should do that, what would happen to my congregation in the meantime? The flock of God would become the softest, sweetest and spongiest group of no-goods that ever came together!

Psalm 23; Psalm 119:67,71; Isaiah 53; 1 Corinthians 13; 1 Corinthians 15:9-10; 2 Corinthians 4:5-7
I Talk Back to the Devil, 128, 129.

1264. Trials: necessity of; Trials: God's presence in; Discipline: corrective

If God has singled you out to be a special object of His grace you may expect Him to honor you with stricter discipline and greater suffering than less favored ones are called upon to endure. . . .

If God sets out to make you an unusual Christian He is not likely to be as gentle as He is usually pictured by the popular teachers. A sculptor does not use a manicure set to reduce the rude, unshapely marble to a thing of beauty. The saw, the hammer and the chisel are cruel tools, but without them the rough stone must remain forever formless and unbeautiful.

To do His supreme work of grace within you He will take from your heart everything you love most. Everything you trust in will go from you. Piles of ashes will lie where your most precious treasures used to be. . . .

But there is a limit to man's ability to live without joy. Even Christ could endure the cross only because of the joy set before Him. The strongest steel breaks if kept too long under unrelieved tension. God knows exactly how much pressure each one of us can take. He knows how long we can endure the night, so He gives the soul relief, first by welcome glimpses of the morning star and then by the fuller light that harbingers the morning.

Psalm 30:5; Psalm 74:16; Romans 8:18-19; Hebrews 12:1-2
That Incredible Christian, 122, 123, 124.

1265. Trials: necessity of; Wounds

It is amazing to me! There are people within the ranks of Christianity who have been taught and who believe that Christ will shield His followers from wounds of every kind.

If the truth were known, the saints of God in every age were only effective after they had been wounded. They experienced the humbling wounds that brought contrition, compassion and a yearning for the knowledge of God. I could only wish that more among the followers of Christ knew what some of the early saints meant when they spoke of being wounded by the Holy Spirit.

Men Who Met God, 59.

1266. Trials: storms; Anchor; Jesus Christ: His sustaining power

We are in the midst of the storm of life. The believing saints of God are on board the ship. Someone looks to the horizon and warns, "We are directly in the path of the typhoon! We are as good as dead. We will surely be dashed to pieces on the rocks!"

But calmly someone else advises, "Look down, look down! We have an anchor!" We look, but the depth is too great. We cannot see the anchor. But the anchor is there. It grips the immovable rock and holds fast. Thus the ship outrides the storm.

The Holy Spirit has assured us that we have an Anchor, steadfast and sure, that keeps the soul. Jesus—Savior, Redeemer and our great High Priest—is that Anchor. He is the One who has gone before us. He has already entered into the calm and quiet harbor, the inner sanctuary behind the curtain.

Where Jesus is now, there we will be—forever.

John 14:3; John 17:20-24; Hebrews 6:17-20
Jesus, Our Man in Glory, 89, 90.

ter. Such a shelter is our high privilege!

Psalm 23; Psalm 61:2-4; John 10:11-15
Jesus, Our Man in Glory, 135.

1267. Trials: storms; Jesus Christ: His sustaining power

When the winter temperature is 50 degrees below zero, it is brave, bold talk to say, "I do not want to hide from the cold. I want to face it, whether I have the proper clothing or not!" When we face abrasive storms of life, it is ridiculous to say, "I do not want a hiding place. I will face the storms."

What we are hiding from is not life. We are hiding from a sinful world, from a sinister devil, from vicious temptation. We are hiding in the only place there is to hide—in God. It is our right and our privilege to know the perfect safety He has promised.

The trusting child of God is safe in Jesus Christ. When the lambs are safe in the fold, the wolf can growl and snarl outside, but he cannot get into the fold. When the child of God enters the Father's house, the enemy of his or her soul can roar and threaten, but he cannot en-

1268. Trials: storms; Jesus Christ: His sustaining power

In the midst of all the turmoil on earth, there is One walking through the storm. His name is Jesus. He is Christ the Lord. We ought never be frightened—even for a moment—because Jesus is the sovereign Lord.

Matthew 14:22-33; John 6:16-21
Faith beyond Reason, 145.

1269. Trials: storms; Jesus Christ: His sustaining power; Christian life

"God hath called you to Christ's side," wrote the saintly Rutherford, "and the wind is now in Christ's face in this land; and seeing ye are with Him, ye cannot expect the leeside or the sunny side of the brae."

With that beautiful feeling for words that characterized Samuel Rutherford's most casual utterance he here crystallizes for us one of the great radical facts of the Christian life. The wind is in Christ's face, and because we go with Him we too shall have the wind in our face. We should not expect less.

The yearning for the sunny side of the brae is natural enough, and for such sensitive creatures as we are it is, I suppose, quite excusable. No one enjoys walking into a cold wind. Yet the church has had to march with the wind in her face through the long centuries. . . .

To accept the call of Christ changes the returning sinner indeed, but it does not change the world. The wind still blows toward hell and the man who is walking in the opposite direction will have the wind in his face. And we had better take this into account when we ponder on spiritual things. If the unsearchable riches of Christ are not worth suffering for, then we should know it now and cease to play at religion.

John 15:18-21; John 16:33;
1 Corinthians 4:10-13
That Incredible Christian, 116, 118.

1270. Trinity; God: His inscrutability

Love and faith are at home in the mystery of the Godhead. Let reason kneel in reverence outside.

Romans 1:19-20; Romans 3:4; Colossians 2:8-9
The Knowledge of the Holy, 32.

1271. Trivialities; Priorities; Distractions

We Christians do so many things that are not really bad; they are just trivial. They are unworthy of us—much as if we discovered Albert Einstein cutting out paper dolls.

Our minds may not be among the six greatest of the ages, but like Einstein's, our minds have endless capabilities. Our spirits were designed by God to communicate with Deity. Yet we consume our time in trivialities. Jesus was never so engaged. He escaped the snare of trivialities. He was separated from the vanities of the human race. Need I remind you in this context that if these words characterized Jesus, they must also characterize each of us who claims to be a follower of Jesus? The runner separates himself from street clothes in order to free himself for the race. The soldier separates himself from civilian garb in order to don equipment that helps his mission of combat. So we as God's loving disciples must separate ourselves from everything that hinders our devotion to God.

2 Corinthians 9:24-25; Ephesians 4:22-24; 2 Timothy 2:3-4; Hebrews 12:1-2
Tragedy in the Church: The Missing Gifts, 111.

1272. True greatness

"*Whosoever will be great among you, let him be your minister,*" said our Lord—(Matt. 20:20-28), and from these words we may properly conclude (and the context strongly supports the conclusion) that there is nothing wrong with the desire to be great provided (1) we seek the right kind of greatness; (2) we allow God to decide what is greatness; (3) we are willing to pay the full price that greatness demands, and (4) we are content to wait for the judgment of God to settle the whole matter of who is great at last. . . .

No one whose heart has had a vision of God, however brief or imperfect that vision may have been, will ever consent to think of himself or anyone else as being great. The sight of God, when He appears in awesome majesty to the wondering eyes of the soul, will bring the worshiper to his knees in fear and gladness and fill him with such an overwhelming sense of divine greatness that he must spontaneously cry "Only God is great!" . . .

Obviously there are two kinds of greatness recognized in the Scriptures—an absolute, uncreated greatness belonging to God alone, and a relative and finite greatness achieved by or bestowed upon certain friends of God and sons of faith who by obedience and self-denial sought to become as much like God as possible.

Deuteronomy 3:24; 1 Chronicles 29:11-13; Matthew 20:20-28
Born after Midnight, 48, 49.

1273. True greatness; Servanthood; Character

The essence of His teaching is that true greatness lies in character, not in ability or position. Men in their blindness had always thought that superior talents made a man great, and so the vast majority believe today. To be endowed with unusual abilities in the field of art or literature or music or statecraft, for instance, is thought to be in itself an evidence of greatness, and the man thus endowed is hailed as a great man. Christ taught, and by His life demonstrated, that greatness lies deeper. . . .

While a few philosophers and religionists of pre-Christian times had seen the fallacy in man's idea of greatness and had exposed it, it was Christ who located true greatness and showed how it could be attained. "Whosoever will be great among you, let him be your minister; and whosoever will be chief among you, let him be your servant." It is that simple and that easy—and that difficult.

Matthew 20:20-28
Born after Midnight, 50.

1274. True religion

To the convinced Christian there can be but one true religion. The half-converted may shy away from the bigotry and intolerance which he fears lie in an exclusive devotion to Christianity, but the wholly converted will have no such apprehensions. To him Christ is all in all and the faith of Christ is God's last word to mankind. To him there is but one God, the Father; one Lord and Savior, one faith, one baptism, one body, one Spirit, one fold and one Shepherd. To him there is none other name under heaven given among men whereby we must be saved. For him Christ is the only way, the only truth and the only life. For him Christ is the only wisdom, the only righteousness, the only sanctification and the only redemption. He knows that his convictions will bring him into disrepute with the so-called liberals, and he knows he will be branded as narrow and "17th century" in his thinking. But he is willing to bear the stigma. What he has seen and heard and experienced precludes any possibility of compromise. He must be true to the heavenly vision.

John 14:6; Acts 4:12; Ephesians 4:3-6
The Price of Neglect, 86, 87.

1275. True spirituality

True spirituality manifests itself in certain dominant desires. These are ever-present, deep-settled wants sufficiently powerful to motivate and control the life. . . .

A man may be considered spiritual when he wants to see the honor of God advanced through his life even if it means that he himself must suffer temporary dishonor or loss. Such a man prays "Hallowed by Thy name," and silently adds, "at any cost to me, Lord." He lives for God's honor by a kind of spiritual reflex. Every choice involving the glory of God is for him already made before it presents itself. He does not need to debate the matter with his own heart; there is nothing to debate. The glory of God is necessary to him; he gasps for it as a suffocating man gasps for air.

Matthew 6:9; Ephesians 3:20-21; Philippians 1:12-18; Jude 24-25
That Incredible Christian, 110, 111.

1276. True spirituality; Eternal perspective

True spirituality manifests itself in certain dominant desires. These are ever-present, deep-settled wants sufficiently powerful to motivate and control the life. . . .

Another desire of the spiritual man is to die right rather than to live wrong. A sure mark of the mature man of God is his nonchalance about living. The earth-loving, body-conscious Christian looks upon death with numb terror in his heart; but as he goes on to live in the Spirit he becomes increasingly indifferent to the number of his years here below, and at the same time increasingly careful of the kind of life he lives while he is here. He will not purchase a few extra days of life at the cost of compromise or failure. He wants most of all to be right, and he is happy to let God decide how long he shall live. He knows that he can afford to die now that he is in Christ, but he knows that he cannot afford to do wrong, and this knowledge becomes a gyroscope to stabilize his thinking and his acting.

Psalm 90:12; Acts 20:24; 1 John 3:2-3
That Incredible Christian, 110, 111, 112.

1277. True spirituality; Eternal perspective

True spirituality manifests itself in certain dominant desires. These are ever-present, deep-settled wants sufficiently powerful to motivate and control the life. . . .

The spiritual man habitually makes eternity-judgments instead of time-judgments. By faith he rises above the tug of earth and the flow of time and learns to think and feel as one who has already left the world and gone to join the innumerable company of angels and the general assembly and church of the First-born which are written in heaven. Such a man would rather be useful than famous and would rather serve than be served.

Matthew 20:20-28; Philippians 1:21-24; Hebrews 12:22-24
That Incredible Christian, 110, 112.

1278. True spirituality; Holiness: first need; Happiness

True spirituality manifests itself in certain dominant desires. These are ever-present, deep-settled wants sufficiently powerful to motivate and control the life. . . .

First is the desire to be holy rather than happy. The yearning after happiness found so widely among Christians professing a superior degree of sanctity is sufficient proof that such sanctity is not indeed present. The truly spiritual man knows that God will give abundance of joy after we have become able to receive it without injury to our souls, but he does not demand it at once. John Wesley said of the members of one of the early Methodist societies that he doubted that they had been made perfect in love because they came to church to enjoy religion instead of to learn how they could become holy.

Leviticus 19:2; 2 Corinthians 7:1;
Ephesians 1:4-6; 1 Peter 1:14-16
That Incredible Christian, 110.

1279. Truth: adulterated

Christianity is rarely found pure. Apart from Christ and His inspired apostles probably no believer or company of believers in the history of the world has ever held the truth in total purity....

The light has shone upon men and nations, and (God be praised) it has shone with sufficient clarity to enable millions to travel home in its glow; but no believer, however pure his heart or however obedient his life, has ever been able to receive it as it shines from the Throne unmodified by his own mental stuff. As a lump of clay when grasped by the human hand remains clay but cannot escape the imprint of the hand, so the truth of God when grasped by the human mind remains truth but bears upon it the image of the mind that grasps it. Truth cannot enter a passive mind. It must be received into the mind by an active mental response, and the act of receiving it tends to alter it to a greater or less degree....

The conclusion of the matter is that we should not assume that we have all the truth and that we are mistaken in nothing. Rather we should kneel in adoration before the pierced feet of Him who is the Truth and honor Him by humble obedience to His words.

Psalm 119:160; John 1:14; John 8:31-32;
John 14:6
Born after Midnight, 76, 77, 79.

1280. Truth: adulterated; Tolerance/Intolerance; Dialogue

So we pool our religious light, which if the truth is told is little more than darkness visible; we discuss religion on television and in the press as a kind of game, much as we discuss art and philosophy, accepting as one of the ground rules of the game that there is no final test of truth and that the best religion is a composite of the best in all religions. So we have truth by majority vote and thus saith the Lord by common consent....

In all our discussions there must never be any trace of intolerance; but we obviously forget that the most fervent devotees of tolerance are invariably intolerant of everyone who speaks about God with certainty. And there must be no bigotry, which is the name given to spiritual assurance by those who do not enjoy it.

Man: The Dwelling Place of God, 113, 114.

1281. Truth: bold proclamation of

The desire to please may be commendable enough under certain circumstances, but when pleasing men means displeasing God it is an unqualified evil and should have no place in the Christian's heart. To be right with God has often meant to be in trouble with men. This is such a common truth that one hesitates to mention it, yet it appears to have been overlooked by the majority of Christians today....

The man who is going in a wrong direction will never be set right by the affable religionist who falls into step beside him and goes the same way. Someone must place himself across the path and insist that the straying man turn around and go in the right direction....

When men believe God they speak boldly. When they doubt they confer....

All great Christian leaders have been dogmatic. To such men two plus two made four. Anyone who insisted upon denying it or suspending judgment upon it was summarily dismissed as frivolous. They were only interested in a meeting of minds if the minds agreed to meet on holy ground. We could use some gentle dogmatists these days.

Galatians 1:9-10; 1 Thessalonians 2:2-4
Man: The Dwelling Place of God, 114, 115.

1282. Truth: bold proclamation of

Then there is the Athanasian Creed, and I thought it might be nice if I took you back about 1,200 or 1,400 years and we listened to our fathers tell who Jesus is. This came into being way back there when a man named Arius stood up and said that Jesus was a good man and a great man but He wasn't God. A man named Athanasius said, "No! The Bible teaches that Jesus is God." There was a great controversy, and some came to Athanasius and said, "The whole world is against you!"

"All right," Athanasius replied, "then I am against the whole world."

The Counselor, 45.

1283. Truth: bold proclamation of; Church: public relations

In our day, churches are trying to offer such a compromise between heaven and hell. Some pastors feel this is the way to get along with people and to improve the church's public relations. Honestly, our Lord would have flunked any such test on public relations. People would not have given Him a grade of 30 percent. He would have flunked the whole thing because He was dealing completely in the area of truth, and truth is just truth—it never has to worry about its image. Truth never worries about the effect it will have, about who is going to hate it or who is going to accept it. It never worries about what there is to lose and what there is to gain.

Matthew 12:30; John 8:44-47; John 15:18-20
Faith beyond Reason, 87, 88.

1284. Truth: carelessness regarding

I cannot determine when I will die. But I hope I do not live to see the day when God has to turn from men and women who have heard His holy truth and have played with it, fooled with it and equated it with fun and entertainment and religious nonsense.

We cannot deny that this attitude is found in much of current Christianity. As a result, people have hardened their hearts to the point that they no longer hear the voice of God.

We ought to be crying out in repentance and prayer: "Oh God, we have heard so much of Your truth, over and over again, yet we are ashamed that we have done so little in giving You our devotion and obedience!"

May God have mercy on us!

John 12:40; Romans 1:18-32; 2 Corinthians 4:4
Jesus Is Victor!, 130.

1285. Truth: carelessness regarding; Apathy; Preaching: response to

We are living in a time of soft, easy Christianity. It is an era marked by a polite, weekly "nibbling" around the edges of the Word of God. Our pews are filled with nice, affable Christians who are willing to listen to outlines from the Bible purporting to be sermons. But they fail to absorb and digest the Word so that it becomes their controlling interest. . . .

In God's realm, the saddest words of tongue or pen may well be, "I failed to take God at His word."

Deuteronomy 6:7-8; Psalm 119:12,18;
2 Timothy 2:14-16; Revelation 10:8-11
Jesus Is Victor!, 157.

1286. Truth: carelessness regarding; Truth/Error

Each generation of Christians must look to its beliefs. While truth itself is unchanging, the minds of men are porous vessels out of which truth can leak and into which error may seep to dilute the truth they contain. The human heart is heretical by nature and runs to error as naturally as a garden to weeds. All a man, a church or a denomination needs to guarantee deterioration of doctrine is to take everything for granted and do nothing. The unattended garden will soon be overrun with weeds; the heart that fails to cultivate truth and root out error will shortly be a theological wilderness; the church or denomination that grows careless on the highway of truth will before long find itself astray, bogged down in some mud flat from which there is no escape.

Proverbs 4:23; Jeremiah 17:9;
1 Timothy 4:13-16
Man: The Dwelling Place of God, 162.

1287. Truth: contextual

Now I have often tried to make the point that truths that are compelled to stand alone never stand straight and are not likely to stand long. Truth is one but truths are many. Scriptural truths are interlocking and interdependent. A truth is rarely valid in isolation. A statement may be true in its relation to other truths and less than true when separated from them.

That Incredible Christian, 36.

1288. Truth: contextual; Doctrinal divisions

Truth is like a bird; it cannot fly on one wing. Yet we are forever trying to take off with one wing flapping furiously and the other tucked neatly out of sight.

I believe it was Dr. G. Campbell Morgan who said that the whole truth does not lie in "It is written," but "It is written" and

"Again it is written." The second text must be placed over against the first to balance it and give it symmetry, just as the right wing must work along with the left to balance the bird and enable it to fly.

Many of the doctrinal divisions among the churches are the result of a blind and stubborn insistence that truth has but one wing. Each side holds tenaciously to one text, refusing grimly to acknowledge the validity of the other....

Lack of balance in the Christian life is often the direct consequence of overemphasis on certain favorite texts, with a corresponding underemphasis on other related ones.

John 17:21-23; Ephesians 4:3-6
That Incredible Christian, 59.

1289. Truth: importance of; Happiness

For myself, I long ago decided that I would rather know the truth than be happy in ignorance. If I cannot have both truth and happiness, give me truth. We'll have a long time to be happy in heaven.

Philippians 3:6-8
Man: The Dwelling Place of God, 22.

1290. Truth: necessity of response

Our response to truth should be eager and instant. We dare not dally with it; we dare not treat it as something we can obey or not obey, at our pleasure. It is a glorious friend, but it is nevertheless a hard master, exacting unquestioning obedience....

The true follower of Christ will not ask, "If I embrace this truth, what will it cost me?" Rather he will say, "This is truth, God help me to walk in it, let come what may!"

Isaiah 30:21; Jeremiah 42:3,6; John 8:31-32
The Set of the Sail, 69, 70.

1291. Truth: necessity of response

We will go far to simplify our religious concepts and unify our lives if we remember these four points: First, truth is a spiritual entity and can be grasped in its inner essence only as the Spirit of truth enlightens our hearts and teaches us in the deep, mysterious recesses of our souls. Secondly, since God is love we must surrender ourselves to love or we can never know the truth of God in its higher meaning. Thirdly, we must come to the Word with the simple faith of a child, ready to believe it whether we can understand it or not. And lastly, we must obey the truth as we see it, trusting God with the consequences.

Psalm 119:130; John 16:13-15; 2 Timothy 3:13-17; 1 John 2:20
The Size of the Soul, 114.

1292. Truth: necessity of response; Bible: study of; Bible: obedience to

You say you are going to take a Bible course. You can take a Bible study course and learn all about synthesis and analysis and all the rest. But if you are holding out on God, you might just as well read Pogo. All the courses in the world will not illuminate you inside. You can fill your head full of knowledge, but the day that you decide you are going to obey God, the knowledge will get down into your heart. You will *know*. Only the servants of truth can ever know truth. Only those who obey can ever have the inward change.

John 14:7; 1 Corinthians 2:12-16; 1 John 4:6
Faith beyond Reason, 31.

1293. Truth: necessity of response; Obedience: need for

Disillusioning people is a thankless task and quite plainly does not come under the category of making friends and thinking positively. Nevertheless it must be done if we are to rescue lost men from the consequences of their delusions. So let me say boldly that it is not the difficulty of discovering truth but the unwillingness to obey it that makes it so rare among men.

Our Lord said, "I am the Truth," and again He said, "The Son of man is come to seek and to save that which was lost." Truth therefore is not hard to find for the very reason that it is seeking us. Truth is not a thing for which we must search, but a Person to whom we must hearken. . . .

We should always remember that we are accountable not only for the light we have but also for the light we might have if we were willing to obey it. Truth is sovereign and will not allow itself to be trifled with. And it is easy to find for it is trying to find us. Obedience is the big problem: and unwillingness to obey is the cause of continued darkness.

Luke 19:10; John 3:19-21; John 14:6
The Set of the Sail, 98, 99, 100.

1294. Truth: necessity of response; Theology; Obedience: need for

For a long time I have believed that truth, to be understood, must be lived; that Bible doctrine is wholly ineffective until it has been digested and assimilated by the total life. I have held this to be an important element in the preaching of the Old Testament prophets, and I have felt it to be near to the heart of the moral teaching of our Lord Jesus Christ. I admit that this belief has made me a little lonely, for not many of my Christian brethren share it with me. While I have not heard anyone deny the truth outright, few have seen fit to teach it with anything approaching emphasis. And by silence a man will reveal his beliefs as surely as by argument. . . .

At what point, then, does a theological fact become for the one who holds it a life-giving truth? *At the point where obedience begins.* When faith gains the consent of the will to make an irrevocable committal to Christ as Lord, truth begins its saving, illuminating work; and not one moment before. . . .

Theological facts are like the altar of Elijah on Carmel before the fire came, correct, properly laid out, but altogether cold. When the heart makes the ultimate surrender, the fire falls and true facts are transmuted into spiritual truth that transforms, enlightens, sanctifies. The church or the individual that is Bible taught without being Spirit taught (and there are many of them) has simply failed to see that truth lies deeper than the theological statement of it.

1 Kings 17:36-38; John 7:17;
1 Corinthians 2:12-16
That Incredible Christian, 92, 93, 94.

1295. Truth/Error

Throughout the whole world error and truth travel the same highways, work in the same fields and factories, attend the same churches, fly in the same planes and shop in the same stores. So skilled is error at imitating truth that the two are constantly being mistaken for each other. It takes a sharp eye these days to know which brother is Cain and which Abel.

We must never take for granted anything that touches our soul's welfare. Isaac felt Jacob's arms and thought they were the arms of Esau. Even the disciples failed to spot the traitor among them; the only one of them who knew who he was was Judas himself. That soft-spoken companion with whom we walk so comfortably and in whose company we take such delight may be an angel of Satan, whereas that rough, plain-spoken man whom we shun may be God's very prophet sent to warn us against danger and eternal loss.

Genesis 27:22; 1 Kings 3:9; John 13:21-22;
Hebrews 5:12-14; 1 John 4:1
That Incredible Christian, 50.

U

1296. Unbelief; Faith: defective

The voice of unbelief says, "Yes, I'm a believer. I believe the Bible. I don't like those modernists, liberals and modern scientists who deny the Bible. I would not do that for the world. I believe in God, and I believe that God will bless." That is, He will bless at some other time, in some other place and some other people. Those are three sleepers that bring the work of God to a halt. We are believers and we can quote the creed with approval. We believe it, but we believe that God will bless some other people, some other place, some other time—but not now, not here and not us. . . .

If we allow the gloomy voice of unbelief to whisper to us that God will bless some other time but not now, some other place but not here, some other people but not us, we might as well turn off the lights because nobody will get anywhere. . . .

The average evangelical church lies under a shadow of quiet doubting. The doubt is not the unbelief that argues against Scripture, but worse than that. It is the chronic unbelief that does not know what faith means.

Isaiah 43:1-3; Jeremiah 33:3; Hebrews 11:1-2
Rut, Rot or Revival: The Condition of the Church, 152, 157.

1297. Unity; Church: unity

. . . unity of mind on the part of the people of God precedes the blessing. I have often heard people pray, "Oh Lord, send the Holy Spirit that we may become a united people." That is all right except it is precisely backwards. The Holy Spirit comes because we are a united people; He does not come to make us a united people. Our prayer should be more like, "Lord, help us to get united in order that the blessing might flow and there might be an outpouring of oil and dew and life." That's the way we should pray. . . .

This teaches us that unity is necessary to the outpouring of the Spirit of God. If you have 120 volts of electricity coming into your house but you have broken wiring, you may turn the switch, but nothing works—no lights come on, the stove doesn't warm, your radio doesn't turn on. Why? Because you have broken wiring. The power is ready to do its work with all the appliances in your home, but where there is broken wiring, you have no power. Unity is necessary among the children of God if we are going to know the flow of power.

Psalm 133:1-3; Acts 2:1-4; Philippians 2:1-4
Success and the Christian, 86, 87.

1298. Unity; Church: unity

I have seen the motto, "In essentials unity; in nonessentials charity," and I have looked for its incarnation in men and churches without finding it, one reason being that Christians cannot agree on what is and what is not essential. Each one believes that his fragment of truth is essential and his neighbor's unessential, and that brings us right back where we started.

Unity among Christians will not, in my opinion, be achieved short of the Second Advent. There are too many factors working against it. But a greater degree of unity might be realized if we all approached the truth with deeper humility. No one knows everything, not saint nor scholar nor reformer nor theologian. Even Solomon in all his glory must have overlooked something.

John 17:20-24; Ephesians 4:3-6
The Warfare of the Spirit, 112, 113.

1299. Unity; Truth: importance of

In a fallen world like ours unity is no treasure to be purchased at the price of compromise. Loyalty to God, faithfulness to truth and the preservation of a good conscience are jewels more precious than gold of Ophir or diamonds from the mine. For these jewels men have suffered the loss of property, imprisonment and even death; for them, even in recent times, behind the various curtains, followers of Christ have paid the last full measure of devotion and quietly died, unknown to and unsung by the great world, but known to God and dear to His Father heart. In the day that shall declare the secrets of all souls these shall come forth to receive the deeds done in the body. Surely such as these are wiser philosophers than the religious camp followers of meaningless unity who have not the courage to stand against current vogues and who bleat for brotherhood only because it happens to be for the time popular.

"Divide and conquer" is the cynical slogan of Machiavellian political leaders, but Satan knows also how to unite and conquer.

Acts 23:1; 1 Timothy 1:5-6; 2 Timothy 3:1-7
God Tells the Man Who Cares, 51, 52.

1300. Unpopularity; Christians: in the world

Popular Judaism slew the prophets and crucified Christ. Popular Christianity killed the Reformers, jailed the Quakers and drove John Wesley into the streets. When it comes to religion, the crowds are always wrong. At any time there are a few who see, and the rest are blinded. To stand by the truth of God against the current religious vogue is always unpopular and may be downright dangerous....

Christianity's scramble for popularity today is an unconscious acknowledgment of spiritual decline. Her eager fawning at the feet of the world's great is a grief to the Holy Spirit and an embarrassment to the sons of God. The lick-spittle attitude of popular Christian leaders toward the world's celebrities would make such men as Elijah or George Fox sick to the stomach....

Lot was a popular believer. He sat in the gates of Sodom. But when trouble struck, he had to send quick for Abraham to get him out of the jam. And where did they find Abraham? Out on the hillside, far away from the fashionable crowds. It has always been so. For every Elijah there have always been 400 popular prophets of Baal. For every Noah there is always a vast multitude who will not believe it is going to rain.

We are sent to bless the world, but never are we told to compromise with it.

Genesis 6:9; 1 Kings 18:18-19; Matthew 5:10-12; Acts 7:52
The Next Chapter after the Last, 20, 21.

V

1301. Vacations; Summer; Commitment

As the sun makes its annual climb up from the south a strange restlessness comes over those of our citizens who live north of the Mason-Dixon Line, and by the time summer has finally arrived this has increased into a pathological condition which turns the country into one vast cage of waltzing mice. A kind of madness grips the populace, and then begins that four-month frenzied effort on everybody's part to get somewhere other than where he is. No one stops to ask what it is all about, but practically everyone who is not in the hospital or in jail joins the general stampede from everywhere to anywhere and return.

An irresistible impulse picks most of us up like grains of dust caught by the wind, and spins and churns us about dizzily and dangerously till the first frost comes to ripen the pumpkin and drive home the trailers....

If most of the population choose to forsake their homes and spend all their spare time scudding between filling stations, there is nothing we can do about it. To protest it is to blow against the wind or shout against the tide. However, some of us old-fashioned throwbacks to a saner if slower age may be forgiven if we indulge in a few honest tears for the havoc this midsummer madness works among the churches of this hectic day....

But the sad truth is that the vacation habit, plus the habit of making weekend trips throughout the summer season, has worked practically to paralyze the church of God for several months out of the year....

It is hard to understand how a follower of Christ can justify himself in laying down his cross so frequently and so shamelessly in this day of the world's judgment. The army of the Lord is the only army on earth where the soldiers expect a four-month furlough in time of war.

God Tells the Man Who Cares, 155, 156, 157, 158.

1302. Values; Sin: consequences of

Sin has done frightful things to us and its effect upon us is all the more deadly because we were born in it and are scarcely aware of what is happening to us.

One thing sin has done is to confuse our values so that we can only with difficulty distinguish a friend from a foe or tell for certain what is and what is not good for us. We walk in a world of shadows where real things appear unreal and things of no consequence are sought after as eagerly as if they were made of the very gold that paves the streets of the City of God.

Psalm 51:5; Isaiah 55:6-8; Matthew 6:19-21
That Incredible Christian, 14.

1303. Values; Truth: carelessness regarding

The fact is that men have never in any numbers sought after truth. If we may judge people's interests by their deeds, then of the young men and women who stream forth from our halls of learning each year the vast majority have no more than a passing and academic interest in truth. They go to college not to satisfy a yearning to discover truth, but to improve their social standing and increase their earning power. These motives are not necessarily to be despised; but they should be known for what they are, and not hidden beneath a pink cloud of specious idealism.

What are people actually seeking? Of course they seek satisfaction for the basic urges such as hunger, sex and social companionship; but beyond these what? Certainly for nothing as high and noble as truth.

Ask the average American what he wants from life and if he is candid he will tell you he wants success in his chosen field; and he wants success both for the prestige it brings him and for the financial security it affords. And why does he want financial security? To guarantee him against the loss of comforts, luxuries and pleasures, which he believes are rightfully his as a part of his American heritage. The ominous thing about all this is that *everything he wants can be bought with money*. It would be hard to think of an indictment more terrible than that.

Matthew 6:33; Luke 12:18-26; 1 Timothy 6:17-19
The Set of the Sail, 95.

1304. Vicarious atonement

At the foundation of the Christian life lies vicarious atonement, which in essence is a transfer of guilt from the sinner to the Saviour. I well know how vigorously this idea is attacked by non-Christians, but I also know that the wise of this world in their pride often miss the treasures which the simple-hearted find on their knees.

2 Corinthians 5:19-21; Galatians 3:13; 1 Peter 2:24
That Incredible Christian, 32.

1305. Vision of God

God had planned a great task and a vital ministry for Isaiah. But as a young man involved in the court life of a successful king, he seemed satisfied with this world and with things as they were. We can say that Isaiah's attention was too strongly focused on King Uzziah.

How was the Lord going to get Isaiah's attention and show him the importance of the world to come? The same way He so frequently does it. He removed the object of Isaiah's interest.

Suddenly, Uzziah, the great and successful king, was gone, taken by death. Isaiah must have been deeply affected, not only as he thought of his own life and career, but as he pondered what Uzziah's passing would mean for the nation of Israel.

I suspect Isaiah stood in tearless grief and looked down at the face of the lifeless king....

The next thing Isaiah did, however, was the wisest thing he could have done. He raised his eyes from viewing the face of the dead king, and suddenly the Lord enabled him to fasten his gaze upon the eternal King of Kings! Isaiah testified that he saw the Lord sitting upon a throne. He saw God's glory filling the Temple. He saw the seraphim, those created heavenly beings, worshiping God.

He heard the adoring ascription of praise around the heavenly throne: "Holy, holy, holy, is the Lord of hosts: the whole earth is full of His glory."

Isaiah 6:1-8
Men Who Met God, 99, 100.

W

1306. Wealth

Brethren, we ought to learn—and learn it very soon—that it is much better to have God first and have God Himself even if we have only a thin dime than to have all the riches and all the influence in the world and not have God with it!

Matthew 6:33; Matthew 16:24-26
I Talk Back to the Devil, 26.

1307. Wealth; Earthly things

The Bible has a great deal to say about wealth. Our Lord dealt with the matter forthrightly, as did also Paul and others of the New Testament writers. What they said is on record and is deserving of a more careful study than most Christians give it. . . .

Knowing the tendency of the human heart to become unduly attached to earthly goods, Christ warned against it. The "things" which the Father gives are to be understood as provisional merely and must never be considered our real treasure. The heart always returns to its real treasure, and if a man holds corn to be a real form of wealth his heart will be where his corn is. Many a man has his heart locked up in a bank vault, and many a woman has her heart in her jewel box or stored at the furrier's. It is a great moral tragedy when anything as wonderful as the human heart comes to rest on the earth and fails to rise to its own proper place in God and in heaven.

Matthew 6:25-34; Colossians 3:1-4;
1 Timothy 6:17-19
Born after Midnight, 104, 106.

1308. Wealth; Materialism; Earthly things

Many of us are forgetting the caution of the Lord Jesus that we ought not to set our hearts on earthly things.

He warned that there is a very real danger involved and He said plenty about it in the New Testament.

Jesus said that when wealth becomes our heart's treasure, our very beings may well be imprisoned within our wealth.

This is the danger: the same heart of man that was made to commune with God and hold fellowship with the Divine Trinity, to soar away to worlds unknown and behold God upon His throne, that same heart may be locked up in a bank vault or in a jewelry box or somewhere else here on earth!

The fashionable woman longing to make the list of the "Ten Best Dressed"—she lives for her jewelry and glamour. And when she puts those jewels into a box at night, she surely imprisons her heart in the same box as she snaps the lid.

So, too, the businessman who doesn't know how to use the money God allows him to get, and who makes an idol out of it. When he snaps the door of his box in the bank vault, he puts his heart there and locks it up.

Matthew 6:19-21; Luke 12:15-21; Colossians 3:1-4; 1 Timothy 6:17-19; 1 John 2:15-17
The Tozer Pulpit, Volume 1, Book 1, 42, 43.

1309. Wealth; Second coming:
    lack of interest in;
    Heaven:
    lack of interest in

Probably the most irritating problem faced by today's western Christians is where to find parking for their shiny automobiles that transported them effortlessly to the house of God, where they hope to prepare their souls for the world to come. In the United States and Canada the middle class today possesses more earthly goods and lives in greater luxury than emperors and Maharajahs did only a century ago.

Since the bulk of Christians comes from this class, it is not difficult to see why the genuine expectation of Christ's return has all but disappeared from among us. About that there can be little argument. It is hard indeed to focus attention on a better world to come when a more comfortable one than this can hardly be imagined. As long as science can make us so cozy in this present world, it is admittedly hard to work up much pleasurable anticipation of a new world order, even if it is God who has promised it.

Matthew 13:20-22; Luke 21:34-36; Acts 1:9-11; Philippians 1:21-24
Tragedy in the Church: The Missing Gifts, 135.

1310. Will: importance of;
    Commitment

That religion lies in the will is an axiom of theology. Not how we feel but what we will determines our spiritual direction. An old poem states it for us:

> One ship drives east and
>   another drives west
> With the selfsame winds
>   that blow;
> 'Tis the set of the sails

And not the gales
Which tells us the way to go.
  —Ella Wheeler Wilcox

Though we do not hear much of it in this age of spineless religion, there is nevertheless much in the Bible about the place of moral determination in the service of the Lord. "Jacob vowed a vow," and it was the beginning of a very wonderful life with God. . . .

Daniel "purposed in his heart," and God honored his purpose. Jesus set his face like a flint and walked straight toward the cross. Paul "determined not to know any thing among you, save Jesus Christ, and him crucified,". . .

These are only a few of the many men and women of the Bible who have left us a record of spiritual greatness born out of a will firmly set to do the will of God. . . .

Let us, then, set our sails in the will of God. If we do this we will certainly find ourselves moving in the right direction, no matter which way the wind blows.

Genesis 28:20; Isaiah 50:7; Daniel 1:8; Matthew 16:21; 1 Corinthians 2:1-5
The Set of the Sail, 11, 12, 13.

1311. Will of God; Choices; Lordship of Christ

One of the problems most frequently encountered by serious-minded Christians is how to discover the will of God in a given situation. . . .

First, it is absolutely essential that we be completely dedicated to God's high honor and surrendered to the Lordship of Jesus Christ. God will not lead us except for His own glory and He cannot lead us if we resist His will. The shepherd cannot lead a stubborn sheep. . . .

Put this down as an unfailing rule: Never seek the leading of the Lord concerning an act that is forbidden in the Word of God. To do so is to convict ourselves of insincerity. . . .

Now, a happy truth too often overlooked in our anxious search for the will of God is that in the majority of decisions touching our earthly lives God expresses no choice, but leaves everything to our own preference. . . .

Except for those things that are specifically commanded or forbidden, it is God's will that we be free to exercise our own intelligent choice. The shepherd will lead the sheep but he does not wish to decide which tuft of grass the sheep shall nibble each moment of the day. In almost everything touching our common life on earth God is pleased when we are pleased. He wills that we be as free as birds to soar and sing our Maker's praise without anxiety. God's choice for us may not be one but any one of a score of possible choices. The man or woman who is wholly and joyously surrendered to Christ cannot make a wrong choice. Any choice will be the right one.

Proverbs 3:5-6; Isaiah 1:16-19; Isaiah 48:7; Matthew 22:37-39; James 1:5-6
The Set of the Sail, 75, 76, 77.

1312. Will of God; Cross: personal

At the risk of repeating a religious cliche, I must point out that the will of God is always best, whatever the circumstances. Jesus refused the crown and deliberately took the cross because the cross was in the will of God, both for Him and for humankind.

Let us not be afraid to take that cross ourselves and trust God to provide the crown in His own time.

John 6:15; Philippians 2:9-11; Hebrews 11:24-26
Faith beyond Reason, 149, 150.

1313. Will of God; Opposition; Self-denial

Few sights are more depressing than that of a professed Christian defending his or her supposed rights and bitterly resisting any attempt to violate them. Such a Christian has never accepted the way of the cross. . . .

The only cure for this sort of thing is to die to self and rise with Christ into newness of life. The man or woman who sets the will of God as his or her goal will reach that goal not by self-defense but by self-abnegation. Then no matter what sort of treatment that person receives from other people, he or she will be altogether at peace. The will of God has been done—this Christian does not care whether it comes with curses or compliments, for he or she does not seek one or the other, but wants to do the will of God at any cost. Then, whether riding the crest of public favor or wallowing in the depths of obscurity, he or she will be content. If there be some who take pleasure in holding this Christian down, still he or she will not resent them, for he or she seeks not advancement but the will of God.

Isaiah 53:7; Romans 6:4-7; 1 Peter 5:5
This World: Playground or Battleground?, 81, 82.

1314. Women

I think there is a great contradiction apparent among us. Many women are working so hard in all kinds of jobs that they are making themselves old in the effort to get money enough to buy the clothes and cosmetics that are supposed to make them look young.

1 Timothy 2:9-10; 1 Peter 3:1-7
I Call It Heresy!, 131.

1315. Women's apparel

... what does the Bible really teach here about the outward adorning of the person?

It says that the woman is not to seek to be attractive by outward adorning and dress. Does it expressly forbid the plaiting of the hair, the wearing of gold and the putting on of fine clothes? This is a question often asked.

Let's say "yes" and then go on from there and see where we stand. ...

Does the Bible say, then, that a woman must not be adorned with braided hair?

If we say, "Yes, that's what it means"—that rules out the braiding of your hair.

The advice continues: "Let it not be the wearing of gold."

Does that mean that gold can never be worn in any way by a Christian woman?

We will agree for the moment and say that gold is out!

"Nor the putting on of fine clothes."

Now, wait a minute! We are in trouble with our reasoning here, because this certainly does not mean that the woman is not to put on any nice clothes.

If it doesn't mean a strict ban on fixing the hair or wearing of gold or putting on of fine clothes, what does it mean?

It means the true attractiveness of the person is not outward but inward! Therefore, the Christian woman should remember that she cannot buy true attractiveness—that radiance which really shines forth in beauty is of the heart and spirit and not of the body!

1 Timothy 2:9-10; 1 Peter 3:1-7
I Call It Heresy!, 126, 127, 128.

1316. World: contempt for Christians

The world's spirit is strong, and it clings to us as close as the smell of smoke to our garments. It can change its face to suit any circumstance and so deceive many a simple Christian whose senses are not exercised to discern good and evil. It can play at religion with every appearance of sincerity. It can have fits of conscience (particularly during Lent) and even confess its evil ways in the public press. It will praise religion and fawn on the Church for its ends. It will contribute to charitable causes and promote campaigns to furnish clothing for the poor. *Only let Christ keep His distance and never assert His Lordship over it.* This it will positively not endure. And toward the true Spirit of Christ it will show only antagonism. The world's press (which is always its real mouthpiece) will seldom give a child of God a fair deal. If the facts compel a favorable report, the tone is apt to be condescending and ironic. The note of contempt sounds through.

John 14:15-17; John 15:18-20;
Hebrews 5:12-14
The Pursuit of Man, 121.

1317. World: contentment with

In the early days, when Christianity exercised a dominant influence over American thinking, men conceived the world to be a battleground. Our fathers believed in sin and the devil and hell as constituting one force; and they believed in God and righteousness and heaven as the other. These were opposed to each other in the nature of them forever in deep, grave, irreconcilable hostility. Man, so our fathers held, had to choose sides; he could not be neutral. For him it must be life or death, heaven or hell, and if he chose to come out on God's side he could expect open war with God's enemies. The fight would be real and deadly and would last as long as life continued here below. Men looked forward to heaven as a return from the wars, a laying down of the sword to enjoy in peace the home prepared for them. . . .

How different today. The fact remains the same but the interpretation has changed completely. Men think of the world, not as a battleground but as a playground. We are not here to fight, we are here to frolic. We are not in a foreign land, we are at home. We are not getting ready to live, we are already living, and the best we can do is to rid ourselves of our inhibitions and our frustrations and live this life to the full.

Deuteronomy 30:19; Joshua 24:14-15;
2 Corinthians 6:17-18; 1 John 2:15-17
God Tells the Man Who Cares, 191, 192.

1318. World: contentment with; Eternal perspective

The answer is that we are too comfortable, too rich, too contented. We hold the faith of our fathers, but it does not hold us. We are suffering from judicial blindness visited upon us because of our sins. To us has been committed the most precious of all treasures, but we are not committed to it. We insist upon making our religion a form of amusement and will have fun whether or not. We are afflicted with religious myopia and see only things near at hand.

God has set eternity in our hearts and we have chosen time instead. He is trying to interest us in a glorious tomorrow and we are settling for an inglorious today. We are bogged down in local interests and have lost sight of eternal purposes. We improvise and muddle along, hoping for heaven at last but showing no eagerness to get there, correct in doctrine but weary of prayer and bored with God.

John 14:1-3; 2 Corinthians 4:5-7; Ephesians 4:17-24; Revelation 5:8-14
The Set of the Sail, 93.

1319. World: contentment with; Pilgrims; Earthly things

You are a Christian. That you admit. You go to church nearly every Sunday. "Just ask the minister; he will confirm it."

You have been working and earning, getting and spending, and now you are enjoying the creature comforts known to modern human beings in this land.

You bristle a little and ask, "Is there anything wrong with being comfortable?"

Let me answer in this way: If you are a Christian and you are comfortable "at home" in Chicago or Toronto, in Iowa or Alberta—or any other address on planet earth—the signs are evident that you are in spiritual trouble.

The spiritual equation reads like this: The greater your contentment with your daily circumstances in this world, the greater your defection from the ranks of God's pilgrims en route to a city whose architect and builder is God Himself! . . .

One of the most telling indictments against many of us who comprise our Christian churches today is the almost complete acceptance of the contemporary scene as our permanent home. We say that we are followers of Christ, but we have already settled down and we are comfortably at home. We are satisfied to be natives and citizens of this world's society—we are no longer "aliens and strangers."

Luke 12:19-21; Philippians 3:18-21; Hebrews 11:10-16
Jesus, Author of Our Faith, 53, 54.

1320. World: corruption of

This was no fallen man Satan was attempting to seduce; it was a sinless Man full of the Holy Ghost and wisdom, whose penetrating glance pierced the world's attractive exterior and saw what was inside. What He saw revolted Him. He would have no part of it.

Our Lord saw in the world's glory not what other men saw and, conversely, He saw what other men could not see. He saw not beauty but death, a garish death that must be purchased at the price of the soul. Beneath its gaudy allurements He saw corruption and decay. He knew its glory was but bait to catch foolish victims, He knew its bright promises were all lies.

Matthew 4:8-10; 1 John 2:15-17
God Tells the Man Who Cares, 19, 20.

1321. World: love not; Separation

With the Bible open before us and a long tradition of truth behind us there would seem to be no reason for our present tragic failure to recognize the world's deceptive appeal and to stay clear of it. For there must not be any denial of the facts: the church has been captured by the kingdoms of the world and the glory of them. In spite of the prophetic voices that are raised here and there among us, present-day believers are drawn to the world with irresistible force.

That world which our Saviour once refused to buy at the price of disobedience to God is now wooing His professed followers with every sly, deceptive artifice. The glory which our Lord once rejected with cold scorn is now being admired and sought after by multitudes who make a loud profession of accepting the gospel. The old trick which our Lord saw through so easily is charming His present-day followers into smiling acquiescence.

Matthew 4:8-10; Matthew 6:19-21;
1 John 2:15-17
God Tells the Man Who Cares, 20, 21.

1322. World: love not; Worship: meaningless

The idea that this world is a playground instead of a battleground has now been accepted in practice by the vast majority of fundamentalist Christians. They might hedge around the question if they were asked bluntly to declare their position, but their conduct gives them away. They are facing both ways, enjoying

Christ *and* the world, gleefully telling everyone that accepting Jesus does not require them to give up their fun—Christianity is just the jolliest thing imaginable. The "worship" growing out of such a view of life is as far off center as the view itself—a sort of sanctified nightclub without the champagne and the dressed-up drunks.

2 Corinthians 6:17-18
This World: Playground or Battleground?, 5, 6.

1323. World unity

We confess we should like to go along with the modern movement toward world unity, and we might do it except for two considerations. One is that in their move toward unity, the nations are not being drawn together, they are being *driven* together and that which drives them is *fear*. The 60 nations of the UN do not love each other, they fear each other, and they fear the rest of the world. And if every nation in the world were finally included in one huge superstate, the tie that bound them would be the same—mutual distrust and hate. And human nature being what it is, and God being who He is, *nothing that rests upon fear can be permanent*. . . .

While a few superior men dream of true brotherhood, the masses of mankind are filled with jealousy, envy, hate and greed. World leaders are too often motivated by lust for power or by the selfish desire to gain and hold high position. . . .

The second reason for rejecting the doctrine of world brotherhood is that it is out of accord with the teaching of the Scriptures. Any unity that may be achieved among nations will be but a temporary thing, and will be exploited by the coming Antichrist to secure his evil ends.

Jeremiah 17:9; Romans 3:10-18;
1 Thessalonians 5:1-8
The Next Chapter after the Last, 38, 39.

1324. Worldliness

To any casual observer of the religious scene today, two things will at once be evident: one, that there is very little sense of sin among the unsaved, and two, that the average professed Christian lives a life so worldly and careless that it is difficult to distinguish him from the unconverted man.

2 Corinthians 6:17-18; Ephesians 5:7-8;
Revelation 18:4
Paths to Power, 39.

1325. Worldliness; Church: spiritual condition; Separation

The result over the last 20 years has been a religious debauch hardly equaled since Israel worshiped the golden calf. Of us Bible Christians it may truthfully be said that we "sat down to eat and to drink, and rose up to play." The separating line between the Church and the world has been all but obliterated.

Aside from a few of the grosser sins, the sins of the unregenerated world are now approved by a shocking number of professedly "born-again" Christians, and copied eagerly. Young Christians take as their models the rankest kind of worldlings and try to be as much like them as possible. Religious leaders have adopted the techniques of the advertisers; boasting, baiting, and shameless exaggerating are now carried on as a normal procedure in church work. The moral climate is not that of the New Testament, but that of Hollywood and Broadway.

Exodus 32:6; Romans 12:1-2; 2 Corinthians 6:17-18; 1 Peter 1:14-16
Keys to the Deeper Life, 22.

1326. Worry

He says, "I will do it for you. Why do you worry? I will do it for you. I am God. I am Jehovah. I am your righteousness. I am your provider. I am your healer. I am your banner of victory. I am your shepherd. I am your peace. I am your everything."

If God is all this to us, then there is no reason why anybody should be downhearted in this hour. If God could make a world out of nothing, why can't He make anything He wants now for His people? God invites us to see Him work.

Psalm 23:1; Isaiah 43:1-3; Matthew 6:25-34; Philippians 4:6-7
Rut, Rot or Revival: The Condition of the Church, 161,162.

1327. Worry; Faith: confidence in God

How are we going to escape fear, when there are legitimate dangers that lie all around us?

Well, here's what the man of God says: "Don't be anxious about anything, but in everything by prayer and supplication with thanksgiving let your requests be made known unto God and the peace of God which passeth all understanding shall keep your hearts and minds through Christ Jesus."

Someone is looking after us. The Bible says "He careth for you." Jesus, our Lord, says: "Your Father knows what you have need of before you ask Him." And Jesus said, "Let not your heart be troubled." And in all your afflictions, He was afflicted, it says.

The Bible pictures God as a very careful, tender-hearted Father, busying Himself about the troubles of His people. He looks after them, goes ahead of them, cares for them, and guides them all the way through.

There you see the problem of worry and anxiety is solved by the assurance that while there are things about which to be concerned, why should you worry, when Somebody is taking care of you!

Isaiah 63:9-10; Matthew 6:8; John 14:1; Philippians 4:6-7; 1 Peter 5:7
The Tozer Pulpit, Volume 1, Book 1, 130, 131.

1328. Worry; Peace: inner

Now, the grace of God in the human heart works to calm the agitation that normally accompanies life in such a world as ours. The Holy Spirit acts as a lubricant to reduce the friction to a minimum and to stop the fretting and chafing in their grosser phases. . . .

It was not to the unregenerate that the words, "Fret not" were spoken, but to God-fearing persons capable of understanding spiritual things. We Christians need to watch and pray lest we fall into this temptation and spoil our Christian testimony by an irritable spirit under the stress and strain of life.

Psalm 37:1,7-11; Matthew 6:25-34; Philippians 4:6-7
Man: The Dwelling Place of God, 67, 68.

1329. Worship: acceptable

I can offer no worship wholly pleasing to God if I know that I am harboring elements in my life that are displeasing to Him. I cannot truly and joyfully worship God on Sunday and not worship Him on Monday. I cannot worship God with a glad song on Sunday and then knowingly displease Him in my business dealings on Monday and Tuesday.

I repeat my view of worship—*no worship is wholly pleasing to God until there is nothing in me displeasing to God.*

Psalm 66:18; Proverbs 28:9; John 9:31
Whatever Happened to Worship?, 124, 125.

1330. Worship: acceptable

I have come to believe that no worship is wholly pleasing to God until there is nothing in us displeasing to God. If there is anything within me that does not worship God, then there is nothing in me that worships God perfectly.

Psalm 66:18; Psalm 95:6-7
Renewed Day by Day, Volume 1, Jan. 8.

1331. Worship: admiration; Thanksgiving

Thus the simple love which arises from gratitude, when expressed in any act or conscious utterance, is undoubtedly worship. But the quality of our worship is stepped up as we move away from the thought of what God has done for us and nearer the thought of the excellence of His holy nature. This leads us to admiration.

The dictionary says that to admire is "to regard with wondering esteem accompanied by pleasure and delight; to look at or upon with an elevated feeling of pleasure." According to this definition, God has few admirers among Christians today.

Many are they who are grateful for His goodness in providing salvation. At Thanksgiving time the churches ring with songs of gratitude that "all is safely gathered in." Testimony meetings are mostly devoted to recitations of incidents where someone got into trouble and got out again in answer to prayer. To decry this would be uncharitable and unscriptural, for there is much of the same thing in the Book of Psalms. It is good and right to render unto God thanksgiving for all His mercies to us. But God's admirers, where are they?

The simple truth is that worship is elementary until it begins to take on the quality of admiration. Just as long as the worshiper is engrossed with himself and his good fortune, he is a babe. We begin to grow up when our worship passes from thanksgiving to admiration. As our hearts rise to God in lofty esteem for that which He is ("I AM THAT I AM"), we begin to share a little of the selfless pleasure which is the portion of the blessed in heaven.

Exodus 3:14; Matthew 22:37-39; Hebrews 13:8; Revelation 1:8; Revelation 4:8
That Incredible Christian, 127.

1332. Worship: admiration; Worship: awe

Then there is *admiration*, that is, appreciation of the excellency of God. Man is better qualified to appreciate God than any other creature because he was made in His image and is the only creature who was. This admiration for God grows and grows until it fills the heart with wonder and delight. "In our astonished reverence we confess Thine uncreated loveliness," said the hymn writer. "In our astonished reverence." The God of the modern evangelical rarely astonishes anybody. He manages to stay pretty much within the constitution. Never breaks over our bylaws. He's a very well-behaved God and very denominational and very much one of us, and we ask Him to help us when we're in trouble and look to Him to watch over us when we're asleep. The God of the modern evangelical isn't a God I could have much respect for. But when the Holy Ghost shows us God as He is we admire Him to the point of wonder and delight.

Genesis 1:24-26; 1 Chronicles 29:11-13; Psalm 8:1,9
Worship: The Missing Jewel, 22, 23.

1333. Worship: adoration

The whole import and substance of the Bible teaches us that the God who does not need anything nevertheless desires the adoration and worship of His created children.

Deuteronomy 6:4-9; Proverbs 15:8; Luke 4:8
Whatever Happened to Worship?, 37.

1334. Worship: adoration; Thanksgiving

Sometimes I go to God and say, "God, if Thou dost never answer another prayer while I live on this earth I will still worship Thee as long as I live and in the ages to come for what Thou hast done already." God's already put me so far in debt that if I were to live one million millenniums I couldn't pay Him for what He's done for me.

Worship: The Missing Jewel, 24.

1335. Worship: adoration; Worship: daily

Looking at what John wrote, I wonder how so many present-day Christians can consider an hour of worship Sunday morning as adequate adoration of the holy God who created them and then redeemed them back to Himself....

God is pleased with His people when His praise is continually and joyfully on their lips. The heavenly scene John describes is the unceasing cry of the adoring living creatures, "Holy, holy, holy!" They rest not, day or night. My fear is that too many of God's professing people down here are resting far too often between their efforts at praise.

Psalm 34:1; Isaiah 6:3; Revelation 4:8
Jesus Is Victor!, 67, 68.

1336. Worship: awe; Encounter with God

There is a point in true worship where the mind may cease to understand and goes over to a kind of delightful astonishment—probably to what Carlyle described as "transcendent wonder," a degree of wonder without limit and beyond expression! . . .

It is always true that an encounter with God brings wonderment and awe!

Isaiah 6:1-8; Revelation 1:17
Renewed Day by Day, Volume 1, Feb. 8.

1337. Worship: awe; God: His awesomeness

Webster's Unabridged Dictionary lists 550,000 words. And it is a solemn and beautiful thought that in our worship of God there sometimes rush up from the depths of our souls feelings that all this wealth of words is not sufficient to express. To be articulate at certain times we are compelled to fall back upon "Oh!" or "O!"—a primitive exclamatory sound that is hardly a word at all and that scarcely admits of a definition.

Vocabularies are formed by many minds over long periods and are capable of expressing whatever the mind is capable of entertaining. But when the heart, on its knees, moves into the awesome Presence and hears with fear and wonder things not lawful to utter, then the mind falls flat, and words, previously its faithful servants, become weak and totally incapable of telling what the heart hears and sees. In that awful moment the worshiper can only cry "Oh!" And that simple exclamation becomes more eloquent than learned speech and, I have no doubt, is dearer to God than any oratory.

Jeremiah 1:5-8; Ezekiel 37:3; Romans 11:33-36
Born after Midnight, 84, 85.

1338. Worship: awe; Worship: meaning of; God: His awesomeness

Worship also means to "express in some appropriate manner" what you feel. . . .

And what will be expressed? "A humbling but delightful sense of admiring awe and astonished wonder." It is delightful to worship God, but it is also a humbling thing; and the man who has not been humbled in the presence of God will never be a worshiper of God at all. He may be a church member who keeps the rules and obeys the discipline, and who tithes and goes to conference, but he'll never be a worshiper unless he is deeply humbled. "A humbling but delightful sense of admiring awe." There's an awesomeness about God which is missing in our day altogether; there's little sense of admiring awe in the Church of Christ these days.

Exodus 3:5-6; Isaiah 57:15; Isaiah 66:2; Micah 6:8
Worship: The Missing Jewel, 4, 5.

1339. Worship: awe; Worship: reverence

I've heard all kinds of preachers. I've heard the ignorant boaster; I've heard the dull, dry ones; I've heard the eloquent ones; but the ones that have helped me most were the ones that were awestruck in the presence of the God about whom they spoke. They might have a sense of humor, they might be jovial; but when they talked about God another tone came into their voice altogether; this was something else, something wonderful. I believe we ought to have again the old Biblical concept of God which makes God awful and makes men lie face down and cry, "Holy, holy, holy, Lord God Almighty." That would do more for the church than everything or anything else.

Psalm 72:18-19; Isaiah 6:3; Revelation 1:17
Worship: The Missing Jewel, 22.

1340. Worship: daily

I have to be faithful to what I know to be true, so I must tell you that if you will not worship God seven days a week, you do not worship Him on one day a week. . . .

Too many of us try to discharge our obligations to God Almighty in one day—usually one trip to church. Sometimes, nobly, we make it two trips to church, but it's all on the same day when we have nothing else to do—and that's supposed to be worship. I grant you, sir, that it can be true worship, provided that on Monday and Tuesday and the other days you also experience the blessings of true worship.

I do not say that you must be at church all of the time—how could you be?

You can worship God at your desk, on an elevated train, or driving in traffic. You can worship God washing dishes or ironing clothes. You can worship God in school, on the basketball court. You can worship God in whatever is legitimate and right and good. . . .

So that's all right. We can go to church and worship. But if we go to church and worship one day, it is not true worship unless it is followed by continuing worship in the days that follow.

The Tozer Pulpit, Volume 1, Book 1, 51, 52.

1341. Worship: essence of

The essence of spiritual worship is to love supremely, to trust confidently, to pray without ceasing and to seek to be Christlike and holy and to do all the good we can for Christ's sake.

Matthew 22:37-39; Romans 8:28-30;
1 Thessalonians 5:16-17; 1 Peter 5:7
The Root of the Righteous, 130.

1342. Worship: essence of; Concept of God

The history of mankind will probably show that no people has ever risen above its religion, and man's spiritual history will positively demonstrate that no religion has ever been greater than its idea of God. Worship is pure or base as the worshiper entertains high or low thoughts of God.

The Knowledge of the Holy, 1.

1343. Worship: for eternity

All of the examples that we have in the Bible illustrate that glad and devoted and reverent worship is the normal employment of moral beings. Every glimpse that is given us of heaven and of God's created beings is always a glimpse of worship and rejoicing and praise because God is who He is.

The apostle John in Revelation 4:10-11 gives us a plain portrayal of created beings around the throne of God....

I can safely say, on the authority of all that is revealed in the Word of God, that any man or woman on this earth who is bored and turned off by worship is not ready for heaven.

Revelation 4:8-11; Revelation 5:8-14
Whatever Happened to Worship?, 13.

1344. Worship: meaningless

Years ago in Mexico, I was attracted by the sight of an old, old church. I walked in with my hat removed and found that the church had no floor except the ground itself.

I paused to look around at the statues and the carvings and then noticed that an elderly Mexican lady had come into the building. She was carrying a small shopping bag.

She paid no attention to me but walked straight down to the altar area. I had the feeling she was so familiar with that aisle she could have walked it with her eyes closed.

She walked directly to kneel in front of a statue of the virgin Mary. She looked up into the facial features of that inanimate statue with deep devotion, deep yearning, deep desire. I thought, "That is the kind of spiritual longing and desire that I would like to see turned to the Lord Himself!"

There was no doubt in my mind that she was having an experience of worship. I believe it was very real to her. She was not pretending. She wanted to worship, but her worship was being poured out on a lifeless statue which was only the work of some person's hands.

Matthew 7:22-23; John 4:23-24; Romans 10:1-3
Whatever Happened to Worship?, 40.

1345. Worship: meaningless; Church: concept of God

Worship rises or falls in any church altogether depending upon the attitude we take toward God, whether we see God big or whether we see Him little. Most of us see God too small; our God is too little. David said, "O magnify the Lord with me," and "magnify" doesn't mean to make God big. You can't make God big. But you can *see* Him big.

Worship, I say, rises or falls with our concept of God; that is why I do not believe in these half-converted cowboys who call God the Man Upstairs. I do not think they worship at all because their concept of God is unworthy of God and unworthy of them. And if there is one terrible disease in the Church of Christ, it is that we do not see God as great as He is. We're too familiar with God.

Psalm 8:1; Psalm 34:3; Psalm 93:1,2; Jude 24-25
Worship: The Missing Jewel, 21.

1346. Worship: meaningless; Church: ineffectiveness; Activity: religious

There is probably not another field of human activity where there is so much waste as in the field of religion. . . .

In the average church we hear the same prayers repeated each Sunday year in and year out with, one would suspect, not the remotest expectation that they will be answered. It is enough, it seems, that they have been uttered. The familiar phrase, the religious tone, the emotionally loaded words have their superficial and temporary effect, but the worshiper is no nearer to God, no better morally and no surer of heaven than he was before. Yet every Sunday morning for twenty years he goes through the same routine and, allowing two hours for him to leave his house, sit through a church service and return to his house again, he has wasted 170 twelve-hour days with this exercise in futility. . . .

I need only add that all this tragic waste is unnecessary. The believing Christian will relish every moment in church and will profit by it. The instructed, obedient Christian will yield to God as the clay to the potter, and the result will be not waste but glory everlasting.

Psalm 122:1; Isaiah 1:11-20; Isaiah 64:8; Jeremiah 18:6
Born after Midnight, 100, 101, 103.

1347. Worship: missing in churches

Now, worship is the missing jewel in modern evangelicalism. We're organized; we work; we have our agendas. We have almost everything, but there's one thing that the churches, even the gospel churches, do not have: that is the ability to worship. We are not cultivating the art of worship. It's the one shining gem that is lost to the modern church, and I believe that we ought to search for this until we find it.

Isaiah 6:1-8; Ezekiel 1:1-5; Revelation 4:8-11
Worship: The Missing Jewel, 20.

1348. Worship: missing in churches

It remains only to be said that worship as we have described it here is almost (though, thank God, not quite) a forgotten art in our day. For whatever we can say of modern Bible-believing Christians, it can hardly be denied that we are not remarkable for our spirit of worship. The gospel as preached by good men in our times may save souls, but it does not create worshipers.

Our meetings are characterized by cordiality, humor, affability, zeal and high animal spirits; but hardly anywhere do we find gatherings marked by the overshadowing presence of God. We manage to get along on correct doctrine, fast tunes, pleasing personalities and religious amusements.

How few, how pitifully few are the enraptured souls who languish for love of Christ. . . .

If Bible Christianity is to survive the present world upheaval, we shall need to recapture the spirit of worship. We shall need to have a fresh revelation of the greatness of God and the beauty of Jesus. We shall need to put away our phobias and our prejudices against the deeper life and seek again to be filled with the Holy Spirit. He alone can raise our cold hearts to rapture and restore again the art of true worship.

Psalm 86:8-10; Psalm 145:3-5; Revelation 5:8-14
That Incredible Christian, 130, 131.

1349. Worship: missing in churches

Christian churches have come to the dangerous time predicted long ago. It is a time when we can pat one another on the back, congratulate ourselves and join in the glad refrain, "We are rich, and increased with goods, and have need of nothing!"

It certainly is true that hardly anything is missing from our churches these days—except the most important thing. We are missing the genuine and sacred offering of ourselves and our worship to the God and Father of our Lord Jesus Christ. . . .

We have been surging forward. We are building great churches and large congregations. We are boasting about high standards and we are talking a lot about revival.

But I have a question and it is not just rhetoric: *What has happened to our worship?*

Psalm 51:15-17; Psalm 95:6-7; Revelation 3:15-17
Whatever Happened to Worship?, 9, 10.

1350. Worship: missing in churches; Church: current condition

In my opinion, the great single need of the moment is that light-hearted superficial religionists be struck down with a vision of God high and lifted up, with His train filling the temple. The holy art of worship seems to have passed away like the Shekinah glory from the tabernacle. As a result, we are left to our own devices and forced to make up the lack of spontaneous worship by bringing in countless cheap and tawdry activities to hold the attention of the church people.

1 Samuel 4:21-22; Isaiah 6:1-5; Revelation 5:8-14
Keys to the Deeper Life, 87, 88.

1351. Worship: missing in churches; Church: religious game

I cannot speak for you, but I want to be among those who worship. I do not want just to be a part of some great ecclesiastical machine where the pastor turns the crank and the machine runs. You know—the pastor loves everybody and everybody loves him. He has to do it. He is paid to do it.

I wish that we might get back to worship again. Then when people come into the church they will instantly sense that they have come among holy people, God's people. They can testify, "Of a truth God is in this place."

Genesis 28:16
Whatever Happened to Worship?, 20.

1352. Worship: missing in churches; Church: services

To great sections of the Church the art of worship has been lost entirely, and in its place has come that strange and foreign thing called the "program." This word has been borrowed from the stage and applied with sad wisdom to the type of public service which now passes for worship among us.

The Pursuit of God, 9.

1353. Worship: missing in churches; Church: services; Church: routine

We of the nonliturgical churches tend to look with some disdain upon those churches that follow a carefully prescribed form of service, and certainly there must be a good deal in such services that has little or no meaning for the average participant—this not because it is carefully prescribed but because the average participant is what he is. But I have observed that our familiar impromptu service, planned by the leader 20 minutes before, often tends to follow a ragged and tired order almost as standardized as the Mass. The liturgical service is at least beautiful; ours is often ugly. Theirs has been carefully worked out through the centuries to capture as much of beauty as possible and to preserve a spirit of reverence among the worshipers. Ours is often an off-the-cuff makeshift with nothing to recommend it. Its so-called liberty is often not liberty at all but sheer slovenliness. . . .

. . . mostly there is neither order nor Spirit, just a routine prayer that is, except for minor variations, the same week after week, and a few songs that were never much to start with and have long ago lost all significance by meaningless repetition.

In the majority of our meetings there is scarcely a trace of reverent thought, no recognition of the unity of the body, little sense of the divine Presence, no moment of stillness, no solemnity, no wonder, no holy fear.

Psalm 95:1-7
God Tells the Man Who Cares, 4, 5.

1354. Worship: missing in churches; God: His majesty

I refer to the loss of the concept of majesty from the popular religious mind. The Church has surrendered her once lofty concept of God and has substituted for it one so low, so ignoble, as to be utterly unworthy of thinking, worshiping men. . . .

With our loss of the sense of majesty has come the further loss of religious awe and consciousness of the divine Presence. We have lost our spirit of worship and our ability to withdraw inwardly to meet God in adoring silence.

Isaiah 6:1-8; Habakkuk 2:20; Revelation 4:8-11
The Knowledge of the Holy, vii, viii.

1355. Worship: purpose for existence

Now we were made to worship, but the Scriptures tell us something else again. They tell us that man fell and kept not his first estate; that he forfeited the original glory of God and failed to fulfill the creative purpose, so that he is not worshiping now in the way that God meant him to worship. All else fulfills its design; flowers are still fragrant and lilies are still beautiful and the bees still search for nectar amongst the flowers; the birds still sing with their thousand-voice choir on a summer's day, and the sun and the moon and the stars all move on their rounds doing the will of God.

And from what we can learn from the Scriptures we believe that the seraphim and cherubim and powers and dominions are still fulfilling their design—worshiping God who created them and breathed into them the breath of life. Man alone sulks in his cave. Man alone, with all of his brilliant intelligence, with all of his amazing, indescribable and wonderful equipment, still sulks in his cave. He is either silent, or if he opens his mouth at all, it is to boast and threaten and curse; or it's nervous, ill-considered laughter, or it's humor become big business, or it's songs without joy.

Worship: The Missing Jewel, 6, 7.

1356. Worship: purpose for existence

The one mark, however, which forever distinguishes man from all other forms of life on earth is that he is a worshiper; he has a bent toward and a capacity for worship.

Apart from his position as a worshiper of God, man has no

sure key to his own being; he is but a higher animal, being born much as any other animal, going through the cycle of his life here on earth and dying at last without knowing what the whole thing is about. If that is all for him, if he has no more reason than the beast for living, then it is an odd thing indeed that he is the only one of the animals that worries about himself, that wonders, that asks questions of the universe. The very fact that he does these things tells the wise man that somewhere there is One to whom he owes allegiance, One before whom he should kneel and do homage.

Isaiah 45:23; Romans 14:11; Philippians 2:9-11
That Incredible Christian, 125.

1357. Worship: purpose for existence; Church: focus

I believe a local church exists to do corporately what each Christian believer should be doing—and that is to worship God. It is to show forth the excellencies of Him who has called us out of darkness into His marvelous light. It is to reflect the glories of Christ ever shining upon us through the ministries of the Holy Spirit. . . .

We are saved to worship God. All that Christ has done for us in the past and all that He is doing now leads to this one end.

1 Peter 2:9
Whatever Happened to Worship?, 93, 94.

1358. Worship: purpose for existence; Life purpose

One of the greatest tragedies that we find, even in this most enlightened of all ages, is the utter failure of millions of men and women ever to discover why they were born. . . .

Those who have followed the revelation provided by the Creator God have accepted that God never does anything without a purpose. We do believe, therefore, that God had a noble purpose in mind when He created us. We believe that it was distinctly the will of God that men and women created in His image would desire fellowship with Him above all else.

In His plan, it was to be a perfect fellowship based on adoring worship of the Creator and Sustainer of all things.

If you are acquainted with the Shorter Catechism, you know that it asks an age-old, searching question: "What is the chief end of man?"

The simple yet profound answer provided by the Catechism is based upon the revelation and wisdom of the Word of God: "The chief end of man is to glorify God and to enjoy Him forever.". . .

Yes, worship of the loving God is man's whole reason for existence. That is why we are born and that is why we are born again from above. That is why we were created and that is why we have been recreated. That is why there was a genesis at the beginning, and that is why there is a re-genesis, called regeneration.

That is also why there is a church. The Christian church exists to worship God first of all. Everything else must come second or third or fourth or fifth. . . .

Sad, sad indeed, are the cries of so many today who have never discovered why they were born. It brings to mind the poet Milton's description of the pathetic lostness and loneliness of our first parents. Driven from the garden, he says, "they took hand in hand and through the valley made their solitary way."

Genesis 1:26-27; Genesis 3:24;
Romans 11:33-36; Revelation 4:8-11
Whatever Happened to Worship?, 49, 51, 56, 57.

1359. Worship: purpose for existence; Life purpose

God was saying, "Abraham, I am trying to tell you something—something very important. I want you to listen and to comprehend. Abraham, you were made in My image and you were designed for a single purpose: to worship and glorify Me."

We are surrounded throughout our lifetimes by a multitude of things designed for specific purposes. Without argument, most things are at their best when they are fulfilling their purpose and design.

For instance, a piano is made with a specific purpose: to produce music. However, I happen to know that someone once stood on a piano in order to put a fastener of some kind in the ceiling. Some artistic women have used piano tops as family picture galleries. I have seen piano tops that were cluttered filing cabinets or wide library shelves.

There is an intelligent design in the creation of a piano. The manufacturer did not announce: "This is a good piano. It has at least 19 uses!" No, the designer had only one thought in mind: "This piano will have the purpose and potential of sounding forth beautiful music!" . . .

Do not miss the application of truth here. God was saying to Abraham, "You may have some other idea about the design and purpose for your life, but you are wrong! You were created in My image to worship Me and to glorify Me. If you do not honor this purpose, your life will degenerate into shallow, selfish, humanistic pursuits.

Genesis 1:26-27; Genesis 17:1-5; Revelation 4:8-11
Men Who Met God, 22, 23.

1360. Worship: purpose for existence; Science

Probably David lying on his back on the green meadow at night, brooding over the mystery of the moon and the stars and the littleness of man in the total scheme of things, worshiping the God who had made him only a little lower than the angels, was a truer man than the astronomer who in his high pride weighs and measures the heavenly bodies. Yet the astronomer need not despair. If he will humble himself and confess his deep inward need, the God of David will teach him how to worship, and by so doing will make him a greater man than he could ever have been otherwise.

Psalm 8; Psalm 19; 1 Peter 5:5
The Root of the Righteous, 80.

1361. Worship: purpose for existence; Worship: missing in churches

Man was made to worship God. God gave to man a harp and said, "Here above all the creatures that I have made and created I have given you the largest harp. I put more strings on your instrument and I have given you a wider range than I have given to any other creature. You can worship Me in a manner that no other creature can." And when he sinned man took that instrument and threw it down in the mud and there it has lain for centuries, rusted, broken, unstrung; and man, instead of playing a harp like the angels and seeking to worship God in all of his activities, is ego-centered and turns in on himself and sulks and swears and laughs and sings, but it's all without joy and without worship.

Now, God Almighty sent His Son Jesus Christ into the world for a purpose, and what was the purpose? . . .

The purpose of God in sending His Son to die and rise and live and be at the right hand of God the Father was that He might restore to us the missing jewel, the jewel of worship; that we might come back and learn to do again that which we were created to do in the first place—worship the Lord in the beauty of holiness, to spend our time in awesome wonder and adoration of God, feeling and expressing it, and letting it get into our labors and doing nothing except as an act of worship to Almighty God through His Son Jesus Christ. I say that the greatest tragedy in the world today is that God has made man in His image and made him to worship Him, made him to play the harp of worship before the face of God day and night, but he has failed God and dropped the harp. It lies voiceless at his feet.

1 Chronicles 16:25-29; Psalm 29:2
 Psalm 95:6-7
Worship: The Missing Jewel, 7, 8.

1362. Worship: reverence

Reverence, for one thing, will always be present in the heart of the one who loves Christ in the Spirit. The Spirit gives a holy solemnity to every thought of Jesus, so that it is psychologically impossible to think of the true Christ with humor or levity. Neither can there be any unbecoming familiarity. The Person of Christ precludes all such.

Psalm 2:10-11; Psalm 5:7; Hebrews 12:28
The Next Chapter after the Last, 32.

1363. Worship: reverence

Reverence is a beautiful thing, and it is so rare in this terrible day in which we live.

Churches don't really succeed in trying to "induce" reverence. You can't do it with statues, and beautiful windows, and carpeting on the floor, and everyone talking through his adenoids.

But a man who has passed the veil, and looked even briefly upon the holy face of Isaiah's God can never be irreverent again.

There will be a reverence in his spirit and instead of boasting, he will cover his feet modestly.

Psalm 119:38-40; Isaiah 6:1-5
The Tozer Pulpit, Volume 1, Book 1, 57, 58.

1364. Worship: reverence; Church: presence of God

I am disappointed that we come to church without a sense of God or a feeling of humble reverence. There are false religions, strange religious cults and Christian cults that think they have God in a box someplace, and when they approach that box they feel a sense of awe. Of course, you and I want to be saved from all paganism and false cultism. But we would also like to see a company of people who were so sure that God was with them, not in a box or in a biscuit, but in their midst. They would know that Jesus Christ was truly among them to a point that they would have a sense of humble reverence when they gathered together.

Psalm 95:1-7
Rut, Rot or Revival: The Condition of the Church, 113, 114.

1365. Worship: reverence; Church: presence of God

Do you quietly bow your head in reverence when you step into the average gospel church?

I am not surprised if your answer is no.

There is grief in my spirit when I go into the average church, for we have become a generation rapidly losing all sense of divine sacredness in our worship. Many whom we have raised in our churches no longer think in terms of reverence—which seems to indicate they doubt that God's Presence is there.

In too many of our churches, you can detect the attitude that anything goes. It is my assessment that losing the awareness of God in our midst is a loss too terrible even to be appraised.

Exodus 4:31; 1 Chronicles 29:20; Nehemiah 8:5-6
Whatever Happened to Worship?, 117.

1366. Worship: reverence; Love for God

I once heard Dr. George D. Watson, one of the great Bible teachers of his generation, point out that men can have two kinds of love for God—the love of gratitude or the love of excellence. He urged that we go on from gratefulness to a love of God just because He is God and because of the excellence of His character. . . .

Many of us are strictly "Santa Claus" Christians. We think of God as putting up the Christmas tree and putting our gifts underneath. That is only an elementary kind of love.

We need to go on. We need to know the blessing of worshiping in the presence of God without thought of wanting to rush out again. We need to be delighted in the presence of utter, infinite excellence.

Psalm 16:11; Psalm 21:6
Whatever Happened to Worship?, 87.

1367. Worship: reverence; God: His presence

Protestants are altogether too much inclined to take things for granted. We laugh at those on the other side of the ecclesiastical fence because they bow and scrape and kowtow in the presence of the church. But we lack reverence—not because we are free in the gospel, but because God is absent, and we have no sense of His presence.

Exodus 33:14-16; Psalm 95:1-7
Rut, Rot or Revival: The Condition of the Church, 40.

1368. Worship: supremacy of

But thinking is not enough. Men are made to *worship* also, to bow down and adore in the presence of the Mystery inexpressible. Man's mind is not the top peak of his nature. Higher than his mind is his spirit, that something within him which can engage the supernatural, which under the breath of the Spirit can come alive and enter into conscious communion with heaven, can receive the divine nature and hear and feel and see the ineffable wonder that is God. . . .

The wise of the world who have not learned to worship are but demi-men, unformed and rudimentary. Their further development awaits the life-giving touch of Christ to wake them to spiritual birth and life eternal.

John 3:6-8; Ephesians 2:1-3
The Set of the Sail, 59.

1369. Worship: supremacy of; Encounter with God; Priorities

Ultimately Abraham discovered that only God matters. He discovered in that revelation the greatest concept in the world. We might say he became a "one idea" man. . . .

It is as if Abraham laid hold of God's favor and promise with rejoicing, saying to himself, "When I have God, I need nothing more!"

Abraham was completely satisfied with God's friendship. He becomes to us a faithful example in his willingness to put God first. With Abraham, only God mattered. . . .

In Abraham's encounter with God he learned why he was here upon earth. He was to glorify God in all things and to continually worship. . . .

These truths concerning Abraham and his wholehearted response to God cause me to wonder. How can we bring our lukewarm Christians into a realization that nothing in the world is as important to them as God's love and God's will?

Genesis 17:1-5; Matthew 16:24-26; James 2:23
Men Who Met God, 27, 29, 30.

1370. Worship: supremacy of; New believer

There is a necessity for true worship among us. If God is who He says He is and if we are the believing people of God we claim to be, we must worship Him. . . .

Oh, how I wish I could adequately set forth the glory of that One who is worthy to be the object of our worship! I do believe that if our new converts—the babes in Christ—could be made to see His thousand attributes and even partially comprehend His being, they would become faint with a yearning desire to worship and honor and acknowledge Him, now and forever.

Exodus 3:1-6
Whatever Happened to Worship?, 118.

1371. Worship: supremacy of; Salvation: goal of

Sometimes evangelical Christians seem to be fuzzy and uncertain about the nature of God and His purposes in creation and redemption. In such instances, the preachers often are to blame. There are still preachers and teachers who say that Christ died so we would not drink and not smoke and not go to the theater.

No wonder people are confused! No wonder they fall into the habit of backsliding when such things are held up as the reason for salvation.

Jesus was born of a virgin, suffered under Pontius Pilate, died on the cross and rose from the grave to make worshipers out of rebels!

Romans 5:8; Ephesians 2:4-10
Whatever Happened to Worship?, 11.

1372. Worship: supremacy of; Service: worship first

God wants worshipers before workers; indeed the only acceptable workers are those who have learned the lost art of worship. It is inconceivable that a sovereign and holy God should be so hard up for workers that He would press into service anyone who had been empowered regardless of his moral qualifications. The very stones would praise Him if the need arose and a thousand legions of angels would leap to do His will.

Gifts and power for service the Spirit surely desires to impart; but holiness and spiritual worship come first.

Matthew 26:53; Hebrews 12:10
That Incredible Christian, 37.

1373. Worship: supremacy of;
Service: worship first;
Salvation: goal of

The work of Christ in redemption, for all its mystery, has a simple and understandable end: it is to restore men to the position from which they fell and bring them around again to be admirers and lovers of the Triune God. God saves men to make them worshipers.

This great central fact has been largely forgotten today, not by the liberals and the cults only, but by evangelical Christians as well. By direct teaching, by story, by example, by psychological pressure we force our new converts to "go to work for the Lord." Ignoring the fact that God has redeemed them to make worshipers out of them, we thrust them out into "service," quite as if the Lord were recruiting laborers for a project instead of seeking to restore moral beings to a condition where they can glorify God and enjoy Him forever. . . .

Our Lord commmands us to pray the Lord of the harvest that He will send forth laborers into His harvest field. What we are overlooking is that no one can be a worker who is not first a worshiper. Labor that does not spring out of worship is futile and can only be wood, hay and stubble in the day that shall try every man's works. . . .

Without doubt the emphasis in Christian teaching today should be on worship. There is little danger that we shall become merely worshipers and neglect the practical implications of the gospel. No one can long worship God in spirit and in truth before the obligation to holy service becomes too strong to resist. Fellowship with God leads straight to obedience and good works. That is the divine order and it can never be reversed.

Matthew 9:37-38; John 4:23-24;
1 Corinthians 3:12-14; 2 Corinthians 5:10
Born after Midnight, 125, 126.

1374. Worship: supremacy of;
Worship: purpose for existence

I think that God has given me a little bit of a spirit of a crusader and I am crusading where I can that Christians of all denominations and shades of theological thought might be restored again to our original purpose. We're here to be worshipers first and workers only second. We take a convert and immediately make a worker out of him. God never meant it to be so.

God meant that a convert should learn to be a worshiper, and after that he can learn to be a worker.

Acts 1:4
Worship: The Missing Jewel, 10.

1375. Wrath of God; Sin: consequences of

Since God's first concern for His universe is its moral health, that is, its holiness, whatever is contrary to this is necessarily under His eternal displeasure. Wherever the holiness of God confronts unholiness there is conflict. This conflict arises from the irreconcilable natures of holiness and sin. God's attitude and action in the conflict are His anger. To preserve His creation God must destroy whatever would destroy it. When He arises to put down destruction and save the world from irreparable moral collapse He is said to be angry. Every wrathful judgement of God in the history of the world has been a holy act of preservation.

The holiness of God, the wrath of God and the health of the creation are inseparably united. Not only is it right for God to display anger against sin, but I find it impossible to understand how He could do otherwise.

Romans 1:18; Ephesians 5:6; Colossians 3:5-11
Man: The Dwelling Place of God, 110, 111.

Z

1376. Zeal; Activity: religious

That many Christians in our day are lukewarm and somnolent will not be denied by anyone with an anointed eye, but the cure is not to stir them up to a frenzy of activity. That would be but to take them out of one error and into another. What we need is a zealous hunger for God, an avid thirst after righteousness, a pain-filled longing to be Christlike and holy. We need a zeal that is loving, self-effacing and lowly. No other kind will do.

That pure love for God and men which expresses itself in a burning desire to advance God's glory and leads to poured-out devotion to the temporal and eternal welfare of our fellow men is certainly approved of God; but the nervous, squirrel-cage activity of self-centered and ambitious religious leaders is just as certainly offensive to Him and will prove at last to have been injurious to the souls of countless millions of human beings.

Matthew 5:6; Romans 9:1-3; Revelation 3:15-17
The Size of the Soul, 81, 82.

1377. Zeal; Extremes; Spiritual discernment

It may be said without qualification that there can never be too much fire, if it is the true fire of God; and it can be said as certainly that there cannot be too much cool judgment in religious matters if that judgment is sanctified by the Spirit. The history of revivals in the Church reveals how harmful the hot head can be. . . .

Among the gifts of the Spirit scarcely any one is of greater practical usefulness than the gift of discernment. This gift should be highly valued and frankly sought as being almost indispensable in these critical times. . . .

There will always be those who hesitate to believe that anything is of God unless it has about it some flavor of the weird, or at least of the supernatural. Persons with a certain type of mentality think only in extremes; they can never achieve perspective in anything, but see everything so close as to miss entirely the corrective benefits of distance. They will believe anything as long as it is unusual and just a little mysterious. Their fire is not large, but by holding it always on one fine point they manage to generate a

42:3	858
43:5	415
46:10	3, 44, 84, 328, 691, 725, 728, 1151, 1207
49:10-12	340
50:10-12	488, 786
51	643
51:1	457
51:2	674
51:3-4	1041, 1208, 1254
51:5	1250, 1302
51:10	1088
51:15-17	327, 1035, 1349
55:22	76
57:5, 11	231
61:2-4	1267
62:1	466, 726, 871, 1149, 1175, 1178
62:5-8	466, 726, 1149
62:11	149
63	466, 685
63:1-2	7, 13, 240, 684, 694, 734-735, 742, 796, 871, 1055, 1178
63:5-6	43, 680
63:6-8	507, 741, 925
66:18	1329-1330
69:8	729
71:12-14	415
72:18-19	1339
73:15-20	604
73:25	280, 654, 737, 749, 832
74:16	1264
76:10	477
77:6	1151, 1234
77:11-15	507, 689
78:9	1202
78:40-41	564
85:6	1050, 1064
86:8-10	1348
89:5-9	490, 503, 884
90:1-2	247, 762
90:4-6	250, 364
90:12	362, 366, 1129, 1276
91:11-12	18
92:1-4	743, 752, 1038
92:7	1075
93:1-2	505, 1345
95:1-7	121, 193, 1038, 1353, 1364, 1367
95:1-2	177, 235, 430
95:6-7	66, 279, 487, 847, 1232, 1330, 1349, 1361
96:1-6	122, 503, 744, 1038
96:7-9	486
96:11-13	664
97:6	800
98:1-6	193, 444, 1064
100	193, 279, 752, 1038
100:3	473
100:5	457
103:1-2	61
103:10-12	455, 1090, 1092
103:13-14	86, 321, 512
103:15-17	364
104	259
104:1	503
104:3-4	1144
104:24	525
105:1-5	1232
106:1-2	1232
106:8	456
106:14-15	943
107:6-9	419
107:10-11	1161
111:1-4	122
111:10	449
115:3	506
118:6	982
119	41, 1014
119:1-2	814
119:9-11	45, 48, 953, 1183, 1239
119:12, 18	1285
119:14-16	1015, 1027
119:20, 24	51
119:33	54
119:38-40	953, 1064, 1363
119:66	206
119:67, 71	1263
119:97	42, 47, 52, 725, 996, 1008
119:105	727
119:111-112	953, 1008
119:130-131	1008, 1291
119:147-148	728, 930
119:160	1279
119:162	1008
119:165	448
121:2	938
122:1	1346
123:1-2	404, 409
124:8	938
126:5-6	371-372, 753, 850, 1221
127:1-5	147, 583, 597, 771
130:3-4	539
130:5-6	883
130:7	509

Reference	Pages
133	1054
133:1-3	1297
139	525
139:1-6	512
139:7-12	346, 511, 699
139:13-16	233, 519
139:17-18	501, 927
139:23-24	4, 680, 811, 947, 972, 1131, 1141
143:5-6	689, 742
143:10	811, 892
145:3-5	1042, 1348
145:18	517
146:5-6	705
150	444, 1038

Proverbs

Reference	Pages
1:5	778, 1018
1:7	906, 1162
1:10, 15-16	353
1:17	369
2:3-9	716
3:1-2	448, 892, 937
3:5-6	224, 313, 499, 613, 892, 937, 1311
3:7	764
3:9-10	136
3:12	321
3:24	447
3:27	829
4:5-9	1015
4:7	1019
4:23	82, 631-632, 913, 1214, 1236-1238, 1241, 1286
5:1-23	354
8:33-36	990
9:9	1018
9:10	449
10:17	263
11:24	140
12:12	1180, 1187
12:16	20
14:12-13	57, 350, 541, 789, 905
14:27	452
14:34	1065
15:8	1333
15:10	990
16:16	1019
16:18	985
16:21	1377
18:15	856
18:24	467-468, 1230
20:24	368, 521
21:21	1164
22:8	1179
23:4	390
23:7	1129, 1236
23:20-21	391
23:23	1019
24:3-4	596
24:24	1162
24:30-31	391
25:28	20
27:1	911
27:6	1217
28:9	1329
29:11	20

Ecclesiastes

Reference	Pages
1:4-10	16
2:1-11	350
2:1-2	353, 541
3:11	627, 1193, 1255
4:13	990
9:3	912
9:4	431
12:1-8	285, 364, 474, 723, 761, 1164
12:11	1018
12:12	32, 1014

Song of Solomon

Reference	Pages
2:1	1220
4:16	1187
5:10	659
5:16	26

Isaiah

Reference	Pages
1:3-4	872
1:5-6	1160
1:11-20	7, 327, 1035, 1056, 1346
1:16-19	88, 817, 1043, 1311
2:22	250
3:16-26	484
5:8-23	17
5:11-12	349
5:18-20	790
5:20-23	1162, 1170

6:1-8 .... 179, 486, 679, 886, 1305,
                      1336, 1347, 1354
6:1-5 .... 744, 879-880, 948, 1042,
                      1070, 1350, 1363
6:1-2 19
6:3 .... 496, 710, 800, 1335, 1339
6:5 .... 381, 408, 450-452, 487,
                      615, 884, 1072
6:8 381
6:9-10 378
9:6 222
11:2-4 .... 128, 714
12:2 473
25:8 602
26:3 448
28:16 812
29:13 433
30:1 148
30:15 44
30:21 .... 1231, 1290
40:3 670
40:11 1093
40:12-15 .... 35, 604, 705, 762, 985
40:21-31 247-248
40:25-26 .... 490, 503
40:29-31 1202-1203
41:18 944
42:8 .... 945, 1049, 1128
42:16 418
43:1-3 .... 1296, 1326
43:15, 22 72
44:23 444
45:9 304
45:11-12 1000
45:18 812
45:22 1134
45:23 .... 1010, 1356
46:10 525
48:7 1311
48:8-11 512
50:7 1310
51:1 789
51:16 881
53 1263
53:3 325
53:5 384
53:6 .... 556, 1161
53:7 .... 98, 1249, 1313
54:10 512
55:1-2 .... 5, 7, 79-81, 474, 567
55:6-8 .... 517, 543, 1043,
                      1049, 1302
55:8-9 .... 343, 518, 530, 690, 939

57:15 .... 751, 1338
57:16 29
57:20 759
63:9-10 .... 564, 1327
64:8 .... 31, 1346
66:2 .... 29, 1338

Jeremiah

1:5 .... 12, 519
1:5-8 .... 363, 859, 1232, 1337
1:7-9 .... 882, 981
1:9-10 .... 881, 1070
4:3-4 1262
4:22 1159
5:3 990
7:22-24 327
8:20 1107
9:1 .... 306, 858, 1221
9:12 872
9:23-24 .... 129, 259, 300, 305, 340,
                      499, 558, 607, 638, 695,
                      839, 849, 907, 988
10:8 1022
10:10 985
10:12-15 .... 525, 791, 1022
10:23 .... 368, 812
13:17 1221
15:16 1251
17:9 .... 34, 912, 1286, 1323
18:6 .... 1185, 1346
22:29 56
23:23-24 699
29:13 1123
32:17, 27 .... 427, 924, 1002, 1104
33:3 .... 1062, 1296
35:15 1155
42:3, 6 .... 817, 1290
51:17-18 1022

Lamentations

1:16 306
3:19-23 .... 415, 457, 542
3:23-24 509

Ezekiel

1:1-5 .... 1082, 1137, 1347
1:26-28 660
2:7 881

3:1-4 881
3:17 1249
10:18-19 178
12:2 347
22:30 373
28:2 986
33:8-9 381
34:2-4 162
37:3 .... 1232, 1337

Daniel

1:8 1310
1:10 844
3:17 395
3:27 1255
4:17 .... 477, 986
4:25 340
4:34-35 .... 477, 506
6:10 487
7:9-10 .... 660, 666
7:14 1046
10:5-9 452
10:12-13 951
12:3 777

Hosea

5:6 178
10:12 .... 174, 1069, 1262
12:6-9 709

Amos

3:3 397
5:15 1165
6:1 .... 229, 858, 1199

Jonah

1:3 237
1:17 1104

Micah

6:8 .... 29, 1338

Nahum

1:3 1144
1:7 249

Habakkuk

1:2 1256
2:4 1134
2:20 .... 3, 788, 1354
3:19 776

Zephaniah

1:15 368

Haggai

1:5, 7 979
2:6-7 676

Zechariah

4:6 .... 128, 143, 148, 173, 991
4:10 393

Malachi

1:13-14 1079
3:1 670
3:6 .... 497-498, 513, 1053, 1205
3:10 136

Matthew

1:21 536
2:1-11 105
3:1-4 669
3:4-5 1178
4:8-10 .... 1067, 1320-1321
4:19 77
5-7 9
5:3 .... 337, 704, 709, 1260
5:3-8 692
5:3-12 .... 34, 199, 1037, 1138
5:5 777

5:6 .... 145, 240, 251, 567,
            685-686, 694, 736, 1057,
            1059, 1164, 1376
5:8 .... 694, 1195
5:10-12 .... 98, 878, 1300
5:14-16 .... 132, 379
5:22 254
5:23-24 .... 227, 1023
5:34-37 326
5:43-44 984
5:45 233
5:48 740
6:1-5 .... 923, 945, 994, 1138, 1219
6:6 .... 44, 328, 844, 852,
            923, 994, 1070, 1176
6:8 1327
6:9 .... 1, 491, 1275
6:10 936
6:14-16 .... 227, 1219
6:19-21 .... 339, 360-361, 442, 471,
            480, 722, 745, 773-774,
            900, 915, 1089,1112,
            1115, 1302, 1308, 1321
6:24, 33 .... 91, 108, 221, 225,
            361, 915, 997, 1123-1124,
            1303, 1306
6:25-34 .... 62, 215, 407, 772, 1307,
            1326, 1328
7:1 461
7:7-11 .... 500, 633, 919-920, 952
7:15-16 .... 181, 257, 401, 437, 440
7:20 .... 396, 808
7:21-23 .... 403, 436, 661, 1057,
            1097, 1344
7:24-27 .... 49, 93, 106, 317, 961
8:20 898
8:26 944
9:37-38 1373
10:10-39 815
10:22 110
10:24-25 270
10:34-39 .... 379, 465
10:37-39 .... 269, 333, 388, 746
            10:42, 1145
11:7-19 .... 659, 670
11:23 411
11:26 1254
11:27 234
11:28-30 .... 76, 103, 115, 126, 498,
            524, 612, 659, 901-902,
            919, 1203,1283
12:24 302
12:30 .... 1245, 1249, 1283

12:34-37 .... 8, 68, 616-617, 913, 978,
            1236, 1239
13:3-9 368
13:11, 16-17 577
13:15 1158
13:20-22 .... 368, 1309
13:29-30 555
13:58 412
14:3-4 879
14:22-33 .... 331, 903, 944,
            1152, 1175, 1268
15:1-2 302
15:8 433
15:18-19 .... 1223, 1238, 1241
16:8 62
16:17 423
16:18 .... 124, 127, 159, 167, 833,
            903
16:21 1310
16:22 903
16:23 338
16:24-26 .... 94, 218, 227, 268, 296,
            337, 339, 356, 358-359,
            362, 454, 530, 910, 998-999,
            1021, 1144, 1213, 1306, 1369
18:4 612
18:6 803
18:10 19
18:15-17 214
18:20 .... 167, 177, 1062
19:21-22 .... 339, 534
19:24 .... 552, 898
19:26 1104
20:20-28 .... 120, 166, 1272-1273, 1277
21:6-9 .... 208, 745
21:12-13 .... 189-190, 623, 854, 1056,
            1155, 1165
21:21 919
22:14 1071
22:37-39 .... 13, 219, 315, 341, 658,
            749, 752, 756, 984,
            1311, 1331, 1341
23:2-3 618
23:4 904
23:5 .... 994, 1219
23:10-12 1215
23:14 921
23:15 1141
23:23-24 .... 184, 641
23:27-28 619
24:5, 11, 24 867
24:6-7 .... 312, 676
24:10-12 .... 932, 1079

24:29-30	1005
24:30-36	1111, 1116
24:36-39	1120-1121
24:45	958
25:10	550
25:21, 23	429
25:31-32	216
25:34-40	603, 755
25:44-46	546
26:33	903
26:36	1198
26:39	46
26:40-41	82, 316, 851, 1071, 1192
26:53	1372
26:56	464, 729, 1212
26:69-75	903
27:3-4	555
27:22	1174
27:26	1212
27:27-31	629
28	652
28:1-10	650
28:18-20	125, 172, 202, 277, 651, 782

Mark

1:15	1039, 1169
4:5-6	208
6:8-9	898
6:46	1152
7:21-22	912
8:36-37	552, 654, 1084, 1133
9:23	924
10:29-30	1124
12:30, 33	751
12:34	902
12:42-44	1145
16:15	3, 1147
16:19	651

Luke

1:46	504
1:78	510
2:13	18
2:14	491
2:8-20	105, 732
4:8	1333
4:18-19	105, 145, 784
5:8	450, 903
6:12	1152
6:20-38	136, 898, 1199
6:44-45	406, 808
6:46	403, 1057
7:15	1063
7:28	1178
7:32	297
7:36-50	455
7:40-47	658
7:47-48	495
9:23-25	77, 155, 217, 226, 269, 271, 315, 388, 535, 636, 746, 775, 815, 975, 1024, 1056, 1071, 1098, 1126, 1204, 1216
9:28	1152
9:57-62	225, 476, 815
10:18	216
10:20	1213
10:38-42	5-6, 33, 329, 691, 1177
11:13	707
11:30	1245
11:46	904
12:15-21	723, 1213, 1308
12:19-21	229, 390, 552, 911, 1319
12:18-26	21, 1303
12:24	57
12:33-34	773, 900
13:3, 5	627, 1039
14:26-27	333, 894, 1086, 1204
14:33	314, 483, 894
15:3-10	81
15:18	763
15:20-24	494-495, 1041
16:10-13	623, 704, 772, 998
16:15	166
16:27-28	380
17:17	61
18:1-8	934-935
18:9-14	254, 531, 609, 641, 643, 764, 902
19:10	1293
19:13	1119
19:19	1132
19:41	1221
21:34-36	999, 1309
24:32	347, 585
24:47	1169
24:49	3, 195, 275, 586, 1177

John

1:1	222, 1100
1:3	258

1:4	1193
1:6-7	373, 669, 882, 1143, 1178
1:10	773, 1133
1:11-13	102, 531-532, 537-538, 647, 1083, 1086, 1118
1:14	73, 104, 222, 233, 647-648, 692, 768, 955, 1279
1:16	61, 233
1:18	511, 646, 699, 948, 955
1:20-23	670, 791, 879
1:29	533
1:51	179
2:14-17	1165-1166
2:19	216
3:3	1068
3:6-8	1247, 1368
3:14-15	409, 1083
3:16	371, 500, 502, 667-668, 750, 961, 976
3:17	24
3:19-21	1029-1030, 1133, 1293
3:27	574
3:30	224, 300, 669, 732, 745
4	1063
4:9-10	1244
4:13-14	14
4:23-24	560, 758, 1011, 1344, 1373
4:28-29	114, 1148
5:24-27	2, 657
5:28-29	216
5:36-40	36, 251, 414, 972, 1002
6:3	1177
6:5-7	62
6:15	1152, 1312
6:16-21	159, 1268
6:27	5
6:35	1085, 1134
6:37, 44	424, 533, 1085
6:63-65	50, 55, 57, 149, 1085, 1100
6:68	220, 474, 654, 737, 1099
7:7	1029
7:17	1294
8:7-9	252
8:12	647, 727
8:31-32	342, 382, 458-459, 718, 1011, 1246, 1279, 1290
8:36	458, 718
8:44-47	1089, 1228, 1236, 1283
8:58	216
9:28-29	302
9:31	1329
10:3	634
10:4	475
10:7, 9	1082
10:11-15	656, 847, 1093, 1267
10:27-29	357, 365, 697, 1093
12:21	74, 1220, 145
12:24-26	77, 268, 293, 379
12:40	1284
12:41	880
13:21-22	1295
13:23	608
13:34-35	154, 156, 754
14:1-6	356, 367
14:1-3	215, 335, 472, 549, 1318
14:1	115, 1327
14:2	290
14:3	941, 1266
14:6	69, 536, 573, 1082, 1246, 1248, 1274, 1279, 1293
14:7	1292
14:13-14	779, 920, 939
14:15-17	148, 575, 581, 821, 1027, 1316
14:19	1247
14:21, 24	341, 816, 819, 823, 940
14:26	45, 148, 573, 639, 1011
14:27	328, 445, 673, 890
15:1-7	208, 309, 579, 842, 920, 929
15:8	396, 815
15:10	707, 815
15:13	750
15:14-16	466-469, 920
15:18-21	30, 97-98, 110, 226, 271, 543, 621, 661, 696, 730, 806, 815, 896-897, 1061, 1201, 1269, 1283, 1316
15:26	344, 576
16:8	423, 576, 983, 1097, 1173
16:13-15	53-54, 215, 572, 714, 1011, 1291
16:33	99, 806, 1259, 1269
17	198
17:3	211, 278, 357, 655, 682, 697-698, 702, 741, 1157
17:11	414
17:14-16	110, 696, 1135, 1201
17:15-18	1, 84, 889, 918, 1208
17:20-24	211, 213, 290, 927, 1194, 1266, 1288, 1298
19:26-27	325
20:13	1053
20:27-29	356

21:15-17 .... 738, 847
21:20 795

Acts

1:1-3 650
1:4 .... 782, 1147, 1374
1:8 .... 149-151, 195, 202,
374, 579, 582, 586, 714,
782, 784, 1072
1:9-11 .... 222, 479, 1109, 1309
1:12-14 .... 3, 935
1:25 555
2:1-4 .... 220, 282, 1297
2:14-36 .... 310, 652
2:14 .... 173, 979
2:20, 27 969
2:30 969
2:33 146
2:37-38 .... 971, 983, 1039,
1042, 1169
2:41 1068
2:42-47 .... 127, 135, 190, 196, 212, 253
2:42-44 .... 63, 107, 117, 152, 165,
176, 320, 928
2:46-47 .... 46, 47, 204, 371, 375, 671
3:10 173
3:11 176
3:19 .... 1040, 1169
4:1-2 971
4:3 226
4:12 .... 369, 413, 536, 538, 1083,
1246, 1248, 1274
4:16-17 830
4:20 .... 346, 982
4:23 92
4:29-30 779
4:31-33 .... 173, 176, 202, 253,
375, 649
5:18 226
5:29 598
5:32 344
5:33 983
5:41-42 .... 226, 560, 671
6:2 329
6:3-7 .... 142, 162-163, 204, 685,
713, 831, 852, 867, 931, 933
7:51-60 878
7:52 1300
7:54 983
7:58 226
7:60 292

8:3-4 .... 661, 226
8:18-21 1049
9:3-5 1042
9:6 .... 12, 452
9:15-16 .... 78, 712, 857, 859
10:33 279
10:34-35 .... 60, 254
10:42-43 .... 2, 657
12:5 163
12:7 944
13:22 539
13:36 .... 431, 527, 720-721, 1243
13:38-39 .... 534, 828, 1073
14:22 1259
14:23 783
15 119
15:10 904
15:24-29 .... 470, 781
16:13 928
16:25 .... 430, 516, 794
16:30-31 .... 531, 537
17:6 .... 202, 218, 375, 1061
17:11 .... 414, 439, 441, 711, 778
17:21 438
17:24-25 786
17:26 1148
17:27-28 1158
17:30-31 .... 2, 576, 657, 659, 664
20:18-21 .... 171, 184, 836,
875-876
20:20, 24, 27 .... 976, 9811166
20:24 .... 184, 219, 225, 232,
380, 785, 841, 894,
946, 982, 1276
20:28-31 .... 130, 181, 198, 207,
439, 738, 833, 847, 868,
874, 1066, 1192 1249
20:33 .... 471, 876
21:13 785
23:1 1299
26:13-19 .... 12, 28, 686, 832, 880
26:20 1039
26:24 96
27:14 812
28:25-27 .... 347, 1158

Romans

1 435
1:9-10 853
1:14-16 .... 65, 96, 150, 870, 1154
1:18-32 .... 274, 790, 1029, 1105, 1284

Reference	Pages
1:18	556, 677, 836, 1161, 1375
1:19-20	234, 801, 1270
1:20-23	248-249, 258, 760, 765, 791, 1022, 1030, 1161-1162, 1172
1:24-25	17
1:26-27	391
2:4	492, 508
2:11	60
2:13	93, 961
2:16	2
2:18	470
3:4	417, 1208, 1270
3:10-18	16, 627, 677, 760, 1159, 1174, 1224, 1323
3:19-20	1227
3:23	1021
3:24	1025
3:25	1076
3:28	400, 534, 1031
4:19-21	419, 422, 1002
4:25	649
5:1	890, 1073, 1251
5:3-5	1218, 1253
5:8	500, 502, 763, 1127, 1245, 1371
5:12	286, 434, 1167
5:19	383
5:20	1229
6:1	22
6:2	353
6:4-7	95, 299, 317, 529, 768, 862, 1091, 1098, 1125, 1210, 1313
6:11-14	25, 219, 266, 353, 545, 764, 802, 821, 1197, 1226
6:16-18	322, 459, 1096
6:19	91, 545, 1142
6:23	1167
7:15-25	85, 615, 804, 826, 1160, 1173, 1200
7:18	610, 995
7:24-25	275, 543, 813, 938, 1072, 1196, 1225
8:1	455, 1028, 1092
8:3	828
8:5-7	541, 1184
8:10-11	272
8:13	219, 825, 851
8:15	459, 718
8:16-17	270, 344, 402, 633
8:18-19	21, 405, 523, 731, 1001, 1114, 1258, 1264
8:18-23	294
8:22-25	410, 416, 731
8:25-27	936, 942
8:28-30	521, 721, 763, 1077, 1085, 1184, 1341
8:31	207
8:34	215, 365
8:35-39	446, 602, 743, 891
9:1-3	371-372, 381, 753, 766, 858, 1376
9:14-16	456
9:19-21	31, 518, 747
9:23-24	242
10:1-3	9, 380, 695, 766, 789, 1032, 1344
10:8-10	531, 560, 820, 1097
10:17	420
11:22	492
11:33-36	24, 35, 298, 490, 518, 530, 708, 786, 962, 1254, 1337, 1358
12:1-2	28, 224, 228, 266, 282, 316, 601, 822, 917, 1048, 1078, 1325
12:3-8	151, 432, 587, 589, 592, 607, 610, 834, 837, 877, 993, 1068, 1131
12:9-13	27, 154, 303, 411, 546, 889, 935, 984, 1165
12:14-16	154
12:16-18	255, 889
13:11-14	112, 207, 426, 617, 1004, 1065
14:1-6	781
14:5	460-461, 641
14:7-9	458, 568-569
14:11	1356
14:17-19	256, 781
14:23	460
15:1	628
15:4	827
15:13	413, 599
15:18-19	956
16:17-18	437

First Corinthians

Reference	Pages
1:1-2	1085
1:7	731
1:10-12	23, 1054
1:17	839, 978
1:18	150, 186, 267, 387, 870

1:20-21 .... 150, 267, 330, 791
1:23-25 .... 267, 870, 949, 971
1:26-29 .... 87, 94, 153, 582, 595
1:30-31 654
2:1-5 .... 129, 590, 649, 842, 849,
956, 1310
2:6-8 35
2:9-10 .... 53, 478
2:11-12 .... 234, 695, 758
2:12-16 .... 280, 572, 574, 577, 679,
971, 1254, 1292, 1294
3:1-3 .... 4, 83, 85, 973, 1037
3:5-9 .... 837, 991, 1212
3:12-14 .... 10, 168, 590, 603,
722, 836, 991, 1146,
1206, 1373
3:16-23 .... 362, 788, 907
3:21-4:1 778
4:2-3 .... 303, 429, 432, 769, 845
4:3-5 .... 10, 989, 1140-1141
4:7 .... 210, 337, 610
4:10-13 .... 96, 98, 876, 899, 1269
4:16 .... 157, 715
5:1-2 354
5:6-7 1168
5:11 214
6:9-10 354
6:12 632
6:19-20 .... 232, 236, 568-569,
575, 747, 1239
7:20 710
7:31 334
8:1 708
8:9 .... 462, 719
8:12 803
9:14 137
9:16 .... 172, 830, 859, 1154
9:19 462
9:22-23 11
9:24-27 .... 238, 316, 526, 636,
681, 775, 841, 851, 861, 868,
933, 946, 1094, 1181, 1213
10:6-11 .... 58, 1228
10:11-12 .... 55, 827, 1130, 1139, 1250
10:13 .... 86, 1073, 1225-1226
10:21 187
10:31 .... 71, 230, 710, 792, 988, 1146
11:1 .... 112, 157, 711, 727, 1077
11:23-29 .... 213, 1130
11:31-32 .... 1131, 1186
12 .... 63, 120, 591
12:1-11 .... 87, 205, 587-588,
594-595, 1377

12:12-27 212
12:18-27 .... 431, 473, 834
12:20 1148
12:22-25 363
12:25-27 .... 165, 180, 199
12:28-31 589
13 .... 757, 1263
13:1-3 .... 100, 753
13:10 592
14:1 592
14:20 973
14:26 794
14:27-33 593
14:40 831
15:3-4 .... 650, 653
15:9-10 .... 10, 305, 993, 995, 1087,
1139, 1263
15:19-20 .... 602, 649, 652, 671
15:25-26 .... 287-288, 434
15:51-57 .... 287, 479, 602, 653,
1108, 1110
15:58 .... 147, 363, 405, 429,
1119, 1140
16:10-11 845
16:16 161
16:22 1110

Second Corinthians

1:12 .... 205, 863-866, 957, 1190
2:4 83
2:11 1095
2:14 .... 267, 275, 542, 938, 1197,
1225
2:17 957
3:5-6 .... 304-305, 955-956, 1139
3:12 304
3:14-15 .... 716, 1030
3:15-18 .... 718, 1229
4:2 .... 957, 1191
4:4 .... 80, 99, 276, 377, 951,
1158, 1284
4:5-7 .... 210, 304, 557, 824,
842, 956, 989, 995, 1139,
1212, 1263, 1318
4:8-11 .... 599, 611, 673
4:16-18 .... 294, 395, 416, 418, 548,
599, 1258
5:1-8 .... 289, 293, 418, 472, 485, 549,
761, 888
5:10 .... 2, 351, 482, 909, 1021, 1084,
1145, 1238, 1373

312

5:12-15	26, 172, 372, 750, 766, 769
5:13-17	346, 663, 768, 1087
5:17	28, 85, 387, 402, 601, 807-808, 810, 1080, 1088, 1098, 1210
5:19-21	383, 763, 766, 1076, 1143, 1229, 1304
6:1-2	23, 80, 369, 901, 1083
6:10	511, 674
6:14-15	91, 187
6:16	515
6:17-18	1, 97, 110, 126, 186, 188, 207, 672, 1056, 1066, 1078, 1317, 1322, 1324-1325
7:1	291, 453, 545, 561, 1052, 1278
7:2	866
7:11	239
8:1-3	138
8:2-5	139, 480, 1145
8:2, 9	94
9:6-14	899, 1179
9:7-8	136, 481, 488
9:8-11	140
9:9-10	1218
9:24-25	1271
10:5	67-68, 605, 631, 637, 905, 1226, 1237, 1240
10:10	363
10:17-18	849
11, 12	1087
11:12-15	712
11:23-33	299, 325, 850, 734, 858
12:7	951, 1201
12:8-9	547, 942
12:9-10	94, 129, 607, 745, 840, 842, 916, 1260
12:19	219
12:20-21	83, 1171
13:5	1130
13:11	255

Galatians

1:6-7	244, 274, 355, 836
1:9-10	30, 131, 146, 214, 262, 989, 1190, 1281
1:13-17	273, 843, 1070
2:6	60
2:11	966
2:20	268, 272, 299, 343, 387, 810, 846, 862, 987, 1125-1126, 1209, 1216, 1245, 1257
3:13	891, 1304
3:24	1227
4:4-5	104, 647
4:29	1247
5:1	458-459, 461-462, 718, 781, 1091
5:13	22, 322, 398, 458-459, 462, 719, 818, 1228
5:16	309, 687
5:17	804, 826, 1160, 1200
5:22-23	401, 432, 678, 1116, 1187, 1196
5:24	266, 987, 1125, 1210
6:2-3	628
6:4	1130
6:7-8	1179
6:9	243, 1203, 1255
6:10	135, 829
6:14	129, 265, 529, 854, 988, 1210

Ephesians

1	1080
1:3	298, 1074
1:4-6	385, 491, 796, 1278
1:7	1025
1:12-14	153, 242, 385
1:15-23	1033
1:17	496
1:18-21	278, 298, 649, 651, 663
1:22-23	115, 141, 175, 645, 918
2:1-3	238, 433, 435, 632, 971, 1224, 1226, 1368
2:2-7	254, 501, 508, 510, 810, 971
2:4-10	456, 493, 1026, 1371
2:8-10	102, 374, 377, 398, 400, 417, 423-424, 492, 534, 537-538, 818, 1031-1032, 1142, 1174
2:12-13	436, 494, 767, 836, 1082
2:14-16	1076
2:19-20	135, 433
3:8	962, 967, 1074
3:9	95
3:10-11	172
3:12	1233
3:18	1073
3:19	565

3:20-21	24, 143, 219, 422, 488, 916, 1275
4:1-6	63, 212, 1023
4:3-6	127, 301, 1054, 1274, 1288, 1298
4:11-16	54, 172, 190, 211, 281, 587, 975
4:11-13	199, 324, 834, 952, 962
4:14-16	85, 118, 185, 313, 591, 805, 976, 1182
4:17-24	186, 1030, 1318
4:20-32	1171
4:22-24	813, 1164, 1271
4:25-32	154, 825, 917
4:25	326, 598, 817
4:26-5:2	1196
4:29	243, 256, 616
4:30	564, 584, 819
4:31-32	255, 1023, 1044, 1222
5:3-4	252, 349, 616-617
5:6	67-68, 311, 677, 867, 1375
5:7-8	187, 1324
5:11	187, 966
5:15-18	25, 147, 205, 547, 567-570, 829, 917, 1048, 1129
5:18-19	164, 430, 585, 672, 794, 848, 1260
5:22-33	771, 888
5:23-24	115, 645
5:25-29	75, 283, 611, 757
6:4	117, 596
6:10-18	144, 809, 1200
6:10-12	180, 238, 309, 445, 861, 885, 1206
6:16	428
6:18	25, 82, 713, 783, 925, 934, 1050, 1096, 1198

Philippians

1:9-11	206, 228, 310, 470, 1050
1:12-18	785, 1136, 1275
1:20-26	307, 779
1:21-24	277, 289, 292, 294, 361, 472, 551, 1020, 1194, 1259, 1277, 1309
1:27-28	830
1:29-30	318, 388, 875
2:1-4	253, 1054, 1297
2:3-4	609, 612, 614, 987, 989, 993
2:5	52, 103, 1239-1240
2:5-11	272, 663
2:6-7	605, 646
2:9-11	77, 121, 356, 520, 531, 651, 820, 822, 1006, 1010, 1046, 1111, 1137, 1216, 1312, 1356
2:12-13	10, 227, 305, 404, 594
2:15	132
2:19-22	303, 1136
2:25-30	527, 865, 1037
3:3	343
3:4-11	28
3:6-8	229, 271, 273, 280, 314, 333, 361, 483, 741, 775, 1066, 1080, 1086 1289
3:7-16	217, 636, 693, 698, 701, 721, 1218
3:10-14	108, 681
3:10	211, 270, 299, 300, 454, 655, 700, 708, 742, 846, 854, 1126, 1128, 1157
3:12-14	775-776, 1132
3:12	526, 1186
3:13-14	11, 113, 231, 281, 323, 476, 1072
3:17	157, 715, 1077
3:18-21	338, 485, 551, 731, 733, 807, 1221, 1319
3:29-30	223
4:3	928, 1054
4:4	395, 542, 673, 675
4:6-7	76, 402, 407, 673, 890, 934, 1326-1328
4:8	89, 92, 631, 638, 756, 1129, 1237-1238
4:9	157, 715
4:11-12	215, 359, 395, 745, 824, 838, 892, 899, 943, 1156
4:13	275, 610, 840, 916
4:17	732
4:18-19	140, 481

Colossians

1:3-4	200, 213
1:9-11	89, 203, 811, 853
1:13-14	1026
1:15-17	522, 533, 648, 1000

1:18 ....115, 141, 153, 175,
    191, 224, 528, 591, 645, 745,
    918, 997, 1036, 1123, 1190
1:19-22 ....1024, 1193, 1233
1:24 1138
1:27 ....438, 889
1:28-29 ....10, 107, 199, 310,
    805, 952
2:8-9 ....67-68, 156, 311, 905,
    1101, 1105, 1270
2:13 374
2:15-17 222
3:1-4 ....108, 290, 336, 338,
    359, 367, 454, 529, 621, 731,
    733, 756, 773-774, 807,
    1037, 1075, 1114, 1129,
    1163, 1184, 1307-1308
3:5-11 ....154, 314, 326, 354, 598,
    822, 825, 1043-1044, 1058,
    1171, 1222, 1375
3:12-14 ....207, 212, 987, 1023
3:15 890
3:16-18 ....71, 164, 230, 256, 585,
    792, 794, 824, 1140-1141
3:19 757
3:23 ....27, 109, 297, 788, 792, 868,
    968, 1140-1141, 1214
4:2 ....117, 935
4:3-4 977
4:5-6 ....97, 128, 829, 1188

First Thessalonians

1:2-3 200
1:5 960
1:6-8 ....112, 156-157, 164, 782
1:9 ....273, 622, 971, 1043, 1081
2:2-4 ....146, 262, 838, 840,
    865, 875, 897, 979-980, 982,
    1190, 1206, 1281
2:3-9 131
2:4-6 ....30, 129, 471, 557, 582,
    590, 978
2:6-7 ....210, 769
2:8-9 1138
2:10-12 ....863-864, 977
2:13 ....37, 412, 957
3:3 1259
4:3-7 ....917, 1050
4:11-12 100
4:13-18 ....159, 292, 472, 653,
    1108, 1113

5:1-8 ....319, 428, 1005
    1111, 1323
5:12-13 ....161, 183, 527
5:13-15 ....255, 628, 950
5:16-17 ....253, 309, 925-926, 933,
    1176, 1341
5:19-20 ....570, 580, 593
5:20-21 ....39, 440, 877
5:21-22 1166
5:23-24 ....422, 526, 730,
    1002, 1243

Second Thessalonians

1:3-4 200
2:3-4 1006
3:3 1243
3:10 33

First Timothy

1:3-4 355
1:5-6 ....252, 984, 1299
1:6-7 ....244, 856, 900
1:12-15 ....59, 78, 734, 854,
    857, 995, 1143
1:15-16 ....537, 615, 1128
1:17 ....24, 679
2:1-8 ....152, 310, 713, 906, 1248
2:9-10 ....484, 1314-1315
3:1-7 ....712, 864, 869
3:5 1132
3:16 ....104, 646, 648
4:1-2 ....252, 274
4:6 969
4:7-8 ....10, 322, 528, 1069, 1214
4:8-10 296
4:12 ....160, 262, 845, 862
4:13-16 ....107, 109, 125, 323,
    852, 863, 868-869, 968, 1007,
    1183, 1192, 1214, 1286
5:17-18 ....137, 161, 183, 711
5:20-21 ....966, 1191
5:22 869
6:6-8 1156
6:9-10 390
6:13-16 1121
6:17-19 ....337, 339, 359, 442,
    480-482, 704, 722-723, 773,
    900, 998, 1129, 1303,
    1307-1308

315

6:20-21 .... 170, 311, 330, 905, 1101, 1105

Second Timothy

1:3 853
1:6-7 .... 14, 109, 118, 445-446, 637, 891, 1072, 1202
1:7, 12 .... 65, 99
1:9 .... 102, 1031
1:10 287
1:11-12 .... 331, 413, 475, 621, 896
1:13-14 .... 170, 245-246
2:2 832
2:3-4 .... 174, 184, 319, 325, 544, 861, 868, 1214, 1271
2:5 238
2:14-16 .... 45, 54, 107, 322, 635, 856, 868-869, 968, 1285
2:21-22 .... 132, 565
2:24-26 .... 120, 184
3:1-7 .... 6, 130, 178, 181, 195, 277, 639, 906, 1299
3:12 .... 30, 896-897, 1061, 1259
3:13-17 .... 573, 585, 932, 1065, 1231, 1291
3:16-17 .... 36-38, 48, 55, 251, 827, 848, 950
4:1-5 .... 30, 65, 125, 130-131, 143, 151, 170-171, 194, 198, 319, 738, 882, 960, 965-966, 970, 972, 977, 980, 1191
4:6-8 .... 232, 288, 293, 527, 551, 626, 681, 841, 946-947, 1020, 1094
4:13 1018
4:16 464
4:17 951

Titus

1:2 417
1:5 .... 783, 831
1:7-9 529
1:8-9 205
1:15-16 252
2:7 160
2:11-14 .... 101, 175, 291, 393, 397, 478, 513, 535, 563, 740, 818, 959, 1001, 1003, 1024, 1026, 1047-1048, 1109-1110, 1118-1119, 1121, 1127

3:4-7 .... 95, 102, 400, 493, 501, 1025, 1031-1032

Hebrews

1:1-2 .... 73, 360, 524
1:3 .... 522, 648
1:6-8 .... 19, 1102
1:13-14 .... 18, 634
2:9 .... 663, 1137
3:12-13 242
4:2 412
4:12 .... 37, 56, 143, 209, 522, 950, 958
4:14-16 .... 310, 486, 495, 512, 923, 949, 1090
5:11-12 .... 113, 693, 973
5:11-6:1 281
5:12-14 .... 280, 809, 1295, 1316
6:1 .... 102, 776, 962, 1033
6:11-12 426
6:17-20 .... 600, 1266
7:25 1053
8:1-2 967
8:12 1090
9:27 .... 285-286, 351, 366, 767, 909, 1020-1021, 1172
10:1-2 828
10:19-23 .... 235, 237, 420, 1028, 1081
10:24-25 .... 165, 320
11 .... 58, 469
11:1-2 .... 410, 416, 832, 1010, 1296
11:4 1084
11:5 .... 348, 1120
11:6, 16, 39-40 1194-1195
11:7 814
11:8-10 .... 57, 232, 335-336, 345, 475, 832, 999, 1080
11:10-16 1319
11:13-16 .... 411, 621, 733, 908, 1001, 1112, 1115
11:24-26 .... 318, 424, 483, 774, 1218, 1312
11:32-40 .... 325, 1063, 1258
12:1-2 .... 11, 145, 175, 191, 316, 405, 409, 476, 698, 943, 1078, 1094, 1157, 1176, 1220, 1264, 1271
12:3-6 .... 243, 263
12:5-11 .... 321, 1261
12:8-14 .... 324, 513
12:10 1372
12:11 848

12:14	544
12:15	1044
12:22-24	18, 158, 1277
12:28	1362
12:29	1227
13:1-3	19, 546
13:5	730, 1156, 1230
13:8	517, 1053, 1205, 1243, 1331
13:17	112, 161, 183, 262, 825
13:20-21	665

James

1:2-4	547, 674, 1217, 1253, 1261
1:5-6	331, 613, 716, 919, 937, 949, 1311
1:12	318
1:13-15	286, 1167, 1223
1:17	497-498, 690
1:22-25	48-50, 93, 155, 317, 570, 814, 816, 959, 961
2:1-5	60, 254, 603, 609, 1244
2:14-20	93, 398
2:17	22, 396, 535
2:18-26	398-399, 401
2:19-20	961
2:22	403
2:23	468, 1369
2:26	22, 257, 396, 820
3:1	1168
3:5-6	20, 616
3:6-10	243
3:17	618
4:1-2	312
4:3-4	665, 696, 921, 939, 941, 945, 1060, 1135
4:6	204
4:7-10	203, 562, 885, 1052, 1095, 1215
4:13-14	21, 296, 334, 358, 362, 910-911, 1021, 1107, 1252
5:8	1004
5:12	326
5:13	430
5:15	427, 924
5:16	152, 936
5:17-18	895

First Peter

1:2	521
1:3-5	3, 65, 288, 422, 478, 551, 599, 602, 626, 891, 915, 1088-1089, 1112
1:6-7	523, 658, 1001, 1003
1:6-9, 13	95, 319, 323, 638, 959, 1113-1114, 1200
1:14-16	239, 561, 601, 1278, 1325
1:18-19	1025, 1174
1:19-20	1084
1:22	1142
2:1-2	185, 636, 687, 805, 973, 976, 1171, 1182, 1185
2:9	101, 1357
2:11-12	733, 826, 908, 1067
2:16	462, 719
2:24	1304
3:1-7	484, 771, 969, 1314-1315
3:15	710
3:16-17	100
4:1-2	103
4:7	1004
4:11	71, 230, 792, 837, 980
4:12-13	1114, 1217
4:15-16	100
5:1-4	120, 161-162, 783, 847
5:5	678, 1313, 1360
5:6	1215, 1219, 1255
5:6-10	562
5:7	407, 923, 1327, 1341
5:8-9	124, 180, 809, 885, 951, 1095, 1200-1201, 1249

Second Peter

1:3	1157
1:4	544
1:5-7	89, 635
1:20-21	36
2:12-15	40, 1224
3:9	463, 492
3:10-11	334
3:12	1114
3:14-18	39, 74
3:16	40
3:17	1250
3:18	74, 185, 298, 324, 635, 687, 693, 950, 1182, 1185

First John

1:1-3	235, 278, 466, 516, 655, 727, 795-796, 886

1:4 675
1:6-9 .... 75, 257, 276, 394, 672,
804, 813, 1168, 1173, 1186
2:1-2 .... 276, 1072
2:3-6 .... 707, 816
2:12 456
2:13 697
2:15-17 .... 126, 188, 228, 334, 336,
351, 360, 442, 632, 756, 819,
997, 1067, 1135, 1163, 1308,
1317, 1320-1321
2:19 .... 29, 386, 1097
2:20 .... 195, 577, 1011, 1291
2:27 .... 572, 639
3:1 959
3:2-3 .... 239, 247, 291, 485, 510,
513, 740, 1003, 1047-1048,
1052, 1118, 1142, 1276
3:4 1161
3:7-8 .... 867, 1091
3:13 1201
3:17-19 .... 155, 754-755
3:21-22 .... 665, 920, 940
4:1 .... 39, 130, 244, 275, 355, 414,
439-441, 712, 867, 1295
4:6 1292
4:7-8 .... 446, 754-755
4:10 .... 502, 750, 1096
4:16 .... 86, 755
4:17 909
4:18 .... 90, 446
4:19 .... 748, 1127
5:1 754
5:3 .... 341, 821, 1027
5:3-10 .... 420, 1251
5:11-12 .... 357, 1073
5:14-15 .... 920, 941
5:21 221

Second John

8-9 245-246
10-11 .... 437, 482

Third John

4 .... 1, 245-246
5-6 303
9 .... 160, 313, 1033, 1136

Jude

3 .... 261, 330
14-15 40
24-25 .... 679, 1230, 1275, 1345

Revelation

1:1-3 523
1:1, 19 1045
1:5-6 1090
1:8 1331
1:9 .... 608, 896
1:12-18 .... 209, 1122
1:13-16 .... 660, 664, 666
1:17 .... 449, 1336, 1339
2:4-5 .... 26, 74, 191, 464,
932, 1040
2:7, 11 .... 1197, 1205
2:15-16 1069
3:1-3 .... 426, 1064
3:4 189
3:14-22 .... 168, 709, 1199
3:15-17 .... 34, 144, 197,
206, 619, 776, 1349, 1376
3:17-19 .... 156, 163, 263
3:20 .... 758, 927
3:21 1205
3:22 148
4:1-8 .... 677, 705, 886, 1081
4:8-11 .... 237, 295, 308, 490, 747,
1146, 1343, 1347, 1354,
1358-1359
4:2-3 967
4:8 .... 87, 496, 1331, 1335
5:1-8, 13 520
5:8-14 .... 295, 308, 550, 659, 663,
747, 1318, 1343, 1348, 1350
6:1-8 .... 1005, 1116
6:9-10 1256
6:12-17 .... 676, 836
7:9-14 894
7:14-17 .... 218, 367, 1093
8:2, 6 1006
10:8-11 .... 1251, 1285
11:15 .... 523, 1046
12:11 318
15:3 705
16:7 556
18:4 .... 188, 1324
19:6 1122
19:7 550

318

19:11-16	179, 209, 222, 666
21-22	479, 549
21:2	908
21:4	287
21:6, 7	1005
21:10-27	335
21:21	1115
21:23	704
22:6	1047
22:6-7, 20	1045
22:17	79-80, 901
22:18-19	38
22:20	1109-1111

Topical Index

A

A.B. Simpson..........................427, 717, 860
Absolutes 1, 1246
Accidents 519
Accountability 2, 392, 909
Activity
    Moratorium on 3, 4
    Religious..................5-11, 107, 207, 590,
        1346, 1376
    Test of Godliness 12
Adjustment..128
Adoration...13
Advertising 772
Affections...14
Affluence (see also Wealth)....................552
Ambition 91
Amen..444
America
    Excess..390
    Greatness 2, 596, 909
    Liberty...15
    Problems 16
    Sinfulness 17, 64, 766, 790, 1170
Anchor...1266
Angels
    Denial of 18
    Ignorance about 19
Anger (see also Temper) 20
Anthropology 21
Antinomianism...22
Apathy.............23-28, 297, 567, 629, 1285
Apologetics 423, 576, 577, 1022, 1030
Apostasy..29
Approval 30
Atheism..................................31, 258, 392
Authors..32
Awesomeness of God (see God: His Awesomeness)

B

Backsliding.....................................266, 709
Balance 33
Beatitudes 34
Bible
    Apparent contradictions........................35
    Authority of 36-38, 414
    Difficult passages 39, 40
    Illumination (see Holy Spirit: Illumination)
    Inspiration of 38
    Meditation 41-44, 52
    Memorization of....................................45
    Misapplication of...................................46
    Neglect of...................................47, 1183
    Obedience to 48-50, 1292
    Reading of.....................51-53, 931, 996, 1014
    Study of...............................45, 54, 1292
    Teaching of..959
    Uniqueness of 55
    Unity of 827, 828
    Value of..................................56, 57, 251
Big shots...1219
Biography
    Biblical 58
    Humanness in..59
    Interpretation of 60
Bitterness 1044
Blessings
    Remembrance of 61
    Spiritual 215
    Unlimited 488, 633
Blood of Christ 75
Boards
    Lack of dependence on God..............116
    Lack of vision...62
Body of Christ 63, 120, 135, 180, 458, 591
Boldness 30, 64-66, 125, 812, 840, 873, 874, 875, 876, 879, 896, 969, 975, 981, 982, 1202
Books (see also Reading)
    Evil 67, 68
    Value of..69, 70
Boredom
    From overstimulation...........................71
    Religious...............................72-74, 835
Bride of Christ 75
Burdens...76
Burning bush 217, 514
Busyness 3, 5, 6, 7, 12, 107, 329, 691, 725

C

Call of Christ 77-78
Call of God 79-81, 1143
Calvinism 365
Carelessness 82

Carnality 83-86, 825
Celebrities 87, 129, 153, 157, 160,
    349, 442, 527, 555, 557,
    1037, 1067, 1078, 1136, 1138
Change 23, 88, 601
Character 89, 598, 1273
Charm 849
Child dedication 90
Children 90
Choices 91, 92, 356, 997, 1185, 1311
Christ-like thinking 103
Christian life 93, 405, 1200, 1269
Christian leaders (see Leaders)
Christians
 Contradictions 94, 95
 Fools for Christ 96
 In the world 97-100,
    128, 175, 330, 804, 806, 889,
    1061, 1201, 1247, 1300
 Other-worldly 454, 1112
 Peculiar people 101
 Relationship with Christ 102
 True freedom 459
Christlikeness 98, 100, 513, 529, 1077,
    1118, 1184
Christmas
 True meaning 104
 Worldly celebration 105
Church
 Activities 3, 106-109, 1052
 Age divisions 212
 Apathy 109-114, 174, 201,
    229, 279, 376, 680, 834
 Authority 115, 116, 414
 Boredom 73, 117, 118, 177, 835, 970
 Business meetings 119
 Competition 120
 Concept of God 121, 122, 420,
    1042, 1345
 Conflict 123, 124, 180, 312
 Cultural impact 125, 202, 218
 Current condition 126-132, 185,
    208, 265, 311, 378, 918, 966,
    1058, 1061, 1181, 1350
 Entertainment 117, 118, 133, 134,
    1038
 Family 135
 Finances 62, 136-140, 471, 481,
    838, 1191
 Focus 141-146, 172, 196, 313,
    1052, 1357
 God's judgment 29
 Government 161, 162
 Holy Spirit's work 147-153, 580,
    582-583, 591-592,
    595, 714
 Ineffectiveness 154-157, 897, 1346
 Invincibility 158-159
 Leadership 160-163, 712-713
 Modeling 164
 Necessity of 165, 783
 Numbers 166-171, 245, 1066
 Objectives 172
 Organization 831-832
 Power of God 143, 173-174
 Presence of Christ 175, 191, 209,
    213, 1053
 Presence of God 134, 176-179, 197,
    1055, 1364-1365
 Problems 180-181
 Proper place of 182
 Public relations 1283
 Pulpit committee 183, 845
 Religious game 184, 830, 1035, 1351
 Routine 185, 1353
 Separation 110, 186-190, 1204
 Services 177, 191-195, 504, 1150
    1352-1353
 Social club 196-197
 Spiritual condition 4, 111-112, 144,
    154, 181, 198-207, 584, 592,
    738, 932, 971, 1066-1067,
    1192, 1325
 Success 145, 208-210, 990
 Unity 180, 211-214, 1023, 1054,
    1297-1298
Church Treasurer 140
Circumstances 215
Claims of Christ 216, 576, 1174
Commitment 91, 217-232, 316,
    568, 745, 747, 999,
    1071, 1301, 1310
Common grace 233
Communion with God 33, 234-237,
    249, 515, 687, 692, 698, 730,
    758, 796, 904, 927
Communism 375, 520
Comparison 431, 845
Competition 238, 837
Complacency 239-242, 642-643,
    694, 739, 776, 1113,
    1132, 1262
Complaining 243
Compromise 244-246
Concept of God 247-250, 504-505,
    786, 904, 1342

Confession 276
Confidence 304
Confirmation
　Need for...251
Conscience 252, 274, 424, 718
Consistency 253
Contempt..254
Controversy..255
Convenience 775
Conversation 256
Conversion 257
Conviction 460-461, 1166
Correction
　Unwillingness to hear..........................990
Courage (see also Boldness)......................65
Creation 258-259, 798-799,
　　　　　　　　　　　　　　　1102-1103
Creeds 260-261
Criticism 262-264, 787, 989
Cross
　Current view of..................265, 273, 387
　Demands of.......................266, 746, 775
　Foolishness of 267
　Personal 268-272, 1126, 1137,
　　　　　　　　　　　　　　　1216, 1312
　Power of..273
Cults 39, 274-275, 376, 380
Cultural awareness 877, 880
Current conditions
　Apathy...24, 276
　Evil days 277
　Shallowness..................8, 113, 226, 248,
　　　　　　　　　　278-282, 298, 637,
　　　　　　　　　　　　　　　1013, 1181
Current issues
　Compromise.......................................244
　Loss of freedom 15
　Misuse of freedom 719

D

Dead churches...............................283, 580
Death
　Baby's 284
　Certainty of 285-286, 1020, 1107
　Enemy..287-288
　No fear of....................................289-290, 602
　Preparation for 291-292, 554
　Triumph in 288, 293-295, 308,
　　　　　　　　　　　　　　472, 626, 653
Dedication..296-297
Deeper life..............................298-300, 333

Defensiveness 65
Defiance 31
Denominations 301-302, 528
Dependability 303
Dependence on God 304-305, 1134
Depression 306, 415
Devil (see Satan)
Devotion to God.............................307-308
Devotional life 328, 1175-1176
Devotional mood 309
Dialogue 310-311, 967, 1248, 1280
Differences...312
Direction..313
Discipleship..................219, 266, 269, 299,
　　　　　　　　　　　314-320, 324, 379, 388,
　　　　　　　　　　　397, 402, 635-636, 783,
　　　　　　　　　　　805, 975, 1072, 1126,
　　　　　　　　　　　　　　　1182-1183
Discipline
　Corrective 321, 513, 1263-1264
　Personal 322-325, 868, 1130, 1214
Discouragement 542, 1091
Dishonesty 326
Disobedience 327
Distractions..............47, 328-329, 351, 499,
　　　　　　　　　　　　　　　1175, 1271
Doctrinal divisions...............................1288
Doctrine...814
Dogmatics..330
Doubts..331
Dry spells 332

E

Earthly loves 333
Earthly things 334-339, 358-360,
　　　　　　　　　　　704, 774, 998, 1084, 1156,
　　　　　　　　　　　　　　　1307-1308, 1319
Earthquakes...676
Egos 340
Eloquence 839
Emotionalism 341-342
Emotions................................342-344, 415
Encounter with God..............345-347, 516,
　　　　　　　　　　　　　　　1336, 1369
Enoch...348
Entertainers 349
Entertainment 350-353, 596,
　　　　　　　　　　　　　　　631-632, 996
Eros..354
Error...355
Eternal destiny.......................................356

Eternal life 357
Eternal perspective   146, 277, 296, 336, 358-364, 478, 527, 543, 621, 722, 907, 910, 1047, 1119-1120, 1206, 1276-1277, 1318
Eternal security 365
Eternity 366-369, 384, 479, 543, 626
Evangelicalism 370
Evangelism
   Concern for lost.........371-372, 753, 984, 1148
   Difficult task 150
   Divine power in 373-377
   God first 491
   Humanistic approach to 378-379, 765
   Lack of involvement in 376, 380-381
   True conversion........................382, 1097
   Urgency of 114, 381, 383-384, 812, 1113
   Wrong emphasis.......385-389, 943, 1085
Excess 390-391
Existentialism...392
Expectations 461
Experiencing God................................1074
Externalism...8
Extremes 593, 1377
Extremists 444
Eyes of God...393

F

Failure..................394, 456, 787, 813, 903
Faith
   And feelings................................395, 673
   And works 396-400, 534, 818, 822
   Confidence in God......62, 475, 923-924, 937, 1253-1254, 1327
   Confirmation of 401-403
   Daily walk 348, 359, 404-406, 516-517, 814
   Defective................406-408, 1195, 1296
   Definition of 409
   Expectation 410-412, 416, 476, 526
   Foundation of...........332, 413-422, 1002
   Gift of God........................417, 423-424
   Intellectual only 425, 1097
   Power of God 426, 427
   Shield of 428
Faithfulness....................................429-430
Faithful service 431-432

Fall of man.............................383, 433-435
False front 865
False hope..436
False teachers................................437-438
False teaching 39-40, 67, 355, 439-441
Fame...442
Family 597
Fanatics...443-444, 593
Fatigue 1203
Fear 445-448, 891
Fear of God....................................449-453
Fellowship
   Need for.....................................135, 528
   Not the answer 201
   With God (see Communion with God)
Finishing well 946-947
Flippancy 486, 659
Follow-up...783
Following Christ 220, 226, 454
Forgiveness 455-457, 494-495, 539, 1028, 1092
Free will 463
Freedom 458-462, 560, 719
Friends
   Fair-weather 464
   Right kind 465
Friendship with God 466-469
Fruit of the Spirit 1187
Fund-raising 471, 482
Fundamentalism................370, 1228, 1235
Fundamentals...470
Funerals 292, 472, 554
Futility
   Feelings of 473
   Of the world......................................474
Future 475-479

G

Giving 480-483, 1079, 1145
Glamor..484
Glorified body 485
Goals 313
God
   His awesomeness 451-452, 486-487, 1042, 1337-1338
   His care 521
   His compassion 512
   His gifts 488
   His glory.....................178, 489-491, 800
   His goodness 492, 500

His grace	493-495, 1243
His holiness	496
His immanence	699
His immutability	497-498
His inscrutability	1254, 1270
His kindness	501
His leading	499
His love	249, 446, 500-502, 668, 750, 1229
His majesty	503-507, 705, 762, 801, 1354
His mercy	498, 508-510
His omnipresence	511
His omniscience	512
His perfection	513
His presence	251, 338, 469, 514-517, 692, 1367
His self-sufficiency	1144
His sovereignty	446-447, 477, 506, 518-523, 892, 944, 986
His transcendence	451
His voice	79, 524
His wisdom	525
His work	525-526, 562, 1063
Godliness	527-529, 740
God's ways/ Man's ways	530
Gospel	
Accept Christ	531-533, 1085
Faith alone	534
Moral implications	398, 535, 818
Need for accuracy	531
Need for understanding	536-537
Trust in Christ	538
Grace	455-456, 539, 755
Great preachers	540
Growth emphasis	168-170, 245
Guilt	1092

H

Happiness	343, 541-547, 671, 1024, 1213, 1257, 1278, 1289
Heart	548
Heaven	
Certainty of	288, 418, 602
Glory of	367, 485, 549-550
Lack of interest in	551-552, 1309
Longing for	290, 294, 731, 908
Popular beliefs about	553-554
Rewards	555
Hell	556
Hero worship	557-559

Hindrances	560
History	
Future more important	21
Holiness	
Basis for joy	672
Commanded	561
Conditions for	25, 239, 562
First need	544-546, 848, 1278
Meaning of	529
Unpopular subject	563
Holy Spirit	
Conviction	423
Do not grieve	564, 819
Filling	25, 565-571, 672
Illumination	53, 572-574, 1011
Indwelling	575
Inward witness	344, 576-577
Need for	205, 275, 370, 578-580, 594-595, 639, 714, 991, 1199
Neglect of	581-585
Power of God	45, 586
Revelation of God	84
Spiritual gifts	151, 587-595
Home	596-597
Honesty	598, 866
Honors	77
Hope	478-479, 599-602
Hospitality	603
Human potential	275
Human wisdom	714
Humanism	507, 604-605, 773
Humble service	527, 606-608, 861
Humility	340, 609-615, 837, 846, 992-993, 1136, 1217, 1255
Humor	
Off-color	616
Proper place of	617
Hymnody	192, 794
Hypocrisy	155, 618-620, 1033

I

Identity with Christ	621
Idolatry	622-623
Idols	221
Illness	624
Imagination	625
Immortality	626-627
Imperfections of men	558-559, 628
Incarnation (see Jesus Christ: incarnation)	
Indifference	629

Indispensability
  Prideful thoughts of 630
Influences 631-632, 756
Individual importance 473, 502, 634, 1127
Inheritance...633
Inner reality...548

Insignificance
  Feelings of 634
Instant Christianity..........................635-636
Intellect..637-638
Intellectual snobbery 640
Intellectual stimulation 256
Intellectualism 639
Intolerance..641

J

Jacob
  Moral flaws................................642, 644
  Longing after God........................642-643
Jesus Christ
  His authority.......................................645
  His death...629
  His incarnation 646-648, 768
  His intercession 365
  His loveliness..................................26, 74
  His preeminence 175
  His resurrection 649-653
  His sufficiency 654
  His sustaining power.......522, 1266-1269
  Intimacy with 270, 655-656, 700, 952, 1093, 1157, 1230
  Judge..657, 664
  Love for.......................28, 658-659, 797
  Modern view of..........................660-665
  Paintings of...666
  Response to..............................222, 1174
John, Gospel of 956
John the Baptist....................669-670, 1178
John 3:16..667-668
Joy 671-675, 1229
Judgment of God
  Deserved..556
  Future 676-677, 1005-1006, 1133, 1172
  Present 678
Judgment seat of Christ..............1140, 1145
Judgmentalism.....................................1132

K

Knowledge
  Inadequacy of............................708, 906
Knowledge of God
  Basis for faith....................419-420, 1002
  Basis for love 751
  Church's need...........108, 179, 679-680, 1055
  Continuous pursuit.....681-689, 693, 741
  Divine encounter...............347, 690, 895
  In the Bible..43
  Neglected........................691-694, 1231
  Personal, intimate......695-700, 742, 953, 1232
  Spiritual depth 300
  Supreme value of 337, 701-705, 948, 1123-1124
  Through humble obedience 706-707

L

Lack of enthusiasm 27
Laodicea 709
Law..1227
Law of the leader 847
Layman 710
Leaders
  Attitude toward 711
  Spiritual need 130, 162-163, 712-716, 753, 847
  Visionaries 717
Leadership (see Spiritual leadership)
Legalism 718
Liberty..462, 719
Life change..227
Life purpose..........296, 362, 720-723, 999, 1358-1359
Listening to God...............44, 724-728, 972
Loneliness......................236, 517, 729-733
Longing for God............178, 223, 240-242, 642-643, 688, 694, 734-744, 1184
Lordship of Christ............28, 224-225, 315, 403, 569, 745-747, 820, 1010, 1053, 1099, 1311
Love
  Genuine 984
  Importance of.............................753-754
  Power of 755-756
  Wrong concept...................................757
Love for God.......................748-752, 1366

M

Man
- Alienation from God..........433, 758-760, 767, 1233
- Insignificance of..................250, 761-762
- Rebellion against God.................31, 237, 763-764, 986, 1161
- Self-centeredness of....................765, 913
- Sinfulness of 34, 424, 434, 766, 1172
- Spiritual searching.......................627, 767
- Value of..768

Man's approval.......................................769
Marriage 770-771
Materialism 360, 772-774, 1308
Mediocrity 775-776
Meditation(see also Bible: meditation)....47, 328, 507, 689, 725-726, 1015-1016, 1019, 1153, 1207
Meekness..777
Mentors 778
Mercy 457
Miracles
- Belief in 1104
- Commercialization of 779-780
- Denial of 1106

Missions
- Cautions about 781-782
- Church planting..................................783
- Commanded 784-785
- Motives for 786, 1141, 1144

Mistakes..787
Modern day 16
Monday worship 788
Money (see Personal finances, Wealth)
Moods..673
Moral bearings 789
Moral rot...790-791
Mortality 286
Motives...................................792-793, 876
Music 631, 659, 794
Mystery
- Acceptance of..35

Mysticism..........................33, 639, 795-797

N

Nature 798-801
Negatives 802
New believer 85, 112, 803-809, 1185, 1370

New man 810
New year 811-813
Noah...814
Nonexpectation 193, 204

O

Oaths..326
Obedience
- Cost of...............................225, 569, 815
- Meaning of 821
- Need for.............93, 203, 317, 341, 399, 403, 570, 814, 816-822, 917, 940, 961, 1027, 1056-1058, 1060, 1293-1294
- Test of love 823

Obscurity 824
Old nature 825-826, 1210
Old Testament 827-828
Opportunity 829
Opposition..............99-100, 124, 604, 806, 830, 840, 878, 896, 1094, 1313
Organization 831-832
Origins 258

P

Para-church ministries 833
Passive religion 834
Pastoral ministry
- Challenge 835-836, 859, 950
- Competition 837
- Convictions...............................214, 246
- Dependence on God........143, 305, 727, 838-844
- Expectations 169, 183, 845
- Need for spiritual reality 571, 585, 590, 846-849, 865, 867, 1189, 1220
- Prayer 850-853, 933-934, 1177
- Pride 210, 854, 1190, 1212
- Shallowness........................855-856, 976
- Significance 78, 869
- Spiritual impact 715, 857

Pastors
- Ambition 1190
- Burden for people 858, 1221
- Call of God................................848, 859
- Commitment......................860-862, 982
- Humility 854, 862, 1215
- Integrity..............................863-867, 978

Laziness..868
Ordination..869
Prophetic ministry.............194, 716, 840, 870-882, 887, 960, 966, 983
Renewal 841, 883-884
Satan's opposition......................885, 951
Stress..842, 1191
Vision of God......879-880, 886-887, 977
Pastor's wife 888
Patience
God's timing.............................411, 1255
Peace
False..474, 889
Inner 777, 890, 1251, 1328
In trials 511, 891-892
Penitence..1186
Permanence..................................893, 1252
Persecution.......99-100, 226, 271, 894-897, 1114
Personal finances 898-900
Personal testimony: Tozer 901-902, 1080
Perspective...1240
Pessimism 1001
Peter
Affection for 903
Pharisaism.......................................641, 670
Pharisees...904
Philosophy 905-906, 1105
Philosophy of life..................723, 907, 1000
Pilgrims 368, 733, 908, 1319
Pleasure 674
Pleasures...632
Politics 46, 909-911
Popular beliefs 912
Possessions..774
Potential...913
Poverty 603, 898-899, 914
Power
High price of 915
Power of God 916-917
Pragmatism 208, 665, 918
Prayer
Boldness in 919
Conditions....................................920-921
Diligence in 1059
Expectation 922-924
Fellowship with God..........925-927, 1151
Hindrances..851
Intercession 857, 928
Lifestyle 926, 929
Mere ritual................................930, 1232
Necessity of.........52, 152, 713, 843-844, 852-853, 931-934

Patience in 935-936
Privilege of 937-938
Unanswered.....155, 411, 939-940, 1060
Wrong use of...........................665, 927, 941-945, 994
Prayers.........218, 338, 606, 612, 704, 728, 741, 745, 861, 946-949
Preaching
Awesome task...................836, 855, 857, 881-882, 950-951
Experiencing God.................74, 952-953
Illustrations in 954
Inadequacy for 955-956
Manipulation 342, 957
Need for application...................958-961
Need for freshness......................962-963
Need for skill 968
Originality in......................................964
Preach the Word 965-967, 977
Preparation for 843-844, 968
Problem texts......................................969
Response to..............227, 970-972, 1285
Too deep...973
Watered down 131, 170-171, 316, 738, 743, 974-978
With authority 979-983
Predictions 911
Presence of God (see God: His presence)
Pretense 984
Pride
Human 30, 607, 613-614, 985-989, 1128, 1131, 1134
Pastoral 837, 990-992
Spiritual..............254, 945, 949, 993-995, 1133, 1186
Priorities.........92, 228, 329, 339, 361, 384, 470, 698, 721-723, 792, 996-999, 1271, 1369
Problems....................................1000-1001
Profanity 252
Progress..16, 791
Promises of God............395, 421-422, 705, 1002
Prophecy 277, 478, 676, 1003-1006
Prosperity...483
Public reading of Scripture 1007-1008
Punctuality...1009
Purposelessness......................................767

Q

Quakers 598, 725

R

Rapture (see Second coming)
Rationalism 1010-1011
Reading
    Classics....................................1012-1013
    Dangers of..............................67-68, 631
    Hymnal 1014
    Limitations of 69-70, 1015-1016
    Newspaper 1017
    Secular 1018
    Widely 856, 1019
Realism 1020-1021
Reason 1022, 1105
Reconciliation 1023
Redemption 605, 763, 1024-1026
Reformation 1027, 1061
Regeneration..257
Regret 1028
Rejection 1029-1030
Religion
    Emptiness of 184, 1031-1033, 1248
    In life..1034-1035
    In the news......................................1036
    Popular.....................................352, 1037
Religious entertainment........................1038
Religious language 978
Repentance...............463, 813, 1039-1043,
                           1125, 1169
Resentment..1044
Respectability 96
Resurrection (see Jesus Christ: His resurrection)
Revelation, Book of 1045-1047
Revival
    Conditions for.........174, 297, 940, 1027,
                           1048-1061
    God's work..............................1062-1063
    Hopeful signs of................................744
    Meaning of..............................1064-1065
    Need for..................132, 179, 189, 203,
                  229, 283, 932, 1066-1067
    Personal 317, 1068-1072
Riches in Christ 1073-1074, 1080
Righteous/Wicked 1075
Righteousness......................................1076
Rigidity..204
Rivals of God...623
Role models 903, 1077-1078

S

Sacrifice 1079-1080, 1214
Saintliness (see Godliness)
Salvation
    By faith alone 400, 409, 534,
                               537-538
    From/to 1081
    Goal of 1371, 1373
    God's plan..............................1025-1026
    Holy Spirit's work 377
    Invitation to............80-81, 356, 532-533,
                            1082-1083
    Preparation for eternity............369, 1084
    Sovereign calling.......................763, 1085
    Transformation 257, 807-808, 810,
                       1043, 1086-1088,
                       1098-1099, 1171
Sartre, Jean-Paul............................156, 392
Satan 124, 809, 1089-1096,
                         1200-1201, 1249
Satanism 1006
Satisfaction..14, 66
Saving faith 1097-1099
Science 258, 362, 791, 906,
                       1100-1106, 1360
Scourging 1263
Seasons of life 1107
Second coming
    Contrary views about.......................1121
    Hope for 159, 1108-1111
    Lack of interest in 552, 1112-1115,
                                1309
    Patient waiting for............................1116
    Preparation for 1117-1121
Secularism..1122
Seeking God 1123-1124
Self...987, 1125
    Self-assertion 764
    Self-assurance...................................1217
    Self-denial 1126, 1313
    Self-image...1127
    Self-interest 945, 988, 1128
    Self-knowledge.............1129-1131, 1153
    Self-love 989, 1028
    Self-righteousness 995, 1132
    Self-sufficiency 1133-1134
Selfishness..120
Separation..............330, 1135, 1321, 1325
Sermon on the Mount 9, 34
Servanthood........................153, 462, 608,
                    1136-1138, 1215, 1273

Service
　Insufficiency for 1139
　Motives for 10, 710, 786, 793, 1140-1141
　Possibilities for 1142
　Privilege of 232, 1143-1144
　Sacrificial 230, 318, 1145
　Worship first 1146-1147, 1372-1373
Sex..354
Shallow belief................................379, 389
Sharing..1148
Silence 1149-1153, 1178
Silent Christians..................................1154
Simplicity 108, 328, 470, 1155-1157, 1176
Sin
　Consequences of 154, 327, 627, 759-760, 1158-1161, 1168, 1302, 1375
　Folly of 1162-1164
　Good perverted 391
　Hatred of......................103, 1165, 1166
　Leads to death 1167
　Never private.....................................1168
　Personal responsibility for 1169
　Prevalence of..........435, 790, 791, 1170
　Refined..1171
　Seared conscience 274, 1172
　Victory over 86
Sin problem 1173, 1174
Skeptics 38, 311, 1105-1106
Solitude 1152-1153, 1175, 1176, 1177, 1178, 1234
Sovereignty of God (see God: His sovereignty)
Sowing and reaping.............................1179
Spiritual decline 678
Spiritual depth.....................280, 732, 1180
Spiritual discernment 205-206, 716, 1377
Spiritual disciplines......................207, 1187
Spiritual goals 11
Spiritual growth 113, 242, 281, 282, 636, 694, 776, 1072, 1181, 1182, 1183, 1184, 1185, 1186, 1187, 1188, 1262
Spiritual leadership..........1189, 1190, 1191
Spiritual neglect...................................1192
Spiritual philosophy.............................1193
Spiritual reality 1194, 1195
Spiritual victory 144, 231, 505, 523, 542, 675, 917, 938, 1188, 1196, 1197, 1198, 1225, 1226, 1256, 1257

Spiritual warfare 238, 319, 325, 614, 656, 809, 826, 951, 1091, 1095, 1096, 1199, 1200, 1201, 1202, 1249
Staleness 1203
Standards 1204
Standing firm.............................1205, 1206
Status symbols......................................209
Status quo 88
Stewardship 899, 900
Stillness 1207
Submission 452, 747, 822, 1208, 1209, 1210
Success 608, 1213, 1214, 1215
Success/Failure 1211, 1212
Suffering................325, 1114, 1137, 1216, 1217, 1218
Summer 1301
Sunday Christians 320, 1219

T

Teachers 1220
Tears..1221
Temper
　Attempts to excuse 1222, 1223
　Loss of control 1224
　Loss of credibility.................................20
　Provocation 1223
Temptation 1225, 1226
Ten Commandments...........................1227
Testimonials 87, 389, 577
Textualism.......................574, 1011, 1228, 1229
Thanksgiving 1230, 1331, 1334
Theology..........................1231-1233, 1294
Thinking
　Avoidance of 1234
　Need for..............638, 1015, 1016, 1235
Thirst for God (see Longing for God)
Thoughts....................................1236-1242
Timidity...1202
Today...1243
Tolerance/ Intolerance........214, 897, 1166, 1244-1249, 1280
Tongue..252
Total depravity 1250
Tranquility...1251
Transiency...1252
Trials
　Attitude toward 76, 485, 523, 547, 562, 892, 1001, 1253, 1254, 1255

330

Difficulty of 271, 1256, 1257
God's presence in.............511, 521, 891, 1264
Inevitability of..............1218, 1258, 1259
Necessity of 270, 272, 325, 1216, 1260, 1261, 1262, 1263, 1264, 1265
Storms............................159, 1266-1269
Trinity 1270
Trivialities..1271
True greatness....................432, 1272-1273
True religion...1274
True spirituality 1275-1278
Truth
    Adulterated 1279-1280
    Bold proclamation of......125, 1281-1283
    Carelessness regarding 326, 1284-1286, 1303
    Contextual..............................1287, 1288
    Importance of........................1289, 1299
    Necessity of response........377, 830, 961, 1290-1294
    Truth/Error 1286, 1295

U

Unbelief...............................412, 939, 1296
Uncertainty 232
Unity 63, 754, 1297-1299
Unpopularity..1300
Unsaved 554, 1020-1021, 1029, 1030, 1107
Unsung heroes 363, 430, 824, 1138
Unworthiness 615

V

Vacations 1301
Values 92, 361, 364, 598, 1241, 1302-1303
Vicarious atonement 1304
Violence...1224
Virtue..89
Vision of God 1305

W

Walk humbly...29
Walk with God......................................348
Wars 312
Wealth..1306-1309

Will
    Importance of..................................1310
Will of God 448, 1311-1313
Wisdom 949
Witnessing (see Evangelism)
Women..928, 1314
Women's apparel.................................1315
Wonder 259, 625, 690, 1242
Workplace 788
World
    Contempt for Christians 1162, 1316
    Contentment with 294, 351, 353, 733, 1112, 1115, 1317-1319
    Corruption of...................................1320
    Imitation of......................157, 637, 1078
    Love not........................1135, 1321-1322
World unity..1323
Worldliness 110, 132, 190, 206, 266, 1163, 1228, 1324-1325
Worry 1326-1328
Worship
    Acceptable 1329, 1330
    Admiration 752, 1331, 1332
    Adoration 13, 122, 1333, 1334, 1335
    Awe..........487, 1332, 1336, 1337, 1338, 1339
    Daily 1335, 1340
    Essence of..............................1341, 1342
    For eternity....................295, 1081, 1343
    Meaningless.......7, 108, 195, 1322, 1344, 1345, 1346
    Meaning of 1338
    Missing in churches 163, 1347-1354, 1361
    Purpose for existence 1355-1361, 1374
    Reverence 1339, 1362-1367
    Reverential fear 453
    Supremacy of 998, 1368-1374
Wounds 1265
Wrath of God..............................677, 1375
Writing..32

Y

Youth 1164, 1226

Z

Zeal 1166, 1376, 1377

Titles by A.W. Tozer available
through your local Christian bookstore:

The Attributes of God
The Attributes of God Journal
The Best of A.W. Tozer
Born after Midnight
The Christian Book of
　Mystical Verse
Christ the Eternal Son
The Counselor
The Early Tozer:
　A Word in Season
Echoes from Eden
Faith Beyond Reason
Gems from Tozer
God Tells the Man Who Cares
How to Be Filled
　with the Holy Spirit
I Call It Heresy!
I Talk Back to the Devil
Jesus, Author of Our Faith
Jesus Is Victor
Jesus, Our Man in Glory
Let My People Go, A biography
　of Robert A. Jaffray
Man: The Dwelling Place of God
Men Who Met God
The Next Chapter after the Last
Of God and Men
Paths to Power
The Price of Neglect

The Pursuit of God
The Pursuit of Man (formerly
　The Divine Conquest)
The Quotable Tozer
Renewed Day by Day, Vol. 1
Renewed Day by Day, Vol. 2
The Root of the Righteous
Rut, Rot or Revival
The Set of the Sail
The Size of the Soul
Success and the Christian
That Incredible Christian
This World:
　Playground or Battleground?
Tozer on Worship
　and Entertainment
The Tozer Pulpit 1
The Tozer Pulpit 2
Tozer Speaks to Students
Tozer Topical Reader
Tragedy in the Church:
　The Missing Gifts
A Treasury of A.W. Tozer
The Warfare of the Spirit
We Travel an Appointed Way
Whatever Happened to Worship?
Who Put Jesus on the Cross?
Wingspread, A biography of
　A.B. Simpson

For information on these and other titles by
Christian Publications, contact us on the web at
www.cpi-horizon.com.